Building the foundation, defining a Christian Marriage and providing the tools and resources to fortify your marriage.

A wise man builds his house on the rock.
Matthew 7:24

Fortified Marriages Ministries

www.fortifiedmarriages.com

Chris & Carmen Garner

This Workbook belongs to: ______________________

Fortified Marriages

Cover design by Adolfo Blanco.
Castle: Casa Loma, Toronto, Ontario, Canada
Couple: Bobby and Claudia Magallanes

Original cartoons and illustrations by Ricardo "Rocky" Balboa.
After Eden illustrations used by permission; Answers in Gensis; Hebron, KY
www.AnswersinGenesis.org

Edited by: Jerry Cruz, Alice Garner, Jon Waterhouse

Library of Congress Cataloging-in-Publication Data
Garner, Chris, 1954—
Fortified Marriages: Marriage Manual & Workbook / Chris Garner
Includes bibliographical references.

ISBN: 0-9772160-0-4
1. Marriage—Religious aspects—Christianity. 2. Spouses– Religious life.
3. Spiritual life—Christianity

Library of Congress Control Number: 2005911279

Printed in the United States of America.

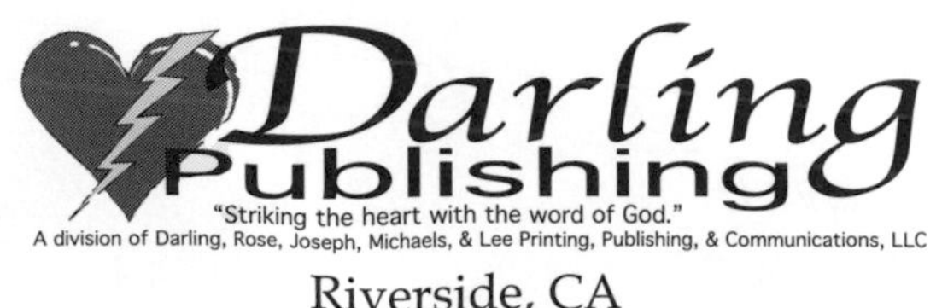

Riverside, CA

Fortified Marriages Ministry

Building Strong Marriages

www.fortifiedmarriages.com

Our Purpose: To be used by God to fortify marriages. To make a difference in lives, marriages and families.

Our Vision: To see marriages become healthy, productive, able to withstand the storms of life and used by God to strengthen other marriages.

Our Mission: To provide resources, training and direction to individuals, couples and churches to help them build the foundation, define a Christian marriage and use sound tools to fortify marriages. To work with the local church to provide marriage education.

Any marriage can become strong to withstand the storms that will come against it. It can become a flourishing, growing marriage fulfilling to both husband and wife.

Acknowledgements: Great is the God of Abraham, Isaac and Jacob and praise be to His Son, Jesus Christ. In twenty-four years of marriage, we have experienced many problems and learned many Biblical principles the hard way. The Lord has held us together, grown our marriage and made it productive and a joy. My wife, Carmen has stood with me and worked to keep our marriage together. I am incredibly blessed with a wonderful wife. Together we are a great team.

God used my friend and mentor, Scott Darling to challenge and push me to make this book a reality. Victor Machiche and Pastor Jonathan Gonzalez' vision for marriage classes to begin strengthening marriages encouraged me to collate this material into one book. I appreciate Pastor Juan Ramos' support and encouragement to see the first marriage classes form and begin to be used by God in couples' lives and marriages.

My children, Michelle, Steven and Michael and grandchildren are wonderful blessings! The Lord has used them to mold me and teach me about being a husband, father and grandfather. There is not enough room to thank all of the people who have made this book possible. My parents, the couples in our Bible studies, mentors, teachers, counselors; God has used many people to bring this project together. Thank you all; may the Lord bless you abundantly!

The Author: Chris Garner is a writer, researcher and teacher. He has studied marriage for many years and has applied these studies to his own marriage and in helping other marriages. He has been a leader in his church for many years as men's ministry director, prayer director and coordinator of men's and couple's retreats. For five years he wrote and published a monthly men's newsletter with a nationwide distribution and for the past five years has published a weekly E-votion, an electronic men's devotion emailed throughout the United States and beyond.

Chris led a couples Bible study for five years with his wife Carmen. They have counseled and mentored numerous couples and currently facilitate marriage classes in local churches. Chris and Carmen's passion for helping couples and families comes from the many years of struggles they experienced in their own marriage and a desire to be used by God to help couples experience the joy that comes from a growing, fruitful marriage. They strongly believe that good marriages don't just happen on their own, but are a product of God's work in lives and marriages and couples working together. The Bible is the blueprint for marriage; this manual is a guide to help couples understand what God wants for their lives and marriages.

Dedicated to my wife, Carmen.
My partner, helper, counselor,
friend and lover...

You have always believed in me
and only wanted the best for me.

You have encouraged me to serve the Lord
and be the person He wants me to be.

Through you, the Lord has encouraged me,
challenged me, pruned me and given me a
blessing far greater than all the
riches in the world.

My Lady, My Love...
You are the greatest!

Table of Contents

Using the Fortified Marriages Manual and Workbook

There are more books and help available for marriages today than at any other period in history, yet marriages still continue to break up at an appalling rate. A couple can know all there is to know about marriage, yet live in a dysfunctional, unhealthy marriage. Fortified Marriages is an excellent resource to assist you as you work toward protecting and strengthening your marriage. Continue your study by reading the books referred to in the Endnotes at the end of each chapter and the Marriage Resources section to help you further strengthen the areas in your marriage that may need additional work. The Crisis Resource section at the end of the manual presents information to aid you in specific areas of immediate need. Through your continued perseverance, commitment, ongoing study, prayer and being open to God's direction and work in your life you can attain a strong, healthy growing marriage.

Working Through the Manual as a Couple

Your marriage will grow much more by working through the 52 studies as a couple. Work through the manual from beginning to end. There is a natural progression as you build the foundation for marriage and then work on the principles of marriage. Read all of the studies, even if it does not directly apply to you now. There may be some information you can use in the future to minister to someone else. Read one study, answer the questions and then share your answers with your spouse. The discussion will help you apply the material to your marriage and gain understanding of your spouse. You may purchase a manual for each spouse or purchase one manual as a couple and copy the questions at the end of each study so that you can answer the questions separately before discussing them. Using the manual in a couples' small group study is an excellent way to work together with other couples to grow in your marriage relationship. The small group setting allows you to learn from the experiences of the other couples.

Pray together as a couple before beginning your studies and as you go through this manual, be open and honest with the Lord, yourself and your spouse. Discussions will not always be easy; at times it will be uncomfortable and can become very emotional. When you encounter difficult situations, you may want to set the study down and return to it later. Do not criticize your spouse's answers. This is an opportunity for you to learn more about your spouse and grow toward oneness as you discuss the studies together.

When Only One Will Try

You cannot change your spouse and any attempt to do so will only cause frustration and stress for both of you. With God's power, you can change yourself, and that action will do much to change your marriage. Work through the manual and apply the principles to your life and your interaction with your spouse. It is very likely that they will become interested once they begin to see changes in you. Use the questions as discussion points between you and your spouse. You may want to ask their "opinion" on certain aspects of the manual. Any discussion based on the material in the manual will enhance your relationship. If your spouse gets defensive, do not press him. Continually pray for your spouse and patiently wait on the Lord to work in his life and change him. You can accomplish a lot on your own if you are willing to try and allow the Lord to work in your life.

The Foundation of the Word of God

Remember, the Word of God is the foundation for all knowledge. Anything you read must be considered in the context of Biblical truth. Studying the Bible and making it a part of your life is most important. Without the work of the Holy Spirit in your life, it is almost impossible to change; God is the Potter, you are the clay. He will mold you and shape you into the person He wants you to become as you surrender your life and allow Him to work.

Keep Learning - Keep Seeking - Keep Growing.

May God bless you richly as you fortify your marriage!

Introduction

The Fortified Marriage

Be on your guard; stand firm in the faith; be men of courage; be strong.
1 Corinthians 16:13

A Marriage on the Rocks

Joe and Martha stand at the brink of a divorce. They don't want to divorce, but don't know what else to do. Raw emotions and poor attitudes make it a strain to get through each day. Their life together seems to be filled with anger and hurt and the children are insecure because of the constant bickering. Divorce seems to be the only option available to rectify the disaster their life together has become.

Six years ago, this couple was very in love. Sure, it was a second marriage for both of them, but they were in love, and love would surely conquer any storm that came their way. Their romantic dream slowly became a nightmare as their differences and the stresses of parenting, career and blending their own lives together worked against them. Feelings of love dwindled until there was more contempt than love.

Joe and Martha communicate well with other people, but communication with each other is strained and difficult. Conversations often become arguments, and the simplest request can result in a fight spanning several days. They thought they were better prepared for this marriage, since they had been through it before, but now they are not so sure. Separately, they don't understand what went wrong, and together, they can't get past the hurt long enough to hold a meaningful discussion. There is no intimacy, and their sexual relationship only adds to the hurt of living together. They had not even considered marriage education or pre-marital counseling. Their communication and marriage concepts were learned watching their parents and through their own life experiences. This couple is not unlike the many thousands of couples considering divorce every day. Their relationship may even be very similar to yours or someone you know.

Marriages Breaking Up

Marriages dissolve today at an alarming rate. Too many marriages end in divorce and it is a shame that divorce also happens within the Christian Church. According to George Barna of The Barna Group, people claiming to be Christians divorce at virtually the same rate that non-Christians divorce.[1] Many people justify divorce by saying that they are going to stop hurting one another, or that it is not right to stay together just because of the children. They rationalize away the fact that, while divorce ends the marriage, it does not end the relationship. They believe the hurt will be left behind, but it is not!

A great number of married couples exist in marriages that are dysfunctional and unproductive. Their marriage is unhappy and unsatisfying and it is not a testimony for God and it certainly does not glorify Him. Their children are insecure and not achieving their potential; their family hangs together by a thread. Why? Because they do not have the marriage relationship that God intended them to have. They are too wrapped up in things and self to be the spouse God desires them to be.

Many marriages are stuck in the vicious cycle of hurt and disappointment Joe and Martha experienced. Dr. John Gottman's research has identified the following six signs that a marriage is headed for disaster:

- ***Harsh startup:*** the way a conversation begins. A couple in trouble will have conversation's that become harsh very quickly.
- ***The Four Horsemen of the Apocalypse:*** negative interaction that includes: criticism, contempt, defensiveness or stonewalling.
- ***Flooding:*** one spouse's negativity—whether criticism or contempt is so overwhelming and so sudden that it leaves the other shell shocked.
- ***Body language:*** negative physical signs during the couple's interaction.
- ***Failed repair attempts:*** one spouse or the other tries to fix the situation and the attempt isn't even noticed. The negativity continues.
- ***Bad memories:*** the couple focuses on the hurt in their marriage and tend to only remember the bad things—they don't remember all the good experiences that have occurred in their marriage.[2]

These signs are indicators of a marriage that is dried up and possibly even dead. Dr. Gottman states that 91% of the time, he can correctly predict whether a couple will divorce based on these six factors.[3] Satan and a person's own selfish desires can lead a couple down this path. Even now, you may find yourself stuck in a very negative relationship. The good news is that God has saved many marriages on the brink of divorce and He can save any marriage when the couple will turn to Him.

Marriage Takes Work

No marriage can survive without work. Marriages must be fortified to withstand the assaults that will come against them. To fortify means to: strengthen and secure; reinforce; invigorate; give emotional, moral or mental strength to; or enrich.[4] Husbands and wives must be pro-active to strengthen their marriages and keep them from failing like so many other marriages today. Today's culture does not care about marriage, and Satan has a great desire to see marriages fail. When a marriage fails, generations suffer. No matter how amicable the divorce might be—children will be permanently affected.

Marriage is the second most important relationship in a person's life; only the relationship with God is more important. It is so important, that in Ephesians 5:31-32, Paul compares the marriage relationship to the relationship of Jesus Christ and the church.

Marriage can be (and often is) the most difficult relationship a person can enter into. Couples enter this relationship without counting the cost as Jesus tells people to do in Luke, chapter 14. They enter into marriage thinking they are in love, only to find they really don't have any idea what love is or what they have gotten themselves into. Divorce is the culture's answer to fixing this "mistake." It is sad to see that many in the Church also condone divorce when life gets too hard together or if they fall out of love.

A successful, flourishing marriage is possible, but it takes work. A married couple must leave their parents, cleave to their spouse and strive for a growing relationship with the Lord and their spouse. Oneness and intimacy with a spouse takes time and continued effort.

A marriage can be compared to a garden. To create and maintain a beautiful, growing garden, one must continue to do the work necessary to care for it. It takes the proper tools, water, fertilizer and weed killer to keep a garden in shape. The marriage relationship also requires the proper care to maintain it and keep it growing and beautiful.

The Bible, books, classes, conferences, tapes and videos are the tools to help educate and inform. Love, nurture and acceptance are the fertilizer to keep the marriage alive. Communication is the weed killer to keep problems from taking over the relationship. As you progress through this manual, you will learn about the many relationship tools available to strengthen your marriage, and also about how to apply the "fertilizer" and "weed killer" to the garden of your marriage. Working through the manual with your spouse, you will gain knowledge, understanding and experience with the relationship tools.

Do you want a dried up, unproductive, dead marriage? Do nothing. It will die on it's own without any work at all. Without nurturing, caring and effort, any marriage will wither and die. You may think you didn't marry the right person or married for the wrong reasons, but please understand that God is able and wants to bless you and this marriage. Divorce and remarriage is not the answer and will hurt rather than help your chances for building the marriage you desire. Negative thinking and attitudes destroys marriages. Your life and marriage can become all that it can and should be with God's guidance.

Building a Fortified Marriage

> ***They replied, "Let us start rebuilding." So they began this good work.***
> ***~ Nehemiah 2:18b***

The walls around a city guard and protect the people inside. Similarly, a fortified marriage guards and protects the family within the marriage relationship. Building strong marriages today can be compared to Nehemiah's building of the wall around Jerusalem several thousand years ago.

Broken down walls and burned gates provided no protection for the people of Jerusalem and they had no refuge from attack. Nehemiah faced opposition and trouble as he organized the Israelites for the task of rebuilding the walls. They had to build and at the same time, remain prepared to fight should an attack come from the enemies around them. Each family had responsibility for one section of the wall, and they worked together to both build and defend from attack. Side by side, they faced the trouble and were able to complete the building to provide protection for the people of Jerusalem.

Couples also must build for protection while defending their marriage relationship from attack. It takes teamwork, diligence and hard work to build a strong marriage and protect your family.

Any marriage can overcome opposition and trouble to become strong and secure with God's direction, guidance and strength. The walls of your marriage may be:

- *Broken down.* Similar to Joe and Martha's marriage, you may be on the brink of divorce.
- *Cracked and crumbling.* The walls of your marriage may need to be repaired and strengthened.
- Strong and secure. Built on the strong foundation, your marriage may be used by God to help others.

Whatever state your marriage is in now; it can be built up to become strong and fortified against the storms and attacks you will face.

Learning God's Plan for Your Marriage

People will spend money, time and energy on many things in life, such as education, career, hobbies, sports and learning to drive a vehicle. However, most people do not seek any training for one of the most important aspects of their life on earth—being a husband, wife or parent. Just as you invest time and money for retirement, homes, cars or property, you need to invest time and money into learning to be the spouse and parent God wants you to be. It is necessary that you fortify your marriage and strengthen it against the crisis, attacks and dryness that can creep into a marriage or broadside it without any notice.

The purpose of this manual is to help you build the foundation for a strong marriage, define a Christian Marriage and provide tools and resources to fortify your marriage. There is a necessary progression in this manual. While the information at the end of the manual is very important, one can not fully grasp those principles without understanding the foundational principles from the previous studies. The Biblical principles in this manual—when applied—will strengthen your marriage, help your family to grow and improve your walk with the Lord. It is really pretty simple—do the work and your marriage will get better; don't do the work and your marriage will not change.

Understanding Biblical responsibilities in the marriage and working toward fulfilling those responsibilities is critical to the growth of a marriage. The goal of marriage is oneness. Oneness between a man and woman is similar to taking a piece of metal and a piece of wood and trying to make them one. In the temporal view it can not be done. Even though they may fit together very smoothly, there is still a seam where the wood and metal come together. Yet, God created the marriage relationship to be a relationship of oneness where a man and woman complement and fulfill each other. When the marriage relationship operates on God's principles and a couple function as the husband and wife God designed them to be, oneness will occur. Oneness in marriage is a great mystery (Ephesians 5:32) and difficult to understand. It is based on commitment and growth together, not on euphoric "feelings" of love.

The marriage lived according to God's design is too rarely seen in today's culture. It is only by God's grace and His work that a marriage can be what He designed it to be, but there are principles everyone must follow. This manual will guide you in the steps you can take to keep your marriage growing in the right direction.

Hard work? Yes! Some pain? Surely! But this will be good pain that brings growth. Will there be enrichment and blessings? Certainly! As you work through this manual with your spouse, you will gain insight into what God wants for you and your marriage. You will grow closer to the man or woman you promised to stay with until death do you part. You will build a fortified marriage—a marriage fortified against the attacks of the world and Satan. There are no formulas to ensure a good marriage; it takes commitment, hard work, great desire and obedience to God's Word. It is the relationship you build with the Lord and His promises, protection and guidance that will fortify your marriage. Everyone goes through trials— it is how one goes through the trials that shape their character and the direction of his marriage.

The Fortified Marriage weathers the storms of trials and emerges stronger with each one. A fortified marriage grows and becomes a beacon in this dark, self-indulging culture, drawing people to Jesus Christ. God will use you to touch others as you grow in your marriage.

> ***Therefore encourage one another and build each other up, just as in fact you are doing.***
> ***~ 1 Thessalonians ~ 5:11***

For Discussion as a Couple

1. What does the term Fortified Marriage mean to you?

____
____
____
____

2. What can you do to fortify your marriage? Is it your work or God's work?

____
____
____
____

3. Is your marriage a thriving garden or a weed patch? Why?

____
____
____
____

4. Does your marriage have any of John Gottman's six signs of a troubled marriage? Which one (s)?

____
____
____
____

5. What are your expectations for going through this manual? What do you think you will get out of it?

____
____
____
____

Fortified Marriages
Introduction Endnotes

Introduction: *The Fortified Marriage*

1. George Barna, The Barna Group, www.barna.org, September 8, 2004
2. Dr. John Gottman & Nan Silver, The Seven Principles for Making Marriage Work (NY, NY; Crown Publishers, 1999) pp 26-43
3. Ibid, p 2
4. The American Heritage Dictionary of the English Language, Fourth Edition; Copyright 2000 by Houghton Mifflin Company.

Recommended for further reading:

- The Seven Principles for Making Marriage Work by John M. Gottman and Nan Silver
- The Christ Centered Marriage by Dr. Neil T. Anderson & Charles Mylander
- Creating a Successful Marriage by Cleveland McDonald & Philip McDonald
- Good Marriages Take Time, Bad Marriages Take More Time by David & Carole Hocking

Marital Health Inventory

Thinking about your marriage relationship, circle the number that best reflects your view of each statement below.

	Never	Rarely	Sometimes	Often	Almost Always
1. I know that I am a forgiven child of God:	1	2	3	4	5
2. I see God working in our marriage:	1	2	3	4	5
3. I understand my spouse:	1	2	3	4	5
4. We complement each other and work together:	1	2	3	4	5
5. Our differences enhance our marriage:	1	2	3	4	5
6. It seems that we are going in the same direction:	1	2	3	4	5
7. The will of God is a priority in our marriage:	1	2	3	4	5
8. We share the same goals and objectives:	1	2	3	4	5
9. My spouse listens attentively when I speak:	1	2	3	4	5
10. We can discuss differences without arguing:	1	2	3	4	5
11. We have times of deep sharing of feelings:	1	2	3	4	5
12. I am able to freely share my hurts and feelings:	1	2	3	4	5
13. I can say no if I don't want to do something:	1	2	3	4	5
14. I feel respected by my spouse:	1	2	3	4	5
15. I trust my spouse:	1	2	3	4	5
16. I feel appreciated:	1	2	3	4	5
17. My spouse understands my needs:	1	2	3	4	5
18. I feel loved:	1	2	3	4	5
19. We meet each other's needs:	1	2	3	4	5
20. Hurts are quickly resolved:	1	2	3	4	5
21. I feel needed by my spouse:	1	2	3	4	5
22. We use a budget for our finances:	1	2	3	4	5

	Never	Rarely	Sometimes	Often	Almost Always
23. We plan major purchases together:	1	2	3	4	5
24. We make good financial decisions:	1	2	3	4	5
25. We have intimacy in our relationship::	1	2	3	4	5
26. We have passion in our relationship:	1	2	3	4	5
27. My sexual needs are met:	1	2	3	4	5
28. We share spiritual insights with each other:	1	2	3	4	5
29. We have time together for just the two of us:	1	2	3	4	5
30. Our marriage roles are defined and understood:	1	2	3	4	5
31. We have healthy "in-laws" relationships:	1	2	3	4	5
32. We enjoy doing things together:	1	2	3	4	5
33. We pray together:	1	2	3	4	5
34. We work together to overcome problems:	1	2	3	4	5
35. We reflect on special times we've had together:	1	2	3	4	5
36. Our relationship has brought me closer to God:	1	2	3	4	5
37. I feel satisfied with my marriage overall:	1	2	3	4	5
38. I can visualize our marriage continuing for life:	1	2	3	4	5

Enter your total score here: ___________

This inventory will give you a picture of where your marital relationship stands now. A score above 150 indicates a strong, growing relationship. Continue to work at it! A score between 120 and 149 shows a growing relationship that could use some attention. A score between 100 and 119 means you have some work to do to improve your marriage and with a score below 100 you may need some counseling and a lot of work will be required to strengthen your marriage. Remember, no marriage is beyond becoming a healthy, strong marriage—God wants to work a miracle in your relationship!

Chapter 1
Created by God

Study 1
Who is Jesus Christ?

Christian beliefs begin with the answer to the question; "Who is Jesus Christ?"

A Christian Marriage

The basis of a Christian Marriage is the person of Jesus Christ. People must understand who Jesus is before they can understand their place in the world, in a family or in the marriage relationship. A Christian simply is a Follower of Christ. Many people claim to be Christians, yet the fruit of that claim is not seen in their lives. In John 14:15, Jesus says; "If you love me, you will obey what I command." This does not mean that you will be perfect, but it does mean that your life is headed in a different direction; that you desire to live your life for Jesus, not for yourself.

Who is Jesus Christ?

In Matthew 16:15, Jesus asked the disciples who they thought He was. When Peter answered, "You are the Christ, the Son of the living God." Jesus replied, "Blessed are you, Simon, son of Jonah; for this was not revealed to you by man, but by My Father in heaven."

Speaking of Jesus, John 1:1 states that Jesus is God. Jesus healed the sick, gave life to the dead and sight to the blind. He forgave sins as seen in Mark 2:5-10 and Luke 7:48,49. In Colossians 1:15-18, Romans 9:5 and Hebrews 1:3, 8 there is further confirmation of Jesus' Godhood.

In the beginning was the Word, and the Word was with God, and the Word was God. He was with God in the beginning. ~ John 1:1-2

Jesus also was man. He was born of a virgin as prophesied in Isaiah and the Psalms and fulfilled in the Gospels. Jesus lived and walked among men and women some 2,000 years ago. Matthew 13:55 states that Jesus had brothers, a mother and was known as the carpenter's son.

The Gospels all record Jesus' physical death on the cross. Roman soldiers verified His death and Jesus was buried in the tomb of a rich man. As prophesied in the Old Testament and by Jesus Himself, He rose on the third day. John 20:28-29 records the meeting of Jesus and Thomas, one of the Disciples. Jesus had physically risen from the dead and displayed to Thomas the wounds of the cross to prove that He was indeed the same person who had died. He appeared to hundreds before he ascended into heaven as recorded in Acts, chapter 1.

Jesus is the Way, the Truth, and the Life

Jesus stated, "I am the way the truth and the life. No one comes to the Father except through Me" (John 14:6). People only have life, eternal life, through Jesus Christ. He was the perfect sacrifice: God became man, giving His life so that all who believe in Him might be saved. Acts 4:12 states, Salvation is found in no one else, for there is no other name under heaven given to men by which we must be saved.

There is nothing one can do to earn salvation (Ephesians 2:8, 9); it is the gift of God. Salvation is only found in Jesus Christ; trusting self or anything else has no value.

Christians revere Jesus as God and worship Him, but He is also a friend as stated in John 15:15. He desires a close intimate relationship with His people and reaches out to them in love and humility.

Jesus will return one day. He stated this fact Himself in John 14:28 and Matthew 24:30. An angel also testifies to this fact in Acts 1:11, and the book of Revelation gives the account how He will return.

Who is Jesus?

1. He is God, He always was always will be.
2. He was born of a virgin.
3. He was a man, he physically walked the earth.
4. He died for the sins of mankind.
5. He physically rose from the dead.
6. He ascended into heaven.
7. He is Lord.
8. He is Teacher.
9. He is a friend.
10. He is the ONLY way to salvation.
11. He will return one day.

Do You Know Jesus Christ?

If your answer to this question is "yes" and Jesus is your Lord and Savior, praise God for what He has done for you! If your answer is "no," or you aren't sure, please consider Jesus' claims as you read this section.

God created mankind in His own image and to have a relationship with Him. He also created people with the ability to choose between right and wrong and whether or not they desire a relationship with God. The problem is that, beginning with Adam and Eve, mankind has chosen to reject God's laws. Sin separates man from a relationship with God.

> ***...all have sinned and fall short of the glory of God.***
> ***~ Romans 3:23***

God's holiness demands justice, and sin must be paid for. There is no way around the penalty for sin. People cannot adequately pay the price for their sin and God's rejection, so God provided a sacrifice for Himself. Jesus Christ willingly took on human form and died so that mankind could be reconciled to God. He was the perfect sacrifice that paid the price for the sins of all mankind.

> ***"For God so loved the world that he gave his one and only Son, that whoever believes in him shall not perish but have eternal life.***
> ***~ John 3:16***
>
> ***God demonstrates his own love for us in this: While we were still sinners, Christ died for us.***
> ***~Romans 5:8***

Jesus paid the price for sin and people only have to ask for forgiveness of their sin and accept Him as Lord and Savior to be saved from their sins. A person's faith in Jesus Christ saves him from eternal separation from God and opens God's promise of eternal life; spending all of eternity with Him in heaven.

> ***For it is by grace you have been saved, through faith-and this not from yourselves, it is the gift of God - not by works, so that no one can boast .***
> ***~ Ephesians 2:8-9***

Do you have this assurance of salvation from your sins and the promise of eternal life? God desires a relationship with you now and forever. Jesus gave Himself as the sacrifice for your sin, all of your sins. You can begin this relationship now with a simple, heartfelt prayer. Speaking to God, say something like; "Jesus, I need You. I have sinned and fallen short of your glory. Forgive my sins and renew my heart. Thank you for dying on the cross for me. Take control of my life and make me the person You want me to be."

> ***That if you confess with your mouth, "Jesus is Lord," and believe in your heart that God raised him from the dead, you will be saved. For it is with your heart that you believe and are justified, and it is with your mouth that you confess and are saved.***
> ***~ Romans 10:9-10***

Not only do you have the promise of eternal life, your relationship with the Lord will change your life dramatically here on earth. As you grow in your relationship with God, He will change you and mold you into His image. Now you are ready to move forward!

For Discussion as a Couple

1. Briefly give your testimony; how and when did you become a Christian?

____

____

____

____

2. In your own words, who is Jesus Christ?

____

____

____

____

3. Why is belief in Jesus Christ necessary for salvation?

____

____

____

____

4. Do you and your spouse have the same views of who Jesus Christ is? What are the differences?

____

____

____

____

5. Why is it important in marriage to know who Jesus Christ is?

____

____

____

____

Created by God
Study 2
Who are You?

The Lord God formed man of dust from the ground and breathed into his nostrils the breath of life, and the man became a living being.
~Genesis 2:7

Then the Lord God made a woman from the rib he had taken out of the man and He brought her to the man. ~ Genesis 2:22

'Yes, man was created in God's image regardless of what we see here.'

You are Physical, Created by God

God created mankind, and physically, He molds and shapes everyone into the person they are. Adam was created from the dust of the earth, Eve was created from Adam, and the sexual union of the first man and woman created the rest of mankind.

People have an outer self, a physical body which relates to the world through the five senses. As long as one lives in the physical world, he must do so in a physical body. But is that all there is to it? Are humans defined as a physical entity, a name, a number and a physical description as seen on a driver's license?

People tend to identify themselves and others by what they look like, what they do, and perhaps even by their theological position, denominational preference, or role in the church. Is who you are determined by what you do, look like and believe in? Or is what you do, look like and believe in determined by who you are?

Who are you? It sounds like a simple question, but attempting to answer it soon reveals the complexity of the issue. People are physical beings created by God, but also much more than that.

You are Your Inner Self: Mind, Emotions and Will

The inner self contains the mind (allowing a person to think), emotions (allowing feelings), and the will (allowing choice). God gives people minds to think with, and He desires that they use their minds wisely. The book of Proverbs highlights the need for wisdom, how people need to pursue and use it to live a Godly life. Just as God gave Adam and Eve the choice to obey or disobey His command to not eat the fruit of the Tree of Knowledge of Good and Evil, He allows everyone the choice of how to live their lives. They make choices based on how they think, feel and react to the environment they live in. The inner self, the heart, determines how people react to the physical world around them and shapes their personality. Without thoughts and emotions, the physical body is only a lump of flesh.

You are Spiritual

You are spiritual, and it is the spirit that lives on forever. Once the physical body dies, Christians have an eternal body in heaven. To be away from the body is to be at home with the Lord (2 Cor 5:8). Christians have the hope and the promise that their spirit will live with God forever. Yet, it is not something that only happens in the afterlife. People are spiritual now on earth. When a person accepts Jesus Christ as Savior, he chooses to live by the Spirit rather than by the flesh. So I say, live by the Spirit, and you will not gratify the desires of the sinful nature (Galatians 5:16).

Adam and Eve experienced a closeness with God that has never been experienced since. They were created physically and spiritually in perfect union with God, but they sinned; they disobeyed God and as a result, they died spiritually. They were then separated from God. People today are spiritually dead before they come to know Jesus Christ as Savior. Through Christ and a trust in Him, people are now alive spiritually.

A New Life in Christ

Many Christians identify only with the first Adam, the one who failed and was separated from God. As a Christian, you are now identified with the last Adam - Jesus Christ. Originally, you were born in sin, not in Christ. The moment you said yes to Christ, your old self was crucified with Christ and you were born again. You are now spiritually alive.

It is not what you do as a Christian that determines who you are; it's who you are as a Christian that determines who you are, and it is who you are that determines what you do.

Dr. Neil Anderson tells the story of a couple that came to see him for marital counseling. Their marriage was in such bad shape and their view of themselves and each other so wrong that he counseled them to forget about their marriage until they could understand who they were in Christ. They each went off

(continued on the next page)

Who You Are:

You are a child of God; a saint. No one, not even Satan, can damage your position and identity in Christ. Satan will attempt to deceive you into believing that you are not acceptable to God, but through Christ you are acceptable.

In Christ you are:

A child of God.~ John 1:12
Christ's friend.~ John 15:15
A new creation.~ 2 Corinthians 5:17
A member of Christ's body. ~ 1 Corinthians 12:27
A son of God; an heir. ~ Galations 4:6,7
A saint.~ Ephesians 1:1, Philippians 1:1
Gods workmanship.~ Ephesians 2:10
Righteous and holy. ~ Ephesians 4:24
Born of God. ~ 1 John 5:18
A partaker of Christ. ~Hebrews 3:14
Chosen, holy and dearly loved. ~Colossians 3:12

Therefore, if anyone is in Christ, he is a new creation; the old has gone, the new has come! ~ 2 Corinthians 5:17

Since you are in Christ, by the grace of God:

You are justified - completely forgiven and made righteous. ~Romans 5:1
You are free forever from condemnation. ~Romans 8:1
You have the mind of Christ. ~ 1 Corinthians 2:16
You have been made righteous. ~ 2 Corinthians 5:21
You have been redeemed and forgiven, and are a recipient of His lavish grace. ~ Ephesians 2:5
You have been made alive together with Christ.~Ephesians 2:5
You have been redeemed and forgiven of all your sins. The debt against you has been canceled. ~ Colossians 1:14
You are firmly rooted in Christ and are now being built in Him. ~ Colosssians 2:7
You have been made complete in Christ. ~ Colossians 2:10
You have been given a spirit of power, love and self-discipline. ~ 2 Timothy 1:7
You have been saved and set apart according to God's doing. ~ 2 Timothy 1:9
You have the right to come boldly before the throne of God to find mercy and grace in time of need. ~ Hebrews 4:16
You have been given exceedingly great and precious promises by God by which you are a partaker of God's divine nature. ~ 2 Peter 1:4

It is important that you see yourself for who you really are - a new creation in Jesus Christ.

alone and studied the Scriptures and sought the Lord. Six months later, their marriage was better than they could have ever dreamed because they understood their position in God's view. Only then could they be the husband and wife God called them to be.[1]

Who You Really Are

> ***But you are a chosen people, a royal priesthood, a holy nation, a people belonging to God, that you may declare the praises of Him who called you out of darkness into His wonderful light. Once you were not a people, but now you are the people of God; once you had not received mercy, but now you have received mercy ~ 1 Peter 2:9,10***

God does not call you a sinner; He calls you a saint - a holy one. If you think of yourself as a sinner, you'll tend to live like a sinner. Why not identify yourself for who you really are; a saint who occasionally sins? The goal, as a Christian, is to live a life that corresponds to who you are positionally because of what Jesus Christ has done for you.

> ***Your hope for growth, meaning and fulfillment as a Christian is based on understanding who you are - specifically your identity in Christ as a child of God.***

For Discussion as a Couple

1. What does the phrase in Christ mean to you personally as you live out your daily life?

____
____
____
____

2. How can the truths about who you are in Christ make your marriage different?

____
____
____
____

3. How can a wholehearted acceptance of the truth that God loves you help you through marital problems?

____
____
____
____

4. Think about your relationship with your spouse. What is it about that relationship that frees you to give and receive?

____
____
____
____

5. What changes have occurred in you since accepting Jesus as your Lord and Savior?

____
____
____
____

Biblical truth is important to a Fortified Marriage. The Word of God, the Bible, is the foundation of all wisdom and knowledge. It is important to understand that there is an Order of Scripture. Feelings are not to rule one's life, Biblical truth is. Use the information below as you continue to grow in your relationship with God. Refer to it as you progress through this manual; it will make a difference in your life and your marriage.

The Order of Scripture:

1. **Know the Truth:** *To the Jews who had believed him, Jesus said, "If you hold to my teaching, you are really my disciples. Then you will know the truth, and the truth will set you free." ~ John 8:31-32*

2. **Believe the Truth:** *For it is with your heart that you believe and are justified, and it is with your mouth that you confess and are saved. ~ Romans 10:10*

3. **Obey the Truth (walk according to the truth):** *Now that you know these things, you will be blessed if you do them. ~ John 13:17*

4. **Feel the Truth (let your emotions be a product of your obedience):** *...but on Cain and his offering he did not look with favor. So Cain was very angry, and his face was downcast. Then the LORD said to Cain, "Why are you angry? Why is your face downcast? If you do what is right, will you not be accepted? But if you do not do what is right, sin is crouching at your door; it desires to have you, but you must master it." ~ Genesis 4:5-7*

Christ has won the battle. Your part is to:[2]

1. **Be transformed by the renewing of your mind:** *Do not conform any longer to the pattern of this world, but be transformed by the renewing of your mind. Then you will be able to test and approve what God's will is -- His good, pleasing and perfect will. ~ Romans 12:2*

2. **Prepare your mind for action (do away with fruitless fantasy):** *Therefore, prepare your minds for action; be self-controlled; set your hope fully on the grace to be given you when Jesus Christ is revealed. ~ 1 Peter 1:13*

3. **Take every thought captive in obedience to Christ:** *We demolish arguments and every pretension that sets itself up against the knowledge of God, and we take captive every thought to make it obedient to Christ. ~ 2 Corinthians 10:5*

4. **Turn to God:** *Do not be anxious about anything, but in everything, by prayer and petition, with thanksgiving, present your requests to God. ~ Philippians 4:6*

5. **Assume your responsibility and choose truth**: *Finally, brothers, whatever is true, whatever is noble, whatever is right, whatever is pure, whatever is lovely, whatever is admirable-if anything is excellent or praiseworthy-think about such things. Whatever you have learned or received or heard from me, or seen in me-put it into practice. And the God of peace will be with you. ~ Philippians 4:8-9*

Victory in the battle for your mind is the undisputed inheritance of everyone who is in Christ!

Created by God
Study 3
Knowing Your Differences

So God created man in his own image, in the image of God he created him; male and female he created them.
~ Genesis 1:27

It is important to understand the differences between men and women for a relationship to grow.

People are Different!

When dating and falling in love, couples tend to focus on their similarities. Usually, those similarities are few, but as it is often said, love is blind. Once married, couples begin to see their differences and they become points of contention in the marriage relationship. All couples face some basic differences:

- Genders: Male and female; it's not a minor difference, it is major. Biologically, there are great differences.
- Genes: Parents give their children a set of genes unique in history. Those genes will bring about physical, emotional and social differences.
- Backgrounds: Social, economic, cultural, and geographical environment causes differences.
- Personality types: Usually, couples will have very different personalities.

These four primary differences bring about several other differences that often cause conflict in marriage. These differences are:

- Communication style
- Ways of thinking
- Strengths
- Weaknesses
- Struggles
- Emotions
- Values
- Styles
- Convictions
- Desires
- Expectations
- Experiences
- Interests
- Views of sexuality

Differences cause division between husbands and wives and can lead to conflict and at times, even death of the marriage. What can you do about your differences?

1. ***Recognize your differences:*** Learn your spouse.
2. ***Work to understand your differences:*** It is your lifetime assignment to gain understanding to know your spouse.
3. ***Learn to appreciate your differences:*** As Ruth Graham says, "If you were exactly alike, one of you would be unnecessary."
4. ***Utilize your differences:*** God created you just as you are and the two of you are better than one alone. When you work together, your differences fill in each other's weaknesses rather than being points of contention.[1]

It is important to recognize and understand your spouse's differences. The Life History Inventory on pages 23 and 24 will help you discover some differences the two of you brought into your marriage.

Men and Women are Different

The study of differences has become big business recently and many books and much information are now available. Whether one subscribes to Men are from Mars, Women are from Venus, Men are Like Waffles, Women are Like Spaghetti, Men are from Israel, Woman are from Moab, or some other analogy, people are beginning to learn about the differences between men and women.

The original man and woman had a perfect understanding of each other. Sin brought the curse. The curse brought many books.

Biblically, God created humans male and female and based only on this fact of life it is obvious that men and women are fundamentally different. They are different anatomically, sexually, emotionally, psychologically and bio-chemically. It is important to be consciously aware of these differences and to recognize that is how you are created. Many tend to think that different is not a good thing, but Genesis states that God created humans male and female and in His image. Understanding differences will aid interaction and help a couple work toward common goals rather than fighting against each other.

Biological differences affect every aspect of a couple's lives; from intellectual abilities, to how children are treated, to how one responds to danger. Physically, mankind is more aware of male-female differences than any other distinction seen in the world. Chromosomes, cells, hormones, brains and bodies differ between the sexes. For instance, the male brain is 10% larger than the female brain, but the female brain is more efficient and any advantages that might be gained in size are negated.

The male brain is predominantly hard-wired for systemizing—analyzing, understanding and building systems, while the female brain predominantly is hard-wired for empathy. Empathizing is the drive to identify another person's emotions and to respond to them with an appropriate emotion.[2]

Testosterone makes men more aggressive, builds muscle, increases the formation of red blood cells, speeds up recovery after injuries or illness and stimulates the metabolism to burn body fat. In short, the male is leaner and better poised to be a hunter, warrior and provider.

Female estrogen plays a role in sexual development, broadening the pelvis, increasing fat tissue and promoting blood clotting. It also has an effect on the female emotions, the softness of her skin and her caring and nurturing of children.

Emotional Differences

Men tend to feel driven to generate, build and procreate. Ask men who they are and they will respond in terms of their occupations. Women generally seek to nurture, care and shelter. They often see themselves as settlers, peacemakers and designers. They feel driven to relate, associate and cultivate. Ask women who they are and they will often respond in terms of their relationships.[3]

While some may scoff at Dr. John Gray's best selling book, Men are from Mars, Women are from Venus as silly or too simplistic, he has done much to increase people's understanding of gender differences.

Martians value power, competency, efficiency and achievement. They are always doing things to prove themselves and develop their power and skills. Their sense of self is defined through their ability to achieve results. They experience fulfillment primarily through success and accomplishment.[4]

Venusians value love, communication, beauty and relationships. They spend a lot of time supporting, helping and nurturing one another. Their sense of self is defined through their feelings and the quality of their relationships. They experience fulfillment through sharing and relating.[5]

Women do seem to be more complicated...

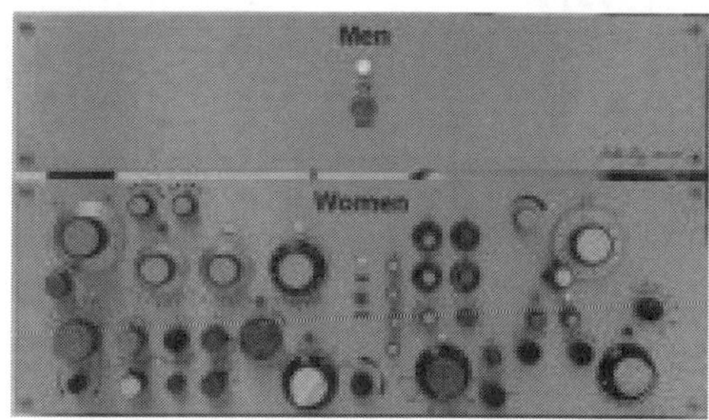

People tend to joke about how complicated women are, but in reality, God has made both men and women very complicated. There are many factors involved in how men and women react to situations such as danger, attack, emotional situations, or joy and happiness. It is important to understand that each person reacts to situations differently than his spouse.

Men and women handle stress very differently. When a woman is under stress, she sees all the problems and may tend to use absolute statements like, always or never; she may appear to overreact or have a certain amount of resentment. She wants to talk it out, but does not want someone to fix her.[6]

Men need to respond by listening without trying to fix her or offering solutions and without invalidating, taking it personally, getting defensive or turning it around and making it about him. Instead, the husband needs to be emotionally supportive by maintaining consistent eye contact, validating, and offering empathetic gestures and responses that show interest and listening.

When a man is stressed, he is focused on a problem—he will detach himself and either try to solve the problem or forget the problem. Many men need down time to transition from work to home—to forget about the problems of the day or to work them out. Often a man will detach when a couple has a difficult conversation.[7]

Women need to realize that detachment is how men deal with problems and stress. She needs to allow him down time and not give disapproval, offer solutions, try to nurture him, push him to communicate or worry about him.

A man must remember to assure his wife that he will return from his detachment time, and to discuss the situation with her once he does.

Both men and women need to stop offering the method of caring they would prefer and begin to learn the different ways their spouses think, feel and react.

Women usually will desire more of a relationship with their husbands. Men need to work at providing more of a relationship and women need to be patient and help their husbands, not demand more.

Communication

A woman typically uses 6,000 to 8,000 words a day, while a man will use only 2,000 to 4,000 words.[8] Not only is there a difference in how many words men and women use, but also in how they use those words. Just watch boys and girls play. Boys will use many more sounds such as "brrrmmm", while girls will be much more articulate and interactive in their play.

Men want the facts and normally communicate to share information and solve problems. Women are much more dramatic and share feelings. They communicate to build relationship. Women tend to be much more active listeners giving more than men.

Spirituality

Women generally are more spiritual than men. While they were not created more spiritual than men, statistically and in reality, women are more in tune to spiritual things. Women are more likely to be involved with discipleship, participate in a small group, volunteer at church, read the Bible, pray and identify themselves as "Christian".[9]

The importance of understanding differences can not be overstated. Without the knowledge that they are supposed to be different, men and women are usually at odds with each other. People want their spouse to want what they want and to feel the way they feel. Everyone likes the fact that men and women are different until some point of contention arises; then they wonder why their spouse can't just be like them! Clearly recognizing and respecting the differences between men and women can dramatically reduce confusion when dealing with the opposite sex. Men and women are incredibly different; yet not so different that couples cannot understand each other.

> ***The marital relationship will grow when couples understand, respect and accept their differences.***

For Discussion as a Couple

1. What are some of the differences you see between you and your spouse?

   ____
   ____
   ____
   ____

2. Why is it important to do something about your differences? What will you do?

   ____
   ____
   ____
   ____

3. Why is it important to understand the differences between men and women?

   ____
   ____
   ____
   ____

4. What are your thoughts regarding how to deal with the stress of your mate?

   ____
   ____
   ____
   ____

5. How do you think you and your spouse's differences can help you grow in your marriage relationship?

   ____
   ____
   ____
   ____

Life History Inventory

Complete the following inventory honestly and completely and then share this information with your spouse. The purpose is to help your spouse understand who you are and where you came from. As he learns, you may also learn some things about your self. Use additional paper, if necessary.

1. Describe where you grew up: your neighborhood and the area where you lived. Did you move a lot? What affect did that have on you? What type of house did you live in? What were the sleeping arrangements? ______

2. In general, describe your family as you were growing up. ______

3. Describe your holidays as a family growing up. What was your favorite holiday? ______

4. Describe your relationship with your mother growing up. ______

5. Describe your relationship with your father growing up. ______

6. Describe your relationship with your sibling(s). ______

7. Did you have pets growing up? Did you have a favorite? Describe the pets in your childhood home.

8. Describe your family's economic situation as you were growing up.

9. Describe your friends and your friendships you had as a child.

10. What types of schools did you attend? Describe your experience with school.

11. Describe your spiritual life growing up. Church life. Spirituality in the home.

12. How do you think this background affected you; making you the person you are today?

Created by God

Study 4

Understanding Personality

God creates people differently. They communicate and interact better when they understand their differences.

For you created my inmost being; you knit me together in my mother's womb. ~ Psalms 139:13

The personality test on page 33 will help you determine your personality type. Take the test before continuing in this study.

Personality is shaped by several factors; the way God creates each person, biological factors inherited from parents, the environment they grew up in, and choices made in their life. Environment includes family and the roles and interactions within it and the social environment: school, church and neighborhood.

The Differences

It is important to know and understand the differences in personalities. Those differences attract couples to each other, but then they cause friction once a couple is married. Biblical oneness requires that a couple know each other well to effectively accomplish what the Lord desires of them.

Essentially, there are four personality types or styles. There are many tests and many variations of names for these personality styles, but no matter what label is given, the basic personalities are the same:

1. The take charge, dominant person
2. The fun loving, influencing person
3. The peaceful, steady person
4. The analytical, perfectionist person

One of the four personality types usually dominates, but everyone is a mix that usually includes parts of all four. The differences in the mix are what make people so unique. The information on pages 26-28 will help you understand the personality types.

Once the personality type is determined, people can achieve a better understanding of themselves and their spouse. With a little study, they can also see how personalities can work together and how they tend to cause friction. With this knowledge comes responsibility. A couple needs to utilize this information to strengthen their marriage and to work together with their spouse to accomplish God's purposes in their lives, marriage and family.

It is important to realize that, while there are certain tendencies with each personality type, a spouse should not be stereotyped by their personality type. God creates people much more complicated than just four types of people. Learning your spouse's personality type is just the beginning of learning about who they really are.

Look at the information about your spouse's personality type and then discuss it to find out what factors there might be in their particular personality. Learning your spouse is like mining for gold. Sometimes it takes a lot of digging to find one little nugget. At times there might be a cave in—a set back that requires more digging to get back to where you were. Through hard work and some patience people are able to uncover golden information about their spouse that will help one understand and know them better.

Personality Style Comparison

Steadiness
Let's do it the easy way
Amiable
Steady & Cooperative
Affiliation oriented
Feeler
Follow Through
Loyal friend
Peaceful Phlegmatic

Golden Retriever

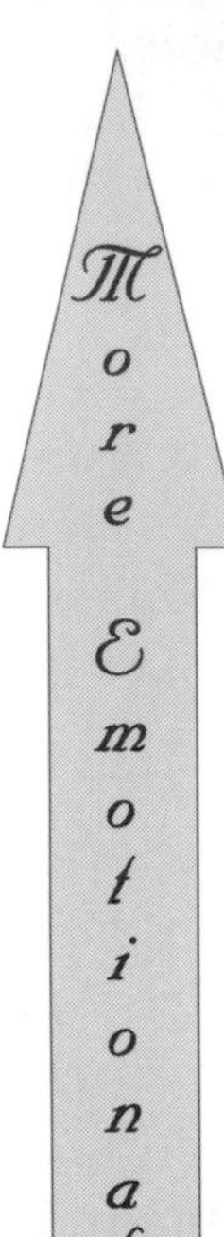

Influencing
Let's do it the fun way
Extrovert
Interested & Lively
Recognition oriented
Sensor
Implementer
Fun Loving
Popular Sanguine

Otter

Desires Safety

What Personality Are You?

More Assertive

Beaver

Compliance
Let's do it the right way
Analytical
Concerned & Correct
Order oriented
Thinker
Fact Finder
Let's be right
Perfect Melancholy

Less Emotional

Lion

Dominant
Let's do it my way
Pragmatic
Direct & Active
Achievement oriented
Intuitor
Quick Start
Take Charge
Powerful Choleric

The Golden Retriever and Beaver will tend to want safety, while the Otter and Lion will tend to be more assertive and aggressive. The Golden Retriever and Otter will tend to more emotional, while the Beaver and Lion will tend to be less emotional.

Personality Style Information

Fearless: the Lion - "Let's do it now!"

1. Fearless people lead, whether you want them to or not! They're notorious for making plans on other's behalf.
2. They thrive on confrontation, competition, and pressure. Those things let them test their capabilities. The greater the odds stacked against them, the better.
3. They have no difficulty making decisions. They'll make all the decisions pertaining to their lives - and all those pertaining to yours if you let them. They can't fathom how you could think that anything but their plan is best.
4. They don't mince words. If you're going to converse with them, you might want to save the flowery orations for someone else.
5. They like quick results. Their favorite time frame is now!
6. They don't give up easily. They are enterprising, determined, and daring. Once they know what they want, it's hard to distract them.

Spontaneous: the Otter - "Trust Me, We'll Make it!"

1. They are parties looking for a place to happen. More than anything, they just want to have fun.
2. They can't wait to see what's just over the horizon. They give the word visionary its meaning.
3. They love the sound of their own voices. Enough said.
4. They wake up smiling. They are civilization's "born optimists."
5. They never read the directions. The fine print bores them.
6. They can mobilize and motivate others with ease. They love to build people up and help their dreams come true.

Loyal: the Golden Retriever - "Let's not change anything, Okay?"

1. They are great listeners. This enables them to accommodate their need for close relationships.
2. They are emotional first-aid kits. They are innately compassionate.
3. They love to please their peers. Conflict intimidates them. They are notorious for saying yes to every idea or request from their friends.
4. They are intensely sensitive. They're tenacious friends - overwhelmingly thoughtful.
5. They can put up with a lot. They are uniquely gifted with the ability to love the one they're with. Although they despise change, they are such strong people-pleasers that they'll grit their teeth and bear it.
6. They don't compromise the things that really matter to them. They stubbornly hold on to what they feel is right.

Deliberate: the Beaver - "Wait while I read the directions."

1. They guard their hearts. They are often difficult to read because they conceal their emotions.
2. They go by the book. They read the owner's manual and hate to deviate from the plan. One of their favorite sayings is "Let's do it correctly."
3. They hate change. If it's not part of the original plan, forget it.
4. They stuff their anger. To show it would be to expose their hearts too much. They'd rather suffer in silence than fight.
5. They love to solve problems. It enables them to use their vast analytical skills.
6. They ask lots of questions. They're never satisfied with how much they know.

The Golden Retriever: Peaceful Phlegmatic

Above all, Golden Retrievers are loyal. They have hearts full of compassion and generally get along with everybody. They enjoy helping people. Retrievers will avoid conflict when possible and are the definition of the word adaptable. Yet, they will stubbornly hold to what they feel is right. Stress is not the Retriever's friend; they do not function well under stress.

Golden Retrievers like predictable routines and do not react well to sudden changes. They are patient, good listeners and like to hear all the details of a story. They do not respond well to pushy, loud, expectant people.

Retrievers need to feel good about their selves; they need respect, tolerance, attention and praise. They need reasons for big changes in their life and time to adjust to the change. They need encouragement to motivate them, not challenges. They need a place of peace to retreat to.

The Otter: Popular Sanguine

Otters want to have fun. As long as it's fun, they will do anything. They love people, but they will get depressed if everyone is too serious. They enjoy telling stories and entertaining people and have enough enthusiasm to motivate just about anybody. Otters are not very organized and do not respond well to demands to fit into a certain mold. They are very susceptible to peer pressure.

Otters can talk about anything at any time. If there is no one else around, they can have a great conversation with themselves. They are very open about their feelings. They may need help to stay on the subject being discussed.

Otters need activity. They need attention, approval, affection and praise. They need change in their life. Otters function well in a certain amount of chaos. They cannot handle too many details and don't function well without talking things out. They do not receive criticism very well.

The Beaver: Perfect Melancholy

Beavers actually read instructions! They want to get it right and do what it takes to make sure a job is done correctly. They usually do not share emotions and will often turn anger inward. Beavers tend to be very serious and meticulous. They focus on details and think analytically, weighing all the pros and cons before making a decision. They set high personal standards.

When Beavers speak, they usually have thought about what they were going to say first. They do not talk just to talk; they speak when there is something to say. Beavers can be very critical and speak logically.

Beavers need to be understood and appreciated. They want quality, and they want to see everything done correctly. They need stability in their life and will resist change for the sake of change. They need clear rules and assignments and need time to analyze a situation before making a decision.

The Lion: Powerful Choleric

Lions want control; they think that the best way to do things is their way. They want productivity and get frustrated if nothing is getting done. If you want to see near miraculous things happen, tell a lion, "You can't do it." They will practically move heaven and earth to prove you wrong. They like challenges and are not afraid of pressure or confrontation.

Lions do not like to be questioned and often perceive questions as a threat. They are not patient when it comes to long, flowery stories that take a long time to get the point. They prefer communication to be short and to the point.

Lions need appreciation for their achievements, approval from a select few, respect, a challenge to accomplish, and to be right (at least on occasion). They need to have some authority and the opportunity to grow and advance. They need new and varied activities.

Knowing Your Spouse

Learning that one is supposed to be different from his spouse is a big responsibility. Now you have to do something about it! What good is this knowledge if you continue to fight and quarrel about your differences? You have discovered that you and your spouse are very different. Those differences affect virtually every aspect of your life together, from how to discipline the children to going on vacation to spending money.

> ***Anyone who listens to the word but does not do what it says is like a man who looks at his face in a mirror and, after looking at himself, goes away and immediately forgets what he looks like.* ~ *James 1:23-24***

If your spouse is a Lion, you now know why control is so important to them. Lions naturally want control of everything around them. You also know that they want the condensed version of stories. A lion will have a hard time sitting through a five-minute story leading up to why one of the children skinned his knee playing outside. They want to know the outcome; what happened? Is everything all right now? Does anything have to be done?

Lions are great to have around in a crisis. They will take charge, get to the bottom of the problem and fix it in the fastest way possible. Lions will get a lot done in a hurry, but don't usually have patience for those who don't work as fast as they do. Lions want to know the answer to "what" questions; "what's going on?", "what are we doing about it?"

If your spouse is a Golden Retriever, you now understand why it takes them a while to get motivated and accomplish projects. They don't make decisions quickly and don't like change—especially quick change. Your Golden Retriever spouse will want all the details of the story and information about each of the participants.

Golden Retrievers are great to have around during a crisis. They will care for people and help with the hurts; physical or emotional. The easy going Golden Retriever normally will help with any work that needs to be done. Golden Retrievers want the answers to the "how" questions; "how did this happen?"

Is your spouse the non-stop whirlwind of energy and emotions? You now know he is an Otter and that being the life of the party is natural for him. Keeping Otters going in one direction can be a challenge, but those married to them know that life is never boring. Give an Otter all the details to a story and you will lose them very quickly. Things have to keep moving for them to retain their interest.

Crisis? Otters probably caused it in the first place (just kidding!). Otters will get people motivated; whether it is dealing with a crisis, going on an outing, a party, or something serious like an outreach event. They will also ensure that whatever you are doing is fun. If everyone is all right, they want to move on to the next adventure. Otters want the answers to "who" questions; "who's involved?"

If your spouse is a Beaver, you now know they were born with a set of rules and regulations. If you want a job done right, turn it over to the Beaver. They will do whatever it takes to accomplish their tasks correctly. Beavers want all the details of a situation so they can analyze it and sort everything out. They want the answer to the "why" questions; "why did this happen?"

Beavers are great to have around after a crisis, they will find out why it happened and put the procedures into place to keep it from happening again.

Personality Traits Before and After Marriage[1]

Before marriage, a fiance tends to be viewed as:		*After marriage, a spouse tends to be viewed as:*
☺ Decisive ☺ Independent ☺ Efficient ☺ Competitive ☺ Determined	**Lion** 	☹ Impatient ☹ Self-sufficient ☹ Never slows down ☹ Attacks first ☹ Stubborn
☺ Enthusiastic ☺ Talkative ☺ Optimistic ☺ Outgoing ☺ Personable	**Otter**	☹ Excitable ☹ Talks too much ☹ Unrealistic ☹ Disorganized ☹ Undisciplined
☺ Steadfast ☺ Stable ☺ Systematic ☺ Easy-going ☺ Agreeable	**Golden Retriever**	☹ Resistant to change ☹ Indecisive ☹ Slow ☹ Unwilling to initiate ☹ Over accommodating
☺ Analytical ☺ Serious ☺ Conscientious ☺ Intuitive ☺ Industrious	**Beaver** 	☹ Critical ☹ Unsociable ☹ Worries too much ☹ Overly sensitive ☹ Perfectionist

- ***Differences are not right or wrong—they are just different.***
- ***A spouse must be received as a gift from God, just as he or she is.***
- ***Respect your mate's uniqueness and differences as that which God has designed to complement and complete you. Together, you are more effective than you would be alone.***

Some accommodation required

Now that you know your spouse's personality style, you can better realize why they are the way they are. Their personality attracted you to them, but people have a tendency to look at those same traits negatively after marriage as seen in the chart to the left. God created them the way they are—it is not your job to change them. It is God's job—He is the Potter, not you. This study is an excellent opportunity to discuss the shortcomings of your spouse's personality style and how some of the negative aspects might be changed, but you must remember that it is the Lord who will do the changing. It is for a couple to utilize their newfound knowledge about their spouse to better be used by God in their life—to encourage, uphold and love—just as they are.

Some change required

At the same time, now that you know your personality style, you can not say "well, God created me this way" and not be open to change. You need to offer your strengths to the Lord and say, "use them" and to also offer up your weaknesses to Him and say "change them." As you investigate and learn about your spouse and how you can be a better spouse for them, you also need to understand your own personality and how you need to change to be a more complete and balanced person. This all takes time—in fact a lifetime! The process of knowing your spouse and growing in your love for them does not end.

People cannot ever stop learning about their spouse. Everyone passes through seasons in life and personality styles will adapt. There also will be a tempering of the negative aspects of personality and even a tempering of the positive aspects. As the Lord works in your life and you mature in Him, the Lion will become less competitive, the Otter will have a somewhat tempered enthusiasm, the Golden Retriever a loyalty tempered by wisdom and the Beaver will have the ability to at least smile at mistakes, if not laugh at them.

Wives... Your beauty should not come from outward adornment, such as braided hair and the wearing of gold jewelry and fine clothes. Instead, it should be that of your inner self, the unfading beauty of a gentle and quiet spirit, which is of great worth in God's sight... Husbands, in the same way be considerate as you live with your wives, and treat them with respect as the weaker partner and as heirs with you of the gracious gift of life, so that nothing will hinder your prayers. Finally, all of you, live in harmony with one another; be sympathetic, love as brothers, be compassionate and humble. Do not repay evil with evil or insult with insult, but with blessing, because to this you were called so that you may inherit a blessing.
~ 1Peter 3:3-4,7-9

For Discussion as a Couple

1. Where did you get your personality? How was it formed?

____
____
____
____

2. Why is it important to understand your own and your spouse's personalities?

____
____
____
____

3. What is your personality type? What are its strengths and weaknesses?

____
____
____
____

4. What is your spouse's personality type? What are its strengths and weaknesses?

____
____
____
____

5. What can you do to utilize your personality differences to fortify your marriage?

____
____
____
____

Please Note:

Copyright for The Personality Profile and Word Definitions appearing on the following pages belongs to CLASServices Inc. This information is used by permission and may only be used in conjunction with this manual. You may order Personality Profiles from:

CLASServices Inc.
3311 Candelaria NE Suite 1
Albuquerque, NM 87107
800-433-6633
www.classervices.com

Personality Profile

(Created by Fred Littauer)

Directions—In each of the following rows of four words across, place an X next to the word that most often applies to you. If you are not sure which word most applies, look at the word definitions on the following pages or ask your spouse. Once finished, transfer your X's to the corresponding words on page 38 and add up the total number of X's you have in each column.

Strengths

Adventurous ____	Adaptable ____	Animated ____	Analytical ____
Persistent ____	Playful ____	Persuasive ____	Peaceful ____
Submissive ____	Self-sacrificing ____	Sociable ____	Strong-willed ____
Considerate ____	Controlled ____	Competitive ____	Convincing ____
Refreshing ____	Respectful ____	Reserved ____	Resourceful ____
Satisfied ____	Sensitive ____	Self-reliant ____	Spirited ____
Planner ____	Patient ____	Positive ____	Promoter ____
Sure ____	Spontaneous ____	Scheduled ____	Shy ____
Orderly ____	Obliging ____	Outspoken ____	Optimistic ____
Friendly ____	Faithful ____	Funny ____	Forceful ____
Daring ____	Delightful ____	Diplomatic ____	Detailed ____
Cheerful ____	Consistent ____	Cultured ____	Confident ____
Idealistic ____	Independent ____	Inoffensive ____	Inspiring ____
Demonstrative ____	Decisive ____	Dry humor ____	Deep ____
Mediator ____	Musical ____	Mover ____	Mixes easily ____
Thoughtful ____	Tenacious ____	Talker ____	Tolerant ____
Listener ____	Loyal ____	Leader ____	Lively ____
Contented ____	Chief ____	Chart maker ____	Cute ____
Perfectionist ____	Pleasant ____	Productive ____	Popular ____
Bouncy ____	Bold ____	Behaved ____	Balanced ____

Weaknesses

Blank ____	Bashful ____	Brassy ____	Bossy ____
Undisciplined ____	Unsympathetic ____	Unenthusiastic ____	Unforgiving ____
Reticent ____	Resentful ____	Resistant ____	Repetitious ____
Fussy ____	Fearful ____	Forgetful ____	Frank ____
Impatient ____	Insecure ____	Indecisive ____	Interrupts ____
Unpopular ____	Uninvolved ____	Unpredictable ____	Unaffectionate ____
Headstrong ____	Haphazard ____	Hard to please ____	Hesitant ____
Plain ____	Pessimistic ____	Proud ____	Permissive ____
Angered easily ____	Aimless ____	Argumentative ____	Alienated ____
Naïve ____	Negative attitude ____	Nervy ____	Nonchalant ____
Worrier ____	Withdrawn ____	Workaholic ____	Wants credit ____
Too sensitive ____	Tactless ____	Timid ____	Talkative ____
Doubtful ____	Disorganized ____	Domineering ____	Depressed ____
Inconsistent ____	Introvert ____	Intolerant ____	Indifferent ____
Messy ____	Moody ____	Mumbles ____	Manipulative ____
Slow ____	Stubborn ____	Show-off ____	Skeptical ____
Loner ____	Lord over others ____	Lazy ____	Loud ____
Sluggish ____	Suspicious ____	Short-tempered ____	Scatterbrained ____
Revengeful ____	Restless ____	Reluctant ____	Rash ____
Compromising ____	Critical ____	Crafty ____	Changeable ____

Personality Test Word Definitions

Strengths

—1—

Adventurous. Takes on new and daring enterprises in any situation with a determination to master them.

Adaptable. Easily fits and is comfortable in any situation.

Animated. Full of life; lively use of hand, arm, and facial gestures.

Analytical. Likes to examine the parts for their logical and proper relationships.

—2—

Persistent. Sees one project through to completion before starting another.

Playful. Full of fun and good humor.

Persuasive. Convinces through logic and fact rather than charm or power.

Peaceful. Seems undisturbed and tranquil and retreats from any form of strife.

—3—

Submissive. Easily accepts any other's point of view or desire with little need to assert his own opinion.

Self-sacrificing. Willingly gives up own personal needs for the sake of, or meets the needs of others.

Sociable. Sees being with others as an opportunity to be cute and entertaining rather than as a challenge or business opportunity.

Strong-willed. Determined to have his own way.

—4—

Considerate. Has regard for the needs and feelings of others.

Controlled. Has emotional feelings but rarely displays them.

Competitive. Turns every situation, happening, or game into a contest and always plays to win!

Convincing. Can win you over to anything through the sheer charm of her personality.

—5—

Refreshing. Renews and stimulates or makes others feel good.

Respectful. Treats others with deference, honor, and esteem.

Reserved. Self-restrained in expression of emotion or enthusiasm.

Resourceful. Able to act quickly and effectively in virtually all situations.

—6—

Satisfied. Easily accepts any circumstance or situation.

Sensitive. Intensively cares about others and about what happens.

Self-reliant. Can fully rely on his own capabilities, judgment and resources.

Spirited. Full of life and excitement.

—7—

Planner. Prefers to work out a detailed arrangement beforehand for the accomplishment of a project or goal and prefers involvement with the planning stages and the finished product rather than the carrying out of the task.

Patient. Unmoved by delay, remains calm and tolerant.

Positive. Knows a situation will turn out right if they are in charge.

Promoter. Urges or compels others to go along. Join, or invest through the charm of their personality.

—8—

Sure. Confident, rarely hesitates or wavers.

Spontaneous. Prefers all of life to be impulsive, unpremeditated activity, not restricted by plans.

Scheduled. Makes and lives according to a daily plan, dislikes their plan to be interrupted.

Shy. Quiet, doesn't easily initiate a conversation.

—9—

Orderly. Has a methodical, systematic arrangement of things.

Obliging. Accommodating, quick to do a task another's way.

Outspoken. Speaks frankly and without reserve.

Optimistic. Sunny disposition, convinces self and others that everything will turn out all right.

—10—

Friendly. Responds rather than initiates, seldom starts a conversation.

Faithful. Consistently reliable, steadfast, loyal, and devoted, sometimes beyond reason.

Funny. Sparkling sense of humor that can make virtually any story into a hilarious event.

Forceful. A commanding personality against whom others would hesitate to take a stand.

—11—

Daring. Willing to take risks, fearless, bold.

Delightful. Upbeat and fun to be with.

Diplomatic. Deals with people tactfully, sensitively, and patiently.
Detailed. Does everything in proper order with a clear memory of all the things that happen.

—12—

Cheerful. Consistently in good spirits and promoting happiness in others.
Consistent. Stays emotionally on an even keel, responding as one might expect.
Cultured. Interests involve both intellectual and artistic pursuits, such as theater, symphony, ballet.
Confident. Self-assured and certain of own ability and success.

—13—

Idealistic. Visualizes things in their perfect form and has a need to measure up to that standard.
Independent. Self-sufficient, self-supporting, self-confident, and seems to have little need of help.
Inoffensive. Never says or causes anything unpleasant or objectionable.
Inspiring. Encourages others to work, join, or be involved, and makes the whole thing fun.

—14—

Demonstrative. Openly expresses emotion, especially affection, and doesn't hesitate to touch others while speaking to them.
Decisive. Quick, conclusive, judgment-making ability.
Dry Humor. Exhibits "dry wit," usually one-liners that can be sarcastic in nature.
Deep. Intense and often introspective with a distaste for surface conversation and pursuits.

—15—

Mediator. Consistently finds himself in the role of reconciling differences to avoid conflict.
Musical. Participates in or has a deep appreciation for music, is committed to music as an art form rather than for the fun of performance.
Mover. Driven by a need to be productive, a leader whom others follow, finds it difficult to sit still.
Mixes easily. Loves a party and can't wait to meet everyone in the room, never meets a stranger.

—16—

Thoughtful. Considerate, remembers special occasions and is quick to make a kind gesture.
Tenacious. Holds on firmly, stubbornly, and won't let go until the goal is accomplished.
Talker. Constantly talking, generally telling funny stories & entertaining everyone around, feeling the need to fill the silence to make others comfortable.
Tolerant. Easily accepts the thoughts and ways of others without the need to disagree with or change them.

—17—

Listener. Always seems willing to hear what you have to say.
Loyal. Faithful to a person, ideal, or job, sometimes beyond reason.
Leader. A natural-born director who is driven to be in charge and often finds it difficult to believe that anyone else can do the job as well.
Lively. Full of life, vigorous, energetic.

—18—

Contented. Easily satisfied with what she has, rarely envious.
Chief. Commands leadership and expects people to follow.
Chart maker. Organizes life, tasks, and problem solving by making lists, forms or graphs.
Cute. Precious, adorable, center of attention.

—19—

Perfectionist. Places high standards on self, and often on others, desiring that everything be in proper order at all times.
Pleasant. Easygoing, easy to be around, easy to talk with.
Productive. Must constantly be working or achieving, often finds it very difficult to rest.
Popular. Life of the party and therefore much desired as a party guest.

—20—

Bouncy. A bubbly, lively personality, full of energy.
Bold. Fearless, daring, forward, unafraid of risk.
Behaved. Consistently desires to conduct himself within the realm of what he feels is proper.
Balanced. Stable, middle-of-the-road personality, not subject to sharp highs or lows.

Weaknesses

—21—

Blank. Shows little facial expression or emotion.

Bashful. Shrinks from getting attention, resulting from self-consciousness.

Brassy. Showy, flashy, comes on strong, too loud.

Bossy. Commanding, domineering, sometimes over bearing in adult relationships.

—22—

Undisciplined. Lack of order permeates most every area of her life.

Unsympathetic. Finds it difficult to relate to the problems or hurts of others.

Unenthusiastic. Tends to not get excited, often feeling it won't work anyway.

Unforgiving. Has difficulty forgiving or forgetting a hurt or injustice done to him, apt to hold on to a grudge.

—23—

Reticent. Unwilling or struggles against getting involved, especially in complex situations.

Resentful. Often holds ill feelings as a result of real or imagined offenses.

Resistant. Strives, works against, or hesitates to accept any way other than her own.

Repetitious. Retells stories and incidents to entertain you without realizing he has already told the story several times before, is constantly needing something to say.

—24—

Fussy. Insistent over petty matters or details, calls for great attention to trivial details.

Fearful. Often experiences feelings of deep concern, apprehension, or anxiety.

Forgetful. Lack of memory, which is usually tied to a lack of discipline and not bothering to mentally record things that aren't fun.

Frank. Straightforward, outspoken, doesn't mind telling you exactly what she thinks.

—25—

Impatient. Finds it difficult to endure irritation or wait for others.

Insecure. Apprehensive or lacks confidence.

Indecisive. Finds it difficult to make any decision at all. (Not the personality that labors long over each decision to make the perfect one.)

Interrupts. More of a talker than a listener, starts speaking without even realizing someone else is already speaking.

—26—

Unpopular. Intensity and demand for perfection can push others away.

Uninvolved. Has no desire to listen or become interested in clubs, groups, activities, or other people's lives.

Unpredictable. May be ecstatic one moment and down the next, or willing to help but then disappears, or promises to come but forgets to show up.

Unaffectionate. Finds it difficult to verbally or physically demonstrate tenderness.

—27—

Headstrong. Insists on having his own way.

Haphazard. Has no consistent way of doing things.

Hard to please. Standards are set so high that it is difficult to ever satisfy her.

Hesitant. Slow to get moving & hard to get involved.

—28—

Plain. A middle-of-the-road personality without highs or lows and showing little, if any, emotion.

Pessimistic. While hoping for the best, generally sees the down side of a situation first.

Proud. Has great self-esteem and sees self as always right and the best person for the job.

Permissive. Allows others (including children) to do as they please to keep from being disliked.

—29—

Angered easily. Has a childlike flash-in-the-pan temper that expresses itself in tantrum style and is over and forgotten almost instantly.

Aimless. Not a goal setter, with little desire to be one.

Argumentative. Incites arguments generally because he is right no matter what the situation may be.

Alienated. Easily feels estranged from others, often because of insecurity or fear that others don't really enjoy their company.

—30—

Naïve. Simple and childlike perspective, lacking sophistication or comprehension of what the deeper levels of life are really about.

Negative attitude. Attitude is seldom positive and is often able to see only the down or dark side of each situation.

Nervy. Full of confidence, fortitude, and sheer guts, often in a negative sense.

Nonchalant. Easygoing, unconcerned, indifferent.

—31—

Worrier. Consistently feels uncertain, troubled, or

anxious.

Withdrawn. Pulls back and needs a great deal of alone or isolation time.

Workaholic. An aggressive goal setter who must be constantly productive and feels very guilty when resting, is not driven by a need for perfection or completion but by a need for accomplishment and reward.

Wants credit. Thrives on the credit or approval of others; as an entertainer, this person feeds on the applause, laughter, and/or acceptance of an audience.

—32—

Too sensitive. Overly introspective and easily offended when misunderstood.

Tactless. Sometimes expresses himself in a some what offensive and inconsiderate way.

Timid. Shrinks from difficult situations.

Talkative. An entertaining, compulsive talker who finds it difficult to listen.

—33—

Doubtful. Characterized by uncertainty and lack of confidence that a problem situation will ever work out.

Disorganized. Lacks ability to get life in order.

Domineering. Compulsively takes control of situations and/or people, telling others what to do.

Depressed. Feels down much of the time.

—34—

Inconsistent. Erratic, contradictory, with actions and emotions not based on logic.

Introvert. Thoughts and interests are directed inward, lives within herself.

Intolerant. Appears unable to withstand or accept another's attitudes, point of view, or way of doing things.

Indifferent. Most things don't matter one way or the other.

—35—

Messy. Lives in a state of disorder, unable to find things.

Moody. Doesn't get very high emotionally, but easily slips into low lows, often when feeling unappreciated.

Mumbles. Will talk quietly under the breath when pushed, doesn't bother to speak clearly.

Manipulative. Influences or manages shrewdly or deviously for his own advantage, will get his way somehow.

—36—

Slow. Doesn't often act or think quickly, too much of a bother.

Stubborn. Determined to exert their own will, not easily persuaded, obstinate.

Show-off. Needs to be the center of attention, wants to be watched.

Skeptical. Disbelieving, questioning the motive behind the words.

—37—

Loner. Requires a lot of private time and tends to avoid other people.

Lord over others. Doesn't hesitate to let you know that he is right and in control.

Lazy. Evaluates work or activity in terms of how much energy it will take.

Loud. Laugh or voice can be heard above others in the room.

—38—

Sluggish. Slow to get started, needs push to be motivated.

Suspicious. Tends to suspect or distrust others or their ideas.

Short-tempered. Has a demanding impatience-based anger and a short fuse, anger is expressed when others are not moving fast enough or have not completed what they have been asked to do.

Scatterbrained. Lack the power of concentration or attention, flighty.

—39—

Revengeful. Knowingly or otherwise holds a grudge and punishes the offender, often by subtly withholding friendship or affection.

Restless. Likes constant new activity because it isn't fun to do the same things all the time.

Reluctant. Unwilling to or struggles against getting involved.

Rash. May act hastily, without thinking things through, generally because of impatience.

—40—

Compromising. Will often relax their position, even when right, in order to avoid conflict.

Critical. Constantly evaluating and making judgments, frequently thinking or expressing negative reactions.

Crafty. Shrewd, can always find a way to get to the desired end.

Changeable. Has a childlike, short attention span, needs a lot of change and variety to keep from getting bored.

Personality Profile Scoring Sheet

Strengths

Animated	____	Adventurous	____	Analytical	____	Adaptable	____
Playful	____	Persuasive	____	Persistent	____	Peaceful	____
Sociable	____	Strong-willed	____	Self-sacrificing	____	Submissive	____
Convincing	____	Competitive	____	Considerate	____	Controlled	____
Refreshing	____	Resourceful	____	Respectful	____	Reserved	____
Spirited	____	Self-reliant	____	Sensitive	____	Satisfied	____
Promoter	____	Positive	____	Planner	____	Patient	____
Spontaneous	____	Sure	____	Scheduled	____	Shy	____
Optimistic	____	Outspoken	____	Orderly	____	Obliging	____
Funny	____	Forceful	____	Faithful	____	Friendly	____
Delightful	____	Daring	____	Detailed	____	Diplomatic	____
Cheerful	____	Confident	____	Cultured	____	Consistent	____
Inspiring	____	Independent	____	Idealistic	____	Inoffensive	____
Demonstrative	____	Decisive	____	Deep	____	Dry humor	____
Mixes easily	____	Mover	____	Musical	____	Mediator	____
Talker	____	Tenacious	____	Thoughtful	____	Tolerant	____
Lively	____	Leader	____	Loyal	____	Listener	____
Cute	____	Chief	____	Chart maker	____	Contented	____
Popular	____	Productive	____	Perfectionist	____	Pleasant	____
Bouncy	____	Bold	____	Behaved	____	Balanced	____
Strengths Totals:	____		____		____		____

Weaknesses

Brassy	____	Bossy	____	Bashful	____	Blank	____
Undisciplined	____	Unsympathetic	____	Unforgiving	____	Unenthusiastic	____
Repetitious	____	Resistant	____	Resentful	____	Reticent	____
Forgetful	____	Frank	____	Fussy	____	Fearful	____
Interrupts	____	Impatient	____	Insecure	____	Indecisive	____
Unpredictable	____	Unaffectionate	____	Unpopular	____	Uninvolved	____
Haphazard	____	Headstrong	____	Hard to please	____	Hesitant	____
Permissive	____	Proud	____	Pessimistic	____	Plain	____
Angered easily	____	Argumentative	____	Alienated	____	Aimless	____
Naïve	____	Nervy	____	Negative attitude	____	Nonchalant	____
Wants credit	____	Workaholic	____	Withdrawn	____	Worrier	____
Talkative	____	Tactless	____	Too sensitive	____	Timid	____
Disorganized	____	Domineering	____	Depressed	____	Doubtful	____
Inconsistent	____	Intolerant	____	Introvert	____	Indifferent	____
Messy	____	Manipulative	____	Moody	____	Mumbles	____
Show-off	____	Stubborn	____	Skeptical	____	Slow	____
Loud	____	Lord over others	____	Loner	____	Lazy	____
Scatterbrained	____	Short-tempered	____	Suspicious	____	Sluggish	____
Restless	____	Rash	____	Revengeful	____	Reluctant	____
Changeable	____	Crafty	____	Critical	____	Compromising	____
Weakness Totals:	____		____		____		____
Combined Totals:	____		____		____		____
Popular/Sanguine Otter		***Powerful/Choleric Lion***		***Perfect/Melancholy Beaver***		***Peaceful/Phlegmatic Golden Retreiver***	

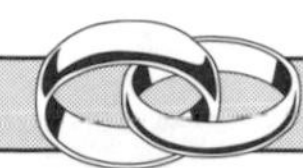

Created by God

Study 5

Spiritual Gifts

Spiritual Gifts are special gifts bestowed by the Holy Spirit upon Christians for the purpose of building up the church.[1] Another definition is a God-given, spirit-empowered ability for Christian ministry.[2] They are the God given abilities to be used for the growth of the Body of Jesus Christ.

Knowing one's Spiritual Gifts and those of his spouse will help a couple better understand each other and how each will desire to serve the Lord. As husband and wife, couples may differ dramatically in the gifts that God has given them and not knowing their spouse's gifts can cause friction in marriage. Spiritual Gifts are given by God's grace—it is not something people choose to have or not have. God has created everyone in a certain way, and the natural bents of personality may have some effect on one's gifts. However, you should not confuse natural talents and abilities with Spiritual Gifts. Often (but not always) God gives gifts to husbands and wives that complement each other. Whether your gifts are complementary or not, they can enhance your relationship and ministry together.

Now about spiritual gifts, brothers, I do not want you to be ignorant. ...There are different kinds of gifts, but the same Spirit. There are different kinds of service, but the same Lord. There are different kinds of working, but the same God works all of them in all men. Now to each one the manifestation of the Spirit is given for the common good.
~ 1 Corinthians 12:1-7

The Spiritual Gifts: People differ on the number of gifts depending how they define and classify them or the version of the Bible they use. The list on the next page was extracted from the Scriptures below (NIV).

Romans 12:6-8	*1 Corinthians 12:7-10*	*1 Corinthians 12:28-30*	*Ephesians 4:11*	*1 Peter 4:9-11*
Prophecy	Prophecy	Prophecy	Prophecy	
Serving				Serving
Teaching			Teaching	
Encouraging				
Giving				
Leadership				
Mercy				
	Wisdom			
	Knowledge			
	Faith			
	Healing	Healing		
	Miracles	Miracles		
	Discernment			
	Tongues	Tongues		
	Interpretation of tongues	Interpretation of tongues		
		Apostleship	Apostleship	
		Helps		
		Administration		
			Evangelism	
			Pastoring	
				Hospitality

Determining your Spiritual Gifts

The desire to know your Spiritual Gifts is the first step toward discovering how God has endowed you with gifts. Surveys or inventories are beneficial, but should not be your only resource. As you seek the Lord and ask Him to reveal your gifts, you will begin to gain the understanding you need.

> ***If any of you lacks wisdom, he should ask God, who gives generously to all without finding fault, and it will be given to him. ~ James 1:5***

Determining your Spiritual Gifts will take some effort on your part. There are ten steps to be taken as you seek to identify the gifts God has given you.[3]

1. Pray for direction and help.
2. Study God's Word.
3. Reflect on your desires and feelings.
4. Expose yourself to various ministries.
5. Take note of the areas that feel natural to you.
6. Watch for the successes.
7. Ask for input; be open to what others see in you.
8. Search out needs and opportunities.
9. Find the areas that give you joy.
10. Be aware of the areas where perseverance comes easily.

Spiritual Gift Definitions

1. Administration; organizing and supervising.
2. Apostleship; messenger, missionary, servant with a message.
3. Discernment; the ability to tell what is of the Holy Spirit and what is of an evil spirit.
4. Evangelism; the special ability to lead the unsaved to a personal knowledge of Christ.
5. Encouragement; coming alongside to offer comfort, counsel, exhortation and help. (Also called the gift of Exhortation)
6. Faith; utter dependence on the Lord.
7. Giving; discerning the material or financial needs of others and meeting those needs.
8. Healing; functioning as an instrument of God's healing grace in the lives of others.
9. Helps; giving assistance or relief from distress where needed.
10. Hospitality; providing an open home and a warm welcome to those in need of food and lodging.
11. Knowledge; knowing a fact or the truth about a person or a situation that is directly revealed by the Holy Spirit.
12. Leadership; able to set goals and communicate those goals such that others will voluntarily and harmoniously work together to accomplish the goals.
13. Mercy; to show compassion or feel sympathy of heart. Enables a person to empathize with others.
14. Miracles; superceding natural law—supernatural power.
15. Pastoring; leading and equipping the believers.
16. Prophecy; presenting God's word with clarity and power.
17. Serving; task-oriented ministry to provide material and temporal services to others.
18. Teaching; explaining God's truths clearly to others.
19. Tongues; speaking in unlearned languages or in ecstatic utterances.
20. Tongues, Interpretation; translating the un known language of someone else.
21. Wisdom; special illumination that enables one in a specific instance to grasp divine in sight regarding a fact, situation or context.

The Spiritual Gifts Inventory below and on the following pages will help you in your quest to understand your spiritual gifts. While this inventory does not include all of the gifts described on the previous page, it will give you a good idea about where God has gifted you. Pray for God's guidance and complete the inventory to continue the process of seeking the Lord for how He has gifted you.

Spiritual Gifts Inventory[4]

Answer each of the following questions by placing the corresponding number in the appropriate blank.

	Much (3)	Some (2)	Little (1)	Not At All (0)
1. Have people told you that you are an effective public speaker?	____	____	____	____
2. Do you find it relatively easy and enjoyable to spend time in intense study and research of the Bible?	____	____	____	____
3. Do you enjoy having people share their personal and emotional problems with you?	____	____	____	____
4. Do you find yourself more concerned with how to apply God's Word than in simply trying to understand its message?	____	____	____	____
5. Have you sensed that God has given you a special ability to learn and acquire knowledge concerning His Word?	____	____	____	____
6. Do you enjoy working to get other people involved in various tasks and ministries?	____	____	____	____
7. Would other people describe you as a person who makes decisions easily?	____	____	____	____
8. Do you seem to concentrate more on practical things that need to be done rather than on why they should be done?	____	____	____	____
9. When you hear of someone who needs help, do you immediately offer your services if it is possible?	____	____	____	____
10. Would you rather give money to help than perform some manual task?	____	____	____	____
11. Do you enjoy visiting people who are sick, disabled, or suffering physically?	____	____	____	____
12. Is your home the kind that most people feel comfortable in and will often drop by to visit with you unannounced?	____	____	____	____
13. Do you find that you have the ability to believe things that other believers cannot seem to accept or see?	____	____	____	____
14. Do other believers often tell you that you seem to always know whether something is right or wrong?	____	____	____	____
15. When situations are not right, do you feel a burden to speak up about them in order to correct them?	____	____	____	____
16. Do you love to prove and answer difficult issues and questions?	____	____	____	____

	Much (3)	Some (2)	Little (1)	Not At All (0)
17. Have you found that people often seek you out to get your advice about their personal problems?	____	____	____	____
18. Do you find that you often know immediately what to do in a situation where other believers are not so clear as to what should be done?	____	____	____	____
19. Do you find that people will often come to you with difficult problems and questions from the Bible, seeking your understanding?	____	____	____	____
20. Do you find yourself setting personal goals and objectives for yourself and your ministry as a believer?	____	____	____	____
21. Do you sense a great deal of responsibility to make decisions on behalf of others?	____	____	____	____
22. Do you usually have a great deal of joy in just doing things that need to be done, no matter how small or trivial the task?	____	____	____	____
23. Do you sense a special ministry in helping other Christians to become more effective in their ministries?	____	____	____	____
24. When you hear of someone in need, do you immediately think of sending them some money?	____	____	____	____
25. When you hear of someone in the hospital, do you desire to bring them some encouragement and cheer?	____	____	____	____
26. Do you feel that something is really missing in your life when you cannot have guests into your home?	____	____	____	____
27. When people say that something cannot be done or is impossible, do you feel the burden to believe it and trust God for it?	____	____	____	____
28. Do you seem to have an understanding of people and their motivations that proves to be correct, even though you do not know them well?	____	____	____	____
29. Do you have a tendency to speak up when issues are being dealt with in a group, rather than remain silent and listen?	____	____	____	____
30. When you hear a question or problem, are you anxious to find and give an answer?	____	____	____	____
31. Would you rather talk personally with someone about their problems rather than send them to someone else for help?	____	____	____	____
32. Do people often seek your advice in difficult situations as to what you would do or how you would handle it?	____	____	____	____
33. In your study of God's Word have you observed that new insights and understanding of difficult passages and subjects seem to come easy to you?	____	____	____	____

	Much (3)	Some (2)	Little (1)	Not At All (0)
34. When someone is not doing their ministry well, do you feel concerned to help them become more effective in what they are doing?	____	____	____	____
35. Do you sense a moral responsibility when giving direction and guidance to people, always thinking of how this will affect others?	____	____	____	____
36. Do you find satisfaction in doing a task regardless of what others thought of what you did?	____	____	____	____
37. Do you enjoy being in a supportive ministry to others rather than in being in a place of leadership?	____	____	____	____
38. Do you find yourself looking for opportunities to give your money without hearing any appeals?	____	____	____	____
39. Do you find it easy to express joy in the presence of those who are suffering physically?	____	____	____	____
40. Do you enjoy entertaining people that you do not know in your home?	____	____	____	____
41. Do you find that you usually have a problem with someone who feels that something cannot be done or accomplished?	____	____	____	____
42. Do you sense often that what is being said is produced by the devil rather than God, and has your judgment proved to be correct?	____	____	____	____
43. Have you sensed that people feel conviction about wrong practices or doctrinal error when you share with them what the Bible says?	____	____	____	____
44. Have people often said to you that you have an ability to explain difficult problems to them, usually giving reasons for what you believe?	____	____	____	____
45. Do you really get much joy out of encouraging people who are going through personal problems and trials?	____	____	____	____
46. Do you find that people usually ask you what you think about a situation with the belief that you will know what to do?	____	____	____	____
47. Have you noticed that you have the ability to understand difficult teachings of God's Word without a great volume of research and study?	____	____	____	____
48. Would you rather show someone else how to do a task than do it yourself?	____	____	____	____
49. Do you enjoy giving direction to others and making decisions for them?	____	____	____	____
50. Is it true of you that when you are asked to do a particular task that you usually feel no pressure or obligation?	____	____	____	____

	Much (3)	Some (2)	Little (1)	Not At All (0)
51. Do you feel a special burden to relieve others of their duties in order to free them to do their most important work?	____	____	____	____
52. Do you find yourself responding immediately to financial needs by giving your money without a great deal of planning to do so?	____	____	____	____
53. Is it easy for you to talk with those who are suffering physically and to experience response on their part?	____	____	____	____
54. Do you consider your home as a real place of ministry to others?	____	____	____	____
55. Have you discovered that you do not have to wait for clear evidence and direction before you make a decision?	____	____	____	____
56. Do you find that you often evaluate people and the things they say as to whether it is right or wrong?	____	____	____	____
57. When you speak God's Word do you usually think of how this is going to challenge and motivate those to whom you are speaking?	____	____	____	____
58. Have people expressed to you how much they appreciate the way you explain things from the Bible?	____	____	____	____
59. Do you find it easy to deal with people who are depressed or discouraged, experiencing a certain joy in what can be accomplished?	____	____	____	____
60. Have other believers referred to decisions you have made or advice you have given as being the right thing to do and the best for everyone?	____	____	____	____
61. Do you seem to understand things about God's Word that other believers with the same background and experience don't seem to know?	____	____	____	____
62. Do you have a special concern to train and disciple other believers to become leaders?	____	____	____	____
63. Do you find yourself constantly thinking of decisions that need to be made in giving overall direction to a group or organization?	____	____	____	____
64. Would you rather do a job yourself than work with a group in trying to accomplish it?	____	____	____	____
65. Do you believe that you would help almost anyone who had a need, if it was possible for you to do so?	____	____	____	____
66. Do you sense a great deal of joy in giving, regardless of the response of the one to whom you gave?	____	____	____	____
67. Do you often think of ways to minister and help those who are suffering physically?	____	____	____	____

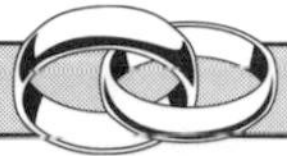

	Much (3)	Some (2)	Little (1)	Not At All (0)
68. Would you like to have a regular ministry entertaining people in your home regardless of who they are?	____	____	____	____
69. Do you feel that you are able to trust God in difficult circumstances without hesitation or indecision?	____	____	____	____
70. Do you feel a great responsibility toward God whenever you sense that something is not right which other believers do not seem to understand?	____	____	____	____
71. Have other believers shared with you that you have the ability to communicate God's Word with great effectiveness?	____	____	____	____
72. Do people come to you often, seeking your answers to specific questions or problems from the Bible?	____	____	____	____
73. Do you sense a great deal of love and compassion for people having personal and emotional problems?	____	____	____	____
74. When you give your advice to someone, do you seem to emphasize more in the area of "how" it should be done, rather than "why" it should be done?	____	____	____	____
75. Have other believers frequently pointed out to you that you have an ability to know and understand the things of God's Word?	____	____	____	____
76. Do you have a special concern for people in helping them to reach their goals and objectives in their lives?	____	____	____	____
77. Do people seem to depend upon you to make the major decisions for the group or organization?	____	____	____	____
78. When you hear of a specific job that needs to be done, are you anxious to do it yourself?	____	____	____	____
79. Are you satisfied more with how a person has been helped by what you did, than by simply doing it?	____	____	____	____
80. When you give your money to someone or something, do you usually desire to avoid letting others know what you did?	____	____	____	____
81. Would you enjoy a regular ministry to those who are suffering physically?	____	____	____	____
82. Do you look at having people into your home as an exciting ministry more than the fact that you have a responsibility to do this?	____	____	____	____
83. Have other believers often shared with you that you seem to have the ability to trust God in difficult situations?	____	____	____	____
84. Have other people often asked your opinion of someone or something that has been said as to whether you thought it was right or wrong?	____	____	____	____

	Much (3)	Some (2)	Little (1)	Not At All (0)
85. Do you believe that you are gifted in communicating to others?	____	____	____	____
86. Would you rather explain the meaning of a word than simply share a verse by quoting it to someone?	____	____	____	____
87. Do you usually desire to hear others share their personal problems rather than being able to share yours with someone else?	____	____	____	____
88. Do other believers seem to follow your advice in difficult situations?	____	____	____	____
89. Have you found in studying God's Word that you seem to know what a passage is saying before other believers discover it, even though you are studying it at the same time?	____	____	____	____
90. Do you usually take the leadership in a group where none exists?	____	____	____	____
91. Do you usually feel morally responsible for the long-range effects of your decisions?	____	____	____	____
92. Would you rather do a particular job than spend time talking with people about their problems and needs?	____	____	____	____
93. When someone asks for your help, do you have great difficulty in saying "no" to that person?	____	____	____	____
94. When you give some money to someone, do you find that you do not expect any appreciation in return?	____	____	____	____
95. Do you feel a great deal of compassion upon those who are suffering physically that makes you want to help them in some way?	____	____	____	____
96. Do you find that you can easily have people into your home without being overly concerned about how it looks?	____	____	____	____
97. Do you feel a burden to encourage people to trust God when you see them defeated and discouraged?	____	____	____	____
98. Have you felt a special responsibility to protect the truth of God's Word by exposing what is wrong and sinful?	____	____	____	____
99. Would you rather speak God's Word to others without much explanation than taking the time to explain every detail?	____	____	____	____
100. Do you usually organize your thoughts in a systematic way?	____	____	____	____
101. When you hear of some believer who has "sinned" or "fallen away," are you anxious to go to them instantly and try to help them?	____	____	____	____
102. Have the decisions and the advice you have given in difficult situations proven to be the right thing to do in most cases?	____	____	____	____

	Much (3)	Some (2)	Little (1)	Not At All (0)
103. Do you have a great desire to share with other believers what the meaning of a difficult verse or passage is?	____	____	____	____
104. Do you sense a great deal of joy in a leadership position, rather than frustration and difficulty?	____	____	____	____
105. Have you had experience in being responsible to make decisions on behalf of a group or organization that would affect everyone?	____	____	____	____
106. Do you find that you enjoy doing things that need to be done with out being asked to do them?	____	____	____	____
107. Do you find yourself looking for opportunities to help other people?	____	____	____	____
108. Do you see the matter of giving money as a tremendous spiritual ministry and one you believe God has given to you?	____	____	____	____
109. Do you find that when visiting those who are suffering physically that it brings you joy rather than depressing you?	____	____	____	____
110. Have other believers often referred to the way God has used you in your home?	____	____	____	____
111. Have you seen God do mighty things in your life that other believers said could not be done but which you believed He would do?	____	____	____	____
112. Do you feel that you are helping other believers when you discern that something is wrong, and have they readily accepted your evaluation?	____	____	____	____
113. When an opportunity is given to you to speak to other believers do you find that you would rather share verses than to share your personal experiences?	____	____	____	____
114. Have other believers told you often that you should have a regular teaching ministry and have you felt the same?	____	____	____	____
115. Do you enjoy a person-to-person ministry more than ministering to a group?	____	____	____	____
116. Have you sensed a special ability in your life to know what to do when dealing with difficult problems and situations?	____	____	____	____
117. When you see other believers confused and lacking in understanding about some difficult teaching of the Bible, have you sensed a responsibility to speak to them about what it means?	____	____	____	____
118. Do you seem to know how to meet people's needs, goals, and desires without too much study and planning?	____	____	____	____
119. Do you enjoy being the "final voice" or the one with the overall responsibility for the direction and success of a group or organization?	____	____	____	____

	Much (3)	Some (2)	Little (1)	Not At All (0)
120. Do you find that it is not necessary for you to have a "job description" when you are asked to do a particular task?	___	___	___	___
121. Have people often expressed to you how you have helped them in doing a particular job that relieved them of that responsibility in order to do something else?	___	___	___	___
122. Are you really excited when someone asks you to help financially in some worthwhile project, seeing this as a great honor and privilege?	___	___	___	___
123. Are you willing and eager to spend time, money, and resources, in order to help those who are suffering physically?	___	___	___	___
124. Do you find a great joy in having people into your home rather than sensing that it is a burden or responsibility that will entail too much work?	___	___	___	___
125. Have you discovered an effective prayer ministry in your life with many wonderful answers to prayer that from a human point of view seem impossible or unlikely?	___	___	___	___
126. Have you often made an evaluation of someone or something that was said that others did not see, but yet proved to be correct?	___	___	___	___

Spiritual Gifts Inventory Scoring

Transfer the value you entered for each question to the corresponding boxes below. Total the rows across.

Values									Total	Gift
1	15	29	43	57	71	85	99	113		Prophecy
2	16	30	44	58	72	86	100	114		Teaching
3	17	31	45	59	73	87	101	115		Exhortation
4	18	32	46	60	74	88	102	116		Wisdom
5	19	33	47	61	75	89	103	117		Knowledge
6	20	34	48	62	76	90	104	118		Leadership
7	21	35	49	63	77	91	105	119		Administration
8	22	36	50	64	78	92	106	120		Serving
9	23	37	51	65	79	93	107	121		Helps
10	24	38	52	66	80	94	108	122		Giving
11	25	39	53	67	81	95	109	123		Mercy
12	26	40	54	68	82	96	110	124		Hospitality
13	27	41	55	69	83	97	111	125		Faith
14	28	42	56	70	84	98	112	126		Discernment

Using the results of the chart, enter below your three highest-rated gifts. This will give you a tentative evaluation of where your gifts may lie.

1. ____________________ 2. ____________________ 3. ____________________

Using Your Spiritual Gifts

The inventory and list of Spiritual Gifts is meant to help you begin the process of determining the Spiritual Gifts God has given you. They are not necessarily definitive; you must continue the process outlined on page 40.

> ***Each one should use whatever gift he has received to serve others, faithfully administering God's grace in its various forms. ~ 1 Peter 4:10***

Once discovered, the gifts are to be used to serve others. It begins with spouse and children; one is to use their gifts to build up and encourage their family in their walk with the Lord. It is a matter of examining one's gifts, understanding them and looking for ways to use them for the family's benefit and to the benefit of others. God does not give Spiritual Gifts without reason or purpose; they are to be used! As you administer God's grace in its various forms (extending God's grace to others through the gifts He has given you), you are accomplishing His purpose, serving the Lord, and extending His kingdom.

For Discussion as a Couple

1. What do you think are your Spiritual Gifts? Are you using them? How?

____

____

____

____

2. What do you think are your spouse's Spiritual Gifts? How is he or she using them?

____

____

____

____

3. How can yours and your spouse's Spiritual Gifts cause problems in your marriage?

____

____

____

____

4. What can you do to use your Spiritual Gifts as a couple to begin or enhance your ministry together?

____

____

____

____

5. How can you use your Spiritual Gifts to serve your spouse and children?

____

____

____

____

Fortified Marriages
Chapter 1 Endnotes

Study 1: *Who is Jesus Christ?*

Recommended for further reading:
- Evidence that Demands a Verdict by Josh McDowell
- More Than a Carpenter by Josh McDowell
- The Case for Christ by Lee Strobel

For further infromation, see:
- Campus Crusade for Christ: www.ccci.org

Study 2: *Created by God*

1. Neil T. Anderson; Victory Over the Darkness (Ventura, CA; Regal, 2000) pp 61-62
2. Ibid., pp 162-164

Recommended for further reading:
- Victory Over the Darkness by Neil T. Anderson
- How to Succeed at Being Yourself by Joyce Meyer
- The Practice of Godliness by Jerry Bridges
- The Wonderful Spirit Filled Life by Charles Stanley
- Victorious Christian Faith by Alan Redpath

For further information, see:
- Campus Crusade for Christ: www.ccci.org
- Freedom in Christ Ministries: www.freedominchrist.com

Study 3: *Knowing Your Differences*

1. Adapted from, Marriage Clues for the Clueless; The Livingstone Corporation (Uhrichsville, OH; Promise Press, 1999) pp 22- 25
2. Simon Baron-Cohen; The Essential Difference; The Truth about the Male and Female Brain (NY, NY; Basic Books, 2003) pp 1-3
3. Neil T. Anderson & Charles Mylander; The Christ Centered Marriage (Ventura, CA, Regal books, 1996) pp 114—115
4. John Gray; Men are from Mars, Women are from Venus (NY, NY; HarperCollins, 1992) p16
5. Ibid., p18
6. Neil T. Anderson & Charles Mylander; The Christ Centered Marriage (Ventura, CA, Regal books, 1996) pp 122- 123
7. Ibid., pp 120- 121
8. Barbara & Allan Pease; Why Men Don't Listen and Women Can't Read Maps (NY, NY; Welcome Rain Publishers, 2000) p 80
9. Women Are the Backbone of the Christian Congregations in America; The Barna Group, Ventura, CA, March 6, 2000

Recommended for further reading:

- Marriage Clues for the Clueless; Developed and produced by the Livingstone Corporation.
- Men are from Mars, Women are From Venus by John Gray, Ph.D.
- The Christ Centered Marriage by Neil T. Anderson & Charles Mylander.
- If Only He Knew by Gary Smalley
- Making Sense of the Men in Your Life by Dr. Kevin Leman
- What Does She Want From Me, Anyway? by Holly Faith Phillips

For further information, see:

- FamilyLife Ministries: www.familylife.com
- Focus on the Family: www.family.org
- Mars & Venus; Dr. John Gray: www.marsvenus.com

Study 4: *Understanding Personality*

1. FamilyLife Marriage Conference—Alumni Sessions, p 3
2. The Personality Profile and Word Definitions by Fred Littauer are used by permission of CLASServices Inc. Ordering information can be found on page 32 of this manual.

Recommended for further reading:

- Personality Plus by Florence Littauer
- Personality Plus for Couples by Florence Littauer
- The Two Sides of Love Gary Smalley and John Trent
- A Woman's Guide to the Personality Types by Donna Partow

For further information, see:

- Classervices Inc.: www.classervices.com
- DISC: www.discprofile.com

Study 5: *Spiritual Gifts*

1. Nelson's Illustrated Bible Dictionary; Copyright 1986, Thomas Nelsons Publishers
2. Identifying & Deploying Your Spiritual Gifts; Dr. Lindsey Garmon. www.theseeker.ort/gifts.
3. Ibid.
4. Spiritual Gifts Inventory by LifeQuest Church, Phoenix, AZ. Used with permission.

Recommended for further reading:

- Finding Your Spiritual Gifts Questionnaire by C. Peter Wagner.
- Discovering Your Spiritual Gifts by J. E. O'Day.
- Discover Your God-Given Gifts by Don & Katie Fortune.

For further information, see:

- Building Church: www.buildingchurch.net
- The Seeker Bible Study: www.theseeker.org/gifts
- Ministry Tools Resource Center: www.mintools.com
- Computers for Christ: www.cforc.com/sgifts.html
- Eleven Talents: www.eleventalents.com/gifts.htm

Chapter 2
Direction in Life

Study 6
Purpose in Life

Jesus replied: "'Love the Lord your God with all your heart and with all your soul and with all your mind.' This is the first and greatest commandment. And the second is like it: 'Love your neighbor as yourself.'"
~ Matthew 22:37-39

"Too long you have been listening to the voice of the diplomat, the scientist, the psychiatrist, the sociologist and the military commander. It is time you listened to the voice of Almighty God."
~ Billy Graham

Knowing your purpose in life is important to your marriage relationship. You need to understand your purpose individually before you can know where you are going together as a couple.

Why Are You Here?

Society today lives at a pace unheard of in earlier generations. Technology has not freed people from the drudgery of work as much as it has enslaved them to a life lived at the edge. Many people run through each day so quickly that they rarely have time to reflect on their life and where it is going. They purchase and consume their way through life with little thought about the meaning of life and their purpose in it.

Did humans evolve out of some primordial ooze, only to gather a lot of possessions and then pass them on to their children or the government when they die? Or is there a larger plan and design for life? Life does not offer much hope without a relationship with God. It becomes a sum of what one achieves; whether it is possessions or position. When a person dies without God, it is over, and contrary to what the bumper sticker says, he who dies with the most toys does not win.

"Unless you assume a God, the question of life's purpose is meaningless."
~Bertrand Russell, atheist

Faith in God changes everything for the believer. Unfortunately, many people do not live out their faith and do not realize who they are as children of God. Chapter One explored identity; who you are in Christ, as male or female and how you were created. At this point, who you are should not be the question. Now it is time to see what you are to do with the life you have been given. God created people just as they are and for a purpose, but what is that purpose? And how does one determine what his purpose is in life?

Purpose Begins with a New Life in Christ

Christians are born again; they have a new life in Jesus Christ. The old, worldly thinking person is dead and the new spiritual person is alive. Christians are followers of Jesus Christ. They are representatives of Christ in this world—God's ambassadors according to Second Corinthians. People are created to do God's will (Mark 3:35), to know God (Ephesians 1:17), to worship and serve God (Luke 4:8), to love God and people (Matthew 22:37-39), and to use their Spiritual Gifts (Romans 12:7). While these commands are very general and broad, they serve as a starting point for knowing God's specific purpose for your life.

> *"Nothing matters more than knowing God's purposes for your life, and nothing can compensate for not knowing them." ~ Rick Warren*

God wants His people to know their purpose in life; it is not some great mystical secret that takes a lifetime to understand. Christians will begin to see purpose in their life when they live life as they are rather than as they or someone else thinks they should be. God will reveal your specific purpose in life as you search the Scriptures and seek His will.

Doing versus Being

> *If any of you lacks wisdom , he should ask God, who gives generously to all without finding fault, and it will be given to him. ~ James 1:5*

Very often people get caught up in doing things rather than being who they are. The Christian life becomes nothing more than a cleaned up, sanitized version of the worldly rat-race. Many use Christian terminology and live by a list of do's and don'ts and think their lives are different than the non-Christian's life. It may be different in some ways, but in many ways it is the same. Christians often wear out faster than non-Christians because they attempt to do all of the things they should be doing trying to measure up as the Christian they think they should be. They are not living out who they are as a person and as a child of God. Christianity does not consist of the things people do, but rather being who they are because of what Jesus Christ has done for them.

In practical terms; if you want to have a great marriage, you have to be a great spouse. If you want to have a more pleasant, cooperative teenager, you need to be a more understanding, consistent, loving parent. If you want to be trusted, you must be trustworthy.[1]

People tend to worry about the other person or their circumstances when they should be concerned about themselves. They point the finger at their spouses and blame him for their poor behavior. They focus on their spouse, parents, employer, even God as the problem, rather than looking at themselves. If they would become the person God created them to be, many of their problems would cease to exist. The Christian life and being married do not have to be the burden many people tend to make them. Both can be joyous and rewarding. In Matthew 11:30, Jesus said that His burden is light. Yet, many drive themselves to exhaustion attempting to have the so called "good life."

Driven versus Called

People are driven to accomplish, excel and perform and do not examine their purposes. Often they arrive at a point where they see how fruitless their quest is. Rick Warren's books, The Purpose Driven Life and The Purpose Driven Church have sold millions of copies. Yet, Gordon MacDonald writes that the driven person will tend to have health problems and an unsatisfied life, while the called person will be less stressed and more productive.[2] Both men speak of the same process from different points of view. According to Rick Warren, the purpose driven life is a life lived for God and according to God's leading. Gordon Macdonald defines driven as the drive to achieve for a purpose other than God's purpose.[3] Both men share the same ideal; that God should be leading and mankind should be following.

"Kiss, Kiss, Gotta Run!"

Direction as a Couple

Many marriages today are not fulfilling because the husband and wife's driving purposes in life are completely different. He is focused on attaining a certain level of achievement in the business world while her whole world revolves around raising children. They may both be pursuing the dream of corporate success, but their dreams do not fit together, or they may attempt to find fulfillment and purpose separately through different people or family. A couple must be going in the same direction or they will experience a dry, fruitless marital relationship.

> *There is a way that seems right to a man, but in the end it leads to death.* ~ *Proverbs 16:25*

A marriage is no better than it's purpose.[4] God's purposes must be at the core of a person individually and as a couple. Scripture says that above all things people are to love the Lord their God with all their heart, soul and mind. When Christians are intent on that purpose, they can begin searching out God's specific purpose for their lives. When God is first in your life and all things are tested according to His will, your ways will be His ways.

Knowing the Will of God

> *Therefore do not be foolish, but understand what the Lord's will is.* ~ *Ephesians 5:17*

When you live your life and conduct your marriage your own way or the world's way, it will be hard at best, miserable and doomed to failure at worst. The fruit (end result) of loving Jesus Christ is obedience to His will (John 14:15). Knowing the will of God sometimes seems to be one of the great mysteries of the universe, but it is not that hard. Ephesians 5 states that people are not to be foolish, but to understand what the Lord's will is. God's will is a great mystery when Christians live their lives for themselves and do not seek Him.

> *Do not conform any longer to the pattern of this world, but be transformed by the renewing of your mind. Then you will be able to test and approve what God's will is-- his good, pleasing and perfect will.* ~ *Romans 12:2*

The mind is renewed through the Word of God, prayer, worship and fellowship with other believers. Studying the Word and making it a part of one's life and spending time in prayer, and worship with the Lord will help people better know God's will for their lives. Fellowship or the close association with other Christians helps bring proper perspective into lives. Proverbs 3:5-6 reminds God's people to lean not on your own understanding, but in all your ways acknowledge Him and He will make your paths straight. Will you know God's will for every decision you need to make? Maybe not directly, but if you search Scripture, pray and seek the advice of Godly friends, decisions can be made with confidence of God's direction.

"Honey, maybe if you move this way, you can get out of the rain."

It is important to be open to the Lord's use of people or circumstances to reveal His will for you. It is wise to be wary of the person who approaches you saying; "The Lord says to you...," but it is also wise to consider what that person has to say. The Lord may have someone speak to you about something in your life, but He will also confirm the message through other means. Unless you are not listening, why would God use someone else to speak to you when He can speak directly to you? The key is being open, listening to Him and seeking His will for your life.

> *"There are many ways by which God leads us, but it is only when our minds and hearts have surrendered to Him, that we sometimes hear His voice." ~ Billy Graham*

You may have already sought God's purpose and will for your life and marriage. If so, that's great! For those who have not sought God's purpose for their life and marriage, now is a great time to begin seeking His wisdom and insight for your life. This is foundational to a strong, fortified marriage. Begin thinking about your purpose in life as you explore this aspect of your marriage more in the next two studies. Know that God does have a plan for your life, good plans for you and your marriage.

> *"For I know the plans I have for you," declares the LORD, "plans to prosper you and not to harm you, plans to give you hope and a future."*
> *~Jeremiah 29:11*

> *"When two people love each other, they don't look at each other, they look in the same direction." ~ Ginger Rogers*

> *For we are God's workmanship, created in Christ Jesus to do good works, which God prepared in advance for us to do. ~ Ephesians 2:10*

For Discussion as a Couple

1. How is your love for God reflected in your daily life? Do people see that God is first in your life? How?

____

____

____

____

2. Are you living the Christian life (being)? Or are you trying to do all the things you should be doing? What is the difference?

____

____

____

____

3. Do you live your life as a driven person or a called person? What is the difference?

____

____

____

____

4. Is it necessary to seek God's will for every decision in your life or only the major decisions? Explain.

____

____

____

____

5. What do you think your purpose is in life? Do you think there is a purpose for your marriage? What is it?

____

____

____

____

Purpose in Life Questionnaire

Answer the following questions honestly as individuals and then discuss your answers together when you have time alone.

1. What evidence is there in your life that God is most important to you?

2. How does the daily grind of life affect you? Does it challenge you? Depress you? Wear you out?

3. How much time do you spend with the Lord on a regular basis? How do you spend that time?

4. How do you attempt to control your life?

5. What are three things you would like to accomplish in life, that you have not already done?

6. How do you find out God's will for your life? In the past have you taken the time to understand if your actions are in God's will? Why or why not?

7. Have you attempted to live up to someone else's (parent or other person) expectations for your life? Have you attempted to get past someone's prediction of failure for your life? What is your experience in this area?

8. Did you pray about whether it was God's will for you to marry your spouse? Do you believe it was your destiny to marry your spouse? Why or why not? ______

9. Is your job fulfilling? Why or why not? Will you remain in your career field or change? ______

10. How do you spend your time? Honestly look at a typical week in your life; how much time do you spend in the following categories? We know approximately 50 hours a week (including lunch and travel) are required for work and approximately 56 hours are required for sleep; what do you do with the other 62 hours a week available to you?

My typical week:

Sleep (above 56 hours)	______	Housework	______
Work (above 50 hours)	______	Yard work	______
Eating	______	Time with spouse	______
Watching Television	______	Time with children	______
Exercise	______	Personal Development	______
Hobbies: ______	______	Ministry	______
______	______	God's Word	______
______	______	Worshipping God	______
		Prayer	______

What are your thoughts about your use of time? ______

Direction in Life
Study 7
The Importance of Change

Yet, O LORD, you are our Father. We are the clay, you are the potter; we are all the work of your hand. Isaiah 64:8

"Sure, I can accept you for who you are, you are someone I need to change."

Blessed is the man who has discovered that there is nothing permanent in life but change.

God Wants His People to Change

God loves His people totally and unconditionally, but He loves them so much that He does not want them to remain the same. The Bible consistently points out the importance God places on change. The Lord told Cain to turn from the sin that desired to have him. He used the prophets throughout the Old Testament to plead with the Israelites to turn from their sinful behavior. Jesus challenged the Pharisees to turn from their traditions. He did not condemn the woman caught in adultery, but did tell her to 'go and sin no more'. The book of Revelation is a final call to repentance; turning from sin to God before the end of time. Today, the Lord desires to mold His children into His image and this requires change.

You used to walk in these ways, in the life you once lived. But now you must rid yourselves of all such things as these... since you have taken off your old self with its practices and have put on the new self, which is being renewed in knowledge in the image of its Creator. ~ Colossians 3:7-10

God is the Potter; He molds and shapes people as He desires. While it is the Lord who shapes and changes, it is important that people are open to change and make choices that will work the Lord's change into their lives. One must allow Him to do the work of molding and shaping.

Everyone has sin in their lives - no one is perfect. People have undesirable patterns, ruts and wrong behavior ingrained into them. Christians are new creatures in Christ, but they need to replace old habits with new Spirit driven behaviors. Conforming into the image of Christ is a life-long process. The journey begins with accepting Jesus Christ as Lord and Savior and continues throughout life.

"Haven't you read," he replied, "that at the beginning the Creator 'made them male and female,' and said, 'For this reason a man will leave his father and mother and be united to his wife, and the two will become one flesh'? ~ Matthew 19:4-5

Change is Important to Marriage

A couple does not become *one* at the wedding ceremony and does not become *one* naturally. They become one as they both grow in their relationship together. Change will happen in this growth process and both must be open to change. The rigid attitude of, "this is how I am, I can't change" (actually won't), will stifle growth individually and in the marriage relationship.

The Lord will often use your spouse to challenge you to change. Too often people reject their spouse's requests or observations, when they should take what they have to say to heart. That doesn't mean that a person has license to point out every little wrong thing that he sees in his spouse (that's criticism). A spouse may also attempt to change his spouse, rather than allow the Lord to do the changing. You cannot change your spouse, only God can do that. People can only change themselves with God's help. As you develop oneness and transparency in your marriage, the Lord will use you to affect each other.

As iron sharpens iron, so one man sharpens another. ~ Proverbs 27:17

A couple must be willing to change for their marriage to grow. How can a marriage grow if both partners are unwilling to change? They will not experience the fullness of marriage if they are constantly looking for their spouse to change and not making room for change in their own life.

People today spend thousands of dollars on cars, weddings or toys. They invest in homes, retirement, the stockmarket, but they will not invest in their marriage nor will they spend the time and energy required to improve their marriage. They won't spend the money for training or the marital counseling that could help their relationship.

Are people so unwilling to commit to a marriage, that they won't take the steps needed to strengthen it? Has marriage as an institution become so degraded that people - even Christians will not do whatever it takes to save their marriage? Are they that unwilling to change?

How Does Change Occur?

Jesus tells people to have the simple faith of children, but they tend to make life more complicated than it should be. They often spend a lot of time, money and energy attempting to figure out life, rather than trusting God for every aspect of their lives. Living by faith is the first step toward change. It is important to trust God that He will make the changes needed. One must trust in His power, His knowledge and His love.

And he said: "I tell you the truth, unless you change and become like little children, you will never enter the kingdom of heaven.
~ Matthew 18:3

Change takes obedience and submission to God's will. You know His will by growing in your relationship with Him. A growing relationship with the Lord requires a transformation by the renewing of the mind (Romans 12:2). Conforming into God's image takes study of His Word and spending time with Him in prayer and fellowship. It does take discipline and some work. No relationship grows without effort. The Lord will change you, but you must be willing to do your part.

Admit our need
Seek the Lord's help
Keep the faith

Your part includes being willing to ASK for help and seek the counsel of other Christian couples, pastors or professional Christian counselors if necessary. Marriage classes, seminars and conferences provide information to challenge and help couples change. God gives direction in many ways. The Bible says that the wise man seeks understanding, instruction and advice. It is the fool who rejects advice and sound counsel and relies only on himself. (See Proverbs 12:15, 15:14, 18:2, 19:20)

"On our program today, we will learn how to be happy and carefree."

Marriage is not easy. It does take effort and work - a couple will get out of it what they put into it. Are you willing to put the effort into your marriage to make it great? Are you willing to change to make your marriage better?

> *Changing one thing for the better does more good than proving a dozen things are wrong.*

The Challenge:

Make the commitment to change. Commit to the Lord and your spouse that you will strive to change to be the husband or wife the Lord has called you to be. Don't look at your spouse, look at yourself! What do you need to change to make your marriage better?

> *If you do what you have always done, you are liable to get what you have always gotten. ~ Anonymous*

For Discussion as a Couple

1. Do you believe God wants you to change? Why or why not?

   ____
   ____
   ____
   ____

2. What does it mean to invest in your marriage?

   ____
   ____
   ____
   ____

3. Do you try to change your spouse? Can you change them? Why or why not? ____________________

   ____
   ____
   ____
   ____

4. How can you change?

   ____
   ____
   ____
   ____

5. What would a commitment to change do for your marriage?

   ____
   ____
   ____
   ____
   ____

Direction in Life

Study 8

A Vision for the Future

> *For I know the plans I have for you," declares the LORD, "plans to prosper you and not to harm you, plans to give you hope and a future. Then you will call upon me and come and pray to me, and I will listen to you. You will seek me and find me when you seek me with all your heart.*
> *~ Jeremiah 29: 11-13*

> *A person who aims at nothing is sure to hit it.*
> *~ Anonymous*

Begin with a Vision

The Bible says that where there is no vision, the people perish. The Hebrew word for perish is also translated to go unrestrained ... each to his own way. Without a vision, people tend to go their own way. A couple going their own ways can not grow in intimacy and become one. They can not fulfill God's purpose for their marriage, and may end up going their own ways to the point of ending the marriage. One of the biggest differences in couples before and after the wedding ceremony is the fact that they stop dreaming together. They stop looking to the future; setting goals and making plans.[1] They lose their vision.

Your vision, where you are going in life, is the fulfillment of your purpose. An effective way to think of vision is to consider what you would like written on your tombstone when you die. Maybe not something people like to contemplate, but everyone will die sooner or later. Thinking about how one would like to be remembered when he is gone can help maintain the focus to fulfill that desire. Think of your purpose in life; what does it mean to be completed? That is your vision.

A vision statement is a short statement of where your life is going. It may even be past tense; the statement you want on your tombstone. My vision statement is: "He ran the race marked out for him with perseverance" from Hebrews 12:1. My desire is to be remembered as a man who stayed the course—God's course, and finished it no matter what came along in life.

What is your vision for your marriage? For your family? Once you have your individual vision statements, sit down together as a couple to create a vision statement for your marriage. If your children are old enough, share your vision and include them in the process of formulating a vision statement for your family. If the children are very young or still in the future, write a family vision statement that can be shared with your children as they get older.

Perhaps today, more than ever, individuals and families need a sense of direction and purpose, a guiding structure in their life around which they can make decisions, and set goals to work toward. Every day life brings many pressing decisions to be made: where to put time, attention, energy and money. With an established vision, mission and goals, one can ask, "Will this option move us toward accomplishing our mission or hinder it?" Depending on that answer, they can make a good decision that will fit the direction they are going.

"Sure, I'd like to have a vision for my life, but I'm too busy living it to figure out what I want to do with it."

Establish the Mission

> ***A mission points you in the direction of your vision.***

Once you have a vision, you can begin work on a personal mission statement. This is the statement of how you will fulfill your vision. It is your philosophy or creed; built on the values and principles upon which all that you do in life is based. The mission statement will reflect what your life is about, what you stand for and how you are going to reach your vision. Outside influences should not affect your mission. It is to be solely dependant on your decisions, actions and God's work in your life.

The mission statement should be short, easily understandable and memorized. It is to be part of a person's life; something they live on a daily basis. Unlike the vision statement, the mission statement is about the present; what you are doing now to attain your vision. My mission statement is "To serve God with a whole heart - To be repentant and willing to change."

A mission of attaining a college degree can be frustrated by any number of factors and often is. Failure to fulfill that mission could result in anxiety and even depression. A degree is a worthy desire and may be an objective, but to make it a mission in life is to set yourself up for disappointment.

The marriage or family mission statement will be different than a personal mission statement, but must be in harmony with it. It's accomplishment will be dependant on the actions of the couple or their family as a whole. As much as possible, a couple must work together and involve the family as they create mission statements that affect the family unit.

Goals Fulfill the Mission

Once the vision and mission statements are created, you can begin thinking about goals. Goals specify the accomplishments to be achieved to realize your mission. A goal is defined as; "The purpose toward which an endeavor is directed; an objective."[2] Goals are set in the different areas of life to maintain the direction you have set with your mission statement.

It is important to differentiate between goals that are reached through a person's efforts alone and goals that require external events or other people to cooperate. No one has total control of the events in their life. One can have a worthy—even godly goal that may not happen. You may want a family member to accept Christ into his life. It is a worthy goal, but if you make this a goal that must be accomplished, its lack of fulfillment can result in anxiety, anger and even depression. His acceptance of Christ is not within your power to make happen.

Both goals that can not be blocked and goals that can be blocked will be set. The primary difference is the focus. Certain goals may not come to pass and if they don't, you re-evaluate, adjust and move on. If you become frustrated and angry when a goal is blocked, that frustration will very often cause problems and damage intimacy in the marriage relationship.

Keeping this differentiation in mind as you begin setting goals for your life will ease frustration with the process. Remember that emotions are God's feedback system and may indicate problems with the way that you are facing a situation. When an experience or relationship leaves you feeling angry, anxious, or depressed, those emotional signposts are there to alert you to the possibility that you may be holding onto a faulty goal which is based on a wrong belief.[3] At times, the most well-intentioned goals are not in accord with God's plans for a person's life and frustration over their failure to materialize can hinder growth. You cannot base your self-worth or personal success on goals that you do not have total control over, no matter how Godly they may be, because you cannot control their fulfillment.[4]

It is very easy in this demanding world for a married couple to become distant and begin going in different directions. A shared life vision, mutual mission and realistic goals and objectives helps a couple remain on track and going in the same direction.

Setting Goals

> ***Your goals are the road maps that guide you and show you what is possible for your life. ~ Les Brown***

Setting goals and objectives resembles a pyramid. Work down from your Vision and Mission Statement to set goals and objectives. There will be more activities to accomplish as you move through the process.

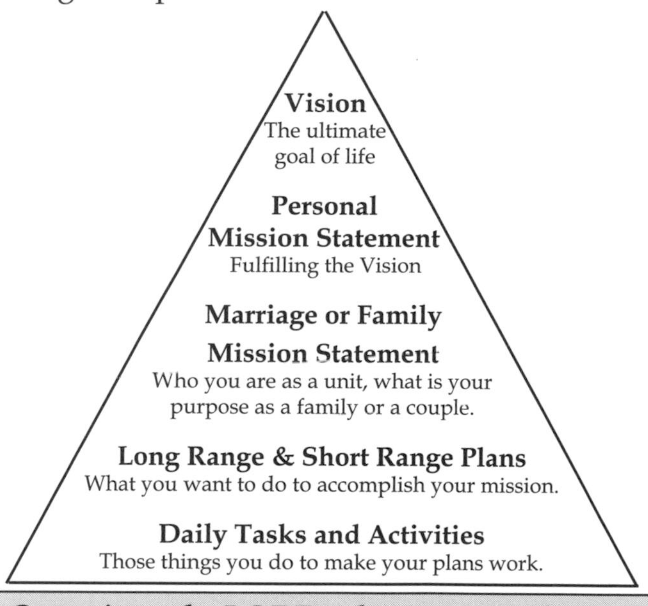

> ***Commit to the LORD whatever you do, and your plans will succeed. ~ Proverbs 16:3***

It is important to continue in the process and set goals and objectives. You may want to get away for a planning retreat; a weekend away without distractions to make plans. My wife and I do this yearly on our anniversary. We get away and review our goals and objectives. It is wonderful to see what the Lord has done in our lives over the past year, but also is a time to reflect on what we need to get serious about in our lives. Be sure to include time for prayer in your planning. Set your goals and objectives with God's Word and His will for your life in mind.

Objectives are the "what" you will do, plans are the "how" you do it and the schedule is when you will complete it. Use the Goal Setting/Planning Worksheet on page 68 as an example to help you begin to put your vision and mission into action. There are seven areas to look at as you work together to create a plan for your lives, marriage and family. This is not an all-inclusive list and you may want to add areas or change areas according to your personal preferences and needs. Goals in the following areas are important:

Spiritual; how are you going to grow in your walk with the Lord, personally and as a couple? What areas can you improve?

Marriage; what can you do to improve your marriage? What do you need to do to grow in oneness?

Family; what do you want to do as a family? Where can you improve and grow?

Financial; what do you need to accomplish financially? What are you saving for? What bills do you need to pay off?

Personal; what personal things do you want to accomplish? Areas might be: read more; lose weight, exercise, education or training, connecting with other couples or people.

Career; what do you want to accomplish on your job? Are you going the direction you want to be going? What can you change? What about retirement?

Ministry; Are you ministering where God wants you? Where can you get involved?

Remember, to build a future on goals that can be blocked can spell disaster. Pray for the things you would like to have and assume responsibility for those things you know God wants you to do.

Also, set long-range goals – dream together! What do you want to be doing in five, ten, twenty years? When do you want to retire? What do you want to do when you retire? It is important to see a future together as a couple. Write your goals down. They may change over time, but that is all right. Goals and objectives must be flexible. Rigid, inflexible goals will be frustrating and divisive in your marriage and family.

A benefit of going through the goal setting exercise is the intimacy it will build into your marriage. The more you plan, dream and work together, the more you will grow together in your relationship.

Maintaining the Balance

There must be a balance as you make plans and trust in the Lord for everything. The book of James says that, no one knows what tomorrow holds. Make plans and set goals, but do not trust in those plans and goals—trust in the Lord. First, seek His kingdom and let Him direct you as you look to the future—as a couple striving to serve Him.

> ***Now listen, you who say, "Today or tomorrow we will go to this or that city, spend a year there, carry on business and make money." Why, you do not even know what will happen tomorrow. What is your life? You are a mist that appears for a little while and then vanishes. ~ James 4:13-14***

For Discussion as a Couple

1. What is a vision? Do you agree that couples tend to have a vision before marriage and lose it afterward? Why or why not?

____

____

____

____

2. Have you experienced frustration with goals that have been blocked? How can this cause frustration in your marriage?

____

____

____

____

3. Do you have a mission statement? Do you think it is a valuable tool in your marriage? Why or why not?

____

____

____

____

4. How can you balance planning and setting goals and objectives with trusting in the Lord and not relying on your own strength and plans?

____

____

____

____

5. How might you begin setting goals and objectives as a couple?

____

____

____

____

What is Your Vision?

Individually

Husband

____

____

____

Wife

____

____

____

Husband's Mission Statement

____

____

____

Wife's Mission Statement

____

____

____

Your Vision as a Couple

____

____

____

Your Vision as a Family

____

____

____

Where are you going?

Couple's Mission Statement

____

____

____

Family Mission Statement

____

____

____

Goal Setting/Planning Worksheet

Commit to the LORD whatever you do, and your plans will succeed. ~ Proverbs 16:3

Mission Statement: ______________________________

____

Goal Setting Areas	**Objectives** What is to be done	**Plan** How it will be done	**Schedule** Date to accomplish
Spiritual			
Marriage			
Family			
Financial			
Personal			
Career			
Ministry			

Fortified Marriages
Chapter 2 Endnotes

Study 6: *Purpose in Life*

1. Adapted from Stephen Covey; The 7 Habits of Highly Effective People (NY, NY, Fireside) p 43
2. Gordon MacDonald; Ordering Your Private World (Nashville, TN, Oliver Nelson)
3. Ibid Chapters 3 and 4.
4. Dan Allender and Tremper Longman; Intimate Allies (Wheaton, IL, Tyndale House) p 74

Recommended for further reading:
- The Purpose Driven Life by Rick Warren
- First Things First by Stephen Covey
- Ordering Your Private World by Gordon MacDonald

Study 8: *A Vision for the Future*

1. Neil Clark Warren; Learning to Live With the Love of Your Life (Wheaton, IL, Tyndale House)
2. The American Heritage Dictionary of the English Language, Fourth Edition; Copyright 2000 by Houghton Mifflin Company.
3. Larry Crabb; The Marriage Builder (Grand Rapids, MI, Zondervan) p 74
4. Neil Anderson; Victory Over the Darkness (Ventura, CA; Regal, 2000) p 126

Recommended for further reading:
- Intimate Encounters by David & Teresa Ferguson and Chris & Holly Thurman
- Learning to Live With the Love of Your Life by Neil Clark Warren
- The Marriage Builder by Larry Crabb

Chapter 3
Boundaries

Study 9

Understanding Boundaries

Above all else, guard your heart, for it is the wellspring of life.
~ Proverbs 4:23

"Having an awareness of boundaries and limits helps me discover who I am. Until I know who I am, it will be difficult for me to have healthy relationships, whether they may be casual acquaintances, friends, close relationships or intimate relationships."
~ Charles Whitfield[1]

What are Boundaries?

Simply stated, a boundary is a limit or edge. A fence marking a property line is a boundary. Walls, hedges or signs also serve as physical boundaries as they mark property that belongs to a person. There are privileges and responsibilities that go with owning the property within a boundary. This is standard and accepted in society today.

There are also personal boundaries that differentiate people from one another. Skin is a boundary line; it defines where one physically begins and ends as a person. Personal boundaries also extend beyond the skin to the space around a person. One may physically back away from another when he feels the other person is too close and crowding his space.

Many people are not aware of how much these personal boundaries affect their lives. In addition to defining a person physically, boundaries define people emotionally, spiritually and intellectually. They define who a person is and also what does or does not belong to him. Feelings, attitudes and reactions to events and people fall within a person's boundaries. People respond to their environment based on who they are and where they came from. Attempted invasion of a person's boundaries or having boundaries that do not protect a person can both have negative affects in a person's life. Healthy, protective boundaries are not the standard today.

Personal boundaries are not as acceptable in society as property boundaries. Most people are not taught about boundaries as children, and they are often taught that their boundaries are not important. Many children are forced to kiss and hug people they do not want to kiss and hug. They are told to do things simply because a parent or an adult says to do them. Appropriate boundaries are not set in relationships, and many people continue through life with a distorted view of personal boundaries in their lives.

God and Boundaries

The concept of boundaries is not a man-made idea; it comes from God Himself. God differentiates Himself from angels and mankind. In the Bible, God defines Himself and takes ownership and responsibility for what is His. He tells others what He feels and thinks and lets His likes and dislikes be known. There are things God allows and things He does not allow.

God introduces boundaries to mankind in the Book of Genesis when He told Adam that he could eat of any tree, but not of the tree of the knowledge of good and evil. God said that if Adam ate of that tree he would die. When Adam and Eve ate the fruit of the tree of knowledge, they brought death into the world. God set the boundary; man violated the boundary and then had to endure the consequences.

Examples of God's boundaries can be seen throughout the Bible (as well as the fact that He does not violate man's boundaries). Jesus stands at the door of the heart and knocks, but He does not enter unless each person opens the door (Revelation 3:20). God does not force people to obey His commands; He allows them the choice. Adam and Eve made their own choices to disobey and eat the fruit. Every person has the choice to live life God's way or their own way.

Taking Responsibility

The concept of boundaries means that each person takes responsibility for the areas of his life that belongs to him. These areas include:

- Actions
- Behaviors
- Choices
- Decisions
- Sexuality
- Attitudes
- Beliefs
- Emotions
- Desires
- Feelings
- Love
- Needs
- Reactions
- Spirituality
- Talents
- Thoughts
- Values

Throughout history people have blamed others for problems that belong within their own boundaries. This is seen in the story of the fall. God confronted Adam, and he blamed the woman God had given him. Then, Eve blamed the serpent. People must quit blaming others for their problems, sin and failures and take responsibility for that which belongs to them. Yes, there may be times when someone may violate your boundaries. You cannot change the wrong done, but you are responsible for how you proceed from that point.

A person is not responsible for the abuse he may have received as a child, but he must take responsibility for his behavior as an adult and not blame present poor behavior on the evil done to him years before. A husband may wrong his wife in some way, treating her disrespectfully or in a demeaning way. His behavior is wrong, but she must take responsibility for her response and not blame her husband if she responds in anger or by attempting to return the hurt.

Boundaries & Relationship

Understanding boundaries is important to healthy relationships. Relationships occur at the point where people have contact with other people, at their boundaries. Without an understanding of boundaries, people will find relationships difficult and often unhealthy. Once healthy boundaries are built, relationships will have the opportunity to grow stronger and healthier.

Very often boundaries are used inappropriately. A husband will put up with a nagging, criticizing wife for years and then set a boundary and leave her. Or a wife may put up with an abusive or immoral husband and finally set a boundary and throw him out of the house. The purpose of boundaries is to take ownership and responsibility for self, not to change others or end unhealthy relationships.

Do everything in love. ~ 1 Corinthians 16:14

The foundation of boundaries is love. Love of God, self and others motivates people to set healthy boundaries. God has boundaries with His people because He loves them. He will not violate their boundaries, but expects that they will not violate His. It is not unreasonable to expect a spouse, children or others to respect your boundaries as you respect theirs. With healthy boundaries people have the freedom to love others as God created them and respect their differences. It becomes what Drs. Cloud and Townsend call the *Triangle of Boundaries*.[2] People take responsibility for their own freedom, live free, love God, spouse, family members and others they are in relationship with. Life and relationships become healthier and more productive.

People often do not have healthy boundaries because they do not understand the concept of boundaries and have not experienced healthy boundaries in their lives. They think that setting boundaries is selfish and hurtful. Christians are especially susceptible to this confusion because of God's call to love and serve others. They think boundaries are incompatible with a humble, loving attitude. Actually, it is not loving to allow others to violate your boundaries at will. God is a God of love and a God of boundaries. He is a God of balance and people need to strive for balance in their lives. There may be a time when one will turn the other cheek, but at another time he will take the appropriate action to protect himself. Healthy boundaries in lives mean that people have the choice, depending on God's will for their lives at that time. "NO" is not a bad word. It is usually the first word children learn and it can be the point at which you begin to set healthy boundaries in your life.

Some husbands don't understand the 'shower before romance' boundary.

For Discussion as a Couple

1. Do you agree that personal boundaries are not as acceptable as property boundaries in society? What are your thoughts?

____

____

____

____

2. How does the fact that God sets boundaries affect your life?

____

____

____

____

3. What can you do to take responsibility for those areas within your boundaries?

____

____

____

____

4. How can boundaries be misused? What can you do to keep from misusing them in your relationships and marriage?

____

____

____

____

5. Why do you think Christians are especially susceptible to confusion about boundaries?

____

____

____

____

____

Boundary Setting Inventory

Think about your relationships with family, friends and co-workers. Circle "YES" or "NO" for each of the following questions as they apply generally to those relationships. Please answer honestly and with some thought. Your relationships can improve if you will look honestly at how well you set boundaries in your life.

1. Do you find it difficult to say no to people, even when you want to? YES NO
2. Do you tend to have relationships with people who hurt you? YES NO
3. Do you feel that your success depends on others? YES NO
4. Do you find yourself attempting to find ways to fix the situation when someone is upset? YES NO
5. Do you lie for others to cover for their mistakes or irresponsibility? YES NO
6. Do you tend to look at others' potential and overlook their consistently irresponsible behavior? YES NO
7. Do you try to fix other people? YES NO
8. Do you take care of the hurts of others while neglecting your own? YES NO
9. Do you find yourself taking responsibility for others' lives? YES NO
10. Do you find that you are manipulated or controlled by others? YES NO
11. Do you have problems being honest with those you are close to? YES NO
12. Do you find it hard to confront others? YES NO
13. Do you find that your conflicts are not usually resolved productively? YES NO
14. Do you have trouble asking for what you want or need? YES NO
15. Do you tend to lend money and not get it back? YES NO
16. Do you trust people only to have them take advantage of you? YES NO
17. Do you tend to be in the middle of problems between other people? YES NO
18. Do you generally put more into relationships than you get out of them? YES NO
19. Do you have trouble following through with your commitments? YES NO
20. Do you have trouble saying "no" to the bad habits in your own life? YES NO

Most people have some boundaries problems in their life. No "YES" answers may mean overly rigid or strict boundaries in your life. A number of "YES" (more than six or eight) answers indicate a problem setting boundaries. Many "YES" answers only indicate that you have not grown up with an awareness of boundaries. This is not a test; it is an inventory you can use to help you understand where you are with your relationships. It is never too late to begin setting boundaries in your life. It may not always be easy, but the effort is worthwhile as you experience healthy, productive relationships.

Boundaries Study 10

Establishing Healthy Boundaries

Above all else, guard your heart, for it is the wellspring of life.
~ Proverbs 4:23

"A good fence makes good neighbors."
~ Robert Frost

"NO" is Not a Four Letter Word and Other Boundaries Concepts

A child's first word often is "no" because, realizing it or not, parents are teaching their children boundaries. A parent's "no" protects the child and protects the parents' possessions from destruction in unstable hands. The problem is that parents do not understand healthy boundaries and do not continue boundary training with their children. It is never too late to learn about boundaries and begin using them to guard yourself.

People must realize that boundaries are not about changing or fixing others and their behavior. Boundaries are about self, not others. One does not set boundaries to keep others out. To have relationships with others, you must let others into your life. Boundaries help protect a person from the hurts of the world. Setting boundaries is a process. It's not just sitting down, writing a list of things one will and will not allow, posting them on the door of the house and then thinks he is done. Any change takes time and there will be some setbacks and hurt along the way. Perseverance and continuing to work on healthy boundaries will help a person gain victory in their life and relationships.

Words are the most basic personal boundary. Through the words of parents people learn at a very young age what was acceptable and unacceptable in their family. Words such as "no", "don't" and "stop" help define self and what is not acceptable. Other words, "yes", "do" and "go for it!" can help define what is acceptable in life. Physical and emotional distance helps protect a person and establish boundaries. Emotional or physical distance may be necessary with a person who continues hurtful or unsafe behavior. Suffering consequences, learning from failures may be necessary in one's own life or for others he is in relationship with. Time is important; everyone must carve out time to grow his relationship with the Lord, spouse, children and others. Yet, time is needed for self. Time boundaries help maintain balance and keep priorities right.

Boundaries Begin With One's Self

The purpose of boundaries is to provide a context in which the people in relationship can grow. Before one can think of boundaries in the context of others, he must develop boundaries in his own life. First, it is important to take responsibility for those things that belong to self (from Study 9). People cannot change anyone but themselves and even that cannot be done without God. Taking ownership for the areas of one's life allows God to work maturity and growth into their life. Seeking to conform into the image of God will change your life.

Knowing self, who one is and how he was formed is important to establishing healthy boundaries. It is necessary to understand one's own struggles, insecurities, problems, strengths and weaknesses, and with that understanding, work on those problem areas and setting boundaries where needed. It is a matter of discipline. Discipline is not a popular word in today's culture, but Biblically, it is an important part of a walk with the Lord.

> *Like a city whose walls are broken down is a man who lacks self-control.*
> *~ Proverbs 25:28*

One may need to set boundaries in the areas of self-control, self-centeredness, judging others, or irresponsibility. Other potential areas are eating, spending, time, task completion, the way one speaks, sexuality, alcohol or substance abuse. This is not about setting up a lot of rules and regulations in life to control behavior. It is about living life for God and what is good for a person. Many Christians condemn smoking cigarettes as sin because it destroys the temple of the Holy Spirit. But what about overeating? Overuse of sugar, salt, caffeine or anything else that harms their health? When one is out of balance, he is out of God's will.

> *"Everything is permissible for me"- but not everything is beneficial . "Everything is permissible for me"- but I will not be mastered by anything. ~ 1 Corinthians 6:12*

Christians do not have to be mastered by their desires or in bondage to the things of the world. Establishing boundaries in life will help bring discipline into one's life. They help people say, "Yes, I could do that, but it's not good for me and I choose not to." Or, "I could be angry and unforgiving, but in God's strength, I can choose to be loving and forgiving." It is a matter of choice for the Christian.

Developed vision, mission, goals and objectives help set healthy boundaries with self and in life overall. It is all right to say "no" to the things that are not conducive to fulfilling one's mission in life and achieving his vision. Saying "no" to a ministry opportunity is not selfish when a person knows that God has called him to do something different and he is working in that direction.

> *"It's easy to say 'no!' when there's a deeper 'yes!' burning inside." ~ Stephen R. Covey*[1]

Establishing Boundaries

The process of setting boundaries will sound easy on paper. In the real world, it is not so easy. It involves honestly looking at yourself, your relationships and seriously evaluating your life and how you interact with the people in your life. You will need support in this effort. It can be a very emotional and difficult exercise. It may be necessary for spouses to work separately in this process if working together is too hurtful and difficult. It is important that there is communication between the two of you during the process and that the support you receive should be from a mature Christian of the same sex who will provide a safe place for you to turn in time of need. Steps to setting boundaries are:

1. Increase your self understanding. Who are you as a child of God, your personality, talents and gifts.
2. Understand God's purpose for your life, your vision for your life and your mission in life.
3. Recognize serious violations of your boundaries, your feelings about those violations and if necessary, get help for the hurt.
4. Examine the boundaries in your present relationships. Are they healthy? Unhealthy? Hurtful? Are they currently being violated or ignored? How?
5. Identify the changes you need to make in your life to establish healthy boundaries.
6. Implement the behavior needed to establish healthy boundaries.
7. Perform ongoing maintenance to ensure your boundaries are healthy and balanced.

Healthy Boundary Characteristics

Healthy boundaries are clearly communicated. Fences, walls and signs communicate property boundaries. They tell people where a property line begins. Personal boundaries also need to be communicated. Words will effectively communicate boundaries in most situations, but there are times when other forms of communication may be appropriate. Maintaining emotional or physical distance will also communicate a boundary. Remember, it is unreasonable to expect a spouse or others to respect uncommunicated boundaries.

Boundaries must be appropriate for the situation. If someone has a problem with alcohol, going into a bar (but not drinking of course) is too lax a boundary. Leaving a relationship when the other person has agreed to get the help they need may be too strict a boundary. Divorce usually is an inappropriate boundary. Rather than set healthy boundaries and work on their relationship, people tend to leave unhealthy marriages.

Healthy boundaries are not set to punish others. Withholding love from a spouse or child because of inappropriate behavior or creating emotional distance because they have caused hurt is punishment, not boundaries. Setting boundaries to force someone to behave a certain way is controlling and manipulating, not setting healthy boundaries. People may not like boundaries and may choose to get angry about them, but healthy boundaries will not hurt or harm others.

Boundaries are not to be set by others. It seems strange to bring this up, but how often do spouses or others tell a person what they are going to do or not do? Parents sometimes will attempt to set boundaries for their adult children. Or even children setting boundaries for their parents; telling them how they are to behave in their relationships. It is appropriate for parents to set boundaries for their small children, but it is inappropriate for parents to set boundaries for their adult children.

Healthy boundaries are flexible. Life constantly changes and boundaries may change over time. A person may set a strict boundary to protect himself in a hurtful relationship. Once the relationship becomes healthy, he can relax that boundary and in some cases choose to remove it. Boundaries belong to the person setting them; he can change them whenever he deems it appropriate to make changes.

Love is the foundation for healthy boundaries. The Bible says that Christians are to do all things in love. An attitude of love and concern for others is important, even as boundaries are set for protection. Allowing others to suffer the consequences of their poor behavior does not mean one doesn't love them. They may experience pain, but that will be because of the choices they make, not because of boundaries. Boundaries set in anger, hurt or disappointment will not be healthy boundaries. Motives and attitudes must be examined while setting boundaries.

Be aware of your feelings. If you feel uncomfortable about a situation, talk about the feelings with your support person. While you should not allow feelings to drive your behavior, you need to be aware of them and examine what might be causing them. An uncomfortable feeling may point out a boundary that is too rigid. Fear may be warning you of danger that a person will not respond well to your boundaries. Being aware of your feelings will help you establish and maintain healthy boundaries.

"My dad says he's helping me learn about boundaries by limiting my time on the computer, but I think he just likes having the computer to himself."

Maintaining Balance

Boundaries help develop the discipline to balance lives and relationships. Setting boundaries does not mean to close off relationships and avoid the work required to maintain them. On the contrary, by exercising freedom, people are able to be free and open in their relationships and do the things that will help them grow and accomplish what God wants them to accomplish. Healthy boundaries help bring about healthy priorities and increased productivity in all areas of life.

Some people will balk at the idea of setting a boundary and going home from work to be available for their spouse and children. They are not willing to accept the fact that the company will function just fine without their twelve-hour days. There are many blessings to having healthy boundaries in your life, and there is great peace when you have your life in order and operating according to God's will.

Serenity Prayer

God grant me the serenity

To accept the things
I cannot change

Courage to change
the things I can

And wisdom to
know the difference.

~ Reinhold Niebuhr

For Discussion as a Couple

1. How are words the most basic personal boundary? How are they used to set boundaries ?

2. What does it mean to take responsibility for the areas of your life? What are some of those areas?

3. How does understanding who you are and your vision in life help you set boundaries?

4. Relate a couple of times in your past when your boundaries have been violated. How have you worked through those violations?

5. What is the difference between healthy and unhealthy boundaries? What can you do to ensure your boundaries are healthy?

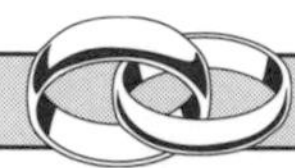

Boundaries
Study 11
Boundaries and Relationships

If it is possible, as far as it depends on you, live at peace with everyone.
~ Romans 12:18

"I don't know the key to success, but the key to failure is trying to please everybody" ~ Bill Cosby

If our brother has something against us, we are to go to him.
~ Matthew 5:23

If our brother sins against us, we are to go to him. ~ Matthew 18:15

The Bible teaches about relationships. Relationship between God and people, people and God and between each other. Boundaries are essential to all relationships The Bible says to live at peace with everyone—as far as it depends on us. Relationships do not totally depend on one person. Each person must do his part in the relationship. If you go to the person who has a problem with you to reconcile and are rejected, you have done your part. Likewise, you are to go to the person who has offended you to seek reconciliation. If he will not accept responsibility for the offense and does not want to restore the relationship, you have done your part. People can only do their part to build healthy relationships. They cannot force others to do their part.

Healthy Relationships

Relationships are a part of life. Whether good or bad, life consists of the relationships a person has. While boundaries protect and help people to care for themselves, the purpose of boundaries is healthy relationships. Relationships are necessary for growth, personal and spiritual. Constructive interaction with other individuals will aid your growth and help you become the person God wants you to be. A clear definition of individual identity is necessary for healthy relationships to occur. A strong understanding of who a person is helps growth in the relationships with spouse, children, family, friends, co-workers and anyone God brings into their life. Boundaries help define that understanding of who one is.

Again, people do not set boundaries on others. Boundaries are about the individual and are set around them. It takes discipline, but it has nothing to do with legalism. A healthy system of boundaries allows people to give themselves fully to those things God has called them to do. They are able to say "no" to the things that are not good for them or that do not fit into God's plan for their life. Healthy boundaries are about freedom, responsibility, ownership and love. Setting boundaries with a planned outcome is manipulation. Healthy boundaries leave the results to the Lord and allow Him to work in the lives of people, rather than attempting to bring the results one desires.

Burdens and Loads

Carry each other's burdens, and in this way you will fulfill the law of Christ... each one should carry his own load. ~ Galatians 6:2,5

The Bible says to carry each other's burdens. This is a weight, a load, or abundance.[1] Christians are to help others with the cares and burdens of life or the problems they experience. They are to extend compassion and love to those weighed down. Yet, each one should carry his own load. The Greek word for load is the diminutive of the word for something carried like the cargo

of a ship. It is a small cargo; task or service.[2] The load is something one must do, his responsibility. The concept is that people are to support and help those who are weighed down by the cares of life, but not to take on their responsibilities.

This concept of burdens and loads aids the setting of healthy boundaries. It is good to listen, care and pray for those who have burdens and problems; who are experiencing troubles in their life. It is inappropriate to take those burdens as one's own. Do not take their responsibilities, those physical, emotional, relational and spiritual areas that do not belong to you. When people take those things, they are not helping and even could be hindering another's growth and maturity.

> ***Do not move your neighbor's boundary stone set up by your predecessors in the inheritance you receive in the land the LORD your God is giving you to possess.***
> ***~ Deuteronomy 19:14***

Respecting Other's Boundaries

Often, people do not respect others' boundaries because they do not understand the concept of boundaries and people have not respected their boundaries throughout their lives. They do not understand how to set boundaries or how to ask others to respect the boundaries they do have. It is important to be aware of others' boundaries. Respecting their boundaries will help them to learn about boundaries and to appreciate the boundaries of others.

Respecting other's boundaries means:

- Taking responsibility for the areas of one's life within his boundaries.
- Accepting confrontation without defensiveness or attacking.
- Acknowledging wrong and asking for forgiveness when appropriate.
- Demonstrating love and acceptance.
- Valuing others' freedom.
- Accepting another person's "no".
- Allowing others to be who they are and not attempt to mold them into the people they should be.
- Allowing others to accept responsibility for the areas that are within their boundaries (carrying their own load).
- Being concerned with one's own growth rather than the growth of others.

Everyone knows people who have a problem saying "no" to any request made of them and people who allow others to manage their lives. Be proactive about respecting others' boundaries and accepting their "no" as you begin setting healthy boundaries. You may help a person learn to set boundaries by saying, "I understand that saying 'no' can be hard for you sometimes and I want to let you know that saying 'no' is all right and I will not be hurt by it." In a non-threatening way, this will help them learn about boundaries.

Gaining Respect for One's Own Boundaries

> ***"The definition of insanity is doing the same thing over and over again and expecting different results." ~ Albert Einstein***

Healthy boundaries will not occur without change. It is unreasonable to expect others to accept or respect one's boundaries without change on their part. One must set boundaries in his life and then enforce those boundaries. This task will not always be easy, but perseverance and continued work will pay off.

Boundaries must be clearly communicated. When possible, boundaries should be communicated before relationship problems arise. A person allergic to certain types of food is a great example of this concept. If he is invited to a friend's house for dinner, he can inform his friend immediately that he is allergic to certain foods or risk having to tell his friend he cannot eat what has been prepared. The person having trouble setting boundaries may even eat the food, not wanting to hurt his friend's feelings… and then suffer the consequences.

There may not be allergies in the emotional, relational, intellectual and spiritual areas of lives, but the concept is the same. It is possible to inform people of boundaries at three points: prior to a situation, during the situation or the boundary can be ignored and consequences suffered. The consequences can range from the minimal of not completing a project to help another person to serious suffering for helping someone do something illegal or immoral.

There was a young man who did not stand up to his friends and received life imprisonment because he was present when they robbed a store and killed the owner in the process. This young man reaped terrible consequences because he did not set boundaries in his life. While the consequences you reap may not be as drastic as this young man, the personal injury received can be very traumatic in your life. It can retard your personal, emotional and spiritual growth, and it can establish a pattern that continues for years and keeps you from being the person God has called you to be.

A boundary is not rejection. Some people may attempt to circumvent boundaries by claiming they are rejected because another's boundaries. A couple may agree to alternate Christmas holidays with their parents. One set of parents may be used to having the whole family at their house every Christmas and treat the couple's boundary as rejection. The couple must remember that no matter what the parents may say, they have set a reasonable boundary and they are not rejecting their parents.

> *"Boundaries are a 'litmus test' for the quality of our relationships."*[3]

People in healthy relationships will be mutually respectful of each other's boundaries. This mutual respect for boundaries represents the quality of the relationship. Is the relationship strong and healthy, helping each other to grow and flourish? Or is it a shallow relationship characterized by disrespect and dysfunctional behavior? Healthy relationships don't usually just happen on their own. They take work and continual enforcement of boundaries even when people react badly to them.

You must realize that there will be some failure as you begin to set boundaries. You may set boundaries too strict or too relaxed, or you may just give in and allow your boundaries to be violated. It is important that you do not give up. Analyze the setback, seek Godly direction and continue the work of setting healthy boundaries. Remember it is critical that you have a support person or group to help you through the boundary setting process in your life.

"What do you mean you're setting a boundary and not playing hockey? I thought playing hockey would be a great activity for us to do together."

Some people will resist your boundaries. A few will even fight against them. It takes a lot of work to change dysfunctional relationships and they do not change quickly. People may react in anger to boundaries. They do not get what they want and they are mad about it! They may rant and rave and threaten in their attempt to violate your boundaries. They may even break off the relationship. That is their choice and you must remember that if they will not accept your boundaries, the relationship was only on their terms and not much of a relationship anyway. It is important that you do not allow the emotions of their anger to control you. Do not get angry and do not allow them to violate your boundaries.

There are people who will attempt to manipulate their way around your boundaries. They may attempt to make you feel guilty about setting boundaries; questioning your love, relating the damage you have done to them or how they would never do such a thing to you. They may even pull out the big weapon; questioning your

Christianity because you are not giving yourself as Jesus did. Again, they may break off the relationship to manipulate you into doing what they want rather than what you know you have to do. People will attempt to get around your boundaries any way they can. For the sake of attaining healthy relationships, persevere and keep working at your boundaries. Evaluate and adjust them if necessary, but keep working at it.

A person owns his boundaries; boundaries do not own the person. Boundaries can be changed when it makes sense to change them. Healthy boundaries are essential to healthy relationships. Prayerfully seek God's help in formulating and setting appropriate boundaries in your life.

For Discussion as a Couple

1. What does Romans 12:18 mean to you? Are you to make peace at all costs?

____

____

____

____

2. Why are healthy boundaries necessary for healthy relationships?

____

____

____

____

3. What is the difference between a burden and a load? How does this affect setting boundaries?

____

____

____

____

4. Why is it important to respect others' boundaries? How do you do this?

____

____

____

____

5. What are some ways people will try to get around your boundaries? What can you do to enforce your boundaries?

____

____

____

____

Boundaries

Study 12

Boundaries in Marriage

If it is possible, as far as it depends on you, live at peace with everyone.
~ Romans 12:18

Genesis math

Boundaries can be especially confusing in the marriage relationship. The ideas of oneness, loving as Christ loved, giving of self, and submission seem to argue against boundaries. Yet, the concept of boundaries does not refute these ideas and actually works to increase their effectiveness in marriage. Lack of boundaries is a major problem in marriages. A husband or wife may suffer through the problems of the spouse until they have had enough and then leave the marriage. They think freedom from their spouse's problems means freedom from their spouse. Yet, very often they have contributed to their spouse's problems by never setting healthy boundaries that would allow the Lord to work in their spouse's life.

A healthy marriage relationship takes the work of two people. One can only do his part in the relationship; the rest must be left up to the Lord. Setting boundaries to change a spouse will not work, that is manipulation. Setting impossibly difficult boundaries will drive a spouse away rather than help build a healthy relationship. Husbands and wives do many things to injure and even destroy their marriage relationship, but it does not have to be this way. Healthy boundaries are a cornerstone of a healthy, fortified marriage that will grow and flourish.

It Takes Two to Become One

"For this reason a man will leave his father and mother and be united to his wife, and the two will become one flesh."
~ Ephesians 5:31

Becoming one seems to be contrary to the whole idea of boundaries, but there can not be one without there first being two. A couple is different; in gender, genes, personalities, gifts and talents. They are raised in different environments and grow up affected by the world in different ways. Every aspect of life works to make a person who he is. People do not lose their identity and become someone else when they marry. When Joe Smith, single man marries Martha, and becomes Mr. Joe Smith, married man, he is the same person. Will marriage change a person? Most certainly! Many aspects of life will change, and, over time, there will even be some subtle changes in personality, but a person's basic identity remains the same.

When a couple enters the marriage relationship, there will be some pressure to change. During courtship, they tend only to see the strengths of each other's personalities. It does not take long before the weaknesses begin to surface. Remember that retaining identity is not the same as using identity to justify wrong behavior. The forcefulness of a Lion can be a wonderful asset, but also a terrible weakness when that forcefulness hurts his spouse. Boundaries help define the marriage relationship and enable a couple to freely meet the needs of each other and also to help them grow into the people God wants them to be.

> *"Boundaries operate best when both spouses restrict their freedoms so as to better love each other."*[1]

It takes two complete people to become one in marriage. It is important to know who one is before he can give of himself to his spouse. Being able to say "no" frees a person to give to his spouse. There is no freedom to give love if there is no freedom to say "no." Personal freedoms are not to be at the expense of the marriage relationship. Being in relationship means that two people are concerned about each other and each other's needs. Your spouse's needs are not your responsibility, but to not care about his needs is to not care about the marriage. Both spouses have needs, desires, wants, dreams and aspirations. It is important for couples to work together to accomplish all that God wants them to accomplish. In the marriage ceremony, they committed to their relationship for life. There are some things that will have to be given up because of that commitment.

Protecting the Marriage

The marriage relationship must be protected. The idea of "open" marriages is neither Christian nor workable in reality. Yes, a person should have the freedom to say "no" to the things he does not want to do. But the reality is that certain things will destroy the relationship. Proper boundaries protect love and are not set to get one's own way, do his own thing, or change, punish or admonish one's spouse.

Healthy boundaries will protect the marriage. They will fortify the marriage against the attacks of the outside world. Both spouses must be willing to work on the relationship and give to make the relationship work. There are times when one must choose to die to self and give in to his spouse. Boundaries give the choice to say "yes" or "no"; making the choice to give demonstrates Christ working in one's life.

Protecting the marriage relationship means that other relationships will change. Going out with friends and extended family relationships take lower priority. It is not possible to have the same relationships with people of the opposite sex as prior to marriage. This is basic to a healthy marital relationship and is part of the commitment a couple makes. The marriage must be protected from all outside intruders whether they are people or things. Some of these possible intruders could be: television, work, hobbies, outside interests, in-laws, friends, secrets (relationships or sin), even children or church. It is important to work together to set proper boundaries and guard the relationship from being attacked in these areas.

Taking what is Not Yours

A person with healthy boundaries takes responsibility for what is his, but also does not take what is not his. Often, spouses will take responsibility for his spouse's emotions. Even though she has done nothing wrong, a wife may take responsibility for her husband's anger or poor attitude and attempt to fix him. Boundaries release her from that responsibility. His anger is his responsibility and she cannot fix him. Often her attempts to fix him will even cause conflict in their relationship. As much as it may hurt, there are times when one must allow his spouse to work things out himself or suffer the consequences of his poor behavior or bad choices. It is good to carry his burden, but he must carry his own load.

"I don't think I like this idea of boundaries. I like being able to eat my dinner and part of yours too."

When a Spouse Resists

It is not unusual for a spouse to vigorously resist the attempt to set boundaries. This will especially happen when there have not been healthy boundaries previously in the marriage. Love, patience and perseverance are required to bring about healthy boundaries. Your spouse may get angry, threaten to leave, manipulate, retaliate, any number of things; but you must continue the path of setting healthy boundaries. Do take responsibility for your part in problems you are facing. State the problem; being specific and use "I" rather than "you" statements. Ask your spouse for change and implement appropriate consequences. Remain committed to the relationship, but do not allow your spouse to derail the boundary-setting process. In the end, you will both experience tremendous personal growth. Your marriage will also grow and become stronger.

Realize that even when both spouses want to establish healthy boundaries, it won't be easy. It still will take work and commitment to make it happen.

> ***Loving your spouse means that you will say "no" to some things.***

For Discussion as a Couple

1. Do you agree that boundaries actually increase the effectiveness of oneness, loving as Christ loved, giving of self, and submission in your marriage? Why or why not?

____

____

____

____

2. How can boundaries strengthen and fortify your marriage?

____

____

____

____

3. How do boundaries help you to be the person God created you to be?

____

____

____

____

4. Why is it important to protect your marriage? How do you protect it?

____

____

____

____

5. What do you need to do if your spouse resists your boundaries?

____

____

____

____

____

Fortified Marriages
Chapter 3 Endnotes

Study 9: Understanding Boundaries

1. Charles L. Whitfield, M.D.; Boundaries and Relationships (Deerfield Beach, FL; Health Communications Inc., 1993) p 2
2. Dr. Henry Cloud & Dr. John Townsend; Boundaries in Marriage (Grand Rapids, MI; Zondervan Publishing House, 1999) p 24

Recommended for further reading:
- Boundaries by Dr. Henry Cloud and Dr. John Townsend.

For further information, see:
- Cloud-Townsend Resources: www.cloudtownsend.com

Study 10: *Establishing Healthy Boundaries*

1. Stephen Covey; First Things First (NY,NY, Simon & Schuster, 1994) p 103

Study 11: *Boundaries and Relationships*

1. Biblesoft's New Exhaustive Strong's Numbers and Concordance with Expanded Greek-Hebrew Dictionary. Copyright © 1994, 2003 Biblesoft, Inc. and International Bible Translators, Inc.
2. Ibid
3. Dr. Henry Cloud & Dr. John Townsend; Boundaries (Grand Rapids, MI; Zondervan Publishing House, 1992) p 108

Recommended for further reading:
- Powerful Personalities by Tim Kimmel.

Study 12: *Boundaries and Marriage*

1. Dr. Henry Cloud & Dr. John Townsend; Boundaries (Grand Rapids, MI; Zondervan Publishing House, 1992) p 202

Recommended for further reading:
- Boundaries in Marriage, by Dr. Henry Cloud and Dr. John Townsend.

Chapter 4
Communication

Study 13
Understanding One Another

Do not let any unwholesome talk come out of your mouths, but only what is helpful for building others up according to their needs, that it may benefit those who listen. ~ Ephesians 4:29

Effective communication is vital to a fortified marriage.

Communication is critically important to any relationship as people develop and grow. Strong communication characterizes a healthy, fortified marriage. Yet, people usually do not learn good communication skills. They have learned by the example of their parents and the environment they were raised in. Prior to marriage, most people attempt to communicate well, but after the wedding, couples very often quit trying and fall into bad communication habits. Couples do not take the time to understand each other and often are not careful how they communicate with each other.

Biblical Communication

According to the Bible, communication should build people up, not tear them down (Ephesians 4:29). The tongue has great power; Death and life are in the power of the tongue (Proverbs 18:21). Communication can make a difference in others' lives; even to the point of life or death. Controlling the tongue needs to be a continuing aim for everyone, because everything that is said either helps or hinders, heals or scars, builds up or tears down.

Words are powerful! Proverbs 16:24 says Pleasant words are a honeycomb, sweet to the soul and healing to the bones, Proverbs 12:18 says Reckless words pierce like a sword, but the tongue of the wise brings healing and 1 Peter 3:10 states For, whoever would love life and see good days must keep his tongue from evil and his lips from deceitful speech. As the Living Bible summarizes; If you want a happy, good life, keep control of your tongue, and guard your lips. There is great power in communication and couples need to be aware of how they use it.

The world's first language barrier problems actually came much earlier than the Tower of Babel.

Understanding Your Spouse

Communication is a process (either verbal or nonverbal) of sharing information with another person in such a way that he understands what is being said.[1] Communicating thoughts and feelings sometimes can be complicated and is not always easy. A couple must work at all aspects of communication to gain understanding. Non-verbal communication such as gestures, facial expressions, and body language play an important part in communication. It is important to understand that

non-verbal communication may contradict verbal communication. Outside influences also can complicate communication and often hinder understanding. Prejudice, attitude, focus, health, lack of sleep and stress will all affect the ability to communicate effectively. One's perception of what another person said is not always what was meant!

I know you believe you understand what I said, but I'm not sure you realize that what you heard is not what I said."[2]

Effective communication occurs when another person understands the meaning of the message sent. Often, someone does not communicate his message well or his spouse will not hear the message sent because of one or more outside influences. There are a variety of factors that will hinder understanding.

Differences contribute greatly to miscommunication. Childhood environment, gender and personality all influence how a person communicates. You can send a Lion, Otter, Beaver and Golden Retriever the same message and they each may receive it very differently. Communication can be difficult with another person, but it can be accomplished if you remember that he may communicate very differently than you.

Typically, women are more verbal and use many more words per day than men, but differences do not stop there. Men and women fundamentally do not think alike and also communicate very differently. Women tend to express feelings, while men tend to convey information. Joe Friday of the old television program Dragnet spoke for most men when he said, "The facts madam, just the facts." Men often will retreat from emotional discussions or will react with anger or defensiveness when pushed into them. Healthy boundaries and an understanding of who their spouse is will help husbands and wives keep the discussion focused on the issues rather than degenerating into an argument. It is also important that a couple keep emotions from taking over the discussion and keep the conversation constructive and moving toward a resolution. It takes understanding and work on the part of both spouses.

What Wives Say	What Husbands Hear

"Honey, I need you to go to the store, take the trash out, lay the baby down for a nap and clean the rest of the yard, while I clean the house until this evening."	"**HONEY**, blah, blah **GO**... blah, blah **TAKE**... blah, blah, blah **A NAP**... blah, blah **AND**.. blah, blah **REST**... blah, blah, blah **UNTIL THIS EVENING**."

Listen More, Talk Less

The tongue weighs practically nothing, yet so few people can hold it.
~ Anonymous

Before marriage most of people listen intently to their prospective spouse. Listening was a joy, not a chore. Very often, this changes over time and listening becomes a task one must do before he can jump in with their response. It is often said that God gave people two ears and one mouth so that they would listen twice as much as they speak. Many people tend to think that the ability to use words is the prerequisite for effective communication. The ability to speak clearly is important, but developing strong listening skills greatly improves understanding and lessens the number of misunderstandings a couple will have.

James 1:19 tells the Christian to be quick to listen and slow to speak. The Amplified version translates quick to listen as to be a ready listener. Many people are ready talkers, but they have little or no desire to listen. Yet, one of the keys to a successful marriage is wanting to listen to your mate. It is important to take the time to listen well.

Active listening means that you make the effort to engage yourself in the act of listening. It involves stopping what you are doing and paying attention to what the other person is saying. This was demonstrated powerfully many years ago by David Anderson, former President of GTE, California. At a company event, a child approached Mr. Anderson and tugged on his pant leg. This corporate executive squatted down so that he was eye-to-eye with the child and gave him his undivided attention. Why wouldn't a husband and wife give that kind of attention to each other, whom they love more than any person on the planet? Respect and value are given to a person when one listens to them. Active listening also means that when someone is talking the other is not thinking about what he is going to say when the speaker stops. Rather, the listener is totally tuned into what the other person is saying, receives the message and seeks to understand what was really meant.

Giving feedback helps gain understanding of what is said. Asking questions and affirming what was heard will help ensure that what was heard is what the speaker actually intended to communicate. A husband learning these principles had to give feedback four times before his wife could agree that his understanding of what she said was actually what she meant to say. Effective communication takes work and it takes practice to learn the techniques that will improve communication between husband and wife.

Body language is an important part of listening. Turning toward the person speaking, looking at him, and nodding the head appropriately will demonstrate that a person is truly listening. Showing impatience or using gestures to signify that the listener would like the speaker to get to the point are not effective listening skills. It is important to reassure the speaker that you are paying attention and hearing what he is saying.

According to Scripture, the person who blurts out whatever they are thinking or feeling without considering the consequences is foolish: Do you see a man who is hasty in his words? There is more hope for a fool than for him. (Proverbs 29:20) Effective listening is critical to good communication. As a couple learns to listen well, their communication will improve.

Gaining understanding is the goal and effective communication will help a person begin to understand his spouse and his needs. Marriage is an intimate relationship built on mutual understanding, but in order to truly understand your spouse you must be able to communicate with him.

Communication is the weed killer in the garden of the marriage.

Connecting Through Communication

Couples connect through communication. Verbal and non-verbal communication allows a person into another's life. They aid understanding the other person better. Spouses can either build up or tear down each other through communication. How often does a discussion begin with some minor disagreement only to degenerate into a battle, not because of the disagreement, but because of the way a couple communicates with one another?

Weeds are the hurt feelings, misunderstandings, and separation that will occur in marriage. Communication kills these weeds before they grow into the bitterness that chokes out marital intimacy. If a couple does not address and kill (or resolve) these weeds, they will become barriers that can severely damage the relationship.

Communication with a spouse requires a balance of communicating feelings, hurts, and needs and yet, always speaking in love. No matter how right one may be on any given issue, it is not right to communicate in anger or in a demeaning manner.

Traditionally, at one point during FamilyLife marriage conferences the speakers will ask spouses to turn to each other and say, "You are not my enemy." It would be an excellent practice for couples to do this on a regular basis. A married couple is a team, and they need to work together to meet the attacks that will come against their marriage. Communication is the best tool that they have for working together.

Most people learn poor communication practices and have behaved their way into poor communication patterns. It takes practice and work to behave one's way out of those poor habits by exercising constructive communication skills. It is important to give your spouse license to hold you accountable, in a loving way, to help you change any poor communication habits you might have. Correcting communication problems in marriage will aid the ability to solve any other problem that comes up in the marriage relationship.

For Discussion as a Couple

1. How do you define communication? How does this definition relate to your marriage relationship?

____
____
____
____

2. How do your differences hinder communication with your spouse? How can you stop this?

____
____
____
____

3. How do you define listening? How is it important in communication?

____
____
____
____

4. How does non-verbal communication affect communication with your spouse?

____
____
____
____

5. How do you think communication can help you work together to solve problems?

____
____
____
____

Communication Effectiveness Inventory

Circle the best answer ("True" or "False") for each of the statements below continuing to the next page.

1. I feel criticized by my spouse.	TRUE	FALSE
2. When I share my feelings with my spouse, I feel understood and supported.	TRUE	FALSE
3. I feel that my spouse does not listen to me.	TRUE	FALSE
4. My spouse shares his or her insecurities with me.	TRUE	FALSE
5. I would rather tell a small lie than get into an argument.	TRUE	FALSE
6. I feel refreshed when I have time alone with my spouse.	TRUE	FALSE
7. My spouse finishes my sentences for me.	TRUE	FALSE
8. We are generally able to work through disagreements without much trouble.	TRUE	FALSE
9. It is not easy for me to share my feelings with my spouse.	TRUE	FALSE
10. I feel respected by my spouse.	TRUE	FALSE
11. When I bring up a problem with my spouse, he or she often turns it around on me.	TRUE	FALSE
12. I feel appreciated.	TRUE	FALSE
13. We don't agree very often.	TRUE	FALSE
14. We enjoy going out on dates alone.	TRUE	FALSE
15. I feel that my spouse does not give me credit for much.	TRUE	FALSE
16. I feel loved.	TRUE	FALSE
17. My spouse does not like to share what is on his or her mind.	TRUE	FALSE
18. My spouse understands me.	TRUE	FALSE
19. We tend to have unresolved disagreements.	TRUE	FALSE
20. We have effective communication.	TRUE	FALSE
21. My spouse does not give me his undivided attention when I talk to him.	TRUE	FALSE
22. My spouse asks for my opinion.	TRUE	FALSE
23. During disagreements, we will shout at each other.	TRUE	FALSE
24. I feel that we are on the same team most of the time.	TRUE	FALSE
25. We fight in front of our children.	TRUE	FALSE
26. I am honest with my spouse.	TRUE	FALSE
27. Our communication is frustrating to me.	TRUE	FALSE

28. I feel trusted by my spouse. TRUE FALSE
29. My spouse gives me the "silent treatment." TRUE FALSE
30. My spouse values my opinions. TRUE FALSE
31. My spouse interrupts me. TRUE FALSE
32. I am able to give input to my spouse on the projects he or she works on. TRUE FALSE
33. Our communication is mostly superficial. TRUE FALSE
34. I feel encouraged by my spouse. TRUE FALSE
35. I feel that I am not allowed to think for my self. TRUE FALSE
36. My spouse gives me valuable feedback. TRUE FALSE
37. Our personality styles cause conflict in our marriage. TRUE FALSE
38. My spouse has good listening skills. TRUE FALSE
39. My spouse tells me what to do. TRUE FALSE
40. I feel connected with my spouse. TRUE FALSE

Count the odd numbered questions you answered "False" and enter the total here: _____

Count the even numbered questions you answered "True" and enter the total here: _____

Add the scores and enter the total here: _____

Scoring:

30—40: Your communication is excellent; keep it up!
20—29: Your communication is good; continue to work at it.
10—19: Your communication needs work; you may want to do further study in a book from the resource section at the end of this manual.
Below 10: You should seek out a counselor to help you learn some basic communication skills.

The purpose of this inventory is to give you an idea about where your communication skills are presently. Communication is a learned skill; you can improve. Please do not use this inventory to attack your spouse for his or her poor communication habits. Excellent communication takes two strong communicators. Poor communication takes two poor communicators. Your score depends on the two of you and the two of you will be able to improve it.

Communication *Study 14*

Managing Conflict

Therefore each of you must put off falsehood and speak truthfully to his neighbor (or your spouse), for we are all members of one body. "In your anger do not sin": Do not let the sun go down while you are still angry,
~ Ephesians 4:25-26

"A conflict-free marriage is an oxymoron. Every married couple must learn how to deal with differences in ways that suit their style, values, and particular Relationship."
~ Judith Wallerstein[1]

Conflict in marriage arises from differences between spouses, conflicting desires, boundary violations, or sin of a spouse. Conflict is inevitable; differences sooner or later will cause disagreement. There will be occasions when one spouse will desire something different than the other. No one's spouse is perfect, and people will violate boundaries or fail at some point.

The continual avoidance of conflict is a serious problem in a marriage relationship. It has been said that this is the number one predictor of divorce.[2] The absence of conflict can mean one of several things:

- One spouse has given up his or her identity for the other.
- There is nothing more than superficial communication in the marriage.
- One or both spouses simply do not care any longer.

Conflict avoidance is detrimental to the marriage relationship whatever the reason for it. Couples who enter marriage believing they will never disagree are ignorant or self-deceived.

As iron sharpens iron, so one man sharpens another.
~ Proverbs 27:17

Growing and maturing together requires some conflict. The point of Proverbs 27:17 is that it takes the friction of iron against iron to make a blade sharp and true. Similarly, friction sharpens people to help them develop more into the image of God. Oneness in marriage does not happen naturally, it takes work and even the friction that conflict brings to the relationship. When Ruth Graham was asked if she and Billy always agreed on everything, she answered, "My goodness no! If we did, there would be no need for one of us." Ecclesiastes 4:9 says that "two are better than one." Spouses complement and build each other up, and their differences help each other mature individually and as a couple.

When Conflict Hurts

The word conflict brings to mind warfare and battlegrounds. Very often, this describes conflict in a marriage, a marriage between two people who at one time promised to love each other through all circumstances. When conflict arises, people tend to change dramatically, sort of like Dr. Jekyll and Mr. Hyde. Loving, committed people act like enemies, hurting each other and at times damaging their relationship. They will resort to intimidation, attack of their spouse's character, withdrawal, criticism, disrespect, even temper tantrums or physical attack. Some will do almost anything

The Earth's first 'Ice Age'.

to win the argument. The hurt inflicted on each other can remain for a long period of time and, if left unresolved, can lead to emotional withdrawal from the relationship. In this environment, it is not surprising that one spouse withdraws and seeks to avoid conflict. This begins a downward spiral that can lead to emotional separation and even divorce.

Conflict is inevitable in a marriage relationship, yet, conflict hurts and can even lead to breakup of the marriage. It seems like a no-win situation; except for the fact that conflict will strengthen a marriage if a couple disagrees without hurting each another. A couple can discuss any difference and even their deepest feelings without resorting to the warfare that will break-down the relationship rather than build it up.

Disagreeing Without Hurting

> ***Do not let any unwholesome talk come out of your mouths, but only what is helpful for building others up according to their needs, that it may benefit those who listen.***
> ***~ Ephesians 4:29***

A couple will disagree; whether it is about where they are going to live, their relationship with the in-laws, spending, child rearing, household chores, sex, time, or even how they squeeze the toothpaste. The problem is not whether they will disagree, but how they will disagree. When both spouses are committed to building each other up rather than tearing each other down, conflict will improve their relationship. There are five ways to resolve a disagreement and build the marriage relationship:

- Work out a compromise.
- Die to self and allow a spouse to have their way.
- Pray and wait for God's guidance.
- Maintain healthy boundaries and allow God to work in a situation.
- Seek mediation.

Compromise resolves conflict by finding a middle point on which both people can agree. This works in many situations. Disagreement over how to squeeze the toothpaste can easily be resolved by purchasing two tubes of toothpaste. Choosing a home to purchase, deciding how to spend time or what to have for dinner may be resolved by compromise. Couples find it harder to compromise when it comes to relationships with in-laws, how to raise children or faith issues.

Often conflict can be avoided or resolved by dying to self and allowing a spouse to do what he wants. This response usually will honor and bless one's spouse. The problem is that this can become the standard for a person who cannot or will not say "no" to his spouse. When this mode of conflict resolution is one sided or not done in freedom and love, it can become enabling. One spouse enables another when he does not say "no" to hurtful or injurious things.

Conflict resolution in a healthy relationship includes prayer. The Lord should be included in every aspect of a couple's life and they should seek to be in His will as they make decisions. This includes how conflict is resolved. Only the Lord can change a spouse and it is important to take disagreements to the Lord and allow Him to work in your spouse. Waiting for God's guidance can be the hard part of this form of conflict resolution. It took twenty-five years for the Lord to bring the promised child to Abraham and Sarah. Their attempt to fix the problem themselves has caused heartache for many generations. Trusting God to change a spouse can be the toughest test of faith, but sometimes a necessary part of conflict resolution. There are times when finding a resolution to a conflict will be very difficult. It is important to seek the Lord and His will during those times.

Healthy boundaries are essential for strong, growing relationships. Sticking with a boundary may not seem like a way to resolve conflict and build your relationship, but at times it is very important. Compromise or dieing to self will not solve problems with sin. Christians are not to compromise regarding the Word of God, and some issues are non-negotiable. Abuse may require physical separation until the abuser gets the help he needs and may even require intervention by church or government authorities. Boundaries may be an inappropriate way to handle conflict arising out of differences or conflicting desires, but they are essential for handling sin. A spouse can not be controlled, but limits can be set regarding the affects of his behavior. Again, it is important to wait on the Lord and allow Him to work in a spouse's life.

Mediation is important to resolving conflict and keeping the marriage relationship moving in the right direction. If you are not able to work through some disagreement, seek the counsel of another couple or trusted friend, or see a Christian counselor. Once conflict becomes emotional, it is not always easy to find a solution, and a mediator can point out aspects of the disagreement the couple did not see. The solution often is surprisingly simple; it may only take a different perspective to find it.

Conflict can be a good thing in the marriage relationship, but couples must stop hurting each other during disagreements. It is important that a couple endeavor together with a joint desire to work through conflict to benefit their relationship.

> ***Hurtful conflict can not take place without your participation***

Working through Disagreements

An excellent boundary to set in marriage states, "I will seek to build up rather than hurt my spouse during conflict." Another boundary might be refusing to participate in a discussion when a spouse is not communicating rationally and reasonably. Seek to diffuse the emotionally charged atmosphere that often accompanies conflict. Treating a spouse with respect, and seeking understanding and resolution during disagreements helps a couple work through any conflict and strengthens their marriage in the process.

"No, I don't think living in North Dakota is a good compromise."

A vision, mission, goals and objectives in life and marriage aid conflict management. It is easy to solve some conflicts by measuring wants and desires with goals and objectives. A good practice for any disagreement would be to look at goals and objectives to see how possible conflict solutions facilitate their fulfillment.

Healthy conflict resolution is a process that can be learned. It takes work and practice and as a couple works together to develop strong communication skills, their relationship will grow tremendously. The following are some points to consider regarding conflict in the marriage relationship:

1. When possible, prepare the setting before a disagreement.
2. Remember, your spouse is not your enemy.
3. Allow for your gender and personality differences.
4. Maintain your boundaries.
5. Respect your spouse's boundaries.
6. Show love and respect to your spouse.
7. Listen before responding.
8. Clarify anything you do not understand.
9. Use "I", not "you" statements when presenting a problem.
10. Do not criticize.
11. Work to solve the problem, rather than attacking your spouse.
12. Acknowledge your part in contributing to the problem.
13. Stay on the subject; do not bring in other issues.
14. Do not seek to "win" the disagreement.
15. Do not argue in front of your children.

16. Fight fair; do not manipulate, bring up the past, exaggerate, use the silent treatment, sarcasm, name calling, attacking their character or use anger to over-power your spouse.
17. Use a "time out" when necessary and set a time to resume the discussion.
18. Offer possible solutions.
19. Plan for implementation of your solution.
20. Seek mediation when necessary.

Ideally, both spouses would agree to abide by the preceding twenty points during any conflict. If you do, use them as a guide to resolve conflict and begin to make them a part of your marital communication pattern. If one spouse will not agree to all twenty, seek to gain acceptance for as many as they will agree to. Some depend only on one person. You can use those and begin changing communication patterns in your marriage even without your spouse's agreement. Healthy boundaries will also help in this effort. Continue the work and do not give up!

> ***My dear brothers, take note of this: Everyone should be quick to listen, slow to speak and slow to become angry,***
> ***~ James 1:19***

For Discussion as a Couple

1. Is there an absence of conflict in your marriage? If so, why is this?

____

____

____

____

2. How have you been hurt in conflict with your spouse?

____

____

____

____

3. How have you and your spouse resolved conflict in the past? How has that worked for you?

____

____

____

____

4. Why are boundaries important in conflict resolution? How can they help in your relationship?

____

____

____

____

5. What do you need to change to improve your communication skills to achieve better conflict resolution?

____

____

____

____

Communication Study 15

Connecting Emotionally

"For this reason a man will leave his father and mother and be united to his wife, and the two will become one flesh."
~ Ephesians 5:31

Effective communication comes from connection.
~ Carla Kimball

Communication is Necessary for Emotional Connection

The Bible says that in marriage, a man and woman become one flesh. There is the sexual connotation of becoming one when husband and wife join together sexually, but there is also the emotional and spiritual oneness achieved over time as a couple grows and matures together. Communication is how they achieve that oneness; that deep connection that a husband and wife cultivate over time. A couple does not connect watching television or doing non-interactive activities. A spouse simply can not be known deeply without communication.

Interestingly, it also takes connection to achieve effective communication. When a spouse is known intimately, one can communicate their deepest feelings, thoughts and desires. A couple who feels separate and alone in their marriage will not communicate as well as a couple that is close. The problem is that it takes communication to get connected! It is important to begin working toward communication at deeper levels.

Communication Levels

Communication experts say that people communicate at five levels; from shallow, superficial communication to transparent communication that shares deep personal honesty. Much of the communication in daily life is on the superficial level. This is the "how are you, I'm fine" type of communication that tells others nothing about who a person is. Communicating facts may reveal a little bit about people as they communicate information about self or their interaction with the world. A person may share ideas or thoughts about people or things, but it is not until they begin to reveal their feelings that they really begin to communicate who they are. Reaching the deepest level of communication; transparency, can be like mining for gold. It takes perseverance and work to be able to communicate at this level. At this point a person shares their heart; hopes, fears and dreams. Building a fortified, intimate marriage requires communication at all levels. This is how couples really get to know each other.

Usually, one spouse will find it more difficult to communicate at deeper levels, while the other will openly share his heart. Some men are able to share feelings and communicate at deeper levels, but more often, it is the wife who finds it easier to be transparent and communicate her feelings. The spouse who can communicate at deeper levels needs to encourage and help his spouse open up in their communications. Pushing, nagging or demanding deeper communication only makes it harder for the non-communicator to communicate. Often, when the less communicative spouse finally opens up and shares a feeling or some fear, he is told that his feelings are not valid. This response is hurtful, and he will tend to be reluctant to open up again in the future.

There is great risk to transparency and openness with anyone, including a spouse. Yet, the rewards of being able to openly share one's heart with his spouse are great. Transparent communication helps a person know and understand his spouse deeply and allows improved teamwork to meet the challenges of life. This transparency also opens one up to the possibility of emotional pain. It is important that deeper levels of communication remain solely between the two of you. There may be times when God can use your transparency to help other people, but do not discuss marital problems outside the marriage relationship without both spouse's agreement. Maintaining trust is important to continuing open communication.

Lack of Communication

People will not communicate at deeper levels without trust. A spouse's trust must be earned; it is not something gained automatically once a couple marries. Revealing one's deeper self, and not having it used against him, helps him continue to reveal his heart to his spouse. Trusting a spouse is a life-long process. Gains made over a period of time can be a set back if trust is broken. Remember, no one is perfect! A couple can build trust and communicate at deeper levels as they work together.

A dog can be trained with treats. Getting your husband to communicate takes a different approach.

Some people have trouble communicating due to problems in their childhood. There may have been abuse, poor communication skills in their family, physical or emotional problems. Whatever barriers there may be, a person can get past them, though it may require the help of a Christian counselor. It will take work, but a couple can discover what barriers are affecting their communication and seek to work through them to achieve the deep communication that will lead to oneness.

A spouse finds it hard to communicate when he fears criticism and judgment. He may have been raised in a critical household and criticism from his spouse keeps him from communicating at deeper levels. It is important to learn to respond without criticism or judgment. There must be a safe environment for transparent communication to flourish.

Feelings and Emotions

> ***Emotions are never wrong—it is how you react to them that causes conflict. ~ Doyle Barnett***

Men and women often handle feelings and emotions very differently. Men tend to isolate and internalize, while women tend to congregate and verbalize. This is not always true, and there are times when it is reversed, but very rarely will both spouses react alike emotionally. Many men bury their feelings. They do not verbalize emotions and escape pain through distractions. They will tell their wife, "nothing" when asked what is wrong. Women don't understand this process because they want to talk through their feelings and process feelings by talking about them. Feelings and emotions tend to frustrate couples because of their differences, but it does not have to be this way.

Feelings occur without input and are a response to situations encountered in life. People may learn to control their reactions to situations in life, but they cannot entirely suppress their feelings. God created human beings with feelings and God Himself has feelings. He expresses anger, joy and many other emotions. They are not right or wrong, but they do reveal what is going on within a person. Feelings and emotions cause problems when they are allowed to control a person's behavior and life.

It is important to understand that feelings belong to the individual. A spouse or others cannot make a person feel a certain way. Everyone needs to take ownership of feelings and handle them Biblically. If your spouse wrongs you in some way, you may feel hurt, disappointment or anger, but he did not make you feel a certain way. Yes, his behavior may have been wrong, but feelings must be owned by the person experiencing them. They also must be handled in a right way. To explode in anger at a spouse's inconsideration or poor behavior is not the correct way to handle emotions. To state, "I am hurt that you did not follow through with your promise and I feel that I am not important to you," expresses the feelings, but does not attack the spouse.

Revealing feelings and emotions to a spouse can be a frightening thing to do. Yet, it is necessary to a strong marriage relationship. Many people do not have experience with communicating their feelings and tend to do it poorly. They may hide their feelings and refuse to talk about them, or they may dump their feelings, expressing them without reserve. Either tendency will injure emotional closeness with a spouse. People need to utilize positive communication skills to express their emotions.

> ***Seek first his kingdom and his righteousness... ~ Matthew 6:33***

Remember, blocked goals and unmet expectations may evoke strong emotions. Focusing on what one wants and desires rather than on what God wants for him will tend to cause frustration and anger. It is humanly impossible for a spouse to meet all of his mate's expectations. If there are expectations, there will be disappointment. As Larry Crabb says, "Pray for your desires and assume responsibility for your goals."[1] Pray that God will provide the things you desire and take responsibility for the goals that are within your control.

Becoming Transparent

Transparent communication is another indication of a fortified marriage. Couples connect emotionally and work toward oneness in their marriage as they communicate at all levels of communication. If you communicate well at all levels, praise God! Continue to work at it, because communicating feelings and being transparent are not natural for most people. There is hope for those who struggle with deeper communication. They can learn to express their feelings to their spouse and not end up in a fight. It is necessary to create a safe environment that is conducive to being transparent and open. This environment will include:

- Positive communication skills.
- Healthy boundaries.
- Unconditional acceptance.
- Mutual trust.
- Supportive communication.
- Forgiveness.

Working positive communication skills into your marriage relationship will make it easier to communicate at deeper levels. Healthy boundaries are important because they will keep a couple on track. Taking responsibility for one's own feelings and behavior and not for their spouse's feelings and behavior is important. Unconditional acceptance means separating behavior from the person. Love and acceptance of a spouse as a person is not based on their behavior. This is seen throughout the Bible as God expresses His love to His people even when He condemns their behavior.

Mutual trust is critical to transparency. People will not communicate their deepest desires, fears and dreams without trust. Trust must be continually built up in a spouse as one proves himself trustworthy and by faith trusts his spouse. Supportive communication means that a person seeks understanding and supports his spouse rather than being critical and judgmental. Understanding why a spouse feels a certain way is important, and criticizing his feelings should cease, even if they seem unfounded and irrational. Gaining understanding of feelings and where those feelings came from enable a couple to help each other work through the feelings and grow in maturity.

Forgiveness is part of the Christian life and vital to transparent communication. Forgiveness does not mean condoning the transgression, but helps restore the relationship even though wrong has been done. Forgiveness allows the relationship to continue as a couple seeks to work through the transgressions that happen in marriage.

> *Therefore, as God's chosen people, holy and dearly loved, clothe yourselves with compassion, kindness, humility, gentleness and patience. Bear with each other and forgive whatever grievances you may have against one another. Forgive as the Lord forgave you. And over all these virtues put on love, which binds them all together in perfect unity.*
> ~ Colossians 3:12-14

For Discussion as a Couple

1. Why is communication important to emotional connection with your spouse?

2. At what level have you and your spouse tended to communicate? Why is this?

3. How is trust important to communication in your marriage?

4. How can you communicate your feelings and emotions without hurting your spouse?

5. How can you become more transparent with your spouse? Where will you start?

Communication Study 16

Effective Communication

Reckless words pierce like a sword, but the tongue of the wise brings healing. ~ Proverbs 12:18

Pleasant words are a honeycomb, sweet to the soul and healing to the bones. ~ Proverbs 16:24

Help your spouse feel loved and secure in your love so they can open up to you and express feelings and ideas without fear of being attacked. Compliment, praise, and give a hug. Small gestures make the grandest statements.[1]

Feeling Heard, Respected and Understood

The goal of communication understands, although more than just understanding is needed during communication. When a spouse feels heard, respected, and understood, there will be growth personally and in the marriage relationship. This is a difficult task since it is so easy in today's fast paced society to drift apart and communicate only at the superficial or factual levels. The demands of work, family, ministry and the endless onslaught of activities work against intimacy in marriage. A couple must set aside time for just the two of them and they need an environment where open and transparent communication is possible.

A person will feel heard, respected and understood when his spouse communicates:

- That the message sent was received.
- Respect for his thoughts and ideas.
- Empathy for his feelings.

Effective communication begins with the non-verbal. Stopping all activity to give a spouse one's undivided attention is important. This can be accomplished by making eye contact, and being open to him (do not assume a defensive posture; arms crossed or a stern look).

A very effective listening tool uses mirroring, validating and empathizing to gain understanding of what was communicated. Mirroring or repeating what was heard ensures that the information received was actually what the speaker meant. Mirroring is to be without judgment, distortion, sarcasm or argument. Repeat in your own words what you think they said. Validating communicates understanding that the speaker's thoughts and feelings are valid for them, even if the listener has a different perspective. To empathize, one communicates that they understand what the speaker is feeling.

An Example:

Speaker: "It hurt me when you criticized me in front of your mother."

Listener: "I hear you saying that you were hurt when I criticized you in front of my mother. Is that correct?"

Speaker: "Yes, that is what I said."

Listener: "I understand that you would not want to be criticized in front of my mother or anyone else."

Listener: "I imagine you felt disrespected and maybe betrayed."

This type of exchange helps a person truly understand what his spouse communicates. It is not always easy, especially for a spouse that is not comfortable with communicating his feelings. One person calls

this process "the drill" and while he is not comfortable with it, he does it because "it works."

The Pathway to Effective Communication

Achieving effective communication in marriage begins with understanding who you are as a child of God and as a person. Understanding that God accepts you unconditionally helps you accept yourself and then accept others as they are. Knowing your purpose gives a direction and confidence about where you are going in life. You know what belongs to you and what doesn't because of healthy boundaries. Effective communication is a result of your understanding of these principles and then applying positive communications skills. Putting it all into practice helps you toward transparency and growth in your marriage relationship.

Effective Communication Takes Practice

Most people do not naturally know how to communicate well, but they can learn to communicate in such a way that they are able to understand and be understood. The goal here is to improve communication skills. Make a commitment to begin now, right where you are, to make the effort to improve communication in your marriage relationship.

Begin with small steps by using the principles you are learning and taking the time to begin communicating about minor issues. Practice giving your undivided attention to your spouse and ask that he do the same as you communicate with him. Stop what you are doing, turn to your spouse and establish eye contact. Learn to listen patiently; in such a way that your spouse feels that you desire to hear everything he has to say. Wait until he has finished before beginning your response. Respond by mirroring, validating and empathizing rather than defending yourself or attacking him.

It is not usually what is said that hurts, but how it is said. A discussion can instantaneously become an argument when conversation begins harshly and you attack your spouse rather than communicate with him.

> ***What causes fights and quarrels among you? Don't they come from your desires that battle within you? You want something but don't get it. You kill and covet, but you cannot have what you want. You quarrel and fight. You do not have, because you do not ask God. When you ask, you do not receive, because you ask with wrong motives, that you may spend what you get on your pleasures. ~ James 4:1-3***

Disagreement doesn't cause hurt in the relationship. It is selfishness that gets in the way of healthy conflict resolution. When the purpose of communication is to get what you want, conflict will be a hurtful exercise that will tend to tear down intimacy rather than build it up. There will be improvement in your communication as a couple when you begin making changes in how you communicate. One spouse can make a difference alone, but both spouses working together to improve communication is more effective.

If possible, agree on Rules of Engagement by setting up an agreement about how you will resolve conflict in your marriage. Include a rule about what to do when one person violates the rules. Put the agreement into writing and refer to it often. Communicating with structure will feel artificial and mechanical. Do not give up! Yes, it is somewhat restrictive, but it works! You can be heard, respected, and understood in any conflict. When you are at an impasse and emotions are rising, you may want to take a break from your discussion Do not walk away and not come back. Set a time to resume the discussion. If you can not resolve the conflict between the two of you, get help! Talk to a mature Christian couple you both respect, talk to your pastor, or see a Christian counselor. The attitude often is that counselors are for the weak and immature. In reality, it is the mature Christian who realizes that God has given wisdom to people who can help them grow in their relationship with Him and each other.

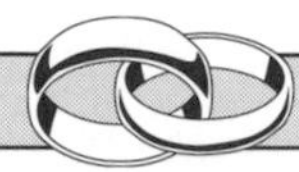

Couples achieve oneness and intimacy through communication and effective communication is absolutely vital to a fortified marriage. It is how one gets to know his spouse; understanding who he is, where he came from and how they can grow together. Effective communication helps solve *any* problem that comes in a marriage. Any couple can be the team God wants them to be with effective communication.

This all takes time and requires investing the energy into the relationship to become skilled communicators. Make time for the two of you and do not allow anything to take it away. Your time alone does not always have to be communicating at the transparency level. Do fun things, play games, go out on dates and enjoy each other. Love your spouse deeply. Die to self and continue to build your relationship. Above all, pray and seek God in everything you do. The blessings you will receive will be great!

> ***Do nothing out of selfish ambition or vain conceit, but in humility consider others better than yourselves. Each of you should look not only to your own interests, but also to the interests of other. Your attitude should be the same as that of Christ Jesus...***
> ***~ Philippians 2:3-5***

For Discussion as a Couple

1. What can you do to make your spouse feel heard, respected and understood?

____

____

____

____

2. Why is The Pathway to Effective Communication important?

____

____

____

____

3. What can you do to begin to make communication in your marriage better?

____

____

____

____

4. What do you think about having Rules of Engagement in your marriage? What are some of the things you would put in it?

____

____

____

____

5. Why is time important to communication and building intimacy?

____

____

____

____

____

Communication Exercise[2]

Follow the instructions below to complete this exercise. Take turns, the wife goes first; once she has completed the exercise, the husband will take his turn. Arrange a time when you can communicate without fear of interruption. Sit so that you are facing each other and are comfortable. Give your spouse your undivided attention and show that you are listening through positive body language. Please to not make a joke of this exercise. It will help you put into practice the principles you have learned in this chapter.

Step 1: Pray together asking for God's wisdom and guidance for your discussion.

Step 2: **Speaker:** State a problem in your relationship without attacking your spouse. Use "I" statements and the principles you have learned in this chapter.

Step 3: **Listener:** Mirror what you heard your spouse say to you in your own words. Once you have it correct, ask, "Is that all? "

Step 4: **Speaker:** Once you have finished and you are sure he has heard you correctly, let your spouse know that you have finished with the issue.

Step 5: **Listener:** Validate your spouse by letting him know that you understand why this is a problem for him. Take ownership for your part with the problem.

Step 6: **Speaker:** Acknowledge your spouse's validation. Correct your spouse's incorrect views of your feelings or thoughts. Remember to be patient and understanding as he attempts to get this right.

Step 7: **Listener:** Empathize with your spouse by relating and identifying with his feelings.

Step 8: **Speaker:** Acknowledge his empathy and thank him for listening.

Step 9: **Speaker:** Share three changes in behavior on your spouse's part that you think will solve the problem.

Step 10: **Listener:** Write down each request and read it back. Change the wording to ensure you have written exactly what the speaker means. Do not argue about perceptions.

Step 11: **Speaker:** Verify that listener has written the requests correctly.

Step 12: **Listener:** Agree to change. You may negotiate, but not to the point of diminishing the Speaker's request for change. The solution must be acceptable to both spouses.

"You tell me that I don't show my feelings, so I made up these signs."

Feelings[3]

Feelings are an important part of life, and they reveal one's reaction to the world around them. It is important to express feelings and attain emotional connection and effective communication in the marriage relationship. The following list of words can help you express your feelings. There are six categories. Identify the category that applies, then get specific with one of the words listed under that category.

Mad	Sad	Glad	Scared	Confused	Serene
angry	devastated	excited	fearful	bewildered	satisfied
furious	hopeless	elated	panicky	directionless	content
seething	depressed	exuberant	afraid	numb	peaceful
enraged	wounded	ecstatic	scared	flustered	satiated
hostile	drained	terrific	shocked	baffled	full
vengeful	defeated	jubilant	overwhelmed	troubled	rested
incensed	worthless	happy	intimidated	ambivalent	composed
abused	helpless	energized	desperate	awkward	calm
hateful	crushed	thrilled	frantic	puzzled	soothed
humiliated	dejected	valued	terrified	disorganized	cool
sabotaged	humbled	relieved	vulnerable	foggy	sober
betrayed	empty	resolved	petrified	perplexed	centered
repulsed	miserable	encouraged	immobilized	hesitant	still
abandoned	distraught	gratified	tense	misunderstood	restful
outraged	grievous	joyful	anxious	doubtful	sheltered
rebellious	demoralized	proud	uneasy	uncertain	protected
spiteful	condemned	cheerful	skeptical	surprised	safe
vindictive	deflated	determined	alarmed	unsettled	unruffled
used	unloved	grateful	frightened	unsure	untroubled
resentful	mournful	accepted	shaken	distracted	undisturbed
ridiculed	disheartened	admired	startled	mixed up	unmoved
disgusted	disappointed	delighted	guarded	overwhelmed	thankful
frustrated	inadequate	hopeful	stunned	blank	
offended	discouraged	fortunate	nervous		
annoyed	ashamed	pleased	unsure		
cheated	lonely	flattered	timid		
provoked	alienated	confident			
	isolated	expectant			
	lost				

Fortified Marriages
Chapter 4 Endnotes

Study 13: *Understanding One Another*

1. H. Norman Wright; Making Your Love Last Forever, A Book for Couples (NY, NY; Inspirational Press, 1998) p 57
2. Cleveland McDonald and Philip M. McDonald; Creating a Successful Christian Marriage (Grand Rapids, MI; Baker Book House Company, 1994) p 151

Recommended for further reading:
- Making Your Love Last Forever, A Book for Couples by H. Norman Wright.

Study 14: *Managing Conflict*

1. Judith Wallerstein, Julia Lewis, and Sandra Blakeslee; The Unexpected Legacy of Divorce: a 25 Year Landmark Study (NY, NY; Hyperion, 2000) p55
2. www.smartmarriages.com/divorcepredictor.html

Recommended for further reading:
- Marriage Clues for the Clueless; Developed and produced by the Livingstone Corporation

Study 15: *Connecting Emotionally*

1. Larry Crabb; The Marriage Builder (Grand Rapids, MI, Zondervan) p 75

Recommended for further reading:
- Intimate Encounters by Dr. David & Teresa Ferguson and Dr. Chris & Holly Thurman.
- The Marriage Builder by Dr. Larry Crabb.

Study 16: *Effective Communication*

1. Secrets of Super-Happy Couples, Ladies Home Journal; www.lhj.com/relationships
2. Adapted from Zach Whaley's "The Marriage Communication Workshop." Contact Zach at 480-855-0075 or zach@zachwhaley.com or visit his website at www.zachwhaley.com.
3. Ibid.

Recommended for further reading:
- Communication; Key to Your Marriage by H. Norman Wright

For further information, see:
- Focus on the Family: www.family.org

Chapter 5
Needs

Study 17

Needs and the Marriage Relationship

> *What good is it, my brothers, if a man claims to have faith but has no deeds? Can such faith save him? Suppose a brother or sister is without clothes and daily food. If one of you says to him, "Go, I wish you well; keep warm and well fed," but does nothing about his physical needs, what good is it? In the same way, faith by itself, if it is not accompanied by action, is dead. ~ James 2:14-17*

Created With Needs

A need is a "lack or absence of something necessary."[1] God created people with needs. This is seen in Genesis 2:20 after God created man and the animals, He said, "but for Adam no suitable helper was found." God created Eve because Adam needed her. God did not make a mistake by creating Adam first without Eve. The order of His creation is part of the awesomeness of that creation.

> *In the Lord, however, woman is not independent of man, nor is man independent of woman. For as woman came from man, so also man is born of woman. But everything comes from God. ~ 1 Corinthians 11:11-12*

Even though people today do all they can to reject God's order, men and women simply are not independent of each other. They are created relationally—with an inborn need for other people. It is a fact that everyone has needs. A person's primary need is to know God. No one but God can meet that need, it is between each individual and God. People also have relational needs that are met by others; God uses people to meet the needs of other people. It is such an important concept that, in the book of James, there is a tie between faith and being used to meet the needs of others. People are saved by faith, not by works, but works demonstrate a person's faith. Those works involve meeting the needs of others.

> *Life isn't worth living, unless it is lived for someone else. ~ Albert Einstein*

The marriage relationship is a special place of meeting needs and having needs met. There are some needs, such as sexual and deep emotional needs, that are only to be met within the marriage relationship. The concept of meeting each other's needs seems to be a contradiction. According to the principles of boundaries, individual needs are each person's own responsibility. It is not a husband or wife's duty to meet the spouse's needs. Yet, the Bible teaches dying to self and putting others before self to meet their needs. What is a major cause of conflict in marriage? Isn't it the selfish desires of the individual (James 4:1)? When a person is focused on getting his needs met, he does not think about how he can meet his spouse's needs. This leads to a vicious cycle of fighting and hurting one another and eventually to emotional distance and relationship breakdown.

Many reasons are given for the break up of marriages today, but the basis of it all is unmet needs. When a person's needs are not being met in the marriage relationship, he will seek to meet those needs by some means, often in ways that will damage the marriage, even to the point of divorce. Jealousy, communication problems, infidelity and sexual problems very often stem from the problem of unmet needs.

One of the biggest myths in today's society is the idea that a fifty-fifty marriage is a normal and good marriage. It may be normal in society, but it is not good. Yet, this myth also flourishes within the Christian church. It is a huge problem. The marriage relationship should be a one hundred—zero relationship. It is a matter of giving everything and expecting nothing in return. Jesus gave everything for mankind without any expectation and Christians are also to give everything for their spouse. Ephesians 5:1-2, John 15:12-14 and other Scriptures bear this truth out. While your spouse's needs are not your responsibility, it is important to make the choice to love him or her by dying to self and putting your needs second. Living a life of giving diminishes or resolves many marital conflicts.

If anyone does not provide for his relatives, and especially for his immediate family, he has denied the faith and is worse than an unbeliever (1Timothy 5:8). This passage generally applies to men meeting the financial needs of their family, but doesn't it also mean that husbands and wives should be available to be used to meet physical, emotional and spiritual needs of their family? It is part of their responsibilities as members of the family unit. This is where dying to self becomes a reality, when people set their needs aside and meet the needs of their spouses.

Everyone has Different Needs

It is vitally important to understand that as husband and wife, couples are two very different people. They are different physically, mentally, emotionally and even spiritually and those differences include needs. Needs differ because of gender, personality and the environment people were raised in. During courtship and early in marriage, couples tend to be focused on meeting each other's needs. It usually does not take long for the focus to change to seeking to have one's own needs met.

It takes time and effort to discover a spouse's needs. Couples must be willing to listen, watch and pay attention to each other to learn their spouse's needs. Everyone's needs are different; you cannot make any assumptions about what your spouse's needs are. It is important that you understand your spouse's needs specific to him or her.

> ***They may forget what you said, but they will never forget how you made them feel.***
> ***~ Carl W. Buechner***

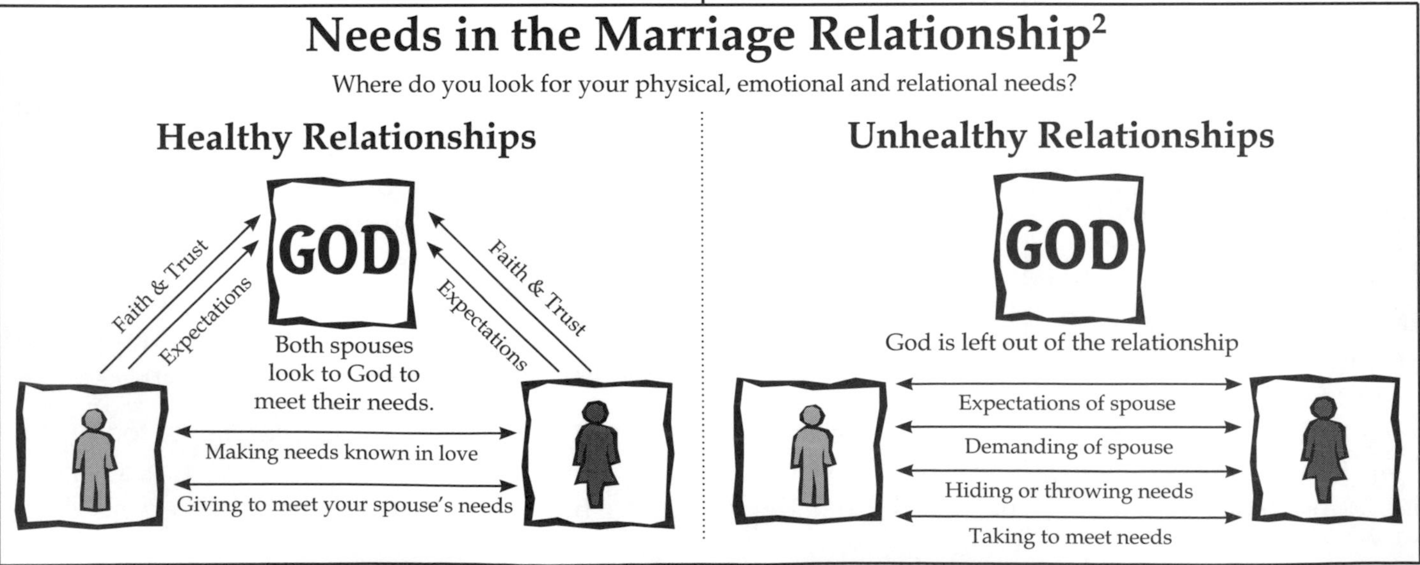

Expectations of God versus Demands on Other People

It is important that both husband and wife focus on God, put their faith and trust in Him, and allow Him to use each other to meet their needs. Often, a spouse may nag, criticize or demand rather than trust God to prompt unselfish behavior in a spouse. The diagram on the previous page illustrates differences between healthy relationships and unhealthy relationships. God should be the focus for needs, not one's spouse as seen in the diagram.

In marriage, each person has genuine, God-given needs. In a healthy relationship, one makes his needs known to God and trusts Him to meet them, without making demands about how, when or through whom. In contrast, people in unhealthy relationships may expect their spouses to meet all their needs. The expectations often become demanding and manipulative, and may result in anger when they are unmet.

No one is perfect; people have expectations and will be disappointed but making a decision to keep expectation levels low can minimize disappointment. A person's level of disappointment correlates to the degree to which his expectations are not met. Even with low expectations, there will be disappointment. The problem isn't the expectations or disappointment; it is how they are handled. Expectations should be directed toward God while communicating needs to one's spouse. When the disappointment of unmet needs is experienced, it is important to cry out to the Lord and communicate to your spouse in love.

It is unfair to criticize a spouse for not recognizing and meeting needs that haven't been communicated. People cannot read minds or guess what their spouses' needs are. A spouse can only connect and respond to needs when they are communicated in love. This will also create intimacy and help a couple grow in oneness as they communicate at deeper levels.

Attacking your spouse for not meeting your needs will only result in hurtful conflict. Remember, it is not his or her responsibility to meet your needs. Yet, it is very damaging to a relationship if one spouse (or both) is not interested in doing anything about his spouse's needs. Selfishness is between your spouse and God, and as you remain focused on the Lord, it becomes easier for you to focus on meeting your spouse's needs rather than looking for him to meet your needs.

Seeking to give sometimes brings very pleasant surprises.

God did not intend for you to find happiness through your spouse or children. People are not free when their happiness depends on other people. God wants you to discover a life of true joy and contentment based on who you are in Jesus Christ.

> Freely you have received, freely give. ~Matthew 10:8b

In a perfect world, couples would not have to deal with most of the problems they face today. God created Adam in a perfect world, but due to sin, that world became imperfect and mankind has had relationship problems ever since. Present problems cannot be blamed on Adam. He did not cause people today to be selfish and self-centered. Nor can Satan be blamed. He may tempt, but the decision to act and do things that cause stress in relationships is made by each person. Many people tend to blame their spouse, but no matter what a spouse has done, he or she did not force a person to behave in any certain way. Tendencies toward poor behaviors are a part of mankind's sin nature; a spouse cannot be blamed for them. It is a matter of making daily, sometimes moment by moment decisions to act the way God wants His people to act rather than the way that feels right or justified at the moment. It is a matter of putting obedience of God before feelings.

It is important to understand needs to continue toward intimacy and moving to oneness in marriage. The goal is to focus on the Lord and allow Him to meet your needs. It also is important to be a tool used to meet the needs of your spouse. There will be growth in the relationship and a couple will move another step toward a fortified marriage when they experience met needs.

> *"If you are looking for someone to meet your needs, make you happy, and make your life worthwhile, you will be greatly disappointed, quickly discouraged, and basically unhappy the rest of your life. But, if you will just be the person God has made you to be, and find out how you can give your life to someone else by meeting their needs and making them happy, you will discover fulfillment, joy, and peace in ways you can't even imagine."*[3]

For Discussion as a Couple

1. Why do you think God created mankind with needs? For what purpose?

____
____
____
____

2. Do you agree that marriage should be a one hundred zero relationship rather than fifty-fifty? Why or why not?

____
____
____
____

3. Where do you find the balance between depending on God for your needs and making your needs known to your spouse?

____
____
____
____

4. What can you do to keep your expectations focused on God rather than your spouse and others?

____
____
____
____

5. What will you do to better meet your spouse's needs?

____
____
____
____

Needs

Study 18

Understanding Needs

God created people with needs and each person's needs are different than those of his spouse. It is important to understand needs before one can be used of God to meet his spouse's needs. Understanding needs will help couples grow in oneness.

"We were never meant to be completely satisfied in this world."
~ Michael Card

"Therefore I tell you, do not worry about your life, what you will eat or drink; or about your body, what you will wear. Is not life more important than food, and the body more important than clothes? Look at the birds of the air; they do not sow or reap or store away in barns, and yet your heavenly Father feeds them. Are you not much more valuable than they? Who of you by worrying can add a single hour to his life? "And why do you worry about clothes? See how the lilies of the field grow. They do not labor or spin. Yet I tell you that not even Solomon in all his splendor was dressed like one of these. If that is how God clothes the grass of the field, which is here today and tomorrow is thrown into the fire, will he not much more clothe you, O you of little faith? So do not worry, saying, 'What shall we eat?' or 'What shall we drink?' or 'What shall we wear?' For the pagans run after all these things, and your heavenly Father knows that you need them. But seek first his kingdom and his righteousness, and all these things will be given to you as well. ~ Matthew 6:25-33

God knows that people have needs and He cares about those needs. Christians don't have to run around like the people of the world attempting to get their needs met anyway they can. They can trust the Lord, seek Him, and be assured that He will provide for them. It is important to remember that a person is not to expect or demand that spouse or others meet his needs. God desires to be the focus for His children's needs and a spouse will only disappoint you if he or she is expected to meet your needs. There are several ways to seek to have needs met. One can:

- Ignore needs and pretend they don't exist.
- Suppress needs and deny them.
- Become enslaved to needs, spending one's life seeking to have them met through achievement, relationships, the flesh or the world.
- Push needs onto one's spouse or others, demanding that they meet needs.
- Make needs known to one's spouse or others.
- Give one's needs to God and allow Him to meet needs His way.

The healthy way is to give your needs to God in prayer and make them known to your spouse and others as appropriate. This will take patience, practice, discipline and prayer. At times, waiting on the Lord will not be easy.

Types of Needs

Needs are an example of the incredible complexity of the human being. God created us physically, emotionally, mentally and spiritually. We have needs in each of these areas and needs within areas may overlap. The sexual needs of men are often viewed as a physical need, but they are emotional needs as well. Men usually need to be desired by their

wives. Likewise, a woman's need for security is both emotional and physical. Women are typically not as strong physically as men and need protection, but the need is an emotional part of them also.

Physical needs are less complex than the other areas. Air, food, and water keep the body functioning. Contrary to what many men may say, human beings can live without sex, although it is a part of God's creation. Cleanliness is important to the body but also not absolutely necessary for life. Mental needs are more complex. Studies show that active seniors live longer than people who are not challenged in life. The brain needs the exercise received from reading, playing complex games, memorization and interacting with people.

Spiritual needs are primarily met in a relationship with God, but there also is a connection between spiritual needs and emotional needs. As a couple grows and matures together spiritually, there will be growth in their marriage relationship. Couples, due to insecurities, poor communication and a lack of intimacy often neglect this area. You will discover a greater closeness and intimacy with God and each other as you begin to seek God individually and as a couple.

Emotional Needs

Emotional needs are much more complex than other areas of need and they are more difficult to identify and meet. Unmet emotional needs cause couples the greatest problems and most conflict. Insecurity, neglect or the lack of support often indicates unmet needs. A couple may think they are fighting about money, coming home late from work, being irresponsible or any number of things, but in fact their conflict usually revolves around unmet emotional needs.

When emotional needs are not met, a couple will not experience intimacy. Unmet needs over time may progress from hurt to anger, fear, guilt and finally to apathy. Negative thoughts and feelings will build until a person feels guilty about those feelings and without a healthy outlet; he will finally stop caring and give up. When one spouse is apathetic about the relationship, it is often only a matter of time before the relationship breaks up.

The progression of unmet needs is a reality of life. God created mankind with needs and unmet needs over a long period of time will block intimacy in the marriage. It is important to look to the Lord to meet your own needs, but it is also important to discover and meet your spouse's needs. Met needs help a couple experience a balanced and healthy relationship.

People tend to do the things they would like done for them and serve their spouse based on their needs rather than their spouse's needs. You cannot meet your spouse's needs by doing what you would want done for you. Men often are oblivious to their wives' needs, while women tend to drop hints about their needs and then are disappointed when their husbands do not figure it out. Typically, needs differ by gender and personality, and it is each spouse's responsibility to learn the needs specific to his or her spouse. The following page will describe needs based on these tendencies. The Needs Inventory on page 116 will help you understand your own needs and assist communicating your needs to your spouse. Discussing your spouse's answers to the Needs Inventory will help you understand his or her specific needs.

Women's Needs:

Affection: Non-sexual physical touch, hugging, caressing.

Caring: Interest in her feelings and concern for her well-being.

Companionship: The need for emotional closeness and openness.

Devotion: Feeling adored and special.

Patience: Waiting calmly or without complaint.

Respect: Treated with dignity, courtesy, and honor.

Security: Protection and provision. A safe environment and relationship.

Sensitivity: Having empathy for her feelings and emotions.

Significance: To know that she is valuable for whom she is.

Spiritual intimacy: Shared spirituality, feeling oneness and openness in the couple's mutual relationship with God.

Trustworthiness: Reliable, faithfulness to your word.

Unconditional love: Absolute, without question.

Understanding: Listening without judgment and with empathy.

Men's Needs:

Acceptance: A favorable reception without rejection.

Admiration: Knowing that he is important and worthwhile.

Appreciation: Gratefulness for what he does.

Approval: To be judged favorably without criticism.

Companionship: Doing things together. Having common interests.

Encouragement: Inspiring with courage, hope or confidence.

Support: Working with him and encouraging him. Being a team.

Physical responsiveness: Demonstrations of affection and sexual responsiveness affirms a man's masculinity.

Respect: To be treated with honor.

To be needed: That he is important to the well being of the family.

Trust: Belief in him and that he knows what he is doing.

Spiritual connection: Serving God together; having a joint purpose and direction in their spirituality.

Unconditional love: Not limited by or subject to conditions.

Needs by Personality[1]

The Lion:

- Appreciation: That their hard work is appreciated.
- Action: They want things to happen and keep moving.
- Opportunity for leadership
- Something to control.

The Otter:

- Attention: They need the attention of people.
- Approval: Praise for what they have done.
- Affection: They love to be loved.
- Activity: Constantly doing things.

The Golden Retriever:

- Peace: Calmness and lack of pressure.
- Self-Worth: They need to feel that they matter; that they are worthwhile.
- Significance: That they have value.

The Beaver:

- Support: That you are on their team.
- Space: They need time for themselves.
- Silence: Time away from the noise and clamor of life.
- Stability: A sense of order in their life.

Love Languages

In his book *The Five Love Languages*, Gary Chapman points out that people speak different love languages.[2] Love languages are the ways people receive love and while they may enjoy receiving love in all ways, usually one way is preferred over the others. The love languages are:

- ***Physical Touch***
- ***Quality Time***
- ***Receiving Gifts***
- ***Acts of Service***
- ***Words of Affirmation***

Love languages are a part of the process of meeting a spouse's needs. A husband and wife seldom have the same primary love language. Couples often make the mistake of speaking their own primary love language to their spouse rather than speaking their spouse's love language. This creates confusion and frustration. Once you identify and learn to speak your spouse's primary love language, you will discover a key way to help him or her feel loved and meet needs.

It is important to understand love languages and learn your spouse's primary love language. Learning his or her love language takes a little time and work, but is well worth the effort. Consciously working to speak your spouse's love language can drastically improve your relationship. Let's take a brief look at the five love languages:

Physical Touch: Holding hands, kissing, embracing and sexual intercourse are all ways to communicate love to your spouse. Touch is not just sex; it is reaching out to your spouse in many ways and at different times.

Quality Time: Not just two bodies in the same room or in the same car. It means communication and mutually enjoyed activities. It does not mean watching TV together, unless you both want to, but rather active listening to one another.

Receiving Gifts: A gift is a physical object that reminds a person that he was thought of. Gifts do not necessarily need to be expensive and can be made or even found. They are visual symbols of love.

Acts of Service: Above all else Jesus demonstrated love through acts of service. Washing the disciple's feet is one of many examples. Acts of service means doing things for your spouse that will make him or her feel loved.

Words of Affirmation: Words penetrate, especially when spoken by someone you are close to or love. Affirming words can touch a soul with extraordinary power. Verbal compliments or words of appreciation are powerful communicators of love.

Discover your spouse's primary and secondary love languages. Look at what he or she does to express love to you and others. Do they give gifts and seem to always think about what they can buy for some one? Do they constantly seek to affirm others? You can often pick out their love language by watching how they express love to others. Think about how they react to various expressions from you. Do they react passively when they receive gifts? Or do they express incredible appreciation for even the smallest gift? Do they pull away from a touch? Or do they seem to melt when you or someone else touches them. Watching and developing an awareness of your spouse will help you learn his love languages.

Once you have discovered your spouse's love language, put that knowledge into practice and speak his love language daily. Form new habits; seek to love your spouse as God intended you to love him. Love him as he is, not as you think he should be.

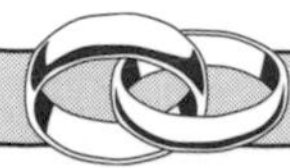

Make a list of things you can do to meet your spouse's need for love in his love language. Do one of those things on a regular, even daily basis to get into the practice of expressing love in his love language.

"Yes, I'm sure. See it says right here on www.selfishmen.org, 'the wife's love language should be the same as her husband's."

For Discussion as a Couple

1. How have you sought to meet your needs?

2. Looking back at your life, would you say that your emotional needs have generally been met? Or have they gone unmet? Why is this?

3. Have you experienced the downward progression of unmet needs? Explain.

4. What did you learn about needs from the explanations on page 113?

5. What is your spouse's primary love language? What can you do to speak it?

Emotional Needs Inventory

Rate your top five needs using "1" for the most important to "5" for your fifth most important need. You may need to refer to the definitions on page 113. Do the same for your spouse and then discuss the results with them. This is a great opportunity to discover what yours and your spouse's primary needs are. It is a way to grow in your relationship with each other as you learn about each other's needs and then seek to meet them.

You		*Your Spouse*
________	*Acceptance*	________
________	*Admiration*	________
________	*Affection*	________
________	*Appreciation*	________
________	*Approval*	________
________	*Caring*	________
________	*Companionship—Emotional closeness*	________
________	*Companionship—Common interests*	________
________	*Devotion*	________
________	*Encouragement*	________
________	*Patience*	________
________	*Physical responsiveness*	________
________	*Respect*	________
________	*Security*	________
________	*Sensitivity*	________
________	*Significance*	________
________	*Spiritual connection*	________
________	*Spiritual intimacy*	________
________	*Support*	________
________	*To be needed*	________
________	*Trust*	________
________	*Trustworthiness*	________
________	*Unconditional love*	________
________	*Understanding*	________

Needs

Study 19

Meeting Needs

Do nothing out of selfish ambition or vain conceit, but in humility consider others better than yourselves. Each of you should look not only to your own interests, but also to the interests of others.
~ Philippians 2:3-4

"Success in life is not in what we get, it is in what we give. Things we obtain, power we possess, fame we achieve will never fill that lasting need we can only find in giving."
~ Kenn Kington

Others before Self

The Word of God says to look to the interests and the needs of others. Biblically, Christians are to put others before themselves. This principle will be seen in marriages in which spouses allow themselves to be used by God to meet each other's needs.

Healthy boundaries allow you the freedom to say no to those things that are not good for you or in the best interest of your marriage. They also give the freedom to say yes to the things that will build up, edify and bless your spouse. Learning your spouse's needs is an incredible relationship builder. Striving to meet your spouse's needs without regard for his or her behavior will change your relationship. Your spouse may be an angry, hurtful, spiteful person. Have you ever wondered why he is that way? Are his needs met? Are his love languages spoken? Is he affirmed and encouraged or is he constantly criticized? If you want to see your spouse change, learn his needs and then seek to meet those needs on a regular basis.

It is a risk to give one hundred percent without expecting anything in return, but the possibility of a strong, flourishing marriage is worth the risk. This is not something you do once and then ignore for the rest of your life. Needs are ongoing and change as people age. Your spouse's needs, at some point, could become significant with age, illness or physical problems. It could try your very commitment to the marriage relationship. It is in those times that couples must remember that they made a vow to love and care for their spouse until death separates them. Far too many people today remain in their marriage as long as it is an agreeable experience. Once marriage becomes work and the romance wears off, they begin to look for a new relationship. Marriage should be a place where a person can take the risk of giving everything without having to worry that his spouse will leave when life is not easy any longer.

Discovering Your Spouse's Needs

In First Corinthians, Paul says that it is better for men and women to remain single so they can serve the Lord wholeheartedly. He knew this was not an option for most people and points out that married people are concerned about how they can please their spouse. To please them, to meet their needs, couples must know each other and each other's needs.

...a married man is concerned about the affairs of this world-how he can please his wife-
~ 1 Corinthians 7:33

...a married woman is concerned about the affairs of this world-how she can please her husband.
~ 1 Corinthians 7:34

Have you taken and discussed the Emotional Needs Inventory with your spouse to find out his or her needs? You cannot assume certain needs because of your spouse's gender or personality type. While the inventory is a great way to begin your needs investigation, it is not all there is to discovering your spouse's needs. Ask your spouse what his needs are, what needs aren't being met and how you might be of help in meeting those needs. There are not very many people who will respond negatively to the question, "Honey, what do you need from me?" You also should consciously observe your spouse in different situations. What brings happiness? What circumstances cause a smile or laugh? You may experiment by trying different things. Use the lists on page 113 as a guide and record your spouse's response to the different activities you try. Trial and error will help you discover what you can do to meet some of your spouse's needs.

The purposes of a man's heart are deep waters, but a man of understanding draws them out. ~ Proverbs 20:5

There's more to just knowing a spouse's needs; husbands and wives need to understand each other. The mystery of the opposite sex is the subject of much discussion and many jokes, but they don't have to be such a mystery. God didn't create humans so complex that they can't be understood. 1 Peter 3:7 tells men to be considerate as they live with their wives; another translation says to dwell with your spouse with understanding. Will men or women feel the same emotions their spouse feels? Most likely, they will not. But that doesn't mean that understanding is impossible. Using learned communication skills, couples can increase their understanding of each other and their spouse needs. You will learn to identify with your spouse's emotions as you mirror, validate and empathize. Empathizing is not feeling exactly what a spouse is feeling, but identifying with his feelings. It is imagining what it would be like to feel what he feels. Understanding will be gained through empathizing.

Give to everyone who asks you, and if anyone takes what belongs to you, do not demand it back. Do to others, as you would have them do to you. ~ Luke 6:30-31

Knowledge and understanding are nothing if nothing is done with them. They must be translated into action. The one hundred – zero principle, giving one hundred percent without expecting anything in return, is unique to Christianity. Talk is meaningless without action. It is important to pick one or two needs and begin working to meet those needs. Speaking a spouse's love language can begin at the same time. It will feel awkward and very contrived at first, but as you continue to work at it, it will become more natural. Many men may feel awkward hugging their wife without trying to fix the problem when she experiences intense emotions. Yet, this action will fulfill a deep emotional need in his wife and do much to build the relationship. New positive habits take time to develop, just as old unproductive patterns take time to change. Be patient and don't stop trying after a week or so and say, "This doesn't work." Gary Chapman tells the story of a woman who spoke her husband's love languages for two months before he even began to respond positively.[1] She gave when she didn't feel like it and in spite of receiving nothing in return. God worked in her husband's heart and he eventually responded to her giving.

Give and it will be given to you. A good measure, pressed down, shaken together and running over, will be poured into your lap. For with the measure you use, it will be measured to you." ~ Luke 6:38

The progression of unmet needs leads to hurt and emotional distance and the progression of met needs leads to intimacy and a strong, healthy marriage. Spouses with fulfilled needs simply are much healthier and happier. They are more apt to be interested in meeting their spouse's needs. Instead of a cycle of hurt and anger, a cycle of consideration and giving begins. One spouse can make a difference if he will begin making changes and giving to his spouse… without expectations.

When your spouse attempts to meet your needs, please do not criticize and put down his or her efforts. There is nothing more demoralizing than to stretch one's self beyond his comfort zone only to receive negative feedback. It will take time to change past behaviors. It is difficult to change and do things that are unnatural and foreign. Praise your spouse's efforts even when they hopelessly make a mess of things. Encouragement and positive reinforcement will help your spouse begin to get it right.

Be Creative

There are many ways to be creative and fun as you seek to meet your spouse's needs. Simply Romantic Nights by Dennis and Barbara Rainey or 101 Nights of Grrreat Romance by Laura Corn are excellent places to get ideas as you begin to bless your spouse by meeting his or her needs.

"My self-esteem is hungry. Do you have any compliments I can snack on?"

For Discussion as a Couple

1. Why is meeting needs not about you? What can you do to remain focused on your spouse's needs?

____
____
____
____

2. What can you do to discover your spouse's needs?

____
____
____
____

3. Why is it important to understand your spouse's needs, rather then just knowing them?

____
____
____
____

4. How can you put your knowledge and understanding of your spouse's needs into action? What will you do to begin meeting their needs?

____
____
____
____

5. How can you encourage your spouse when he or she attempts to meet your needs?

____
____
____
____
____

Fortified Marriages
Chapter 5 Endnotes

Study 17: *Needs and the Marriage Relationship*

1. Collier's Dictionary; William D. Halsey, Editorial Director (NY, NY; Macmillan Educational Company, 1986)
2. Adapted from Intimate Encounters, by Dr. David and Teresa Ferguson and Dr. Chris and Holly Thurman (Nashville, TN; Thomas Nelson, 1994) p 52
3. Kenn Kington; Searching for a Superman, Watching for a Wonder Woman (Marietta, GA; King 2000 Publishing, 1998) p 25

Recommended for further reading:

- His Needs Her Needs by Willard F. Harley, Jr.
- The Five Love Languages by Gary Chapman
- Building Your Mate's Self-Esteem by Dennis and Barbara Rainey
- For Women Only by Shaunti Feldhahn

Study 18: *Understanding Needs*

1. Florence Littauer: Personality Plus for Couples (Grand Rapids, MI; Fleming H. Revell, 2001)
2. Gary Chapman; The Five Love Languages, How to Express Heartfelt Commitment to Your Mate (Chicago, IL; Northfield Publishing, 1992) p 14

Recommended for further reading:

- Intimate Encounters by Dr. David & Teresa Ferguson and Dr. Chris & Holly Thurman.

Study 19: *Meeting Needs*

1. Gary Chapman; The Five Love Languages, How to Express Heartfelt Commitment to Your Mate (Chicago, IL; Northfield Publishing, 1992) pp 148-259

Chapter 6 Finances

Study 20

Finances & Your Relationship with God

> *For where your treasure is, there your heart will be also. ~ Matthew 6:21*

> *"No servant can serve two masters. Either he will hate the one and love the other, or he will be devoted to the one and despise the other. You cannot serve both God and Money." ~ Luke 16:13*

Money is a necessary part of life, and it can be used for tremendous good. Yet, the desire for money drives some people to lie, cheat, steal and even commit murder. Problems with money can cause great hardship and even divorce in marriage.

> ***For the love of money is a root of all kinds of evil. Some people, eager for money, have wandered from the faith and pierced themselves with many griefs. ~ 1 Timothy 6:10***

Money is not the root of all kinds of evil; but the love of money can cause problems, pain and heartache. This is a problem for the poor as well as the rich. Possessions and money can become idols, and idolatry is a grievous sin to a jealous God. He must be first priority in life over all other things. Hebrews 12:1 reminds Christians to throw off everything that hinders and the sin that so easily entangles. Money can be a snare that hinders people from serving God as they should. One rich young man turned away from Jesus because his riches meant more to him than God (Matthew 19:16-24). Many people, rich and poor, have damaged their relationship with God, spouse or family in their pursuit of riches.

> ***"He said to them, 'Beware, and be on your guard against every form of greed; for not even when one has an abundance does his life consist of his possessions'" ~ Luke 12:15***

Scripture contains more than 2,300 references to money and possessions.[1] Many of Jesus' parables are about money and God gives direction regarding finances throughout the Bible. Money and material things are not the problem, but people's attitudes, desires and priorities often cause great problems. People need to guard their hearts against greed, covetousness, ego and pride. Many either want to be like the rich and famous or will condemn them for their richness out of jealousy. "Rich" is a relative term unless a person is one of the few extremely wealthy people in the world. Comparison is pointless, because there will always be someone richer. No amount of money is enough for those whose focus is money. Life does not consist of possessions, yet many people accumulate possessions as if their lives depended on them.

> ***"A man's treatment of money is the most decisive test of his character, how he makes it and how he spends it." - James Moffatt***

The Purpose of Money

What do you use money for? To gain security? For prestige? To achieve something of value? To maintain a life style? To succeed? To accumulate material things? According to the Bible, God is the provider. He cares about His people and promises to meet their needs. (See Matthew 6:25-34) Yes, one needs to work and provide for his family, but money should not be the driving purpose of his life. What is your purpose, your vision and your mission in life? That is what should drive you, not the pursuit of worldly possessions, success or the approval of people. Ron Blue writes that the Bible points to three purposes of money.[2]

- Money as a Tool
- Money as a Test
- Money as a Testimony

> ***Money is a good servant but a bad master. ~ French Proverb***

People can use money for great good when it does not rule them. Everyone brings nothing into the world and takes nothing out of it. Everything received during life is a gift from God. People can spend their money to please themselves or to do God's will. As a tool, money can be used to help bring people to Christ, help the poor and support ministry.

God tests His people to show them where the focus of their hearts are. When people are not faithful with a little, how can they be trusted with much? Jesus told His disciples that "whoever can be trusted with very little can be trusted with much, and whoever is dishonest with very little will also be dishonest with much." (Luke 16:10-11) The use of money reveals a person's trust and faith in the Lord and what is important to him.

People can not be drawn to Jesus Christ when Christians are no different than anyone else. God desires that they be examples so that by their good deeds, God will be praised (Matthew 5:16). Many Christians tend to live no differently than non-Christians and often spend their money in the same ways; purchasing lottery tickets, alcohol, accumulating possessions or gambling. Money is a testimony when people see God glorified by a Christian's spending. Are you different than those in the world? Does your spending reveal your Christianity?

> ***I, the LORD your God, am a jealous God, ~ Deuteronomy 5:9***

Biblical Priorities

Before anything else, God must be first in Christian's lives. He is a jealous God and nothing is to come before Him. If people put money, the earning of money; even the caring for their family before God, it is idolatry. It is something God will not tolerate. This doesn't mean that possessions or caring for your family are evil, but there must be a balance. Again, money and possessions are not the problem, it is the heart. When God is first in a person's life, the rest will fall into place.

> ***Jesus replied: "'Love the Lord your God with all your heart and with all your soul and with all your mind.' This is the first and greatest commandment. And the second is like it: 'Love your neighbor as yourself.' All the Law and the Prophets hang on these two commandments." ~ Matthew 22:37-40***

Jesus says that loving God totally is a Christian's primary responsibility in life and loving one's neighbor is God's second commandment. The Lord says that to wish a person well and not meet his material needs is not good (James 2:15-16). As seen throughout the Bible, God cares about people and uses other people to help those less fortunate or in trouble. Whether one helps the poor or reaches out to their neighbors with the love of Jesus Christ, money should be used to help others.

There is much need in the world today and many good ministries in need of funding. One may not be able to give to every ministry that asks, but Christians are to give to God's work.

Generosity is a quality that God commends; a generous spirit will be blessed. Yet, people need to be wise and discerning about their giving. There are those who claim to love God, but only want money and power for themselves. He will reveal where you should give your money as you seek God and His will for your life. You should give to your home church first. Beyond that, the Lord may want you to give to other ministries or good works.

> ***Remember this: Whoever sows sparingly will also reap sparingly, and whoever sows generously will also reap generously. Each man should give what he has decided in his heart to give, not reluctantly or under compulsion, for God loves a cheerful giver. ~ 2 Corinthians 9:6-7***

People ask if they are to tithe (giving a tenth of one's income). Tithing is a part of the Old Testament law and while Christians are not under the law, the Bible is very clear on several points:

1. Everything people have comes from God.
2. God is to be first in a person's life.
3. God loves the generous person.
4. People are to give what they feel God wants them to give.

Do not give reluctantly or out of compulsion. Remember boundaries; your money is yours to give. Pray, seek God and give what you feel the Lord wants you to give. Take care of your responsibilities and give generously.

> ***But godliness with contentment is great gain. ~ 1 Timothy 6:6***

Christians are to be content with what they have. Envy and covetousness are sin and can be very destructive. When you focus on the Lord rather than possessions, material things become less important. Serving and acting as God's agent to the hurting and lost then becomes rewarding and fulfilling. God desires to bless His people, but that does not necessarily mean that they will become rich. Obedience, faithfulness, and love are more important than riches. When people are content with the blessings they have, their lives will be a testimony of the love of God.

> ***"Do not store up for yourselves treasures on earth, where moth and rust destroy, and where thieves break in and steal. But store up for yourselves treasures in heaven, where moth and rust do not destroy, and where thieves do not break in and steal. ~ Matthew 6:19-21***

Christians are to live for God, not for possessions. Extravagance and opulence are things Jesus neither condoned nor blessed. Wealth is not evil and God does bless people with money, but the people of God are not to flaunt their wealth or indulge themselves. God looks at the heart and is concerned about purpose, motives and attitudes toward possessions.

Debt and living beyond the income people earn is a huge problem today. While it may be necessary to borrow money on occasion, living a life of credit and debt is bondage. Debt will dictate how you spend your money over the life of the loan and the interest you pay on the loan could pay for family essentials. Debt also limits the options you have for serving God and helping others. Trust the Lord for His provision and live within your income.

> ***Keep your lives free from the love of money and be content with what you have ~ Hebrews 13:5***

"God, I'd gladly give up my riches, if I could have Robert's riches."

God may have blessed you with the ability to earn a great deal of money, or you may struggle to earn enough to feed your family. In either case, there are clear Biblical principles regarding finances. You are to put God first in your life, to love Him, love others and be rich in good deeds as you serve the Lord your God with a whole heart. Do not put your hope in wealth. Trust in God and serve Him in all you do.

> ***Command those who are rich in this present world not to be arrogant nor to put their hope in wealth, which is so uncertain, but to put their hope in God, who richly provides us with everything for our enjoyment. Command them to do good, to be rich in good deeds, and to be generous and willing to share. In this way they will lay up treasure for themselves as a firm foundation for the coming age, so that they may take hold of the life that is truly life.***
> ***~ 1 Timothy 6:17-19***

For Discussion as a Couple

1. Where did you learn about money? What are some of the un-Biblical views you have?

2. What are your thoughts about the purpose of money? How does this apply to your life?

3. Based on your finances, would someone see that God is first in your life? Why or why not?

4. Do you tithe? Should you? Why or why not?

5. Are you content with what you have? Do you think God would be pleased with your attitude toward money? Why or why not?

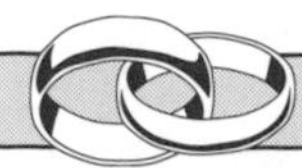

Needs Study 21 Finances & Marriage

> *If anyone does not provide for his relatives, and especially for his immediate family, he has denied the faith and is worse than an unbeliever. ~ 1 Timothy 5:8*

> *Take control of your finances before your finances take control of you and your marriage. ~ Damon Carr*

Most couples do not discuss finances before marriage and often they have no idea of each other's financial health until the honeymoon is over. One or both spouses will bring debt, poor spending habits, or financial problems into the marriage relationship. To compound the problem, spouses often have very different views and abilities regarding finances. This is one of the major areas of conflict in marriage and couples tend to communicate rarely and poorly about finances. One spouse may spend money or incur debt without talking to the other spouse. Some married couples even hide money from each other.

People learn about finances from the example of their parents. They usually do not receive formal training and their parent's example rarely will help them toward financial health and stability. They have no budget and no plans. The irony of a divorce over finances is that divorce causes even greater financial problems.

The area of finances is important to the marriage relationship and marital intimacy because so much of a couple's life revolve around finances. Couples need to be transparent and honest in this area and use the principles of communication to work together regarding finances in the marriage.

Financial Differences

Marriage blends together two very different lives including, for better or worse, their finances. Socioeconomic background, parental views about money and education, as well as natural differences will affect a person's financial outlook. While not true in every case, each personality type will have strong tendencies regarding the use of money. For the Beaver, money often means control; to the Lion, competence; to the Otter, esteem; and to the Golden Retriever, love.[1] More concerned with safety, the Beaver and Golden Retriever will tend to be savers, while the Lion and Otter will tend to be spenders.

Men tend to value money more than women. The person flashing around a thick wad of bills usually is a man. Women are less likely to take financial risks. They tend to be more concerned with security and stability. Again, this is a generalization; you need to know the specifics of how your spouse views money and learn his financial background. Then you can begin working together with the family finances. Use the Financial Background Inventory on pages 129 and 130 to learn more about your spouse's financial views.

> *... a household divided against itself will not stand.*
> *~ Matthew 12:25*

Financial Direction

Financially, a marriage cannot stand strong when spouses are divided. Couples need to work together regarding the family finances. Without a unified financial direction, couples will not get the best use of their money and often will have financial difficulties. Couples need financial goals and objectives in their marriage and those goals and objectives should align with the vision and mission of the couple.

There are many financial choices to make in life.

Utilize sound communication skills to begin working together to develop a financial direction for your marriage. Find the point agreeable to both spouses where you will not spend money without consulting each other. For couples in financial trouble, that may mean that you consult each other for every expenditure. Other couples will have a different point at which they will consult each other before spending. Certainly, major items, such as appliances, vehicles and investing should be planned together. Working together will do two things. First, it will bring the two of you closer to each other as you work as a team to bring your finances into alignment with God's principles. Second, you tend to have fewer financial troubles and a stronger financial position.

> ***Do two walk together unless they have agreed to do so? ~ Amos 3:3***

Family financial stability benefits greatly from husband and wife differences if the couple will utilize their differences and work together. Couples need each other to balance one another to make the best financial decisions possible. Often, one spouse tends to be a spender and the other a saver. One spouse will be a risk taker and the other will desire security and safety. One spouse may want to give to every need they encounter, while the other will be more worried about their needs. Couples tend to fight about these differences. The conflict is a point of contention rather than an opportunity for growth. As a couple works together and learns from each other, they will gain a balance in all areas. Each must be open to change and learning new principles, willing to admit when they are wrong and to deny self when necessary for the good of the family.

> ***... being one in spirit and purpose. ~ Philippians 2:2***

Biblically, there is no such thing as yours, mine and ours. The concept does not hold up when God's Word states that the two will become one. Separate bank accounts or money kept separately just does not fit the Biblical model of oneness. Trust is an integral part of marriage. While it is necessary to trust your spouse, it is more important that both are trustworthy. Trust is earned when people conduct themselves in a way that builds their spouse's trust. Hiding money, spending without telling a spouse, or spending money on frivolous or sinful things will break down trust.

One spouse controlling the finances to the exclusion of the other can cause serious marital problems. A husband who earns the money and keeps it all, giving his wife only a meager allowance does not live according to God's Word. Just as the woman who takes her husband's pay as soon as he brings it home to make sure it is spent wisely is also out of balance with God's Word. Or the wife may be the primary wage earner in the marriage and feel that she needs to control the finances. Whatever the situation, if spouses are not working together regarding finances, there are likely to be problems.

Often, one spouse possesses better financial skills than the other. This can be the husband or

wife, and that person should be primarily responsible for the finances. If neither spouse has sound financial skills, they must get help. Financial counseling and training are available and often can be found for a nominal fee or at no charge. While one spouse may pay the bills and manage the finances on a daily basis, it is still important that both spouses be aware and work together regarding family finances.

> ***The ability to work together is more important to financial health in the marriage than the amount of money a couple has.***

At times money may become a weapon for power and control in the marriage. Unfortunately, there are times when the husband or wife will use money to control or manipulate their spouse. This is not what is meant by money being a tool! The tool, in this case, is to be used to advance the Kingdom of God and accomplish His purposes. When money represents control, power, freedom, love, self-image or self-esteem to one or both spouses, there will not be a balance in the family finances. Keeping a proper perspective about money is important to the financial stability of the family.

"But honey, it was 'on sale' and you never know when we might need a bus. For kids, ministry, something..."

Stewardship and Responsibility

The principle of stewardship first appears in the Bible when God told Adam to subdue the earth in Genesis 1:28-30. Stewards care for the owner's property; the Biblical principle is that God owns everything and has granted mankind stewardship over His property. Responsibility is a key to Biblical stewardship. God gives the resources to be used for His purposes. The responsibility to use those resources accordingly falls on the husband and wife together. What is your vision? What is your mission? Are you using the resources God has given you to achieve those ends? To comprehend the Biblical principle of stewardship and financial responsibility, it is important to understand that mankind's purpose on earth is not to serve self. There is a responsibility to use one's finances for God's purposes.

> ***Give everyone what you owe him: If you owe taxes, pay taxes; if revenue, then revenue; if respect, then respect; if honor, then honor. Let no debt remain outstanding, except the continuing debt to love one another, for he who loves his fellow man has fulfilled the law.***
> ***~ Romans 13:7-8***

Everyone has a responsibility to take care of his family, and also to pay taxes and the debts he incurs. Jesus demonstrated these principles when He said to give to Caesar what is Caesar's (Matthew 22:21), when He paid taxes Himself (Matthew 17:24-27), and when He appointed John to care for His mother (John 19:26-27). Jesus told His disciples to pay their taxes despite the fact that Rome was a terrible, oppressive and corrupt government. He paid the temple tax when it was not His tax to pay. Jesus took care of His responsibility for His mother even while hanging on the cross. Most people would forgive that oversight under the circumstances, but responsibilities were important to Jesus.

The Bible says to let no debt remain outstanding, except the debt to love one another. Christians are to live within their means – if they can't afford to pay for something, the rule should be, don't purchase it. Couples often find themselves in financial difficulties because they do not wait for God's provision. They use credit to make purchases rather than allowing the Lord to provide for them in His timing. People think in terms of how much of a monthly payment they can afford rather than waiting for the money to pay cash for purchases. Paying interest when it is not necessary is an ineffective use of the resources God has given.

Remember the principles of boundaries when working with your finances. Accept responsibility for the areas under your control and do not take responsibility for the areas you do not control. Acting responsibly with your finances is a great boundary to have and will honor God. You cannot force your spouse to work with you or spend money wisely. But you can take measures to keep their irresponsibility from affecting you and the family overall.

If you cannot work through financial problems in your marriage, seek counseling. Get the help you need to get your finances on track and begin working together. Be open and honest with each other and do not give up. Every area of marriage takes work and perseverance to become what God wants it to be.

Remember; your spouse is NOT the enemy

For Discussion as a Couple

1. As a couple, did you discuss finances before you married? Why do you think it is important to understand each other's financial strengths and weaknesses?

____

____

____

____

2. How are you and your spouse different in the area of finances? Who is the spender and the saver?

____

____

____

____

3. Do you and your spouse generally agree or disagree about finances? How can you agree more?

____

____

____

____

4. How can you work together to take care of the family finances?

____

____

____

____

5. How is stewardship important in marriage? Is incurring debt good stewardship?

____

____

____

____

Financial Background Inventory

Answer the following questions honestly and openly. Your spouse should also answer the questions before you discuss them. Discuss your answers and make notes about how you can work together to manage your family's finances.

---

1. Who controlled the finances in your family as you grew up? Your father or mother? Did they work together with the finances? ____________________

2. Did you see gambling in your family growing up? Did anyone in your family have a gambling problem? ____________________

3. As a child, did your parents do anything to teach you about finances? What do you remember learning about finances? ____________________

4. Did your mother work outside of the home? Why or why not? ____________________

5. Did your parents buy you whatever you wanted? Do you remember going without some things? Explain: ____________________

6. Where did you get money as a child? What was your first job? When did you get it? ____________________

7. Which one of your parents was the spender? What do you remember about this? ____________________

8. Did your parents give to charities? Church? Helping people? What are your memories? ____________________

9. What do you know about budgeting? Where did you get your information? ____________________

10. As a teenager, did your parents pay for all of your expenses? When did you begin paying for your own things? ____________

11. Prior to marriage, did you balance your check book? Did you have savings? Investments? What were your finances like? ____________

12. Who has influenced you positively regarding finances? What do you remember about them?

13. Before you were married did you owe money to others? For what? ____________

14. Do you view money as something to spend or something to use for a purpose? Why? ____________

15. Do you tend to worry about finances? How do you handle financial problems? ____________

16. What are your views on debt? Is it acceptable? When? ____________

17. Do you purchase items you don't need just because they are on sale? When shopping, do you shop with a list or a specific goal? Or do you go shopping and impulse buy? ____________

18. Do you want to be rich? Why or why not? ____________

19. Do you and your spouse fight about money? Why? ____________

20. Who should take care of the money? Husband? Wife? Both? Why? ____________

Communication Study 22

Your Financial Future

In his heart a man plans his course, but the LORD determines his steps.
~ Proverbs 16:9

Our financial goal in marriage is not to become rich, but to become content in Christ. Contentment comes from security in Christ and from good stewardship of our money.[1]

Nobody plans to fail, they just fail to plan.
~ Damon Carr

Financial planning is an important aspect of a fortified marriage. Planning will help avoid future financial problems and help a couple grow together. Increased communication and working together will strengthen your marriage and increase intimacy. Working as a financial team does not come naturally. In fact, you may experience increased conflict as you begin working together with the finances. Persevere and your marriage and finances will both grow stronger. It is important to include God in this area of your marriage. His Word has much to say about finances, and there will be blessings for planning according to God's principles.

Obtain Financial Advice

Plans fail for lack of counsel, but with many advisers they succeed.
~ Proverbs 15:22

Managing personal finances, even for those with limited resources can be a complicated task. There are bookkeepers and accountants who track money for large companies and yet possess weak personal financial skills. For most people, finances can be intimidating. Seek a financial advisor, accountant or a Christian that can help you. There are churches and ministries that will help people with their finances with little or no charge. Your pastor may be able to recommend someone knowledgeable about finances to give you advice. Use Christian counselors; they are more likely to share your values and priorities. The advice of several advisors can be helpful as you consider your options.

Even if you obtain professional or volunteer help with your finances, it is important that you educate yourself about financial matters. Even professionals can make mistakes. You need to have enough information to understand the advice you are given and to know if it is the right choice for you and your family. Take a class, attend a seminar, purchase or borrow books about finances. Libraries hold a wealth of information, and governmental information regarding taxes and finances may also be available. No one cares about your finances more than you do. It is important to obtain advice, but it is also important that you have some knowledge yourself.

Analyze Your Present Financial Situation

Complete the Financial Assets Worksheet on page 140 to quickly determine your financial health. Enter amounts honestly to the best of your knowledge. If possible, use exact amounts of outstanding loans and for the value of assets. Conservatively estimate the value of home furnishings and personal property. Except for antiques or very valuable items, you will want to value items quite low to be accurate. List all of your debts on the liability side. Short term liabilities are the amounts

you now owe for utilities and bills due. The goal is to take a snapshot of your net worth at this time. Once assets and liabilities are entered and totaled, subtract liabilities from assets to obtain your net worth. The higher the net worth the better. If your net worth is negative, which is a net liability, much work will be required.

Society may tell people that they deserve vacations, new cars, jewelry and all the possessions they can charge on credit cards, but the reality is that couples must be responsible with the money God has given them. The liability side of the worksheet may be a good source of some financial goals and objectives. Debt is bondage to monthly payments and a lack of flexibility to use your money as you desire or as the Lord directs. If you are in debt, your first financial goal can be to get out of debt.

Get out of debt by doing the following:

1. Stop credit buying.
2. Pay off high interest debt first.
3. Pay off one debt at a time.
4. Continue working through each loan until all debt is paid off.

Getting into debt is a matter of spending more money than you receive. Remaining out of debt requires financial discipline and self-control. Many people do not understand that some sacrifice now will bring great benefits later. Young people today seem to think that there shouldn't be any reasons why they can not have what their parents have. Easy credit makes it possible, but also keeps them from achieving strong financial health.

"The budget only allows five dollars a month for me to go shopping at the mall?"

Establish a Budget

> *"Budget: telling your money where to go instead of wondering where it went."* ~ C.E. Hoover[2]

Many people look at a budget negatively as something controlling their lives and limiting their pleasure. Some don't want to take the time to track expenses nor have the discipline to begin a budget and stick with it. Yet, a budget is not very difficult to establish and maintain. Although it will take sacrifice, dedication and work to make a budget effective and helpful for your finances, the freedom and benefits you will experience are great. A budget will:

1. Increase your control of your money.
2. Give you a sense of security about your finances.
3. Help you set financial goals and objectives.
4. Allow financial success, regardless of your in come level.
5. Improve teamwork and accountability in your marriage.
6. Increase your awareness as a consumer.

Use the Budget Worksheet on page 139 to begin setting up your budget. First determine your income; enter your salary before deductions and any other income you receive regularly. Total your income and then begin entering expenses. Some expenses on the worksheet may not apply to you and there may be others that are not listed. Enter all of your expenses on the worksheet.

Once completed, the Budget Worksheet allows you to see how your expenditures match up with your income. The concept of a budget is that expenditures are allocated according to their priority in a couple's lives and within the income available. If expenses exceed income, either income must be increased or expenses cut. Credit is not the answer as it only prolongs paying the expense and increases the cost because of interest.

Living within a budget takes discipline, but waiting to purchase something desired will be worthwhile for your overall financial health. Trust God and ask Him to provide those things you desire. Take care of your responsibilities first, such as taxes and giving to God's work. Long term or retirement savings is important and will provide support when employment is no longer feasible. Short-term savings provides for the expenses that occur periodically, such as medical bills, insurance premiums, automobile repairs, gifts or vacations. Christian financial experts point out that automobiles should be paid for in cash, not with credit. Once you get into the habit of saving to purchase rather than purchasing and then finding a way to pay the debt, your financial position will improve dramatically. It will take some time and discipline to get to this point, but it will be well worth the effort.

You may need to live a simpler lifestyle and do what you know to be right rather than what feels good. It feels good to get new clothes, jewelry, a new car or things for the house, but it is a temporary feeling that will not benefit you over time. It is very difficult for those who spend to feel good to get ahead financially. Impulse spending tends to incur debt and diminish savings.

> ***Plan for tomorrow by prudence today; make plans in light of present circumstances, not on some future event; and maintain the principle of staying debt free. ~ Larry Burkett***

A Long-term View

People often spend money based on income that they should have if everything remains as it is presently. Larry Burkett says that this is a dangerous way to live. Unless there is a contract guaranteeing income for a specified period of time, there is no promise of income for the future. The person who takes a loan for some purchase, saying they are going to trust God that they will have the income to continue the payments is not really trusting God. Trusting God means waiting on Him to provide the means to make the purchase in cash. Does this mean that people should never use credit? Actually, the preference is to not use credit ever. Realize that if you borrow $2,000 dollars and pay 10% interest over two years, you will pay $215 in interest. It may not seem like a lot, but it is money added to the cost of your purchase. Credit card interest compounds faster and is much higher than standard loans. Most financial experts agree that a home purchase is the only time paying interest makes sense.

> ***A simple man believes anything, but a prudent man gives thought to his steps. ~ Proverbs 14:15***

There are several ways to accumulate savings for the future. Long term saving will help if you encounter physical problems and are unable to work or if you experience company downsizing and have an interruption of income. If available, company matching pension funds are a great way to save for future retirement. Investing in the stock market, real estate or other opportunities brings both risk and benefits. The first rule of investing is that if it seems too good to be true, it most likely is. There is no such thing as a risk-free investment. Diversifying your investments will reduce risk and help protect you from catastrophic loss. Many men will leave their wives out of investment decisions because they think their wives just don't understand. This is a bad decision. Your wife may not understand stocks, bonds and a free market, but if you will take the time to educate her, she may be able to give you invaluable input. There is something to be said for woman's intuition. A wise man will listen to his wife's concerns and take them into account when making financial decisions.

Financial advisors can help with investing, but again, it is your responsibility to obtain sufficient knowledge to ensure wise investments. This is being a good steward of what God has entrusted to you.

Insurance is an important part of financial planning. As a couple, it is necessary to analyze your need for life, medical, homeowner, rental, automobile and possibly mortgage insurance. If the company you work for provides life and medical insurance, great. If not, you need to find affordable insurance in the event of illness or death. It is important that a husband provides for his family now and in the event of an unexpected death. Many families are left destitute at the death of the husband, when inexpensive life insurance could have helped.

It is vital that you have a will or trust drawn up to protect your assets in the event of your death. A will is inexpensive and can be easily drawn up. Also, the Personal & Financial Information pages following this study will help you organize your financial information should one or both spouses pass away. Having this information in a safe place will save much additional heartache during a difficult time. A little planning now will provide for the future of your family

For Discussion as a Couple

1. What are your financial goals in life? What plan do you have for meeting them?

____

____

____

____

2. What is your present financial state? Do you have too much debt?

____

____

____

____

3. How can you get out of debt? What can you do to stay out of debt?

____

____

____

____

4. Do you have a budget? What will it take to create a budget and begin to use it to guide your finances?

____

____

____

____

5. Do you have a will? Life insurance? A retirement account? Is all of your financial information organized? What do you need to do to plan for the future?

____

____

____

____

Personal & Financial Information

Names: ______________________________ Date: ____________

Address: ____________________ City: _____________ St: ___ Zip: _______

	Husband	Wife
Dates of Birth:	____________	___________
Social Security Numbers:	____________	___________
Employer & Address:	____________________	____________________
	____________________	____________________
Parents Names/Age:	____________________	____________________
	____________________	____________________
Brothers/Sisters:	____________________	____________________
	____________________	____________________

Immediate Family Information

Name/Relationship	Address	Ph#	SSN#

Important Names

Name/Relationship	Address	Ph#

Will and/or Trust

Location of Will or Trust: ____

Person designated to carry out its provisions: ______________ Ph #: _________

If that person cannot or will not serve, the alternate is: _________ Ph #: _________

Attorney: ________________ Ph#: __________

Accountant: _______________ Ph#: __________

Income Benefits

Company Benefits (Description): ______________________________________

____

____

Contact: __________________ Ph#: ___________

Social Security Benefits:

Husband and wife's SSN#s: __________________ __________________

To receive Social Security benefits, go in person to the local Social Security office. Take the Social Security card, death certificate, birth certificate, marriage certificate and birth certificates for each child.

Veteran's Benefits

Branch of Service: __________________ Service Number: ______________

Length of service: _________ From: _________ Until: ________ Rank: _____

Information: ____

____

____

____

Insurance Coverage

Insurance Company: ______________________________ Policy #: ____________________

Person Insured: ________________ Beneficiaries: __________________________________

Insurance Company: ______________________________ Policy #: ____________________

Person Insured: ________________ Beneficiaries: __________________________________

Insurance Company: ______________________________ Policy #: ____________________

Person Insured: ________________ Beneficiaries: __________________________________

Insurance Company: ______________________________ Policy #: ____________________

Person Insured: ________________ Beneficiaries: __________________________________

Other Insurance

Insurance Company: ______________________________ Policy #: ____________________

Type of Insurance: ______________ Information: __________________________________

Insurance Company: ______________________________ Policy #: ____________________

Type of Insurance: ______________ Information: __________________________________

Insurance Company: ______________________________ Policy #: ____________________

Type of Insurance: ______________ Information: __________________________________

Insurance Company: ______________________________ Policy #: ____________________

Type of Insurance: ______________ Information: __________________________________

Property Owned

Description	Address
______________________________	____
______________________________	____
______________________________	____

Investments

Company ____________ Account # ____________ Product ____________

Contact Information: ____________

Company ____________ Account # ____________ Product ____________

Contact Information: ____________

Company ____________ Account # ____________ Product ____________

Contact Information: ____________

Company ____________ Account # ____________ Product ____________

Contact Information: ____________

Funeral Instructions

Funeral Home: ____________ Ph#: ____________

Address: ____________

Burial Place: ____________

Instructions: ____________

____

____

____

Memorial gifts to be given to the following organizations:

____________ Address: ____________ Ph#: ____________

____________ Address: ____________ Ph#: ____________

Budget Worksheet

Total Monthly Income: ______

Salary: ______

Other, ______: ______

Other, ______: ______

Less:

1. Giving/Donations: ______
2. Taxes (est. income, etc.) ______

Net Income to Spend: ______

3. Housing: ______
   - Mortgage (rent) ______
   - Insurance: ______
   - Taxes: ______
   - Utilities: ______
   - Telephone: ______
   - Maintenance: ______
   - Other ______: ______
   - Other ______: ______
4. Food ______
5. Short-term Savings: ______
6. Automobile (s): ______
   - Payments: ______
   - Gas & oil: ______
   - Insurance: ______
   - License/Taxes: ______
   - Maint./repair: ______
   - Replacement: ______
7. Insurance: ______
   - Life: ______
   - Medical: ______
   - Other: ______
   - Other: ______
8. Medical: ______
   - Doctor: ______
   - Dentist: ______
   - Prescriptions: ______
9. Debts: ______
   - Credit Card: ______
   - Loans: ______
   - Other: ______
10. Clothing: ______
11. Miscellaneous: ______
    - Toiletries: ______
    - Beauty/barber: ______
    - Laundry: ______
    - Subscriptions: ______
    - Gifts (all): ______
    - Allowances: ______
    - Other ______: ______
    - Other ______: ______
12. School/Child Care: ______
    - Tuition: ______
    - Materials: ______
    - Day Care: ______
    - Other: ______
13. Entertainment & Recreation: ______
    - Eating out: ______
    - Activities: ______
    - Vacation: ______
    - Other: ______
14. Investments: ______

Total Expenses: ______

Income vs. Expenses

Net Income to Spend: ______

Less Expenses: ______

Surplus Income: ______

Financial Assets Worksheet

Assets		**Liabilities**	
Home equity:	________	Amount owed on home:	________
Vehicle value:	________	Amount owed on vehicle:	________
Vehicle value:	________	Amount owed on vehicle:	________
Home furnishings value:	________	Credit card debt:	________
Personal property value:	________	Credit card debt:	________
Life insurance cash value:	________	Other debt:	________
Savings:	________	Other debt:	________
Investment:	________	Other debt:	________
Investment:	________	Short term liabilities:	________
Investment:	________		________
Other assets:	________		________
Other assets:	________		________
	________		________
	________		________
	________		________
Total Assets:	________	**Total Liabilities:**	________

Total Assets—Total Liabilities = Net Worth ____________

Fortified Marriages
Chapter 6 Endnotes

Study 20: *Finances & Your Relationship with God*

1. Ron & Judy Blue; Money Talks and So Can We (Grand Rapids, MI; Zondervan Publishing, 1999) p 12
2. Ibid p 12

Recommended for further reading:
- How to Manage Your Money; by Larry Burkett.
- God's Plans for Your Finances; by Dwight Nichols
- Using Your Money Wisely; by Larry Burkett.

For further information, see:
- Crown Financial Ministries: www.crown.org
- Rob Blue: www.ronblue.com
- Christian Money: www.christianmoney.com

Study 21: *Marriage and Finances*

1. Mike and Jacqueline Powers; Two for the Money (NY, NY; Avon Books, 1999) p 9

Recommended for further reading:
- Money Talks and So Can We by Ron and Judy Blue.
- Becoming One Financially by J. Andre Weisbrod

Study 22: *Your Financial Future*

1. Neil T. Anderson and Charles Mylander; The Christ Centered Marriage (Ventura, CA; Regal Books, 1996) p 170
2. Quoted by; Larry Burkett; World's Easiest Guide to Finances (Chicago, IL; Northfield Publishing, 2000) p 34

Recommended for further reading:
- The World's Easiest Guide to Finances by Larry Burkett with Randy Southern.
- The Complete Idiots Guide to Managing Your Money by Robert K. and Christy Heady

Chapter 7
Christian Marriage

Study 23

Foundations for Marriage

"Therefore everyone who hears these words of mine and puts them into practice is like a wise man who built his house on the rock. The rain came down, the streams rose, and the winds blew and beat against that house; yet it did not fall, because it had its foundation on the rock."
~ Matthew 7:24-25

The Importance of Marriage

Most people do not understand marriage and are ill-equipped to enter into it when they marry. You wouldn't board an airplane with an untrained pilot or allow an uneducated attorney to represent you in court. Yet, like most people, you probably received your marriage license without any formal training. The informal training you received from your parents did not prepare you adequately for marriage and the admonition your pastor gave you just before the wedding had little, if any affect. Understanding the marriage relationship is important to a healthy marriage and learning God's principles is critical to that understanding.

Two very different people affected by different environments come together to form a marriage relationship. Together, a couple can build a relationship that is both productive and fulfilling or they can build a relationship destructive to both themselves and the generations after them. People do not decide one day that they are going to build a dysfunctional marriage. A poor marriage takes shape over time through selfishness, neglect and poor decisions. A healthy, fortified marriage does not become strong by following a formula or twenty rules of a good marriage. You must grow, learn, change and put Biblical principles into practice to build a marriage that will honor God and withstand the storms of life.

People profess a commitment to their marriage and a desire for a permanent, stable relationship. Believing that your marriage can work is much different than a commitment to make your marriage work in spite of any obstacles that may occur. Commitment often subsides when romantic love fades and the routine of day to day life becomes a reality. A fortified marriage has a true commitment for life—no matter what.

The importance of the marital relationship is only eclipsed by your relationship with God. Marriage is important to your emotional and physical well-being and to future generations through your children. The Bible consistently shows how important marriage is to God. At creation, God said; "It is not good for the man to be alone, I will make a helper suitable for him" (Genesis 2:18). God honors marriage and condemns the unfaithfulness which is so prevalent in this sinful, broken world. Marriage is God's idea and when couples build their marriage on His principles, it becomes strong and healthy.

The Foundation

There is only one firm foundation on which to build life and marriage — Jesus Christ. He is the Rock a marriage must be built on to withstand the storms that will come against it. Building a marriage on anything else (love, romance, met needs, fulfillment—anything!) is sand that will give way when the storms of life hit.

> ***For no one can lay any foundation other than the one already laid, which is Jesus Christ.* ~ 1 Corinthians 3:11**

Christ is the foundation of a marriage when a couple understands who He is, who they are in Him and continue growing in their relationship with Him. Christians surrender their lives to Christ—all of their lives; needs, wants, desires and even their spouses. When couples quit playing God through attempts to change a spouse and make him or her who they want them to be, the Lord's work in their lives and marriage will begin to become evident. The marriage built on Jesus Christ will seek to serve, honor and obey Him; living life according to His direction.

> ***By wisdom a house is built, and through understanding it is established; through knowledge its rooms are filled with rare and beautiful treasures.* ~ Proverbs 24:3-4**

Jesus Christ is the foundation of a Christian marriage, but there are also several foundational principles important to the marriage relationship. You need to understand:

- Who you are as God's creation.
- God's will and direction for your life and marriage.
- Concepts of healthy boundaries.
- Principles of communication.
- That you are responsible for your own needs, but also the importance of being used of God to meet your spouse's needs as part of the marriage relationship.
- God's principles of finances.

These principles are the basics needed for a healthy and productive marriage relationship. They will give you the tools and resources to build a strong marriage, but they are not the marriage relationship itself. There is still more to understand about God's design for marriage.

> ***Then the LORD God made a woman from the rib he had taken out of the man, and he brought her to the man. The man said, "This is now bone of my bones and flesh of my flesh; she shall be called 'woman,' for she was taken out of man." For this reason a man will leave his father and mother and be united to his wife, and they will become one flesh.* ~ Genesis 2:22-24**

Man and woman were created separate and different, but created to become one. They become one through sexual intercourse, but oneness also speaks to the monogamous nature of marriage. God instituted marriage to be one man and one woman coming together for life. Marriage is sacred; the marriage relationship is to come before all other relationships other than one's relationship with God.

Leaving and Cleaving

Leaving parents and cleaving to your spouse is essential to a healthy marriage. It is very difficult to become one with your spouse when your parents still control your life. A close family is a good thing, provided there are defined boundaries in the relationship with both sets of parents. Separateness is necessary and healthy to a growing marriage relationship. Parents must realize that their married child probably will not be able to spend every holiday with them. Husband and wife will have to negotiate how they will divide their time between both sets of parents while still maintaining time for themselves.

When "parent" problems arise between husband and wife, it is time to examine parental relationships. Parents do not have a right to meddle in your life and marriage. One caveat to this is when there are financial ties. This is one reason that Christian financial experts suggest remaining free from financial entanglements with parents. If financial aid is necessary to get through a season of life, that is fine, but untangle yourself as soon as possible. Setting clear, firm boundaries will help develop healthy relationships with your parents while allowing space and growth in your marriage relationship.

Leaving your father and mother means independence from your parents. Perhaps, healthy boundaries are more important in the parent relationship than any other outside relationship. Parents can be a wonderful source of wisdom and a refuge during the storms of life, but your primary loyalty is to your spouse and children, not your parents. When one spouse allows his parents to interject too much into his marriage, his parents may cause division in the marriage relationship. There may be a time when one must stand up to his parents and ask them to back off. Taking that step may be the action required to aid the growth of your spouse's relationship with your parents. It is Biblical and healthy to set limits on your parent's involvement in your married life.

Cleaving means to stick fast, adhere to, to remain attached, devoted or faithful.[1] Cleaving (remaining attached, devoted and faithful to your spouse) is foundational to the marriage relationship. It is a commitment, unique in all of human interaction, where two distinct people commit to work together and remain in the relationship for life. Loyalty is an important part of this definition; a husband and wife choose to put each other first before parents, friends, and even their children. A couple cleaves to each other and meets the challenges of life together.

"What do you mean that my parents are too involved in our lives?"

The divorce rate would be lower if instead of marrying for better or worse people would marry for good. ~ Ruby Dee

Strong commitment is also foundational to a healthy marriage. That commitment will get you through the times when you don't feel love for your spouse. In fact, there probably will be times in your marriage when you just don't like your spouse. Human beings are imperfect and it is impossible to live a perfect life. Romance and feelings will not sustain a marriage through the storms that will come. Commitment is the sustaining factor that will hold it together during the hard times.

Commitment is a decision couples make and continue to make throughout their marriage. It is deciding to change, grow and work to make the marriage better. It is letting go of self and focusing on the spouse and what is good for the marriage. Marriage limits individuals in some ways, yes, but the rewards and personal growth each spouse receives is worth far more than the so-called freedoms they lose. Continued commitment strengthens a couple's relationship together.

The Marriage Covenant

Biblically, marriage is a covenant, the commitment of people without reservation. A contract is an agreement that involves the exchange of services. The fifty-fifty or sixty-forty relationship is contractual. One person gives as long as the other person does their part. In contrast, a covenant commitment is a one-hundred-zero relationship. Just as Jesus Christ gave everything for you, you are called to give all without expectations of return in your marriage. Nelson's Bible Dictionary says; "a covenant, in the biblical sense, implies much more than a contract or simple agreement. A contract always has an end date, while a covenant is a permanent arrangement. Another difference is that a contract generally involves only one part of a person, such as

a skill, while a covenant covers a person's total being."[2] It is a choice couples make to commit all of themselves to their marriage for life.

> *Another thing you do: You flood the LORD's altar with tears. You weep and wail because he no longer pays attention to your offerings or accepts them with pleasure from your hands. You ask, "Why?" It is because the LORD is acting as the witness between you and the wife of your youth, because you have broken faith with her, though she is your partner, the wife of your marriage covenant. ~ Malachi 2:13-14*

Marriage as a covenant makes sense. Becoming one doesn't involve part of a person, it involves the whole person; mind, body and soul. Marriage vows should mean more than a loan contract or business agreement. God is serious about the marriage covenant and couples also need to take it seriously. The world may think that a marriage contract works fine, but many people now see the shallowness of a lack of commitment. God established marriage as a covenant not a contract.

The reality of life is that marriage is not easy. Talking about commitment, covenant, and giving one-hundred percent while expecting nothing in return is much easier than living it out on a daily basis. Yet, this is what God calls couples to do. One remains with his spouse, not because he wants to or feels like it, but because he knows it is the right thing to do. Commitment to marriage doesn't mean enduring and living a miserable life of sacrifice. The principles learned in the first six chapters of this manual will help you live out your commitment and even prosper and grow in your love for your spouse.

Jesus Christ is the basis of the marriage covenant. He has bought you with a price and you are loved dearly as you are, and as you live who you are because of what Christ has done for you, you can have the marriage God wants you to have. God will empower you to love your spouse as you surrender your life to Him. Christ, your foundation will enable you and strengthen you.

What's Love got to do with it?

Western culture today has a preoccupation with the need for love to marry. People marry because they are in love, yet love is not the best reason to marry. The prevalent view is that feelings define love and that one must have the feelings of love to have a committed relationship. This kind of love is not the love that will endure the test of time. The *Love Marriage* is a very new concept when studying marriage historically. Marriages were arranged by the parents for most of history and are still arranged in India, China and much of eastern culture. The concept is that love will grow as a result of the marriage relationship growing. In the west, people don't realize that true love takes time to grow. The love a couple has for each other on the wedding day is only the beginning of what is to come.

Love develops between husband and wife over the years as they grow in oneness. Those who marry for love often experience lust more than love. They are enamored with the feelings of love, romance and the attention lavished on them by their prospective mate. Those feelings are not the love that will withstand the pressures that a couple will experience as they live life on a daily basis. As a couple works through problems and experience life together, their love will grow into the type of love that will get them through any crisis that comes into their lives.

It is important to understand the distinctions in the Biblical usages of the word love. The Greek language uses three words to express love. Agape is an unconditional, selfless love. Phileo is a friendly, brotherly love. Eros is the sexual, lustful love. All three types of love are necessary for an intimate, growing marriage.

> ***And now these three remain: faith, hope and love. But the greatest of these is love.***
> ***~ 1 Corinthians 13:13***

Agape is the most important type of love a person can have. It is the love Paul states as *the greatest of these*. Agape love allows one to give one-hundred percent without expecting anything in return. It allows one to remain committed to his spouse through the tough times.

Developing a phileo love builds intimacy and a togetherness that strengthens and matures the marriage relationship. Through phileo, a couple builds the teamwork and loyalty to help them work through problems and experience joy together.

There is good reason that the Bible admonishes couples to save eros love for marriage. Sexual intercourse consummates the covenant of marriage and joins the couple together in physical oneness. The intimacy they share with their spouse through sex is the most intimate experience a person can have with anyone.

Love is important to marriage, but it must be kept in the right perspective. The wedding ceremony begins a life-long growth of love. Love is lived out in your commitment to your spouse. Love is a decision you make, not a feeling you have.

For Discussion as a Couple

1. What training did you have for marriage? Where did you receive your training?

____
____
____
____

2. How is Jesus Christ the foundation of your marriage? How do you see this on a daily basis?

____
____
____
____

3. Why is it important to understand the foundational principles of marriage before talking about marriage?

____
____
____
____

4. Why is it important to leave your parents and cleave to your spouse? How have you demonstrated this to your spouse?

____
____
____
____

5. How can you demonstrate your love to your spouse on an ongoing basis?

____
____
____
____
____

Stories of True Life-Long Commitment

Commitment is not the most popular word in today's culture of *me*. The culture teaches that "I" am the most important person in the world. "I deserve a break, to have it my way, a new car, a new body, a new and better wife or husband;" it is not hard to imagine where all of this leads. Self reigns and everything else must bow to it. The problem is that God calls this idolatry. The Bible teaches people to die to self and live a life committed to God. Commitment may not be a popular concept, but seeing it lived out in life is rewarding and fulfilling.

You have heard the quote; "Behind every great man stands a great woman." There are many stories of women committed to their husbands and supporting their great achievements. Ruth Graham's support of Billy Graham and his evangelistic ministry illustrates the importance of a wife to a ministry even when she is not directly involved. Committed women have taken care of the home front while their men have won wars and achieved greatness in ministry, government, business and sports. But what about the tough times? Does that commitment continue when the times are tough? For women, the answer usually is yes; they stick with their husband when he is maimed, crippled or incapacitated. Yet an increasing number of people, both women and men now leave the relationship rather than endure hardship. The following stories of men who remained totally committed to their wives are significant because many men would not have remained so committed.

Trusted, godly friends counseled Columbia College and seminary president Robertson McQuilkin to institutionalize his wife of forty-two years for the sake of his ministry.[3] The time had come to make a choice between his ministry in Christian education and the ministry of caring for his wife. Alzheimer's disease robs a person of everything; one's mind and body, and Muriel's once vibrant mind would eventually even forget who she was. The decision was not hard to make, he had vowed to love her "in sickness and in health ... until death do us part." Caring for his wife was not a duty to be endured, but a ministry that blessed him and provoked people around the world to renew vows and examine their definition of commitment.

In his book, In Defense of Marriage, Art Carey relates the story of the decline of his grandmother and the commitment of his grandfather to his dearly loved wife. As his grandmother deteriorated physically and mentally, her husband of sixty years remained at her side caring for her needs rather than putting her in a convalescent home and allowing others to care for her. Some time after her death, Art asked his grandfather if there wasn't a part of him that was relieved of the burden of caring for his wife twenty-four hours a day. His grandfather answered; "Artie, with all her incapacities and all that that involved, I'd give anything to see her there now. God, what I wouldn't give."[4]

Chris Spielman put his football career on hold to care for his wife Stephanie and their two children while she fought breast cancer. At thirty-four years old, this star football player sacrificed his career to put his wife and family first. Chris demonstrates marital commitment, denying his own dreams and ambitions to be available to his wife in her time of need.

Do you have a shallow, worldly commitment to marriage that will look for an exit when your needs are not met? Or do you have a true life-long commitment that will bear any and all problems that may come your way? Robertson McQuilken, Edward Lynch and Chris Spielman demonstrate a godly love and commitment even when their wives were not able to give back. Both husbands and wives today need to have that kind of commitment.

Christian Marriage

Study 24

The Christian Marriage

"Haven't you read," he replied, "that at the beginning the Creator 'made them male and female,' and said, 'For this reason a man will leave his father and mother and be united to his wife, and the two will become one flesh'? So they are no longer two, but one. Therefore what God has joined together, let man not separate."
~ Matthew 19:4-6

The Marriage Relationship

Marriage is the most complex relationship we will have in life. It brings together all the diversities of two people into one close relationship as they begin a new life together. Oneness is not something that happens instantly at the wedding ceremony. A couple gradually becomes one as their relationship grows and their lives meld together. Life adds to the complexity of marriage as problems arise, challenges are met and couples continue along the road of life.

The Christian ideal has not been tried and found wanting. It has been found difficult and left untried.
~ G.K. Chesterton

Biblical principles for marriage are not some ancient ideal meant for a culture that is long gone. They pertain to marriage today and, if applied, will strengthen and fortify your marriage. People cannot pick and choose which principles they will apply to their marriage. The whole Word of God; every part of the Bible should be obeyed as one lives his life for God.

The reality of marriage is that it brings together two sin scarred human beings, imperfect and with an inclination to sin. It is necessary to realize that your spouse is different and not perfect. He will fail you and will not measure up to your expectations. If you can accept this premise, you can begin to work to build your marriage.

Marriage is a life-long relationship that must be continually cultivated and cared for or it will die. Men tend to view the wedding as the completion of a quest, while women tend to view the wedding as the beginning of a life long relationship to be nurtured and grown. Both spouses must be committed to working at the relationship and growing in their relationship with God and with each other. The work continues until death takes one partner or the other.

What is a "Christian Marriage?" The simple answer is "a marriage centered on Jesus Christ and based on Christian principles." Christ is the foundation of the marriage, and each couple must build their marriage according to who they are within the guidelines of Scripture. Different personality combinations and environmental factors can make two "Christian" marriages look very different. The problem is that most people do not understand Biblical principles for life and marriage. There are couples that call their marriage "Christian," but they don't understand what God wants for their marriage and don't surrender their lives and marriage to Christ. They conduct their marriage their own way without regard for what God wants for them.

Reality weddings.

> *"A good marriage is not something you find, it's something you work for." ~ Gary Thomas*

The Successful Marriage

There is no clear definition of a successful marriage. Authors, researchers and people in general all have their own idea of a successful marriage. Definitions of a successful marriage range from "we haven't killed each other yet" to a long list of criteria that is impossible for anyone to live up to. Marriage researcher Dr. Judith Wallerstein states; "A good marriage is in a process of continual change as it reflects new issues, deals with problems that arise, and uses the resources available at each stage of life."[1] Essentially, it is a changing, growing marriage. The couple in a successful marriage will work together and be committed to each other for life.

> ***Has not [the LORD] made them one? In flesh and spirit they are his. And why one? Because he was seeking godly offspring. So guard yourself in your spirit, and do not break faith with the wife of your youth. ~ Malachi 2:15***

Biblically, oneness, godly offspring and faithfulness are marks of a successful marriage. Yes, children can and sometimes do choose to reject their parents' values and faith in God. As parents, couples have a certain amount of responsibility for that choice. They need to accept that responsibility, seek God's forgiveness and strive to be the parents God desires them to be. Everyone has varying degrees of faithfulness and oneness. God has made a couple one and the question is; are they living that oneness or living separate lives under the same roof? No one is perfect, but every spouse can be committed to making the effort to succeed in God's strength to achieve His goals for their marriage. A successful marriage may seem impossible to you, but it is your commitment to working to build your marriage relationship that is most important.

All marriages will have dry spells when it feels like a couple only exists together. The romance is gone, communication is unproductive and they may even feel like giving up. The marriage may be in a rut, that dull, fixed routine that they just can't seem to get out of. It takes something radical to get out of ruts. During those times, couples need to disrupt the routine and do something different, even fun. All long-lasting marriages change; it takes change to get out of the dry spells of marriage. If left alone too long, the marriage will dry up and begin to whither and die.

One author published a statistic that only five percent of marriages are truly happy and fulfilling unions.[2] The unhappy, unfulfilling marriage is heartbreaking to see because it does not have to be that way. It may take counseling and some hard work, but a happy, fulfilling marriage is possible. You can have a fulfilling marriage strong enough to withstand the inevitable and ongoing stresses of life. No one has to be a part of this grim statistic.

Attaining a successful, good, flourishing, growing, fortified (whatever you want to call it) marriage can be accomplished. It takes being the person and spouse God wants you to be rather than looking at your spouse's failings. Don't measure your marriage on the happiness you feel, but in the joy you can bring to your spouse. Begin with a commitment to the marriage and then work toward living out that commitment daily. Eliminate the "D word" (divorce) from your vocabulary. Meet your spouse's needs, build them up; work at being the best spouse you can be for them.

> *"There is no more lovely, friendly and charming relationship, communion or company than a good marriage."*
> *~ Martin Luther*

Met needs are an important aspect of a successful marriage. Unmet needs will drive a couple apart, while met needs will draw them together.

Scripture states that husbands and wives are to be concerned about pleasing their spouse (1 Corinthians 7:32-34). Marriage will distract a person from being totally devoted to the ministry of the Lord because he must take care of his spouse and family. Meeting the needs of your family comes before other activities and is your first and most important ministry. Too many Christians allow family to suffer at the expense of serving others. A strong family requires a husband and wife who are concerned about its welfare.

> ***I would like you to be free from concern. An unmarried man is concerned about the Lord's affairs-how he can please the Lord. But a married man is concerned about the affairs of this world-how he can please his wife- and his interests are divided. An unmarried woman or virgin is concerned about the Lord's affairs: Her aim is to be devoted to the Lord in both body and spirit. But a married woman is concerned about the affairs of this world-how she can please her husband.***
> ***~ 1 Corinthians 7:32-34***

Shared Goals

Couples in successful marriages move in the same direction; they can see a future together. Often in today's culture, couples do not have shared goals and live almost totally separate lives. In the past, this was not the case. A couple had to work together just to meet the challenges of daily life. Leisure time has caused great difficulties in marriage. It seems that with so much free time on their hands, people are going in wrong directions. Differences are the basis for some separate activities and goals, but overall, a couple must be going in the same direction or they may eventually part ways completely.

Friendship is an important part of marriage. Couples grow together when they share the joys (and even the heartaches) of life as a couple. Developing friendship in the marriage relationship means that couples will find some common activities they can enjoy together. No matter how different you are, there is something you can do together. There were some commonalities before marriage or you would not have married. Friendship will grow as you minister to others or enjoy a hobby or activity together.

Goals of Marriage

God brings together a man and woman in oneness to produce godly children and for faithfulness. Marriage is the starting point of the family. A strong family cannot exist without a strong marriage. It is important that couples never cease working on their marriage. They must continue to cultivate and grow the marriage relationship.

Contrary to popular opinion, the purpose of marriage is not to make you happy. This false assumption has contributed greatly to the high divorce rates we see in today's culture. People become disillusioned and unhappy with their mate and marriage and become vulnerable. Someone comes along, promises happiness and a husband or wife rips apart the family to pursue *their* happiness. The problem is that the cycle repeats itself until they give up or acknowledge the fact that marriage has a higher purpose than *their* happiness.

"Honey, don't you think we would get farther if we pushed in the same direction?"

Promoting God's kingdom is a higher purpose for marriage. The marriage lived for God's glory draws people to Him. God desires that a couple build the foundation of their marriage on Jesus Christ and strive to live their lives and marriage according to His principles rather than the world's principles. Your marriage will continue to grow as it reflects Jesus Christ to others, as you honor your spouse and work together for God's glory.

Do not compare your marriage to someone else's and make a judgment about whether it is better or worse. No two marriages will be alike. Outward appearance means little. You may own a big house, keep it very clean and have nothing out of place, or your house may be very humble and always a mess. A house becomes a home through the relationships within it. "Each marriage is a different world, a sovereign country unto itself."[3] Your standard is the Word of God and our mirror is each other. What are you doing for each other? How are you working together to accomplish what God wants you to accomplish? Together, with God's strength, you can make your marriage all that it can be for God's glory.

> *Coming together is a beginning,*
> *staying together is progress,*
> *and working together is success.*
> *~ Henry Ford*

For Discussion as a Couple

1. Do you believe Biblical principles apply in marriage today? Why or why not?

____

____

____

____

2. What does the term "Christian Marriage" mean to you? What does it mean to your marriage?

____

____

____

____

3. What is a "successful marriage?" How can you aim for that ideal in your marriage?

____

____

____

____

4. How should the Biblical view of commitment affect your marriage?

____

____

____

____

5. What are the goals of your marriage?

____

____

____

____

Marriage Preconceptions

Answer the following questions honestly and openly. Your spouse should also answer the questions before you discuss them. Discuss your answers and note the differences in your preconceptions about marriage.

1. In your family growing up:

   Who controlled money? ______________________

   Did the house work? ______________________

   Took out the trash? ______________________

   Did your mother work outside the home? ______________________

   What did your parents argue about? ______________________

   Was your father involved in your home life? How? ______________________

   ____

   What were your parents' views on roles in the marriage? ______________________

   ____

   Do you think your parents had a successful marriage? Why or why not? ______________________

   ____

   What was the role of religion in your family? ______________________

   ____

2. About your marriage:

   Why did you get married? ______________________

   ____

   How are decisions made? ______________________

   ____

   What do you think your roles are as husband and wife? ______________________

   ____

   What are the roles of your parents and in-laws in your marriage? Is it what you think it should be? ______________________

   What is God's role in marriage? How is He involved in your marriage? ______________________

   ____

Aspects of a Successful Marriage

Honestly rate each of the following points as they apply overall to your marriage relationship at this point in your life. Individually complete this questionnaire and then discuss the answers together.

We:	Never	Rarely	Sometimes	Often	Almost Always
1. Are growing toward oneness; becoming closer.	1	2	3	4	5
2. Work together to meet the demands of life.	1	2	3	4	5
3. Strive to meet each other's needs.	1	2	3	4	5
4. Are committed to the marriage.	1	2	3	4	5
5. Display mutual love and respect.	1	2	3	4	5
6. Set healthy boundaries.	1	2	3	4	5
7. Trust each other.	1	2	3	4	5
8. Spend time together as a couple.	1	2	3	4	5
9. Solve problems as a team.	1	2	3	4	5
10. Use the strengths and gifts of both spouses.	1	2	3	4	5
11. Have effective communication.	1	2	3	4	5
12. See the future together; dream together.	1	2	3	4	5
13. Have a common vision, goals and objectives.	1	2	3	4	5
14. Consult and seek each other's advice.	1	2	3	4	5
15. Work together with the finances.	1	2	3	4	5
16. Are more positive than negative.	1	2	3	4	5
17. Forgive each other.	1	2	3	4	5
18. Experience fulfilling sex.	1	2	3	4	5
19. Have romance in our relationship.	1	2	3	4	5
20. Laugh and have fun together.	1	2	3	4	5

Total your score here: __________

This is not a test to discover how bad your marriage is, but rather an inventory to see where you can work on your marriage. If you scored above 80, your marriage is great, keep working at it. A score of 60—80 reveals that there are some issues that should be addressed. If you scored below 60, please sit down and have a serious talk with your spouse to see how you can get back on track. You might want to consider seeking counseling to help you.

Christian Marriage

Study 25

Biblical Order

God

Jesus Christ

Now I want you to realize that the head of every man is Christ, and the head of the woman is man, and the head of Christ is God.
~ 1 Corinthians 11:3

A marriage is made up of two equal but profoundly different beings: each reflects the character of God in ways that give a unique picture of His character.[1]

Understanding God's Order in Marriage

Understanding how you were created and the factors in your life that have contributed to your personality make up will help you understand how you fit into God's order for life and marriage. Knowing your gifts, purpose in life and having a vision and a mission in life are also important. If you don't know who you are and where you are going in life, it will be difficult to find your place in the marriage relationship.

Although many people argue against it, there is a Biblical order. Some will go as far to contend that the "head" (kefaleé) of 1 Corinthians 11:3 does not mean "authority over," but means "source."[2] Dr. Wayne Grudem proves that the Greek word kefaleé does, in fact mean, "Person in authority over."[3] God is the head of Christ as Christ is the head of every man and man is the head of the woman. Originated by an all-knowing Creator, this order is not unfair to women and honors both men and women. This is not an interpretation; there is a hierarchy in the Bible.

Then the LORD God made a woman from the rib he had taken out of the man, and he brought her to the man. ~ Genesis 2:22

Family is the first social organization created by God and it is the foundation of society. Male headship is not an idea put forth by men to "keep the woman subjugated," but is a God ordained principle of life that is representative of His relationship with mankind. "The husband's headship over the house neither relieves the wife of responsibility nor makes her passive. Nor does it make her a simple servant in the house. Instead, the wife's subordination to the husband expresses an order of authority with the wife's ruling function carried out subordinate to the husband's."[4] Biblical hierarchy emphasizes equality, differences and unity at the same time.

Problems with the hierarchy came with the fall of mankind to sin. Adam and Eve chose to disobey God and the war of the sexes has continued ever since. People are selfish and sinful. Self-centeredness comes from the fall and is a sin that causes many of the problems in marriage. As Jesus relates in Matthew, chapter 19, it was not this way from the beginning. God's design did not include the problems seen throughout mankind's history.

Jesus consistently pointed the institution of marriage to its foundation; how God created it to be. Men perverted marriage to be male dominated, forcing women into a subordinate role with no rights. Treating women fully as heirs to the Kingdom of God, Jesus caused a change in marriage unprecedented in history. He liberated the wife and allowed the full potential of the marriage union to be realized. Marriage was no longer only an institution for procreation, but also an aspect of the Kingdom and a context in which people could serve God.

Created Equal

> ***There is neither Jew nor Greek, slave nor free, male nor female, for you are all one in Christ Jesus.***
> ***~ Galatians 3:28-29***

Men are not created more in the image of God than women—both are created in the image of God. Both are equally valuable to God, and, contrary to much commentary on both sides, one sex is not better than the other. Peter states that husbands and wives are joint heirs together of the gift of salvation (1 Peter 3:7). Both men and women are the sons of God and called to serve Him.

Couples who work together tend to have a strong marriage, while those who are always fighting tend to have a weak, ineffective marriage. Differences between spouses bring strength and balance to the marriage. It is the different strengths, abilities and gifts that allow couples to accomplish much more together than they could alone. Rather than fighting about who is in charge, couples need to follow Jesus' example of service and giving. Then they can work together to accomplish all that God wants them to accomplish in their lives and marriage.

Roles in Marriage

Often, couples in marriage relationships today fight for power and authority and forget about God's plan and following His direction. Listening to the lie that God's plan may not be best, they operate according to their own plan rather than God's. Rejecting the horrendous abuse of men over the past several thousand years, many women in western society refuse to submit themselves to what they believe will be even more abuse and subjection.

Roleless marriages supposedly correct this inequity between men and women. Equals in everything, the roleless marriage disregards gender differences and seeks to bring justice to the marriage relationship. Yet, women have lost ground rather than gained. Very often, they take care of the home, children and attempt to pursue a career as well. Hardly equal, this arrangement leaves women overworked and undervalued.

Some long for the days of the "traditional marriage" when the husband worked and the wife remained at home and cared for the children. The "traditional marriage" is not necessarily a Biblical marriage. An absentee husband and devalued wife do not fit the Biblical model for marriage and has caused many of the problems seen in society today. Couples sometimes view the activities they perform as roles, but chores and household responsibilities often are different than the Biblical roles of husbands and wives.

Going back even further to the Roman world, society was very similar to today's society. Roman families contended with many of the same issues, stresses and problems faced today. Marriages failed at an alarming rate and family life unraveled despite increasing prosperity. The Roman Empire of the first century was much like today's society and it was into this world that Jesus Christ came and Christianity began.

Paul's letters to Christian churches speaking of the husband's headship and wife's submission probably sounded as out of place then as they do in today's society. Based on Jesus' teaching, Paul's letters presented a distinctively alternative view of the marriage relationship. This message applies as much today as it did 2,000 years ago and will build a marriage strong and flourishing if followed.

A successful, growing marriage depends on the confidence and clarity that Biblical roles bring to the relationship. This is not about tasks; who washes the clothes and who takes the trash out. Roles are "the essential function that God has de-

"Alright then, you can be in charge on Sunday mornings, Mondays, Wednesdays and Saturdays."

signed a man or a woman to fulfill in a marriage relationship."[5] Roles address responsibilities, not rank or position.

God the Father, Jesus Christ and the Holy Spirit are equal, but they have different roles. Likewise, the husband and wife are equal, but they have different roles. The husband is the servant leader; the one who leads guides and protects the family. The wife is the helper— *a helper suitable for her husband*. The Hebrew word helper is not a demeaning term. The woman in Genesis was made to complement the man, to help him populate and rule the earth, and to unite with him as a loving companion-partner.[6] To give you an idea of the importance of this role; the same word is used to describe God as man's helper later in the Old Testament. The connotation of the word is one of strength and power. As God the Father, Jesus Christ and the Holy Spirit work together for one purpose, a husband and wife are to work together with Christ for one purpose.

God's roles for marriage do not limit who you are. Gender, personality, background, strengths and gifts are to be used together to glorify God, work through the problems of life and grow together in your marriage relationship. It is a matter of obedience to God's Word and pursuing His purpose for your life. Couples accomplish much when they work as a team and fulfill their roles in the marriage.

> ***"I used to believe that marriage would diminish me, reduce my options. That you had to be someone less to live with someone else when, of course you have to be someone more."***
> ***~ Candice Bergen***

The "S" Word—Submission

Submission, unfortunately, is an extremely polarizing word in society today. Criticized within and outside the church, people simply do not want to hear that a woman is to submit to her husband. Yet, the Bible clearly states in Ephesians 5:22-23, Colossians 3:18, 1 Timothy 2:9-15, Titus 2:3-5, and 1 Peter 3:1-7 that wives are to submit to their husbands. Christians understood what submission meant for 1900 years and then suddenly, in the second half of the twentieth century, some Christians decided that God didn't really mean for the wife to submit to her husband.[6] Contributing to the problem is the fact the even today, men use this concept for their own self-serving, selfish ways. As Jesus said, it was not this way from the beginning.

Submission is a Christian virtue; as the church submits to Christ, the wife is to submit to her husband. This is not a conditional command that takes place only if the husband submits to God. The wife is to submit; to be subject to or subordinate to her husband. The word implies a relationship of submission to an authority. Yet, submission is not about domination and intimidation. Biblical submission does not put the wife down. It acknowledges God's hierarchy; God the Father is the head of Christ as Christ is the head of the man and the man is the head of the woman. Christ would never ask His people to do something morally questionable and the husband who asks his wife to do anything immoral or illegal, is wrong.

> ***Submission never is to be a mandate to follow human authority into sin.***

An excellent way to think of submission is "aligning one's self" with another or "going in the same direction." The husband and wife must be going in the same direction and it is up to the wife to align herself with the direction God has given her husband. This emphasizes the importance of having purpose, a vision, mission and direction for the marriage and family. The wife can not align herself with her husband if she doesn't know where he is going.

A balanced marriage based on God's hierarchy and Biblical roles will grow and flourish. The husband who guides and leads his family according to God's Word and loves his wife and children as Christ loves the church will draw them to God's love. The wife moving in the same direction as her husband and helping him will strengthen his leadership and walk with God. Together, they will lead their family in ways that will strengthen and protect it from the challenges and attacks that will come in life.

A couple's joint participation in family responsibilities and the joy of a shared life will bring a couple closer together in oneness and intimacy and help them toward a balanced and steady marriage relationship. Husbands and wives who value each other other's differences, gifts, and wisdom will provide a caring, secure environment for their children. They bring glory to God by serving Him and raising their children to love Him.

For Discussion as a Couple

1. Does the husband act as the head in your marriage? Why is male headship important in the marriage relationship?

2. How do you see the affects of the fall in your marriage? What are some of the areas of contention you experience?

3. What arguments do you have regarding roles in your household? How can you change this pattern?

4. How can defining roles according to God's Word help you gain better balance in your marriage?

5. Is submission an issue in your marriage? How?

Christian Marriage

Study 26

The Servant-Leader

> *Sitting down, Jesus called the Twelve and said, "If anyone wants to be first, he must be the very last, and the servant of all."* ~ *Mark 9:35*

> ***Important Note to Wives:*** ***It is useful for you to understand your husband's role in the marriage, but hurtful if you use this information to criticize or put him down.***

Jesus Christ, the Example

Jesus is the example of perfect leadership. He is the lion and the lamb; tough and fierce, yet soft and gentle. This is the definition of the servant-leader; the head of the family. Male domination through the millennia is a product of the fall of mankind to sin and the selfishness of men. The problems society has today with male headship resulted from men forcing their headship upon women rather than leading as Christ would have them to lead. In the beginning, this was not how it was. God's plan was that the husband would be fierce in his protection and provision for his family, yet soft and gentle with his family. Jesus could be harsh, with those who would hurt His people. Yet, He was never harsh or demanding of those who came to Him in humility and need.

> ***Husbands, love your wives, just as Christ loved the church and gave himself up for her to make her holy, cleansing her by the washing with water through the word, and to present her to himself as a radiant church, without stain or wrinkle or any other blemish, but holy and blameless.***
> ***~ Ephesians 5:25-27***

Biblical leadership is about serving, not being served. Jesus Christ is the example as seen in Ephesians, Chapter 5. Jesus loved the church, His people, so much that He gave Himself up and died for her. Similarly, men are to love their wives that much. If a choice had to be made of who would live and who would die, most men would die for their wives. But realize that Jesus spent thirty-three years on earth knowing He was going to die for mankind. At any time, He could have said, "This isn't worth it, Father take me home." He didn't, He continued on toward the cross and died to Himself every day along the way. Men also are to die to self and serve their wives each and every day.

Jesus didn't only die that the church might live. He died that the church would be cleansed and made holy. The husband's role goes beyond just dying to self to something even deeper and more profound. Because of the sacrifice Christ made for mankind, God views His people as holy and blameless. A person's actions don't always measure up to his position in Christ, but that doesn't change his position in God's eyes. The husband also is to present his wife to himself as radiant, without stain or wrinkle or any other blemish, but holy and blameless. Men can not do this on their own, but as they submit to Christ, die to self and as they live for Him, He will empower them to love their wives as He loves them.

This doesn't mean that they overlook sin and poor behavior. Christians are forgiven and holy in God's eyes, but there are often consequences for sinful behavior. Boundaries are foundational to the marriage relationship. There are times when the husband will have to confront sin. He will have to take a stand for righteousness and holiness and confront the

wrong behavior of his wife or children in love.

Prophet, Priest and King[1]

The role of a servant-leader brings a huge responsibility. If this responsibility was properly understood by young men before marriage, many of them would likely choose bachelorhood over marriage. As head of the home, the husband is responsible for the spiritual, emotional and physical welfare of his wife and family. He fulfills his role by being the prophet, priest and king of his home. This responsibility can not be fulfilled when the husband looks to his own needs before those of his family. He must die to self to be the head that God designed him to be.

The *prophet* is one who hears from God and speaks God's Word to the people. He studies the word of God and seeks the Lord in prayer. The prophet builds his relationship with God, and, out of that close relationship, proclaims God's truths to his family. The prophet confronts sin and guides his family according to God's Word.

The *priest* leads people into God's presence through prayer and worship. It is the husband's responsibility to guide his family's spirituality. First, he must model a close relationship with the Lord. Then, he encourages his family in that direction. As priest, the husband should pray for and with his family on a daily basis. He is to live a life set apart for God; openly worshiping God through word and song.

The *king* leads, protects and provides for the safety of his subjects. The reality of the role is one of responsibility and leadership, not of privilege and possessions as we see so often in the world of men. Biblically, the king would judge the nation and lead the nation in their battles (1 Samuel 8:19-20). The husband as king, leads his family, and is their provider and protector. He is the judge who knows and applies the Word of God justly in the home.

Headship is a high and holy calling and is modeled after Christ's headship of His bride, the church. Headship means that the husband seeks his wife's best interests, even at his own expense. It does not mean to dominate or force his headship on the wife. Just as Jesus came to serve, not to be served (Matthew 20:28), the husband also assumes his role as head in humility and as a servant. Biblical Headship is:

- Responsibility, not rank.
- Sacrifice, not selfishness.
- Duty, not domination.[2]

Understanding Your Wife

> ***Husbands, in the same way be considerate as you live with your wives, and treat them with respect as the weaker partner and as heirs with you of the gracious gift of life, so that nothing will hinder your prayers. ~ 1 Peter 3:7***

Servant-leadership involves being considerate of and understanding the wife. Men are to listen and pay attention to their wives and children and discover their particular tendencies. It takes time and effort to know a spouse, but this is the husband's responsibility. Men can gain an understanding of their wives with patience, work and some creativity.

The servant-leader cares about his wife and children. He studies his wife to know her personality, strengths, weaknesses, background, childhood environment, gifts and talents. Meeting her needs and speaking her love language will build her up and empower her to be the wife God has called her to be. Rather than fleeing from relationship with his wife and understanding her, the Godly husband seeks intimacy and to know her deepest fears and desires. He strives to meet her needs, ease her fears and help her achieve her desires.

Biblical Leadership

Leadership is the man's responsibility even if it is not natural for him. Regardless of personality type, the man is the head of the household.

This will be more of a challenge for the Golden Retriever husband with a Lion wife. Leadership can be developed through discipleship and training. Any man can learn leadership and be the husband God calls him to be. Husbands, who reject leadership because it is not their personality or is difficult, reject God's design for their marriage.

Similarly, the take charge, natural leader who misuses his role by subjugating his wife, leads based on his own strength, not the Word of God. Throughout history men have wrongly abused women and treated them as possessions rather than as gifts from God. God's pronouncement of man's rule over woman in Genesis, Chapter 3 was not a command to be followed, but rather a statement of how sin would affect the male—female relationship. Male physical strength has allowed men to exert power over women, but in the beginning it was not this way.

Men must take responsibility for their life and their family. They must quit blaming God, their parents, wife, childhood, and society for their problems and inadequacies and be the godly men God calls them to be. The husband must provide for the emotional, spiritual, physical and mental well being of his wife and family. Husbands need to protect their wives' self-esteem and self-worth and establish Biblical principles as the guiding force of their home. Husbands need to be the initiator spiritually and relationally in the home. The man who begins living a holy life, lived for God is an example to his family and is moving in the direction of Biblical leadership.

"Honey, I don't think Skippy is going to attack me."

This kind of leadership, this headship, will change the destiny of a man's family. Most women would be willing to submit to the leadership of a man living his life for God and giving himself up for her. It may take some time for her to trust the change and get aligned with his leadership, but as he lovingly encourages and works with her, she will come around. Children may take time to get used to life without valueless television programs and ultra-violent video games, but as you invest your time into your children and become the guiding force in their lives, you will see a change in them also.

The Servant-Leader

There are as many ways to lead a family as there are married couples on earth. While there will always be differences from family to family, there are some Biblical principles that will characterize the household of a Biblical servant-leader. The servant-leader's weapons are not man's weapons of the flesh or world, but are faith, prayer, and God's Word (1 Corinthians 10:3-4). Men must depend on the Lord God of Heaven for every aspect of their lives, as this job is too great for any man to accomplish alone. It is a huge responsibility, even overwhelming. Get support, meet with a mentor or a group of men who have the desire to live life God's way. The Lord will provide the tools to help you with this responsibility, but you must seek out those tools and learn to use them.

Your wife is the most important person you can have helping you. Enlist your wife onto your team; she is your helper and must be included in family leadership. Sit down together to plan and coordinate activities that will help your family grow and become what God wants it to be. Utilize her abilities and gifts to help you lead the family. Help your wife develop her leadership skills and encourage her in her spiritual and emotional growth.

The servant-leader must be a learner. Learn your wife and children and continue to learn what it means to be a Godly leader and growing in a Christian marriage. Continue growing spiritually, but also grow intellectually and professionally. Do not be content with where you are, but build learning into your life.

Loving encouragement rather than harsh condemnation will help build up your family. Invest time and energy into each family member to develop their gifts, abilities and interests. Guide your family in their growth and learning and finding fulfillment in Christ. Be willing to admit when you are wrong and apologize and ask forgiveness when needed. Humility and transparency enhances leadership rather than hinders it, as many men tend to believe. If you don't know how to do something, say, "I don't know" and then go out and find how to do it.

> ***A Quick Servant-Leader Self-test:***
>
> ***Can you honestly say your wife and children are growing physically, emotionally and spiritually? If they are, you are succeeding as the spiritual leader. If they are not, what do you need to do to help them begin growing?***

For Discussion as a Couple

1. Why should Jesus' leadership style affect the way the husband leads his family? How can this happen?

   ____
   ____
   ____
   ____

2. How does the husband serve in your household?

   ____
   ____
   ____
   ____

3. How can a husband get to know and understand his wife?

   ____
   ____
   ____
   ____

4. In your home, does the husband lead Biblically? How is this displayed or not displayed?

   ____
   ____
   ____
   ____

5. What are some ways the husband can be the servant-leader in your home?

   ____
   ____
   ____
   ____

Christian Marriage

Study 27

The Helper

The LORD God said, "It is not good for the man to be alone. I will make a helper suitable for him." ~ Genesis 2:18

***Important Note to Husbands:** It is useful for you to understand your wife's role in the marriage, but hurtful if you use this information to criticize or put her down*

The Example of a Helper

The Hebrew word for helper, "ezer," means much more than our modern term for an assistant. There is nothing inferior or negative about this term. Positive and powerful, the helper in the Bible upheld, strengthened and delivered. God uses this word to describe Himself as His peoples':

- Shield, helper and glorious sword (Deuteronomy 33:29).
- Help and deliverer (Psalms 70:5).
- Helper (Hosea 13:9).

The idea that as helper, a woman is inferior to her husband did not come from the Bible. Unfortunately, men have used their physical strength to subdue and subjugate women throughout history. The man who does not utilize the great strengths and abilities of his wife to work together as a team lacks wisdom. She was created to uphold, strengthen and deliver him in the battles they will face as a couple. The ancient Hebrew letter "Vav" was used to represent a nail, peg or wife. It was that which binds or nails things together. The wife is considered the nail of the tent in Ancient Hebrew upholding the family and holding it together.[1] The Biblical importance of the wife cannot be overemphasized.

A wife of noble character who can find? She is worth far more than rubies. Her husband has full confidence in her and lacks nothing of value. She brings him good, not harm, all the days of her life. ~ Proverbs 31:10-12

Proverbs 31 gives a picture of an ideal woman and it is an excellent example of the helper as the term is meant in the Bible. This wife is extremely valuable to her husband; she strengthens and cares for him. She conducts business to benefit and care for her family. She manages and teaches her family and household, and also helps the poor. Her husband is a man of influence because of the strength his wife gives him, empowering him to achieve what God would have him to do.

A wife may wonder how one woman could accomplish all these things; no normal woman could do this much. It is not helpful to compare yourself to others, but it is instructive to understand what can be accomplished with God's power and direction. The Proverbs 31 woman is a woman of confidence. Her heart is at home and she ensures that her husband and children have the proper care. Rather than limiting the woman, this ideal liberates and empowers her to accomplish all that God calls her to do. She uses her talents, abilities and gifts to benefit her home and uphold her husband. He attains a measure of success because he has her on his side working with him.

Husband Lover, Child Lover

> *Then they can train the younger women to love their husbands and children, to be self-controlled and pure, to be busy at home, to be kind, and to be subject to their husbands, so that no one will malign the word of God. ~ Titus 2:4-5*

The most important aspect of the wife's role in the marriage is to be lover of her husband and children. This defines how the wife fulfills her role as helper. It is not all she does in the relationship, but defines the direction of her priorities and activities. Her role is vital to the marriage and the overall health of her husband and children—her role is indispensable.

Children, especially the young, need tremendous amounts of personal attention, support and love. It will be extremely difficult for children to grow into healthy adults without mother pouring her love into her children. The nurturing she gives her children is an investment into future generations. While children need both parents, it is the mother who primarily nurtures (cultivates, develops, encourages) them.

Wives have incredible power over their husbands. Through criticism and disrespect, they can drive their husbands away from the family (*it is better to live on a corner of the roof than in a house with a quarrelsome wife.* Proverbs 21:9) and even into sin. The wife can also empower her husband and help him become a Godly man that is respected in the home and in the community. Most women can rip their husband's ego apart in a matter of seconds with cutting remarks and disrespect in front of the children or friends and family. When a wife rejects the negative and builds him up and encourages her husband positively, she can strengthen him to meet the challenges of his role as servant-leader. The wife must choose daily to be a positive influence on her husband.

Should the Wife Work Outside the Home?

There is no easy answer to this question; a husband and wife must make this decision together after careful consideration. With or without children, the principles for making this decision are the same. Biblically, the wife's responsibilities center on the home. While marriage and a "career" are not necessarily mutually exclusive, it is very difficult for a woman to juggle marriage, family, home and career and be effective in all areas. Many women have found out as they entered the work force in massive numbers that this so-called ideal life is not as fulfilling as was promised. There are many costs associated with being a "working mom." A couple must count those costs to determine if this is something they want to do.

The family must come first; neither the husband nor wife can sacrifice the family for the sake of career and success and be in God's will. If you have chosen to have a family, there are certain sacrifices that must be made. Children take a lot of time and energy, leaving them in the care of other people is not a decision that should be made lightly. Money and possessions will not make up for a lack of parental involvement in children's lives. As a team, a couple must make the right decisions to benefit their family and fulfill their God-given purpose.

A couple must carefully examine the reasons for the wife to work outside the home. A wife working to find self-fulfillment works for the wrong reasons. Likewise, working for luxuries and material possessions is a misplacement of priorities. There may be periods where working outside the home is necessary, but there should be very specific goals established for the wife's income. Too many children have been sacrificed to finance wants and desires when working outside the home has not been a necessity. This decision must be made with great care and a lot of prayer.

"You mean you actually su, sub, subm... do what your husband says?"

Submission is Not a Four Letter Word

> *Wives, submit to your husbands, as is fitting in the Lord.*
> *~ Colossians 3:18*

Independence is a major focus of society today. Women are told that they don't need to depend on anyone and certainly don't have to submit to any man. Yet, many women now see the shallowness and lack of intimacy that comes with their independence. Both Christian and non-Christian women now understand the positive aspects of submission and respecting their husband. Attempting to live independent of your husband undermines the marriage relationship and strains intimacy.

> *Some women work so hard to make good husbands that they never manage to make good wives.*
> *~ Anonymous*

Submission means that many women will have to give up control of their husbands. They control their husbands through a variety of means, using sex, manipulation, emotions, guilt or martyrdom to get their way. Many have emasculated their husbands who will do almost anything to avoid the emotional turmoil caused by disagreements or taking a stand contrary to their wives opinions. Even those women with controlling, domineering husbands often find ways to control him to accomplish their desires. Submitting, as God wants her to submit means that the wife chooses to give up control of her husband, get aligned with his direction, trust God for the outcome and work with her husband as a teammate.

The Godly wife consents to being ruled, she is not forced. She respects and honors her husband; she is not his slave. She supports and encourages her husband rather than mothering him and trying to make him into something she thinks he should be. Using the principles of boundaries, the submissive wife allows God to change her husband as she loves him and strives to meet his needs and encourage him in his leadership of the family.

Submission does not mean that a woman accepts her husband's physical abuse, addictions or continued unfaithfulness. Matthew, chapter 18 gives direction for the confrontation of those in sin and it also applies in the marriage relationship. Healthy boundaries provide protection against the abuse that may result from sin and it is important that the proper steps be taken when necessary.

The helper is valuable and necessary to the health and well being of the family. A couple working together as a team will better provide stability and direction for their family. A supportive and encouraging wife facilitates her husband's ability to meet the demands of his role as servant-leader of the family. It is necessary for the wife to actively seek to fulfill her responsibilities in the marriage. A passive, uninvolved wife will not fulfill those responsibilities as God would want her to fulfill them.

The Godly Helper

A wife is a helper, suitable for her husband. She brings her skills, abilities and gifts alongside him to help build the marriage and family into a strong, fortified unit equipped to meet the challenges of daily life. She affirms her husband and makes him feel like the most important person in the world. She is on his side, upholding him and working with him to fulfill God's purposes for their lives, marriage and family. She provides a balance that a man can never have alone. She stands with her husband through every challenge that comes at them and their family. Her husband is her first priority. Naturally, she will protect her children, if her husband is abusive, but in other aspects, he comes first.

As advisor, counselor and teammate, the wife complements her husband and brings strengths to his weaknesses. She ministers to her husband and is used by God to make him a better person. Her respect and loyalty help him stand strong when he feels like running from the challenges he faces as leader of the home.

A godly helper resists the temptation to take charge of her husband and situations that will come up. God's Word directs the wife, even when she has a Lion/leader personality, to set boundaries and refuse to take leadership of the home. She is to support her husband and help him become the godly leader of the home he is meant to be. Her gentle and quiet spirit provides peace in the storms of daily life and is greatly valued by God (1 Peter 3:4).

> ***A Quick Helper self test:***
>
> ***Can you honestly say your husband and children feel loved? Do they feel your love and support or do they feel criticized and judged? If they feel loved, you are succeeding as a husband-lover, child-lover. If they do not, what do you need to do to help them begin feeling loved?***

For Discussion as a Couple

1. How do you (or your wife) fulfill the role of helper in your marriage?

____

____

____

____

2. How does the wife demonstrate being a husband-lover?

____

____

____

____

3. How is a wife a child-lover? Should the children ever come before the husband in your marriage?

____

____

____

____

4. Does the wife work outside the home in your family? Why or why not?

____

____

____

____

5. What should the wife's submission look like in daily life?

____

____

____

____

Christian Marriage

Study 28

Direction of the Home

> *... But as for me and my household, we will serve the LORD."*
> *~ Joshua 24:15*

> *"We were never meant to be completely satisfied in this world."*
> *~ Michael Card*

Throughout history marriages always faced difficult and trying times. The environment, obstacles and problems may change, but every generation faces challenges to their marriage and family relationships. Noah faced many of the challenges we have today, violence, corruption, godlessness, and moral decay. Yet, Noah and his family made a difference in their world (Genesis, chapter 6). Noah made the decision to obey and trust in God, just as Joshua did many generations later and couples must do the same today. Godly wisdom in the home does not develop naturally; couples must make the decision to commit to serving God, following and trusting in Him. It takes perseverance to remain on the path in spite of the problems a marriage experiences. It is important to hold to the path God has for you and remain faithful to Him through any obstacles, problems and difficult times.

The Husband-Wife Team

The addition of children changes a marriage more than any other event in married life. The change is for life and couples need to be prepared for the challenge before it comes. "Good marriages are designed to hold children together; children are not created to hold their parents together."[1] Working together with common goals and objectives is extremely necessary, especially when a couple is blessed with children. A strong, stable marriage provides a foundation for raising mentally, emotionally and spiritually healthy children. The couple that stands strong together will endure and grow through the challenges that will come in life.

> *The best gift you can give your children is a good marriage. ~ Harville Hendrix*

A God-centered home built on the foundation of Jesus Christ has profound effects on the children and future generations. Producing spiritually healthy, balanced children require a stable environment that is secure and loving. A couple who has respectful communication and expresses praise, affection and appreciation for each other in the presence of the children allows their children to experience the love and strength of a healthy marriage.

Men and women are not independent of each other (1 Corinthians 11:11-12) and contrary to what society may say; marriage is not a separate but equal arrangement. Parenting is not a one-person job and it is important that husbands and wives work together to guide the home in the direction God wants it to go. Establishing goals and objectives, individually, as a couple and as a family is extremely important to keeping the family on track. Including the children in the process will increase their commitment and help them to learn to set goals and objectives for themselves. Posting the family mission statement conspicuously in the home reminds the whole family of their direction.

Clear Biblical roles strengthen the marriage and the family overall. Children learn from their parent's example and experience the security that comes from stability and order. Clear roles also help a couple work together as a team rather than arguing about responsibilities and working against each other. A couple struggling for control in the marriage will not be productive and efficient. Biblical order allows a couple to build a fortified marriage that will be the foundation for a strong family. They complement each other, utilizing each other's strengths to guide and direct the home and family.

> ***Better a hundred enemies outside the house than one inside. ~ Arab Proverb***

A Christian Home

A Christian home certainly *should* feel much different than a non-Christian home. It should be a place of refuge where each member of the family is refreshed and strengthened so they may be able to meet the problems they experience in daily life. Love and respect for everyone in the home brings stability and security. As a couple works together to first love each other and then love their children, there will be a freshness that will set their home apart from the homes that do not care about God's principles.

> ***He must manage his own family well and see that his children obey him with proper respect. ~ 1 Timothy 3:4-5***

Paul writes to Timothy that the overseer or leader in the church must manage his family well. No home is perfect and no child is perfect, but there is a difference in the family that serves the Lord first in their lives. Many parents will not confront the poor behavior of their children and allow their children to dictate how the household will operate. Parents do not have to be tyrants and demand that their children behave perfectly in all situations, but it is not unreasonable to expect obedience and respect from their children.

When Bad Things Happen

Healthy, fortified marriages are better able to handle the inevitable issues that will come in life. All marriages will suffer setbacks, downturns, crises or problems. The presence or absence of issues in marriage is not indicative of how strong the marriage is, but the true measure of the marriage commitment shows when crises occur.

Sin is a reality in the world today. Whether it is the sin of one spouse, children or outsiders that hurt the family, it is likely that sin will affect your family in some way. Sin must be dealt with; it cannot be ignored. Ignoring sin shows the one who was sinned against that he is not worthy of protection and often will give the perpetrator the opportunity to hurt others. Abuse, addictions, infidelity and habitual sin cannot be allowed to continue. It must be confronted and worked through. Get help if necessary.

Sin is not the only factor affecting marriages. Natural disasters, accidents, health problems, infertility and death affect marriages and families tremendously. The husband may lose his job beginning a financial crisis in the home. Each problem presents a different set of issues as a couple tries to work through the problems. As with sin, external problems and crises do not have to destroy the family and in fact, can strengthen a couple and their family.

> ***Love is strengthened by working through conflicts together. ~ Anonymous***

Prior to marriage, couples tend to believe love will conquer all, that there is no problem their love cannot solve. Yet, in reality, love alone does not sustain couples through a crisis. It is their dependence on God, determination, commitment and working together that will not only get them through the problems, but help them to grow in their love for each other as they face and work through the crisis together.

Job of the Old Testament teaches a lot about facing crises. This man lost his means of financial provision and all of his children. In one day, he

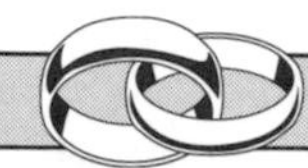

went from being a prosperous, contented man to poor and desolate. Even his health failed and yet he would not accuse God. In answer to his wife's admonition of "Curse God and die," Job responded; "shall we accept good from God, and not trouble?" (Job 2:10) Similar to Job, couples facing crises must remain focused on the Lord and not blame Him for their troubles.

> ***"I am convinced that life is 10 percent what happens to me and 90 percent how I react to it. And so it is with you—we are in charge of our attitudes." ~ Chuck Swindoll***

A couple facing a crisis must focus on getting through the crisis without attacking each other. They need to take responsibility for their actions and attitudes and deal with the issues rather than blaming each other and fighting. Couples facing crises need to trust God, work through the problems together and seek support and help from others to resolve the issues they will face.

"Now can we call for some help?"

The Power of a Godly Home

The direction of a home is a choice a couple makes. Noah, Abraham, Sarah, Moses, Joshua, Rahab, David, Joseph and Mary made the choice to trust in God and walk in His ways and the Lord blessed them for their obedience. None of these people were perfect; there have been no perfect families throughout history. We could discuss the problems of each of the people listed above, but God doesn't look at the problems, He looks at the heart. David, who had a very dysfunctional family, is called the man after God's own heart. The Lord uses imperfect people, people who make the choice to follow Him despite circumstances or problems.

> ***The righteous man leads a blameless life; blessed are his children after him. ~ Proverbs 20:7***

People do not lead perfect and blameless lives, but when they make a choice to follow God and surrender their lives to Him, He will bless them and bless their children also. The Godly home uses God's Word as the standard of how to live life. Couples living their lives for God model prayer, worship and Bible study for their children. The husband leading his family is a role model for how Jesus Christ loves His people. The children experience the love of God and see imperfect parents allowing God to mold and shape them into His image.

Working as a team, the couple guides their children together, without contradiction and disrespect. They don't fight in front of their children and present a united front to the children. The tasks of husband and wife may vary due to many circumstances, but a couple focused on the Lord will work together to accomplish whatever needs to be done in the household.

A God-focused home is a center of care and service, not only to the family living in the home, but to others as well. Characteristics of a God-focused home include love, support, encouragement and forgiveness. A couple with a solid foundation and a fortified marriage working together creates this type of home. People feel safe in their home and it's not unusual to see the neighborhood children gathering there. A growing, caring family will have fun together, spending time playing as well as working together. There is power in this home because Jesus Christ is Lord and serving Him is a priority.

Families serving God make a difference in their church, neighborhood and the world. Learning God's principles for life and marriage and applying them to your marriage brings strength and power to be used by God in other's lives. A couple moving in God's direction is a magnet for troubled marriages that see something they don't have.

A growing, God directed marriage doesn't seem as challenging as it is for so many hurting couples. Interestingly, there will be more growth in the couple committed to serving the Lord than in the lives of those couples who continue to live selfish, self-centered lives. The couple in a committed marriage seeks God's will for their lives and marriage. They seek advice and counsel from others, but rely on the Lord to lead them as they lead their family in His direction.

For Discussion as a Couple

1. Do you and your household serve the Lord? Name five things you and your household do to serve the Lord?

____
____
____
____

2. Why is it important that a couple be a team? Are you and your spouse a team working together?

____
____
____
____

3. Is your home different than a non-Christian home? How?

____
____
____
____

4. How can you keep going in the right direction together when a crisis occurs?

____
____
____
____

5. What difference does your marriage make in the lives of others? How can you be used by God to make a difference?

____
____
____
____

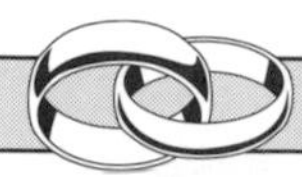

Christian Marriage

Study 29

Leaving a Legacy

A good man leaves an inheritance for his children's children,
~ Proverbs 13:22

There are people who live as if they are never going to die. When they die, it is as if they never have lived. ~ Anonymous

A Legacy Will Be Left

Choosing the direction of your home begins the journey of leaving a legacy. Your legacy is what you have left for future generations once you are dead and buried. It is defined as "anything left by ancestor or predecessor" or "property bequeathed by a will."[1] There is two aspects of this definition, first, the unintentional leaving of property or emotional, social and spiritual attributes. Many people die without giving any thought about what they will leave to their descendants. Whether it is their possessions and a lack of a will to direct distribution or giving no thought to what kind of emotional, social or spiritual legacy they will leave. They live life as though death is the end of it all. It is not the end, because good or bad, there will be some part of you left with your children, grandchildren, family, friends and acquaintances. The second aspect is the intentional leaving of those same things as in a will. It is a matter of setting a vision of how your life will look in retrospect once you are gone and living out that ideal.

"Leaving a godly legacy requires character, commitment, and vision."[2]

To leave a positive legacy, people must live lives that will make a difference in the lives they come in contact with. Leading a life of purpose serving Jesus Christ is a positive way to begin shaping the legacy you will leave. Many men will give their wife and children every thing they want, but not what they need. These men give all the material possessions a person could desire, but do not give of themselves. Their family doesn't know who they are, and yet, these men do not understand that they are leaving a negative legacy. Eli, the high priest of Israel before King Saul's time did not restrain his sons from their ungodly activities. He did not have the character or commitment to leave a positive legacy for his family and he was afraid to confront his sons. The consequences were costly as God took the lives of both sons and Eli himself (1 Samuel 3:11-14).

Fix these words of mine in your hearts and minds; tie them as symbols on your hands and bind them on your foreheads. Teach them to your children, talking about them when you sit at home and when you walk along the road, when you lie down and when you get up. Write them on the doorframes of your houses and on your gates,
~ Deuteronomy 11:18-20

There is a balance involved with leaving a legacy. Some parents attempt to push their will on their children and choose the direction of their children's lives. They demand that the child follow the family tradition of a certain career or they will live out their life through their children. Others will leave all choices to their children, choice of education, career, and whether or not to follow Christ. God desires that parents guide their children to seek Him and His will for their lives. Parents are to train their children in God's love and His principles. This provides a godly foundation for children and, even if they stray, they will come back to the Lord (see Proverbs 22:6).

> *The purposes of a man's heart are deep waters, but a man of understanding draws them out. ~ Proverbs 20:5*

The Legacy Received

People cannot escape the bonds of biology and identity that connect them to their parents, grandparents and the generations before. Those connections to preceding generations may be either positive or negative and may span three, four, or even five generations. They are a part of who a person is; many of the patterns and behaviors passed from previous generations are carried throughout life.

God allows the consequences of ancestral sin to impact several generations, but He also blesses future generations of those who love Him. There are "tendencies" passed from generation to generation. Children raised by alcoholics, abusers or criminals tend to follow those same patterns, and children raised by upright, Godly, productive people tend to follow those patterns. People who desire to break out of the negative patterns of their ancestors, usually have to work hard to make the break. Moral weakness tends to produce moral weakness, just as godliness and strong character tends to produce godliness.

The legacy of divorce affects families for generations. Through divorce, couples think they can rebuild their lives with a clean slate, but they cannot. Children are a permanent legacy of the marriage and there will always be some connection between the parents.[3] Judith Wallerstein studied 131 children of divorce for twenty-five years and found that divorce is a "life-transforming experience."[4] After the divorce, every stage of life is different for children of divorce. Their ability to develop and maintain meaningful relationships and even how they interact with society is affected. One study defending divorce admits that divorce creates approximately 150,000 children each year heading for serious social, emotional or psychological problems. The devastation of divorce touches many thousands of households each year and affects generations.[5]

"You can't be the leader without followers; we're going with you."

Many people have sacrificed their family for career, power, achievement and even ministry. Throughout the history of the Christian church, stories can be told of men who achieved much for the Kingdom of God, but did not fulfill their role as the servant-leader of their family. Some have even boldly proclaimed that marriage would not slow them down one bit from their ministry.[6] It is not right that a man should be out trying to win the world for Christ and not take care of their family. Too many men achieve great things outside the home, but do not leave a positive legacy for their children.

> *What good will it be for a man if he gains the whole world, yet forfeits his soul? ~ Matthew 16:26*

It is possible to achieve great things and also leave a positive legacy. Jonathan Edwards was a pastor and evangelist in Colonial America. He achieved much outside of the home, but he felt that his first ministry was to his family. Jonathan and Sarah Edwards' investment into the welfare of their family paid huge dividends as their children grew and served God in their own ways. A study of 1400 Edwards descendents reveals thirteen college presidents, thirty judges, sixty-six physicians, sixty-five professors and more than one hundred clergymen, missionaries and theology professors.[7] A positive legacy reaches far and may have an affect on the world as the family grows and serves God.

It is important to examine the legacy you and your spouse were left by your ancestors. It will be helpful to look objectively at your childhood to see what kind of legacy your parents and grandparents left you. This information will serve four purposes:

1. Illuminating areas in your life that may need examination and change.
2. Aiding the breaking of generational strongholds of sin.
3. Increasing intimacy and closeness with your spouse.
4. Providing a starting point to begin working together toward leaving a positive legacy for your children.

Complete the legacy worksheet on page 175 to help you determine what kind of legacy you were left. You will be asked to evaluate three areas of your legacy. Through a spiritual legacy, parents model and encourage spiritual principles and truths. A strong emotional legacy helps a person develop healthy emotions and can handle the struggles of life positively. A social legacy builds strong social skills for cultivating healthy, stable relationships.

Look back to the legacy you have been left, then look up to the Lord and ask Him for forgiveness when necessary and for a changed legacy. Finally, look forward; what kind of legacy do you want to leave?

Choosing a Legacy to Leave

What kind of legacy will you leave? Similar to a vision statement, one sets the goal and then works to fulfill that goal. The object is to leave a legacy of your choosing, rather than leaving it to chance and wondering how future generations will view your life and the legacy you left. While not impossible, it is hard to leave a positive legacy if you do not live your life for God. Your priorities and the direction of your life need to be in line with God's purposes for you. It is never too late to make the changes necessary to change a legacy. God is a God of redemption; when His people repent and turn from their wicked ways, He is faithful to restore them. While there may be consequences for the past actions, God will redeem the future.

The memory of the righteous will be a blessing, but the name of the wicked will rot.
~ Proverbs 10:7

Godliness, integrity, and holy living will do a lot to leave a positive legacy. Husbands and wives accepting and living out their roles of servant-leader and helper also will help leave a positive legacy. The home that prays, worships God and studies His word will be stronger than the home that does not consider God's ways. Actions speak louder than words, husbands and wives must put their words into practice.

You can only preach the Christ that you live.

Use the worksheet on page 176 to briefly describe the legacy you desire to leave for your children and future generations. This is another opportunity for husband and wife to work together to decide the future of their family. Many couples have achieved much without sacrificing their family. You can also achieve positive goals while still guiding your children with a strong legacy. It is your choice.

Transmitting the Legacy

It is not impossible to leave a positive legacy for your family. Paul writes that the married person must be concerned about worldly things and how to please his spouse (1 Corinthians 7:27-34). It is necessary for the husband to provide for the spiritual, emotional and physical needs of his family and for the wife to be the helper, and her husband's strength and support as he leads the family. Together they can guide their children and impress upon them a godly legacy. Verbal, symbolic, visual and written opportunities are important to guiding children in the ways of the

Lord and the direction you desire for your family. In the movie *My Big Fat Greek Wedding*, the father took every possible opportunity to explain how all words originated with the Greek language. Similarly, it is vitally important that Christian parents teach their children the Word of God, and make the most of every opportunity to guide and direct them and impress a positive legacy into their lives.

An excellent way to pass on a legacy to the next generation is through formal ceremonies. A child's wedding is an excellent place for this. Parents can use part of the ceremony to formally pass the legacy to their son or daughter and their new spouse. Parents may formally send their child off to college, create a ceremony to instill the legacy as their children move out of the home or develop a legacy ceremony for their children's 18th or 21st birthdays. There are many things a couple can do to impress their legacy into their children's lives.

For Discussion as a Couple

1. Why is it important to have a purpose for your life and a direction for your home when thinking about leaving a legacy?

____

____

____

____

2. Why do you think so many people, even Christians, tend to leave a negative legacy?

____

____

____

____

3. Was the legacy you received from your parents generally positive or negative? How has it affected your life?

____

____

____

____

4. Why is it important to choose to leave a positive legacy? What does Godliness have to do with a legacy?

____

____

____

____

5. What will you do to ensure that you leave a positive legacy for future generations?

____

____

____

____

The Legacy You Were Left

Answer the following questions as honestly and completely as you are able. Share your answers with your spouse.

Your Spiritual Legacy:

1. Were spiritual principles incorporated into your family's daily life? How? ________________

2. Was church life important in your family? Did you attend church regularly? Did you participate in church events other than Sunday services? What? ________________

3. How did your parents view God? How did they relate to Him? ________________

Your Emotional Legacy:

1. Describe your home atmosphere growing up. ________________

2. Did you feel important growing up? How were you treated? With respect? Explain. ________________

3. How did your parents relate to each other and treat each other? ________________

Your Social Legacy:

1. How did your family interact with other people? What were the attitudes like? ________________

2. How were rules set and enforced in your home? ________________

3. How did your parents deal with wrong behavior? ________________

The Legacy You Will Leave

Briefly describe the legacy you desire to leave your children and future generations in the following areas. Work with your spouse to decide a legacy for your family.

The Spiritual Legacy I want to leave: ______

The Emotional Legacy I want to leave: ______

The Social Legacy I want to leave: ______

Fortified Marriages
Chapter 7 Endnotes

Study 23: *Foundations for Marriage*

1. Collier's Dictionary; William D. Halsey, Editorial Director (NY, NY; Macmillan Educational Company, 1986)
2. Nelson's Illustrated Bible Dictionary; Copyright 1986, Thomas Nelsons Publishers
3. Robertson McQuilkin, Living by the Vows; Christianity Today, October 8, 1990
4, Art Carey; In Defense of Marriage, (NY,NY; Walker and Company, 1984) p 153

Recommended for further reading:
- Muriel's Blessing by Robertson McQuilken, Christianity Today, February 5, 1996
- An Outrageous Commitment; The 48 Vows of an Indestructible Marriage by Dr. Ronn Elmore
- The Complete Marriage Book by Dr. David and Jan Stoop

For further information, see:
- FamilyLife: www.familylife-ccc.org
- Covenant Marriage Movement: www.covenantmarriage.com

Study 24: *The Christian Marriage*

1. Judith Wallerstein & Sandra Blakeslee; The Good Marriage, How and Why Love Lasts (NY,NY; Houghton Mifflin Company, 1995) p 24
2. Mike Mason; The Mystery of Marriage (Portland, OR, Multnomah Press, 1985) p 81
3. Judith Wallerstein & Sandra Blakeslee; The Good Marriage, How and Why Love Lasts (NY,NY; Houghton Mifflin Company, 1995) p 240

Recommended for further reading:
- The Christ Centered Marriage by Neil T. Anderson and Charles Mylander
- The Case for Marriage by Linda J. Waite and Maggie Gallagher.
- Whole Marriages in a Broken World by Gary Inrig

For further information, see:
- Focus on the Family: www.family.org

Study 25: *Biblical Order*

1. Dan Allender and Tremper Longman; Intimate Allies (Wheaton, IL; Tyndale House, 1995) p146
2. Wayne Grudem, Editor; Biblical Foundations for Manhood and Womanhood (Wheaton, IL; Crossway Books, 2002) pp 47 - 48
3. Ibid.
4. Stephen B. Clark, Man and Woman in Christ (Ann Arbor, MI; Servant Books, 1980) p 57
5. Robert Lewis and William Hendricks, Rocking the Roles: Building a Win-Win Marriage (Colorado Springs, Co; NavPress, 1991) p 46
6. Alexander Strauch, Men and Women: Equal Yet Different (Colorado Springs, CO, Lewis & Roth Publishers, 1999) p 23

7. Wayne Grudem, Editor; Biblical foundations for Manhood and Womanhood (Wheaton, IL, Crossway Books, 2002) pp 221-222

Recommended for further reading:
- Biblical Foundations for Manhood and Womanhood; Wayne Grudem, Editor
- Men and Women: Equal Yet Different by Alexander Strauch
- Rocking the Roles: Building a Win-Win Marriage by Robert Lewis and William Hendricks
- Man and Woman in Christ by Stephen B. Clark
- Different by Design by John MacArthur

For further information, see:
- Council on Biblical Manhood and Womanhood: www.cbmw.org

Study 26: *The Servant-Leader*

1. Bob Lepine; The Christian Husband (Ann Arbor, MI; Servant Publications, 1999) p 109
2. Robert Lewis and William Hendricks, Rocking the Roles: Building a Win-Win Marriage (Colorado Springs, Co; NavPress, 1991) p 46

Recommended for further reading:
- The Christian Husband by Bob Lepine
- A Man After God's Own Heart by Jim George
- The Man in the Mirror: The 24 Things Men Face by Patrick Morely

For further information, see:
- Promise Keepers: www.pk.org
- Man in the Mirror Ministries: www.maninthemirror.org
- National Coalition of Men's Ministries: www.edcole.org

Study 27: *The Helper*

1. F. Andy Tryon, Ph.D.; Ancient Hebrew: God's Picture Language; Goodyear, AZ, p 16

Recommended for further reading:
- Captivating by John & Stasi Eldredge
- For Women Only by Shaunti Feldhahn
- A Woman After God's Own Heart by Elizabeth George
- Men Who Won't Lead and Women Who Won't Follow by James Walker
- Liberated Through Submission by P.B. Wilson

For further information, see:
- Women by Grace: ww.womenbygrace.com
- Women of Faith: ww.womenoffaith.com

Study 28: *Direction in the Home*

1. James Walker; Husbands Who Won't Lead & Wives Who Won't Follow (Minneapolis, MN; Bethany House Publishers, 2000) p 163

Recommended for further reading:
- Guiding Your Family by Tony Evans
- When Bad Things Happen to Good Marriages by Les and Leslie Parrott
- The Strong Family by Chuck Swindoll
- Before a Bad Goodbye; Dr. Tim Clinton

Study 29: *Leaving a Legacy*

1. Collier's Dictionary; William D. Halsey, Editorial Director (NY, NY; Macmillan Educational Company, 1986)
2. FamilyLife Marriage Conference Manual (Little Rock, AR; FamilyLife, 1997) p 157
3. Judith Wallerstein, Julia Lewis & Sandra Blakeslee; The Unexpected Legacy of Divorce (NY,NY; Hyperion, 2000) p 46
4. Judith Wallerstein, Julia Lewis & Sandra Blakeslee; The Unexpected Legacy of Divorce (NY,NY; Hyperion, 2000) p xxvii
5. E. Mavis Hetherington; cited by Richard Corliss, "Does Divorce Hurt Kids?" Time, January 28.2002
6. John Wesley; quoted by Doreen Moore; Good Christians, Good Husbands? (Ross-Shire, Scotland, Christian Focus Publications, 2004) p 56
7. Dennis & Barbara Rainey, Building Your Mate's Self-Esteem (Nashville, TN; Thomas Nelson, 1995) pp 229—230

Recommended for further reading:
- The Heritage by J. Otis Ledbetter and Kurt Bruner

Chapter 8
Intimacy in Marriage

Study 30

Created for Intimacy

For this reason a man will leave his father and mother and be united to his wife, and they will become one flesh. The man and his wife were both naked, and they felt no shame.
~ Genesis 2:24-25

"Intimacy is what makes a marriage, not a ceremony, not a piece of paper from the state."
~ Kathleen Norris

Marriage is the closest; most intimate human relationship people have the capacity for. Through physical, intellectual, emotional and spiritual connection, a husband and wife become closer to each other than to any other person. Intimacy, simply stated, means, "into-me-see."[1] It is a close personal relationship in which one person allows another to see what is going on inside of him—communicating on a personal level. Couples must make the choice to open up and allow each other inside to experience intimacy. It means that both spouses communicate at the deeper levels of communication to express their emotions, feelings, hurts and desires.

People are created for intimacy and relationship. God created Eve as a helper suitable for Adam. Mankind was not created to be alone and it is through relationship that people mature and flourish. The world today has more ways to communicate and stay in touch with each other than ever before, yet, for all the conveniences available, many people are very lonely. Living for self is not the way to meet relationship needs, yet so many people live only for themselves. Giving one's life to another person, seeking to know him and to be known, is how God created mankind, and it makes life fulfilling.

Usually, one spouse or the other will find it hard to honestly reveal his deeper thoughts and emotions to build intimacy in the relationship. While men typically have a harder time communicating their feelings and showing their emotions, at times the situation is reversed and the husband finds it easier to communicate than the wife. A couple must work together for intimacy to occur. The spouse who expresses himself more easily needs to help the other to open up and the spouse who has a hard time opening up needs to push himself to share his heart with his spouse. Deep, lasting intimacy will not occur unless both spouses are willing to work at it.

Intimacy with God

But the man who loves God is known by God.
~ 1 Corinthians 8:3

True intimacy with one's spouse begins with a close, intimate relationship with Jesus Christ. God desires relationship with His people. This is a reason God uses marriage as an example of His relationship with mankind. Couples will become more intimate in their relationship with each other as they mature in their relationship with the Lord together.

> *Love the Lord your God with all your heart and with all your soul and with all your mind and with all your strength.*
> *~ Mark 12:30*

A relationship with God is not a regimen of things to do and not do; it is loving God totally. The Lord calls believers His friends: He loves them and gave His life for them. It is difficult for Christians to develop a relationship with God through a whirlwind of activity of doing things for Him. The story of Mary and Martha in Luke chapter 10 demonstrates what the Lord thinks about the whirlwind of activity. Reading the Bible, going to church, and serving God aid the development of a relationship with Him, but God places higher value on prayer, worship and listening quietly to His voice.

God is relational. In the Garden of Eden, He walked with Adam and talked with him. His relationships with Noah, Abraham, Moses, David, Elijah and others throughout the Old Testament demonstrate His desire to be close to man. Jesus also demonstrated close, intimate relationships while He walked the earth. His relationships with the disciples, Lazarus, Mary, Martha and others show how He opened up to the people He knew. He took His closest friends with Him to the Garden of Gethsemane during His darkest hour to support Him as He bore the greatest burden of all time. God does not walk and talk with mankind today as He once did, but it does not diminish the fact that He desires relationship with people. The subtle, faith based relationship between mankind and God is just as powerful today as the face-to-face relationships of Biblical times.

The marriage relationship illustrates God's relationship with His people. It is a love relationship. Jesus Christ demonstrated His great love for people by dying for them. He reveals Himself to His people through His Word, miraculous signs, nature, circumstances and other people. Loving the Lord and seeking Him through prayer, worship, study, meditation and service allows people to draw into a deeper, more intimate relationship with God.

The couple that actively brings God into their marriage relationship will be stronger than the couple attempting to build their relationship on their own strength. Individual intimacy with God is crucial to the relationship that hopes to be centered on Jesus Christ. A strong, close—intimate relationship with God is central to the fortified marriage that will grow and strengthen though the seasons of life.

Peter thinks 'becoming one flesh' with Mary sounds pretty strange.

Becoming One Flesh

It is not good for man to be alone. God created man to be relational: first, with God, then with one's spouse and finally, with others. Relationships are an integral part of who people are as human beings, but they do not just happen. You must be purposeful for a relationship to grow. Intimacy is the result of continued work and effort by both husband and wife and is critical to a healthy marriage relationship. Intimacy moves a couple beyond the superficial to a deeper—oneness relationship.

God created Adam and Eve for relationship and oneness. They were naked and felt no shame (Genesis 2:25). The first couple was open with each other emotionally and spiritually. Sin brought shame and the lack of intimacy. Growing apart is easy, but it takes work to build intimacy and move toward oneness in marriage. Sinful mankind naturally tends toward selfishness and self-centeredness. A couple must work on their relationship to make it what God created it to be.

Oneness means that "two shall be one flesh, shall be considered as one body, having no separate or independent rights, privileges, cares, concerns, etc., each being equally interested in all things that concern the marriage state."[2] Two people do not give up who they are as people; oneness is not "sameness." But, when they marry, they choose to give their lives to another person. Both husband and wife give up the right to do whatever they please; they choose to live within the marriage relationship and share their whole life with each other. "Socially, legally, physically, emotionally, every which way, there is just no other means of getting closer to another human being, and never has been, than in marriage."[3] There is a cost to that closeness - giving up the separateness that was a right before marriage.

The mystery of oneness is a difficult concept to grasp. It is a process that begins on the wedding day and continues throughout life together. Husband and wife become bound together in the totality of their lives. Living the concept of oneness on a daily basis is impossible without God's intervention. Participating in the candle lighting ceremony on their wedding day does not prepare a couple for the flames of independence and selfishness that will rise up during the conflict that will come in marriage. Dying to self, trusting an imperfect spouse, giving when you don't want to give, revealing your deepest darkest self and loving your spouse no matter what are all aspects of oneness. Oneness means that two people will cleave to each other and choose to develop and work at intimacy with each other over all other people.

Intimacy gives another person the power to hurt you terribly. No one is potentially more harmful than a spouse to whom you have revealed your inner self. More importantly, intimacy also offers the power to heal one another, the power to bless and minister to one another as no other person on the face of the earth can.

Separateness versus Connectedness

Connection with your spouse is critical to developing intimacy in your relationship. It is not based simply on the amount of time a couple spends together, but the time they spend with a shared life. Doing activities together does not necessarily mean that a couple is connected and building intimacy. Yet, most activities can be a point of connection. Watching television all evening and then going to bed with only some superficial communication is not connection. Watching television and then discussing what was seen and how it relates to life does build connection. Two people can live together for many years and not enjoy intimacy in their life together. There are couples that, after many years together, have very little idea of who their spouse is.

Any marriage relationship can fall into separation and isolation. If a couple does not actively seek connection, they will become isolated from each other. Busy schedules and the demands of career, family, household upkeep, and ministry can keep a couple from connecting with each other. The turmoil of activities in and around the home contributes to separateness not connectedness. A couple must carve out time on a daily basis to connect with each other and be a part of each other's lives.

> ***"Successful couples are those who are in touch with each other's emotional worlds."***
> ***~ John Gottman***

Regular interaction at the deeper levels of communication is necessary to remain connected as a couple. Both spouses must work at including the other in their worlds; work, home, ministry and activities. They must be deliberate and purposeful about including each other in their lives. Couples who share their lives, their emotions, feelings, hurt and desires with each other remain connected and grow in intimacy.

It is possible to establish connection even if you and your spouse are presently disconnected and living separate lives under the same roof. Some couples develop comfortableness in dysfunctional relationships and can be resistant to change. They are not happy, but they don't want to cause problems by initiating change. Achieving genuine intimacy with your spouse is impossible without change. Change begins with one person making the commitment to do things God's way rather than the way he has been doing it. It will take some time, but change will occur once one spouse begins seeking connection.

> *"Everyone has the ability to move from self-consciousness and separation to authentic connection." ~ Carla Kimball*

Take an interest in your spouse. Seek to know and understand who he is and where he is in life. It is interest in each other that kindled the relationship in the first place, and your spouse will respond to your interest in him.

For Discussion as a Couple

1. How do you define intimacy? What does intimacy mean to your marriage?

____
____
____
____

2. Why is it important to develop intimacy with God? How do you do this?

____
____
____
____

3. What does it mean to be "one" with your spouse?

____
____
____
____

4. How do you become one with your spouse?

____
____
____
____

5. How can a husband and wife develop connection in their marriage relationship?

____
____
____
____

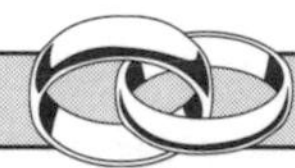

Intimacy in Marriage

Study 31

Reconnecting through Forgiveness

Forgive us our sins, for we also forgive everyone who sins against us.
~ Luke 11:4

"Forgiveness is both a decision and a real change in emotional experience. That change in emotion is related to better mental and physical health."
~ Everett L. Worthington

Many people enter marriage thinking that life will be one of the "happily ever after" stories they read about. They believe love will conquer any problems that come their way, but their fairy tale views of marriage change very quickly as the pressures of life and the reality of a fallen world shake them out of their dream state. No matter how "good" a person is; he cannot be perfect. Sooner or later one spouse will hurt the other. The wedding does not bring together Prince Charming and Cinderella to live happily ever after, but two descendants of Adam and Eve who have a propensity to sin and act very selfishly.

Forgiveness is central to Christianity, and an extremely important part of the marriage relationship. It is only through God's forgiveness of a person's sin that he can have a relationship with Him. Jesus Christ's atoning sacrifice makes it possible for mankind to be reconciled with God. While God's forgiveness covers all sin, when people sin, they damage their connection with God. Repentance restores the connection and the relationship continues to grow. In this same way, sin in the marriage relationship will damage or break the connection between husband and wife. Repentance and forgiveness restores the connection and intimacy to the relationship.

Forgiveness: "The act of excusing or pardoning another in spite of his slights, shortcomings and errors."[1] "Forgiveness is a gracious act, a favor, or a gift. It is something that cannot be earned or demanded from the guilty."[2] When one person forgives another, he lets go of any claim for justice or debt owed. One does not forgive and forget, but he does choose to give up resentment and any opportunity for retaliation. There are two parts of forgiveness: the act of making a conscious decision to forgive one's spouse or other person and the process of working through the pain and hurt resulting from the wrong that was done.

Forgiveness is not just an occasional act: it is a permanent attitude.
~Martin Luther King

The lack of forgiveness is a huge problem in marriages and society as a whole. Many people suffer emotional, psychological, mental and even physical problems due to a lack of forgiveness, either not giving or not accepting forgiveness. Just as sin or emotional injury will break connection, unforgiveness will keep the connection broken. A marriage will wither and die without forgiveness. Only forgiveness will truly restore the connection and begin to repair the intimacy.

Couples must not ignore problems and hurt caused by one spouse or the other as it can lead to bitterness and permanent relationship damage. Addressing hurt in a non-hurtful manner and going through the process to bring about forgiveness will build intimacy and the relationship overall.

Unforgiveness and its psychological baggage of hostility and bitterness can put people at risk for mental illness such as depression and anxiety.[3]

Healing will come to the marriage through forgiveness.

God's Forgiveness

When Adam and Eve disobeyed God and ate of the forbidden fruit, they broke their close relationship with God and changed the world dramatically forever. God's justice requires atonement for sin. In other words, someone has to pay. Every person is born into sin, and, through his own selfish, sinful ways falls short of the perfection that God requires (see Romans 3:23). The bad news is that no human being can measure up. The good news is that God provided His own sacrifice to pay the debt of mankind's sin once and for all through the death of Jesus Christ. Jesus willingly gave Himself as the perfect sacrifice so that the relationship with God could be restored.

God demonstrates his own love for us in this: While we were still sinners, Christ died for us. ~ Romans 5:8

Out of God's grace (getting what you don't deserve) and mercy (not getting what you deserve) Jesus took on the sin of the world and paid the price for mankind's sin. That forgiveness is consummated when a person accepts Jesus Christ as Savior, acknowledges his sin, and asks for God's forgiveness. Undeserved forgiveness sets Christianity apart from all other religions. People do not find this grace anywhere else.

Therefore, my brothers, I want you to know that through Jesus the forgiveness of sins is proclaimed to you. ~ Acts 13:38

When God forgives, He no longer holds a person's sin against him. He is free from sin—all of his sin, forever. Even after becoming Christians, everyone continues to sin, but God's forgiveness is once and for all. He forgave it all and promises not to remember the sin of a person that turns his life over to Him (Hebrews 8:12).

God's Forgiveness in Your Life

Forgiveness is a necessary part of the Christian's life. It is the foundation of a person's relationship with God, and it also should be an integral part of his daily life. The Lord says to forgive as you have been forgiven. God gave His forgiveness unconditionally, and Christians are to do likewise. God has canceled the debt owed to Him, and believers are to cancel the debt owed to them by others.

Bear with each other and forgive whatever grievances you may have against one another. Forgive as the Lord forgave you. ~Colossians 3:13-14

Forgiveness is not easy. In fact, true forgiveness is impossible apart from the power of God. Forgiveness is a choice, a decision to release someone from the penalty of retribution for any crime they have committed against you, but it does not mean that the offense is acceptable. "Forgiveness goes beyond human fairness; it is pardoning those things that can't readily be pardoned at all."[4] The process begins with remembering what God has done for you and deciding that you will conduct yourself as Christ would want you to act, rather than doing what you feel like doing.

The Apostle Peter probably thought he was being very gracious when he asked Jesus if he should forgive his brother up to seven times. It must have been a shock to hear Jesus respond, "not seven times, but seventy times seven."[5] Essentially, Jesus said to forgive as many times as it takes. It is an attitude and way of life Christians are to have, not an act they do when they feel like it.

Tommy really didn't want to hear that he had to forgive Bobby seventy times seven times.

Forgiveness does not necessarily take away the consequences of the injury or sin. Some people hurt another, ask for forgiveness and once granted, expect that everything will be the same as before. Deep emotional hurt may take a long time to completely heal, even though a person has forgiven another for the hurt. Trust takes time to rebuild and the consequences of hurt may have long-term affects on the relationship.

There are many factors that affect forgiveness. One consideration is the nature of the offence. Accidentally stepping on someone's toe is much different than committing adultery. Most offenses require a simple, "I'm sorry, will you forgive me?" Adultery, long term hidden sin that surfaces, or physical abuse may require counseling and even temporary separation before the relationship can be restored. This doesn't mean that the person offended hasn't forgiven; it means that he is protecting himself and utilizing a system of healthy boundaries.

> ***"In your anger do not sin": Do not let the sun go down while you are still angry, and do not give the devil a foothold.***
> ***~ Ephesians 4:26-28***

Many people find Matthew 6:14, 15 a hard Bible passage to understand. It says that if a person does not forgive, God will not forgive him. Biblically, God's forgiveness is unconditional and total; it is past tense and complete. What must be asked of the unforgiving person is; "what difference has God's forgiveness made in your life?" If he refuses to forgive any offense against him, has he really accepted God's forgiveness of the sin in his life? Forgiveness is not an option, God commands Christians to forgive those who offend them. God forgave those who accept Him as their Lord and Savior even though He knows they will continue to sin against Him.

Forgiveness in Marriage

When one spouse offends the other, intimacy is injured or broken depending on the nature of the wrong. Restoring intimacy in the relationship requires that the offending spouse be humble and willing to ask for forgiveness, and that the offended spouse be honest and open about the hurt. Burying the hurt does not build intimacy in the marriage. Both spouses must work together to ensure intimacy is maintained in the relationship. If one is hurt, he needs to speak up, in love.

It is important that the offending spouse ask for forgiveness unconditionally. He must: confess his offense, accept responsibility, offer no excuse or attempt to shift the blame, and acknowledge the hurt and pain caused, demonstrate repentance and change his behavior. When a person asks for forgiveness this way, it is much easier for his spouse to grant forgiveness.

Granting forgiveness is also necessary in the marriage relationship. Forgiveness acknowledges the offense, relates the hurt and pain caused by it and then lets it go. Having granted forgiveness, your life together can continue toward oneness. Is there a cost? Yes, you will give up the right to hold his offense over him, give up the hope that he will completely understand your hurt and give up any hope of retribution. Restoration of trust, feelings of intimacy, love and open communication may take time and work, but it doesn't begin until forgiveness is granted.

> ***Forgiveness is not a feeling but a promise or commitment to three things:***
>
> 1. ***I will not use it against them in the future.***
> 2. ***I will not talk to others about them.***
> 3. ***I will not dwell on it myself.***
>
> ***~ Jay E. Adams***

Forgiveness Sets You Free

Granting forgiveness is more for the forgiver than the offender. The forgiver is not bound by the hurt and a victim of the offense when he forgives. He must give the pain to God, seek counseling if necessary and move forward.

Healthy boundaries are at the heart of a forgiving attitude. The person willing to forgive takes responsibility for his attitude and actions and not the offender's attitude and actions. He forgives, not because he feels like it, but because it is God's desire. The forgiving person gives the offender to God and allows Him to work in his life. Forgiveness sets him free from the bondage of anger, bitterness and resentfulness, and he can live in peace because of this freedom.

It is your choice: forgive and allow God to restore the relationship or don't forgive and allow your flesh to break down intimacy and even tear apart your relationship. You can allow God to work through you, or you can hold onto the hurt and allow it to eat at you, until it destroys you. Choosing forgiveness will bring intimacy to your marriage.

> ***Be kind and compassionate to one another, forgiving each other, just as in Christ God forgave you. ~ Ephesians 4:32***

For Discussion as a Couple

1. Did you marry thinking you would live happily ever after with no problems? What made you realize there would be problems in your marriage?

____

____

____

____

2. Is forgiveness a problem in your marriage? How?

____

____

____

____

3. Why is forgiveness important in the marriage relationship?

____

____

____

____

4. When have you had a problem forgiving your spouse?

____

____

____

____

5. How can you grant forgiveness and still maintain healthy boundaries?

____

____

____

____

Marital Intimacy Inventory

Complete the following inventory by carefully reading each of the twenty statements below and circle the number that is most representative of your response for each statement. Take the inventory separately and then discuss your answers with your spouse.

	Always	Usually	Sometimes	Rarely	Never
1. I share deeply personal information with my spouse.	1	2	3	4	5
2. My spouse shares deeply personal information with me.	1	2	3	4	5
3. I feel heard, understood and validated when I reveal my hurts or disappointments to my spouse.	1	2	3	4	5
4. My spouse and I reserve time of quality communication for just the two of us.	1	2	3	4	5
5. Asking for and giving forgiveness occurs easily in our relationship.	1	2	3	4	5
6. We talk about the good times and blessings we have enjoyed as a couple.	1	2	3	4	5
7. I'm comfortable communicating my sexual desires and preferences to my spouse.	1	2	3	4	5
8. I feel an oneness, a close connection with my spouse.	1	2	3	4	5
9. We have a mutual unconditional acceptance of each other.	1	2	3	4	5
10. Regular displays of affection are a part of our relationship.	1	2	3	4	5
11. We enjoy activities for just the two of us.	1	2	3	4	5
12. We experience connection on a daily basis.	1	2	3	4	5
13. Our marriage is generally positive.	1	2	3	4	5
14. I trust my spouse.	1	2	3	4	5
15. My needs are generally met.	1	2	3	4	5
16. My spouse expresses appreciation for me.	1	2	3	4	5

Continued next page

Marital Intimacy Inventory (continued)

	Always	Usually	Sometimes	Rarely	Never
17. We pray together daily.	1	2	3	4	5
18. I feel respected by my spouse.	1	2	3	4	5
19. We are able to resolve our differences.	1	2	3	4	5
20. I feel close to my spouse.	1	2	3	4	5

Scoring: Add all circled items to derive your total score and enter it here: __________

30 or less:	Your marriage is exceptional, keep working at it!
31 – 50:	Very strong keep improving!
51 – 70:	You need to begin working on developing intimacy.
70 or above:	There is little intimacy in your marriage, seek help or counseling and begin working to build intimacy into your marriage.

What did you learn about yourself from this inventory? Your spouse? ______________________

____

____

What are your thoughts and impressions of this inventory? ______________________________

____

____

____

Discuss this inventory with your spouse as you have time. Do not use this inventory to criticize your spouse, but use this information to constructively build your marital intimacy.

Intimacy in Marriage
Study 32
Building Intimacy

Can two walk together, unless they are agreed? ~ Amos 3:3

Intimacy and the Marriage Relationship

A marriage relationship growing in oneness will be characterized by an increasing interdependence. Both spouses become more dependent on each other as their lives integrate and become one unit. A couple needs to develop oneness in each area of life; spiritually, socially, recreationally, intellectually, sexually and emotionally. There will be fewer separate friends and more mutual friends as the years pass and the melding of their lives will be so complete that people often won't know them individually as much as they know them as a couple.

This type of intimacy, this oneness, doesn't happen naturally or without work—a lot of work. A couple must make a conscious decision to work together to build intimacy in their marriage. Both husband and wife must take the risk of opening up their hearts and learning to relate to each other in ways that draw them together rather than pull them apart. They utilize the knowledge of their differences to cultivate their relationship and not bicker about their differences. It is easy to allow the busyness of life to break down intimacy and ruin the relationship. A couple committed to strengthening their marriage will take the steps necessary to build and maintain intimacy in their relationship.

A strong, solid marriage is not possible without intimacy. Couples could be married for 25, 30, even 50 years and yet not have intimacy in their relationship. They have existed together for many years, raising children and even working through problems, but lack intimacy in their relationship and know very little about each other. A long marriage doesn't prove that it is intimate and fortified. A couple may not know any different and even though they have a dysfunctional, unproductive marriage, they aren't aware that there are other options. The truth of this will usually show up in the next generation through divorce and the broken marriages they experience. Making a difference in the lives of your children and others and leaving a positive legacy requires a strong, intimate marriage relationship.

Differences

Gender, personality and environmental differences greatly affect intimacy in a relationship. People are very different for a variety of reasons and couples do not naturally understand their spouse and the differences between them. Intimacy will grow when both spouses seek to understand each other and use their differences to build their relationship rather than allow their differences to break down the relationship.

Those newly in love focus on their similarities and think their differences are cute, but once married, couples tend to focus on the ways they are different and allow them to cause separation.

Most couples wonder what happened to their relationship after a few years. They enjoyed each other when dating, during courtship and for some period of time after marriage. The caring, respectful, romantic man she knew has disappeared, and in his place is this non-communicative, rude man who works too much and doesn't ever seem to notice her. Similarly, the supportive, appreciative, respectful woman he once knew has been replaced by a nagging, unresponsive woman who tries to change him and never seems to want sex. Couples do not realize that, while a certain amount of change is inevitable, the romance and intimacy in their relationship will die unless it is continually cultivated.

Men and women view their wedding very differently. The wedding day is the end of a quest for a man. He has won the prize and can now relax and return to his old ways. The woman is ready to begin the real work of building their relationship. The resulting conflict drives the couple apart until they learn the principles of building intimacy or they quit the marriage. Once committed to building the marriage and intimacy, the couple can take the steps necessary to build an intimate, lasting marriage that will withstand any storm that comes against it.

Steps to Building Intimacy

> *"Presence is more than just being there."*
> *~ Malcolm Forbes*

Couples must be present physically and emotionally to build intimacy. Overly busy lives and "weekend marriages," where couples spend time together only on weekends, damage rather than help a marriage relationship. Problems cannot be solved and the relationship cannot be nurtured unless there is time to communicate. Interpersonal interaction, communication and working together build intimacy, while emotional distance and busyness breaks down intimacy. It is necessary to make your relationship a priority.

A couple moves either toward or away from intimacy. A continued lack of intimacy in the relationship puts a couple in a downward spiral of pain and hurt that will continue throughout the marriage. Yet, it is never too late to reverse the trend and begin building intimacy in your relationship. Beginning with a commitment to each other, a couple can spend time together and begin working on each of the aspects of intimacy:

- Acceptance
- Respect
- Honesty
- Trust
- Open communication
- Met needs
- Friendship
- Intimacy

Accepting your spouse unconditionally is foundational to intimacy. This doesn't mean that you accept sin in his life, but it does mean that you accept him for who he is and do not attempt to change him or make him into someone you think he should be.

Respect; *to place value on or to treat with consideration or courtesy* builds a person's self esteem and makes him feel important and valued. The respected spouse feels closer and more connected to his spouse.

Complete honesty promotes intimacy as a couple shares their lives together without hiding anything emotionally from each other. Couples must be truthful with each other even when their spouse may not like the truth.

Trust is not a right but must be earned. A person is trusted by proving him self trustworthy. His word, especially to his spouse, should be something that can be trusted and counted on. The only secrets a couple should have are surprises they have for each other on occasion.

Open communication is communicating at the deeper levels openly and honestly. Intimacy in a marriage requires that spouses communicate needs, feelings and desires. It is a matter of letting your spouse into every aspect of your life.

There will not be intimacy when needs are not met. Couples should be concerned about each other's needs. Meeting the needs of your spouse builds intimacy in the relationship.

The Importance of Friendship

> ***Enjoy life with your wife, whom you love, ~ Ecclesiastes 9:9***

Couples usually begin their relationship with friendship. They can talk for hours about anything and the friendship blooms into a romance. Once married, the feelings of romance wear off, they begin pursuing their own interests, and the friendship fades. It becomes more of a business partnership than God's idea for marriage.

Friendship doesn't come naturally, especially with someone as different as a couple tends to be. A couple must make a decision to be friends - to work at it and cultivate the relationship. Some separate interests are natural and healthy, but it is important to develop mutual interests also. What can you do together – as friends? There most-likely will have to be some compromise in this area. It may not be easy to come up with something you both like to do, but the pursuit of mutual interests can expand your horizons individually and as a couple.

Can you serve in ministry together? Joint service projects? Teaching a Sunday school class together? Is there a craft you both might like doing? Working on puzzles together? Bargain shopping together? Exercising together? Doing yard work together? It doesn't have to be expensive; the important thing is to find something you can enjoy together. Try participating in a hobby or activity your spouse has always done without you; you may find that you like it.

It is critical that a couple get time away for just the two of them. Whether it is a "date night," going for a walk, locking yourselves in the bedroom for an hour or going for a drive, your marriage relationship needs time away from the children, family and friends. Take time for just the two of you to nurture your friendship and build intimacy.

Spiritual Intimacy through Prayer

> ***And pray in the Spirit on all occasions with all kinds of prayers and requests. With this in mind, be alert and always keep on praying for all the saints. ~ Ephesians 6:18***

The goal of prayer is intimacy with God. Regularly communicating with God together will also build intimacy with each other. Praying as a couple lets God into your marriage relationship. During those times of prayer and seeking the Lord, God will be near to you. When a couple prays together, life seems safe and secure. The intimate sharing and the deep connecting of prayer together is a very special, intimate time with God and your spouse. Prayer brings intimate knowledge of the shape of one another's souls.

Praying together is not an easy exercise for most couples. Whether it is spiritual immaturity, a lack of the spiritual disciplines, or not seeing the need for prayer, couples often do not want to pray together. It takes time and perseverance for prayer to become a part of a couple's life together. Prayer is important to God. Jesus demonstrated this importance through a strong prayer life. The Lord will bless a couple's efforts with a sense of His closeness, and there will be a new level of intimacy and strength as a couple perseveres in prayer.

Some practical pointers: Start simple; do not have expectations and remember that Jesus commended the man who simply beat his chest and said; "have mercy on me, a sinner." There is no certain way to pray, and grand sounding words are not necessary. Commit to a convenient time for both of you to stop and spend a few minutes in prayer together. You may start with Scripture as part of your prayer; there are many wonderful prayers in the Psalms. Read a portion of scripture to begin your time of prayer. Praise God for what He has done for you and be thankful in all circumstances. Have patience and stick with it; in time prayer will become a vital part of your walk with God and your relationship with each other. Satan and your flesh do not want you to spend time in prayer, alone or with your spouse. Resist the temptation not to pray, especially when you are not happy with each other—persevere!

> ***Finally, brothers, whatever is true, whatever is noble, whatever is right, whatever is pure, whatever is lovely, whatever is admirable—if anything is excellent or praiseworthy—think about such things.***
> ***~ Philippians 4:8***

The Positive Influence

A positive person will draw his spouse into intimacy more than someone with a critical, negative attitude. You will not build intimacy criticizing and pointing out your spouse's deficiencies. Everyone reacts better to encouragement and uplifting than to belittling and put-downs. Marriage researcher, Dr. John Gottman states that negativity can overwhelm the relationship and break it up, and that relationships require a 5 to 1 ratio of positivity to negativity to grow and be fulfilling for both spouses.[1] Couples need to replace negativity in marriage with positivity.

"Honey, you are going to say something encouraging and uplifting, aren't you?"

A person will positively influence his spouse when he shows interest, affection, care, appreciation, concern, empathy, and acceptance. Accomplished even in small ways, these actions will build intimacy and draw couples closer together. This needs to be accomplished on a regular basis and must offset negativity in the relationship. This pattern is seen in healthy marriages and contributes to the positive outlook these couples have.

Positive marriages with strong intimacy usually are characterized by balanced priorities. When priorities are out of balance, couples will struggle with intimacy and in their marriage. A person's priorities should be God is first, spouse second, and then children, provision for the family, extended family and friends, ministry and finally recreation and hobbies. At times, spouses feel that they only receive what is left over after their spouse has accomplished everything else he wants to do. When a spouse feels that he is top priority, it is easier for him to be more positive in return. Balanced priorities build intimacy in the marriage relationship.

At the end of life, few people ever say they wished they had worked more hours or given

more time to ministry. Usually, if they could live life over again, they would slow down and take more time to enjoy life and relationships. No one regrets an intimate relationship with his spouse, but many regret the intimacy they never had. Building intimacy with your spouse takes time and work, but it makes life more meaningful.

Intimacy is a responsibility. When a person allows another into his life and to see the inner most parts of his being, he opens himself up to the possibility of great hurt and pain. Couples must guard their intimacy and keep it between the two of them. One careless conversation with another person can break trust and tear down intimacy. It is beneficial to have a close confidant to turn to in times of trouble, but there should never be intimacy with another person of the opposite sex. Intimacy is to be reserved for the husband and wife only.

For Discussion as a Couple

1. Why is intimacy so important in your marriage relationship? How is intimacy demonstrated between husband and wife?

____

____

____

____

2. How do the differences between you and your spouse affect your intimacy?

____

____

____

____

3. What are some specific things you can do to build intimacy in your marriage relationship?

____

____

____

____

4. Do you pray together regularly? If not, how can you get started?

____

____

____

____

5. Is your marriage relationship generally positive? What can you do to make it more positive?

____

____

____

____

____

Intimacy in Marriage

Study 33

Keeping Romance Alive

I belong to my lover, and his desire is for me.
~ Song of Solomon 7:10

"There is no such thing as the 'naturally romantic' person—like most things, romance is practiced and perfected.
~ Julie Steeper

Romance is an important part of intimacy in the marriage relationship. The feelings of love bloom when spouses intentionally display love and affection toward one another. Intimacy builds as a couple does little things throughout each day to show they are thinking of each other.

Romance in the Marriage Relationship

Many people today have a distorted view of romance. Some think romance is childish and for the young and irresponsible. Others spend their lives chasing the romantic feeling that is felt at the beginning of a new love relationship. Marriage relationships tend to suffer because of a lack of romance and many people divorce seeking that romantic feeling. They don't realize that romance will fade unless it is cultivated and too often they allow the daily activities of life to choke out romance in their marriage. Many couples get to the point where they do not even remember what makes their spouse feel loved.

Do you know what makes your spouse feel loved?

God's plan for marriage includes an ongoing romantic relationship between husband and wife. The Song of Solomon is a book of love relating the story King Solomon, his discovery of a beautiful woman and their love for each other. It is a sensual story and, for that reason, some argue that it should not even be a part of Holy Scripture. This book, written more than 3,000 years ago, gives a glimpse of what God desired when He created man and woman for each other. Above all else, the Song of Solomon is a book of romance.

Romance is the intimate display of love between two people. There are many ways to demonstrate love, but romance is reserved only for a spouse. Couples usually are very romantic before marriage and then often allow romance to die out when the honeymoon is over. Once married, men tend to be romantic only when they want sex from their wife. The wife often doesn't do anything romantic for her husband, but waits for him to romance her. She is disappointed when he isn't romantic or tires of his crude gestures signifying his desire for sex.

There is an important distinction to make between romance and the romantic love stage. The romantic love stage is a period of euphoria at the beginning of a love relationship and will end in a relatively short period of time.[1] Research shows that chemicals in the body are partly responsible for the feelings of love during the romantic love stage.[2] Couples experiencing this love see the world differently and will do virtually anything to spend time with the love of their life. Understanding this difference can help a couple put romance into its proper perspective.

The Romance Does Not Have to End

The romantic love stage of the relationship may fade with familiarity, demands of friends and family, career and the mundane day-to-day responsibilities of life, but romance can continue for the life of the relationship. Far too many marriages experience the death of romance. Their marriage may continue and can even be fruitful and productive, but there is no passion in their relationship. Romance gives life to the relationship and it can be vibrant and alive even when a couple reaches the twilight years of their lives. It takes conscious effort to keep the flames of romance burning in a marriage relationship.

> ***Romance takes ongoing, conscious, daily effort.***

Men have a tendency to understand romance only as a means to initiate sex. They make some nominal effort at romance to indicate to their wife that they are interested in sex. What they don't usually realize is that romance and sex are two different aspects of their marriage relationship. Romance often is a precursor to the sexual act, but is much more than just an initiator of sex. Sex is the physically intimate relationship between husband and wife that takes place when they have time alone. Romance is an all day process of ensuring a spouse knows that he is loved and thought of. Holding hands, a quick kiss on the cheek, a whispered "I love you," phone calls during the day, a wink and a blown kiss—these and hundreds more gestures constitute the romantic relationship.

A woman needs to feel emotionally close to her husband to feel romantic. Sexual precursors usually do not make her feel romantic. Speaking her love language, meeting her needs, displaying non-sexual affection and communicating intimately will make a woman feel loved. Women must also remember that romance is not only the husband's responsibility. She also needs to extend herself to do those things that will make him feel loved. A couple can keep romance in their relationship or bring it back, if it has dwindled. Romance can put the thrill back into a marriage relationship as a couple experiences each other's love.

> ***A successful marriage requires falling in love many times, always with the same person. ~ Mignon McLaughlin***

An On-Going Love Affair

In today's culture many people think of a love affair as something illicit—a secretive, adulterous love. The world has tried to convince people that this type of affair is more exciting and fun than love in marriage. The dictionary defines love affair as "a relationship or episode between lovers, especially a romantic or sexual one."[3] A love affair is not limited to illicit lovers, but can and should be enjoyed within the marriage relationship. God desires that couples enjoy the thrills, joy and lasting satisfaction of a love affair in their marriage. His will is that in every marriage, the couple will love each other with an absorbing spiritual, emotional, and physical attraction that continues to grow throughout their lifetime together.

When love begins between a man and woman, it doesn't take much work. Everything seems to just happen. They very much want only to be with each other, hate to be away from each other, constantly think about each other, and do whatever they can for each other. Sure, a relationship will change over the years, but it does not have to lose the excitement and allure that is characteristic of those first months of being in love. Intimate relationships do not improve spontaneously, and troubled relationships do not get better on their own. Couples must choose to work at their marriage relationship, love their spouse and pursue romance with them.

> ***"If you would be loved, love and be lovable." ~ Benjamin Franklin***

Neil Anderson's Order of Scripture applies to the romantic relationship in marriage; a couple must know the truth, believe the truth, walk in the truth and then the feelings will follow. Knowing that it is God's plan that they love their spouse, a couple believes that truth, makes the choice to walk in love and the feelings will follow. True love comes out of a *decision* to love another person. People who allow their feelings to rule their life tend to lead very unhappy lives.

> ***May your fountain be blessed, and may you rejoice in the wife of your youth. A loving doe, a graceful deer — may her breasts satisfy you always, may you ever be captivated by her love. ~ Proverbs 5:18-19***

The feelings of love can be restored in marriage. The process of that restoration begins with a choice to love your spouse without regard to how you feel. Consistently choosing to love your spouse and do loving things for them will bring the feelings of love back.

Truths about Love:

- The Word of God teaches the truth about love.
- Love is not some mystical experience; it is understandable and rational.
- Love does not come naturally and it is not simple or easy.
- Love is not an uncontrollable feeling.
- People can learn to love.
- People can choose to love.
- Giving love will gain love.
- Love recognizes value in the one loved.
- Love seeks the best for the one loved.
- Love is a choice backed up by action.
- Love is costly.

1 Corinthians 13 clarifies the meaning of love. Living the principles of love in this great chapter will improve romance and intimacy in any marriage relationship. Consider some of the main points from the *Love Chapter*:

- Love is patient.
- Love is kind.
- It does not envy.
- It does not boast.
- It is not proud.
- It is not rude.
- It is not self-seeking.
- It is not easily angered.
- It keeps no record of wrongs.
- Love does not delight in evil but rejoices with the truth.
- It always protects, always trusts, always hopes, and always perseveres.
- Love never fails.

The Romantic

It doesn't take Don Juan, Casanova or a genius to figure romance out. Understanding your spouse's needs and love language provides much of the information one needs to be incredibly romantic. A little thought and creativity will help anyone become an incurably romantic person. Romancing your spouse can be a great deal of fun as you think of new ways to express your love for them. It is not a sin to get help romancing your spouse! Borrow ideas from friends or check out the resources available in this manual. Simply Romantic Nights; by Dennis & Barbara Rainey or 101 Nights of Grrreat Romance; by Laura Corn will give you many excellent ideas for sparking romance in your marriage. There are many inexpensive, fun, romantic things you can do to build intimacy in your marriage, although it takes some thought.

In his first attempt to be romantic, Adam merely states the obvious.

Non-sexual affection is a very important aspect of a romantic relationship. Holding hands, kissing, non-sexual touching of different parts of the body all builds romance into the relationship.

Play with your spouse and flirt with him or her. You are never too old to have fun and having fun with your spouse will strengthen your marriage.

Both spouses need to exert effort to bring romance into their marriage, but as leader of the home, it is primarily the husband's responsibility to cultivate and initiate romance. Solomon and his lover both extended themselves to express love and build romance. Every couple can also have great romance in their relationship.

The Romantic Person:

- Surprises his or her spouse.
- Dates his or her spouse, making plans to go out together.
- Is creative; doing different and new things.
- Expresses daily acts of care, concern, love, speaking his or her spouse's love language and giving personal attention.
- Is committed; doing special things for his or her spouse whether they feel like it or not.
- Writes love letters or poems and sends cards.
- Communicate intimately.
- Touches his or her spouse frequently.

Think about it: babysitters are less expensive than marriage counselors.

For Discussion as a Couple

1. What is romance and why is it important to intimacy in marriage?

____
____
____
____

2. Why is it important that romance only occur between husband and wife? What damage could be done if romance (even if there is no sex) occurs outside the marriage?

____
____
____
____

3. Do you agree that romance does not have to end? Why or why not?

____
____
____
____

4. What can you do to feel love for your spouse? Is it something that happens naturally or does it have to be cultivated?

____
____
____
____

5. What can you do to increase the romance in your marriage?

____
____
____
____

Are You Romantic?

Take the following quiz to test your romantic awareness. Circle the number that best represents the last time you did each of the items. This is a snap shot of how romantic you are now. Don't give yourself extra points if you do something on a continual basis. Take the quiz separately and then discuss it with your spouse.

When was the last time you:	In the past... Week	Month	6 Mos	Year	Never
1. Said, "I love you" to your spouse?	10	7	5	3	0
2. Gave your spouse a hug "just because?"	10	7	5	3	0
3. Send your spouse a card?	10	7	5	3	0
4. Called your spouse during the day to say, "I love you?"	10	7	5	3	0
5. Gave your spouse a gift for no special reason?	10	7	5	3	0
6. Surprised your spouse with something special?	10	7	5	3	0
7. Taken your spouse out on a "date?"	10	7	5	3	0
8. Written a love letter to your spouse?	10	7	5	3	0
9. Given your spouse a back rub?	10	7	5	3	0
10. Purposefully spoken your spouse's love language?	10	7	5	3	0
11. Told your spouse that you appreciate them?	10	7	5	3	0
12. Sat down just the two of you and talked about your dreams and aspirations?	10	7	5	3	0
13. Kissed your spouse passionately for 30 seconds when sex was not involved?	10	7	5	3	0
14. Spent an entire evening together without distractions?	10	7	5	3	0
15. Went out to dinner, just the two of you?	10	7	5	3	0
16. Left a love note for your spouse to find?	10	7	5	3	0

Continued next page

Are You Romantic? (continued)

When was the last time you:	In the past... Week	Month	6 Mos	Year	Never
17. Did an errand for your spouse without them asking?	10	7	5	3	0
18. Whispered, "I love you" into your spouse's ear?	10	7	5	3	0
19. Did something non-verbal in public to tell your spouse "I love you?"	10	7	5	3	0
20. Gone for a walk together?	10	7	5	3	0

Scoring: Add all circled items to derive your total score and enter it here: __________

More than 170:	You are doing a great job, keep it up!
110 – 170:	Very romantic, keep improving!
60 – 110:	You could use some help, us this quiz for ideas of what you can do.
Below 60:	It is never too late to get started!

Did you learn some ways you might bring romance into your marriage? What? ______________

____

____

What are your thoughts and impressions of this quiz? ___________________________

____

____

____

Discuss this quiz with your spouse as you have time. Please do not use this quiz to criticize your spouse, but use this information to constructively build more romance into your marriage. The twenty items in this quiz are great ways to build romance, try them out!

Intimacy in Marriage

Study 34

Intimacy & Sex

Marriage should be honored by all, and the marriage bed kept pure, for God will judge the adulterer and all the sexually immoral. ~ Hebrews 13:4

Sex is an Important Part of Intimacy

Sex also is an important aspect of marital intimacy. The sexual relationship brings a physical and emotional oneness to the marriage that is not found in any other relationship. God created sex for much more than to multiply the human race. Many people find it hard to believe, but God intended sex for pleasure. Proverbs 5:15-15, Song of Solomon 7:10-13 and 1 Corinthians 7:3-5 bears this truth out. It is a pleasure only meant for the marriage relationship and it can build a wonderful intimacy that can continue throughout the life of the marriage.

Humans (both male and female) have twisted and perverted sex into something it was not meant to be. Today's generation may think they have seen the worst perversions of sex, but since the fall, God's plan has been distorted and abused in every way conceivable. The whole idea of temple prostitutes and worshipping gods through sexual activity is appalling. Yet, people very often turn to the culture rather than to the Bible for sexual ideals. The degradation of women through pornography and sex without commitment has continued through history. It is time for both men and women of God to reject the world's view of sex and embrace God's view.

The physical act of sex can be accomplished without any intimacy. Animals have "sex" and in the marriage relationship sex without intimacy does not honor either spouse or God. Very often women will give sex to get love and men will give love to get sex, but this is not what God intended for sex. Sex was meant to be the enactment of a close, intimate and loving relationship between a husband and wife. Sex brings together a man and woman in an act that is the culmination of all that their marriage represents. Godly sex that brings together husband and wife in oneness requires intimacy: spiritual, emotional, intellectual and physical.

The sexual relationship is meant to build up and enrich the marriage relationship. The natural, pleasurable enjoyment of sex is like the frosting on the cake of intimacy, but it is not the cake. A couple's intimate, connected relationship is the cake. A couple secure in their relationship with the Lord and each other give themselves wholly to each other to grow in their relationship and build oneness.

The husband should fulfill his marital duty to his wife, and likewise the wife to her husband. The wife's body does not belong to her alone but also to her husband. In the same way, the husband's body does not belong to him alone but also to his wife. Do not deprive each other except by mutual consent and for a time, so that you may devote yourselves to prayer. Then come together again so that Satan will not tempt you because of your lack of self-control. ~ 1 Corinthians 7:3-5

Marital Responsibility

Husbands and wives have a responsibility to take care of each other sexually. There is a duty to each other, but it is important to remember that God is to be the One to meet your needs. The 1 Corinthians 7 passage is about giving, not taking. A spouse who uses the Bible to justify selfish demands for sex does not take the whole counsel of God into account. The Bible also speaks of dying to self and learning to control one's body in a way that is holy and honorable. Demanding sex from your spouse is not holy or honorable.

> *"Sex should not be a conjugal duty to be endured, but an act of mutual pleasure and union."*
> *~ W.C. "Tres" Tanner*

An intimate, fulfilling sexual relationship will do a lot to keep sexual sin out of the marriage relationship. Using sex as a weapon to get your own way or to punish your spouse does not honor Biblical truths. Refusal of sex usually means there are deeper problems in the marriage. Sexual intimacy is the fulfillment of intimacy in marriage, not intimacy itself.

Male and Female Sexual Differences

Gender differences often are more pronounced in sexuality than any other area of the marriage relationship. These differences cause most of the conflict involving sexuality. Men tend to focus on the physical aspects of sex, while women focus on the emotional aspects. The chart on page 208 identifies the major differences between men's and women's sexuality. This is a generalization and may be different in your relationship, but it is important that you discuss the chart as a couple to discover your specific differences. Use this information to increase intimacy and grow in your sexual relationship.

Couples need to understand each other's sexuality. Far too often, sex is not discussed by anyone. Young people learn about sex from friends and improper experimentation, parents hide their sexuality from their children, and the church only discusses the evils of sexual sin. The result is that couples enter marriage ill-equipped and unprepared for a healthy sexual relationship. It is no wonder that sex is the center of much conflict in marriage.

Men must move beyond sexual intercourse solely for physical release to the total sexual experience. Women need affection and an emotional connection for a fully satisfying sexual encounter. Connecting emotionally through conversation, affirmation and non-sexual affection build a woman's intimate feelings and a desire for her husband. Once men begin to participate in a broader sexual experience, they usually find that it is much more fulfilling for them also.

Women must realize and understand how important sex is to her husband. Sex to a man is not just the physical aspects; there are emotional aspects also. Men need to feel sexually desired by their wives. Often, a woman will cut her husband down with disrespectful and unwarranted remarks. She needs to encourage her husband and build him up.

When a couple seeks to know and understand each other, meet each other's needs, build emotional intimacy, and romance each other, the sexual relationship will grow and flourish. Discussing their sexuality will help a couple improve their sexual relationship and build intimacy overall.

"Is that someone knocking at the neighbor's door?"

Sexual Problems

A majority of couples at one time or another, experience either physical and/or emotional problems in their sexual relationships. "Professionals" call this sexual dysfunction and it is much more than the discomfort or irritability of the wife's monthly menstruation. One spouse may not feel desire for the other, there may be difficulty with arousal, a spouse may not be able to achieve orgasm, or there may be physical pain during intercourse. There is a long list of potential causes for problems in a couple's sexual relationship. It includes:

- Physical problems (disease, nerve damage, organ failure, hormonal deficiencies, etc.).
- Childhood abuse.
- A repressive, legalistic upbringing.
- Inappropriate sex outside of marriage.
- Rape.
- Sexual sin.
- Depression.
- Chronic fatigue.
- Drug or alcohol abuse.
- Poor body image.
- Anxiety.
- Stresses of everyday life.
- An unfulfilling marriage.

It is essential that a couple work together to understand and overcome sexual problems. Some problems can be resolved through communication and providing emotional support. Physical problems may require treatment by a medical doctor and that often is the first course of action to determine any sexual problem. Counseling may be required for deep emotional problems or if problems persist and cannot be treated by a doctor.

> ***"Making love is about enhancing a couple's experience of love on all planes of their relationship and having their sexual union be the truest expression of that love." ~ Christopher McCluskey***

> ***I belong to my lover, and his desire is for me. Come, my lover, let us go to the countryside, let us spend the night in the villages. Let us go early to the vineyards to see if the vines have budded, if their blossoms have opened, and if the pomegranates are in bloom-- there I will give you my love. The mandrakes send out their fragrance, and at our door is every delicacy, both new and old, that I have stored up for you, my lover. ~ Song of Solomon 7:10-13***

A Healthy Sexual Relationship

God intended the sexual relationship between husband and wife to be a romantic, exciting and fulfilling dimension of marriage. It is possible for a couple to experience a passionate sexual relationship throughout their married life together. Yet, many couples do not experience a fulfilling sexual relationship. Once the romantic love stage dies out, sex tends to become mechanical, unexciting and unfulfilling. Couples usually do not understand that they must work at their sexual relationship as they do with the rest of their marriage relationship.

A healthy sexual relationship begins with a relationship with God. A couple needs to understand who they are and how they are created. Knowing your spouse is also important to the health of your sexual relationship. There are two aspects to knowing your spouse: understanding him, who he is, what his needs are and what makes him feel loved. The Bible also uses the term "know" at times to signify sexual relations. God intended that a couple experience a much deeper connection, a knowing of each other that is often experienced in the sexual union.

Healthy boundaries are important also. A person needs to be able to say, "yes" to the things he wants to do and "no" to the things he doesn't want to do. Respecting a spouse's boundaries does much to build intimacy, and, even when it doesn't seem like her "no, I'm tired" is unreasonable, respecting her right to say "no" will tend to

increase her love for you.

It is important that couples take care of themselves physically and attempt to look good for their spouse. This is not about attempting to maintain a perfect body using the plastic beauty seen in the media as an example. You will feel better about yourself if you take care of your body and your spouse will also notice. Men must remember that body odor, bad breath, or an unshaven face is not conducive to their wife feeling sexually open to him.

Intimacy and romance are required for a healthy, fulfilling sexual relationship. Sex is much more than the physical act and both husband and wife need to cultivate the other aspects of the relationship. Intimate, open communication, acceptance, affection, trust, honesty, respect, met needs and friendship will all enhance the sexual relationship. Sex is not a ten-minute exercise to complete the day; it is an all day love affair. A healthy sexual relationship requires daily intimacy and romance. No, you don't necessarily have to stop and devote two hours every day to tend to your spouse, but you do need to be compassionate, kind, humble, gentle and patient with your spouse during encounters with them. Cultivate a romantic love toward each other.

Therefore, as God's chosen people, holy and dearly loved, clothe yourselves with compassion, kindness, humility, gentleness and patience. ~ Colossians 3:12

Talking about sex is not an easy thing to do in most marriages. The culture is saturated with sexual imagery, but it tends to be taboo to talk about sex on a personal level. Sex is not evil, God created it and there is no shame to talk openly about sex in the marriage relationship. Communicate your likes and dislikes, what gets you in the mood for sex and how you can please each other. Discuss how you can put some excitement into your sexual relationship. Change the location and setting or atmosphere for your sexual encounter. Work together to revive your sex life. Plan for time alone without children where you can spend time growing in your sexual relationship.

Good sex doesn't just happen; it takes time and planning.

Drink water from your own cistern, running water from your own well. Should your springs overflow in the streets, your streams of water in the public squares? Let them be yours alone, never to be shared with strangers. May your fountain be blessed, and may you rejoice in the wife of your youth. A loving doe, a graceful deer-- may her breasts satisfy you always, may you ever be captivated by her love. ~ Proverbs. 5:15-19

A healthy sexual relationship will bring physical and emotional closeness. When sex is a profound expression of love, both will feel good about each other and themselves. Mutual giving is very important to this relationship. Both must care for the other and seek to meet each other's needs physically and emotionally. Honor your spouse and raise sex out of the mire of sin and place it before God as it was created to be. Use your imagination and all of your senses to create an exciting sexual relationship fulfilling and satisfying to both husband and wife. Become soul mates in every sense of the term.

"Sex can be a brief, incendiary encounter between relative strangers; it can be a desultory, mechanical act between partners who have grown weary of each other; or it can be a glowing, lasting healing experience between people who have become spiritual soul mates." ~ Dr. Pat Love

Regarding a healthy sexual relationship:

1. *Non-sexual intimacy and romance will build the sexual relationship.*
2. *Sexual fidelity is imperative, physically, mentally and emotionally.*
3. *Be sensitive to each other's needs.*
4. *Never use sex as a weapon.*
5. *Don't hold back unless both agree.*
6. *Be open and honest with each other. If you don't like something or feel uncomfortable with some part of your sexual activity, tell your spouse.*
7. *You have a lifetime to learn. Take the time to learn about each other and your sexual experience.*
8. *Explore and enjoy - but do not violate your spouse's wishes to not do something.*
9. *Have no expectations*
10. *Remember the Crock-Pot vs. Microwave analogy for the differences between men and women. Men are like microwaves and can heat up almost instantaneously. Women are like Crock-Pots; it takes a long time for them to heat up.*

> *"When sexual union expresses love within covenant Christian marriage, God is glorified."*
> *~ Christopher McCluskey*

For Discussion as a Couple

1. Do you feel the sex in your marriage is bringing you closer together or creating more frustration? Why or why not?

____
____
____
____

2. In your opinion, are you having too much or too little sex? Why is this?

____
____
____
____

3. How do you and your spouse differ in sexuality? Is this a source of irritation? Why or why not?

____
____
____
____

4. Can Christians enjoy and even have fun with sex? Why or why not?

____
____
____
____

5. What can you and your spouse do to enhance your sexual relationship?

____
____
____
____
____

Differences in Sexuality[1]

	Men	*Women*
Orientation	Physical Compartmentalized Physical oneness Variety Sex is high priority	Relational Wholistic Emotional oneness Security Other priorities may be higher
Stimulation	Sight Smell Body centered	Touch Attitudes Actions Words Person-centered
Needs	Repect Admiration Physically needed Not to be put down	Understanding Love Emotionally needed Time
Sexual Response	Acyclical Quick excitement Initiates (usually) Difficult to distract	Cyclical Slow excitement Responder (usually) Easily distracted
Orgasm	Propagation of species Shorter, more intense Physically oriented Orgasm usually needed for satisfaction	Propagation of oneness Longer, more in-depth Emotionally-oriented Satisfaction often possible without orgasm

Intimacy in Marriage

Study 35

Maintaining Intimacy

"But at the beginning of creation God 'made them male and female.' 'For this reason a man will leave his father and mother and be united to his wife, and the two will become one flesh.' So they are no longer two, but one. Therefore what God has joined together, let man not separate."
~ Mark 10:6-9

Change is Inevitable

There is one constant in life that everyone can expect; life will change. It is inevitable, natural and will occur whether a couple is ready for it or not. Many people prefer the "status quo" and do not want to think about change coming to their lives. Often, they will live in dysfunctional, unfulfilling marriages and have no desire to change. They have found a level of comfort in their situation and are afraid of what might happen if they initiate change. Time stops for no one, and they can wish their life would remain as is, but change will occur.

Couples usually discover the reality of how life changes very quickly. This discovery may even come during the honeymoon as husband and wife find that the person they wake up with in the morning is very different from the person they thought they married. The wonderful, loving, caring person they fell in love with somehow was replaced by an uncouth ogre or the wicked witch of the west. It usually takes longer than the honeymoon, but sooner or later the husband and wife discover the idiosyncrasies of the person they married. It's not that they are a different person as much as it is the fact that the couple enters a new stage in the marriage relationship. This is the first of many changes the marriage will endure as a couple experiences life together.

...train yourself to be godly. For physical training is of some value, but godliness has value for all things, holding promise for both the present life and the life to come. ~ 1 Timothy 4:7-8

People prepare and train for a lot of things in life, but many neglect preparing for life as a husband, wife or parent. They enter marriage ill-equipped and tend to be especially unprepared for the changes that life will bring. Couples often have expectations of what their life together will look like and are not prepared when reality differs from their vision. A strong foundation built on Jesus Christ and the Word of God will strengthen a couple for their future life together. When a couple relies on God's promises and face the changes together, they are not as dramatic.

Seasons of Life

Life progresses through seasons as a couple ages and matures. Every marriage experiences ongoing change often based on distinct periods or seasons in life. There are natural changes in the marriage relationship as a couple ages or changes may come through events such as illness, injury, death, job loss or the effects of sin. A fortified marriage will withstand the changes that come in the relationship. This couple has built their foundation on Jesus Christ and clings to Him through the trouble and celebrates in Him with the victories. The marriage built on the sand of self or the world will tend to crumble and fall apart when the storms

of life crash against it. The natural changes coming through the seasons of life often are harder to handle because they usually do not come announced and a couple is caught off guard.

Intimacy must be cultivated and built through the seasons of life to keep the marriage relationship growing and strong. A couple can attain high intimacy at one point in their marriage and then get to a point where there is virtually no intimacy. It is important that a couple continue building intimacy throughout their married life. Intimacy needs will change and it will require new and innovative ways to build intimacy through the seasons of life.

The seasons marriages go through can be broken down into several typical stages. These life-cycle stages help explain the constantly changing demands and expectations of family interaction. Being aware of these stages helps a couple to prepare for the inevitable challenges and stresses accompanying them. There are typically four stages in the life-cycle of a marriage.

Stage 1: Newly Married

This is a period of adjustment as a couple adapts to each other and melds their lives together. The tension of this stage can be felt in many areas as the couple learns how different they are. Arguments can arise from seemingly anywhere as they discover that they squeeze the toothpaste differently, have very different tastes and schedules and find out about the family they married into. Usually, they find out that virtually everything is different, from boundaries and communication to views on roles and intimacy. The excitement of their sexual relationship wears off as they settle into the daily grind of life. It is important at this point that a couple establish patterns of healthy interaction. Small problems not dealt with at this point can become serious problems later.

Stage 2: Full Nest

Children arrive and few couples are prepared for how much their lives will change. There are incredible demands on their time, resources and energy as a couple attempts to meet the needs of children, career, home upkeep and each other. Couples usually have little time for each other during this stage and if intimacy is to be kept, they must work hard at remaining close. Sexual intimacy often lacks and unresolved problems from the early years can become major issues.

Stage 3: Full Nest 2

One might think that as children grow and become adolescents or teenagers, there would be fewer demands on a couple. But teenagers still require time and energy and often, the demands of career, civic work and church responsibilities increase. A couple finds less time for each other and must also face that fact of age beginning to affect intimacy. Complacency may set in and the couple begins to take each other for granted. It is important that a couple works as a team through this stage as they meet the challenges of children breaking free. Couples who do not maintain connection through this period may have serious marital problems once the children leave the home.

Stage 4: Empty Nest

The last child leaves the nest, and a couple now has a home with no children for the first time in many years. Often, there is a big adjustment as a couple refocuses on each other rather than on children and activities. At the same time, aging and medical problems may affect their lives greatly. It is important that a couple remain committed to each other as they enter this stage of life. There may be more time for intimacy, but age and health may work against them. Couples must be more creative and work together to rebuild and maintain intimacy.

"I'm not sure you are the same man I married thirty years ago. I need to draw some blood for a blood test to make sure it's you."

Few families travel through the marriage life-cycles in the same way. Divorce, remarriage, blended families, adult children returning home, couples raising grandchildren and other unique circumstances can change aspects of the stages, but in a general sense, the stages will apply to every marriage. However as a couple journeys through the life-cycle, it is important that they remain connected and continue to build intimacy. The work never stops, and, through each stage of life, intimacy will be built in different ways. Intimacy and oneness are not attained one time and kept for life. The work continues until death do us part.

> ***A truly happy marriage is one in which a woman gives the best years of her life to the man who has made them the best.***

Intimacy Disciplines

Discipline is required to maintain intimacy through the stages of life. Intimacy will not occur without work, and a couple must continue the work throughout their marriage. It is a terrible travesty that a couple would remain together through the first three stages of the marriage life-cycle, only to divorce once the children leave home. They now have the opportunity to enjoy life and each other and be used by God to affect younger couples, but they divorce because they lost intimacy many years previously. Couples on an average remain in Stage 1 for two years, Stage 2 for twelve years, Stage 3 for fifteen years and Stage 4 for 28 years.[1] It is unfortunate that too often, a couple doesn't remain together for potentially the longest (and potentially the best) stage of their marriage.

Intimacy must be developed according to how God created mankind; body, soul and spirit. Every couple can continue to build their physical, sexual relationship throughout the life stages. It may take work and creativity, especially if there are physical problems with one spouse or the other. It is possible to maintain vibrant and fulfilling sexual intimacy into old age.

Intimacy at the soul, or inner self level, must also be nourished and strengthened. Maintaining intellectual and emotional intimacy takes joint effort and developing common interests. Couples who divorce because they "have nothing in common" forget what it was like to be in love with their mate. They have allowed feelings to overrule the commitment they made on their wedding day. Building a friendship and continuing the romance in the marriage relationship is not as difficult as many people make it out to be. Does it take time and energy? Sure it does, but the rewards are worth the effort.

Spiritual intimacy also takes some effort, but there is a much greater reward than just increased intimacy between husband and wife. It also builds intimacy with God and a close, growing relationship with the Lord strengthens every area of life. Worship, prayer, study of the Word of God and fellowshipping together is important to an intimate relationship. A couple can go out at sunset (or better, at sunrise) and sing your favorite hymn or praise song together to the God of the universe. Share meaningful insights God gives you with your spouse. Take the time to enter into each other's spiritual worlds.

There is a pattern here; it takes time to build and maintain intimacy. Spending time together in different areas is crucial to intimacy. The key word here is together. It doesn't mean sitting next to each other and being in totally different universes while you read or watch television. You must interact with each other, physically, intellectually, emotionally and spiritually. You must make it a priority to stop all the busyness and take time for just the two of you. Your spouse must be first, before all other worldly things; even ministry. Your spouse is, in fact, your first ministry. Make intimacy with him the priority in your life, second only to your relationship with God.

Christianity is poorly advertised by Christian marriages that are no better than marital relationships governed by secular values and empowered by merely human energy. If the love and power of Christ is to be effectively displayed in Christian marriages today, couples must first realize that nothing less is expected of them than consistent movement toward oneness; oneness in body, soul and spirit.

God created marriage for oneness; it does not happen on its own, a couple must work at it. Just like a beautiful garden must be cultivated and cared for on a daily basis, the marriage relationship must also be tended and cared for daily. The intimacy developed will help you maintain a strong, fortified marriage. A marriage able to withstand any storm or attack that comes against it.

For Discussion as a Couple

1. Do you agree that change is inevitable? What can you do to be prepared for changes in your life and marriage?

2. What stage of the marriage life-cycle is your marriage in now? How is it different than the other stages you've been in?

3. How can intimacy be maintained through the different life-cycle stages?

4. How can you continue to build emotional intimacy in your marriage?

5. What are you doing to build spiritual intimacy in your marriage? If nothing, what could you be doing?

Fortified Marriages
Chapter 8 Endnotes

Study 30: *Created for Intimacy*

1. Drs. David & Jan Stoop; The Complete Marriage Book (Grand Rapids, MI, Fleming H. Revell, 2002) p 83
2. Adam Clarke's Commentary, Electronic Database. Copyright (c) 1996 by Biblesoft
3. Mike Mason; The Mystery of Marriage, As Iron Sharpens Iron (Portland, OR, Multnomah Press, 1985) p71

Recommended for further reading:
- More than Married; the Keys to Intimacy for Lasting Marriage by David & Teresa Ferguson
- Relationship Rescue by Dr. Phil McGraw
- Becoming One/Emotionally, Spiritually, Sexually by Joe Beam

Study 31: *Restoring Intimacy Through Forgiveness*

1. Nelson's Illustrated Bible Dictionary; Copyright 1986, Thomas Nelsons Publishers
2. Charlie "T" Jones and Daniel R. Ledwith; Finding Freedom in Forgiveness (Eugene, OR; Harvest House Publishers, 2005) p21
3. Allison Kitchen; Forgiveness: A Key to Better Health, www.vibrantlife.com/vl/article-24.html
4. C.S. Lewis, quoted in Readings for Meditation and Reflection, ed. By Walter Hooper (NY, NY; Harper Collins, 1996) p 63
5. In Matthew 18:22, the NIV Bible states seventy-seven times., but most other versions and the footnote in the NIV use seventy times seven.

Recommended for further reading:
- Finding Freedom in Forgiveness by Charlie "T" Jones and Daniel R. Ledwith
- Total Forgiveness by R.T. Kendall
- The Power of Forgiveness: Keep Your Heart Free by Joyce Meyer
- Five Steps to Forgiveness: the Art and Science of Forgiving by Everett Worthington

For further information, see:
- Campaign for Forgiveness Research: ww.forgiving.org

Study 32: *Building Intimacy*

1. Dr. John Gottman, Why Marriages Succeed or Fail (NY, NY; Fireside, 1994) p 101

Recommended for further reading:
- Made to be Loved by Steve and Valerie Bell
- Love Life for Parents by David & Claudia Arp
- 100 Fun and Fabulous Ways to Flirt with Your Spouse by Doug Fields
- 400 Creative Ways to Say I Love You by Alice Chapin

For further information, see:
- Marriage Intimacy: www.marriageintimacy.com

Study 33: *Keeping Romance Alive*

1. Dr. Patricia Love & Jo Robinson; Hot Monogamy (NY, NY; Penguin Group, 1994) p 176
2. Larry Russell; Before Love Dies (Denver, CO; Legacy Publishers, 2004) p 180
3. Wordsmyth Dictionary; www.wordsmyth.net

Recommended for further reading:

- Holding onto Romance by H. Norman Wright
- Love Life for Every Married Couple by Ed Wheat
- The Love List/Eight Little Things That Make a Big Difference in Your Marriage by Drs. Les & Leslie Parrott
- 10 Great Dates to Energize Your Marriage by David & Claudia Arp

For further information, see:

- The Romantic: www.theromantic.com
- FamilyLife: www.familylife-ccc.org

Sparking Romance in Your Marriage:

- Simply Romantic Nights by Dennis & Barbara Rainey
- 101 Nights of Grrreat Romance by Laura Corn

Study 34: *Intimacy & Sex*

1. Dennis & Barbara Rainey; How do men and women differ in their view of the sexual relationship in marriage? FamilyLife, www.familylife.org

Recommended for further reading:

- The Gift of Sex by Clifford and Joyce Penner
- When Two Become One; Enhancing Sexual Intimacy in Marriage by Christopher & Rachel McCluskey
- Intended for Pleasure by Ed Wheat
- Sex, Romance and the Glory of God by C.J. Mahaney

For further information, see:

- Passionate Commitment; Clifford & Joyce Penner: www.passionatecommitment.com
- Sexual Wholeness - God's truth about sexuality: ww.sexualwholeness.com

Study 35: *Maintaining Intimacy*

1. David & Teresa Ferguson and Chris & Holly Thurman; Intimate Encounters (Nashville, TN; Thomas Nelson, 1994) p 220

Recommended for further reading:

- Staying Close by Dennis Rainey
- The Second Half by David & Claudia Arp
- 52 Fantastic Dates for You and Your Mate by David & Claudia Arp
- 5 Essentials for Lifelong Intimacy by Dr. James Dobson

For further information, see:

- Marriage Alive Ministries: www.marriagealive.com

Chapter 9
Parenting

Study 36
When Children Arrive

Has not [the LORD] made them one? In flesh and spirit they are his. And why one? Because he was seeking godly offspring. So guard yourself in your spirit, and do not break faith with the wife of your youth.
~ Malachi 2:15

Children Will Change Your Life!

The arrival of children changes a marriage completely and permanently. Rarely do couples realize how much change comes with having children in their marriage. It seems that many couples are like Adam and Eve, who had no role models and no concept of what having children would be like. Parents today know what children are like, and they have an incredible amount of resources available. Yet, seeing the ignorance of so many parents, one would think they are the first couple to ever have children.

Bringing a child into the world is an awesome privilege. God allows mankind to participate in the creation of life. Conception, pregnancy and birth bring about the miracle of a new life. It is an absolute shame that so many people take sex and childbirth so lightly. The creation of life. Think about it for a moment. God created the first two humans and then turned over procreation to them. What has mankind done with this privilege? People do not take sex seriously and society accepts "recreational sex" with no commitments. Abortion is common and often accepted as a form of birth control. People have children, but do not take responsibility for them. Divorce is acceptable available for any and every reason. People desire the freedom to do what they want, but they do not want to take the responsibility for their actions.

Parenting requires sacrifices of both husband and wife. Yet, many people do not want to make the sacrifice it takes to be a parent. Marriage changes the way a man and woman interact with the world. They do not have the same freedoms they had as single people. Parents also give up some of their "rights" as adults. A couple must be concerned about each other's needs and now they have a child (or children) to be concerned about. Parenting gives people the opportunity to learn more about dying to self and living Christ-like lives.

Responsible Parenting

Parenting is the most important task a person can have in the world. Molding and shaping a child and preparing him for adulthood is a huge responsibility. Many people take this responsibility too lightly, as if chil-

dren can prepare themselves for life. They may abdicate responsibility to childcare providers, church, the school system, and allow others to decide what is best for their children. Parents need to understand that every aspect of their child's training and education is their responsibility.

Educating your children is not the school system's responsibility. They certainly can help you train your children in the academic disciplines, but schools should be the support, not the primary educator. Parents need to be involved in their children's education and know what the school system is teaching. Teachers should know that the parents care about their children's education and will get involved when issues arise.

Parents are also responsible for the faith of their children. One hour a week in Sunday School will not build faith into a child. God brings a couple together in oneness to produce Godly offspring. It is not the church's responsibility to bring children to a saving knowledge of Jesus Christ. Parents cannot teach their children about faith if they do not display faith in their daily lives. Children will see through hypocrisy and will know whether their parent's faith is genuine.

Children are a gift from God, and they are to be handled with care and treated with respect. Parents only have stewardship of their children for a short while and need to make the most of the time that they have. It is impossible to fulfill this huge responsibility without God's help. He will give parents wisdom and guidance as they seek His direction in their parenting.

God the Father, the Model Parent

God is the ideal parent. He loves His children with an everlasting love and accepts them unconditionally. The story of the prodigal son in Luke, chapter 15, could better be titled the story of the loving father. It is a picture of God the Father as He accepts His repentant son without condition. God is a merciful and gracious Father who always loves his children, but He never accepts sin. He sets healthy boundaries and will discipline those He loves.

The Marriage First

The first responsibility parents have is to ensure their marriage is healthy and strong. Effective parenting occurs in the context of a flourishing marriage. The wife who puts her children before her husband and does not seek to meet his needs rejects Biblical values and may push him to look elsewhere to get his needs met. Similarly, the husband who only accepts responsibility for providing the family's financial needs and neglects caring for his wife also rejects Biblical values. Both must make their marriage relationship a priority and work together raising their children.

> *"The relationship between a husband and wife is the foundation on which kids build their sense of security, their identity, and learn to relate to others."*
> *~ Jay Kesler*

A healthy marriage is important to raising healthy, well-adjusted children. Children feel secure when their parents exhibit closeness in their relationship. The quality of a couple's marriage has a direct influence on the quality of their child's future marriage.[1] Children in healthy homes do better in school and are better able to resist the temptations of sin that will come their way. A couple who neglects their marriage may potentially set up their children for future unhealthy marriage relationships by their example.

Spending time away from the children benefits both the children and marriage relationship. The children are able to experience new environments and a measure of freedom from Mom and Dad. Parents' time alone allows them to relax and enjoy each other without worrying about the children. Sending the children to Grandma's house for a night or a weekend is win-win situation or couples can work with another couple or a group of trusted, Christian couples to take turns watching each other's children for a night or the weekend.

"Whew! They are finally all in bed. Now we can have some time for the two of us."

An important word of caution. Parents must know whom they are allowing their children to stay with. You need to make sure they have the same values you have and adhere to the same guidelines you set in your household. Unfortunately, you cannot make any assumptions about the behavior of others, even if they are Christians. You do not want to unknowingly expose your children to an unacceptable or even dangerous environment.

Working Together as a Team

Parenting also demonstrates the differences between husband and wife. Often, one parent tends to be a strict disciplinarian while the other tends to be soft. A couple will see differences in many areas and it is important that they work out their differences before situations arise with the children. Children benefit by having parents with different backgrounds and personalities because they can gain from the strengths of both parents. This won't happen unless the parents are moving in the same direction and working together.

Unity as a couple is important to raising healthy children. A husband and wife who do not support one another weaken their influence on their children. This is not the time for one spouse to demand his way because, "it worked in our family," or "I'm the head of the house, I'll decide what to do." Compromise not only works, but also often produces the best results in parenting. Children reap benefits from the best of both parents' wisdom, background and personalities.

Parents must never contradict each other in front of the children. Demonstrating conflict resolution by deciding which restaurant or which movie the family will go will help children, but arguing about issues involving the children must not happen in front of the children. Take the discussion to your room, outside or for a drive, but do not argue in front of the children. It causes division, disrespect and insecurity. Some couples may wonder why their children are so argumentative when that is what their marriage relationship models for the children.

Parenting is a joint responsibility that requires both parents' participation. Biblical roles are important to raising healthy children. The husband as servant-leader, prophet, priest and king serves, leads and protects his family. The wife as helper and husband-lover—child-lover, supports, encourages and nourishes her family. Together they share the work and responsibilities to help their children learn to love God, develop healthy boundaries and learn self-discipline.

Parenting by Example

> *"Don't worry that children never listen to you; worry that they are always watching you."*
> *~ Robert Fulghum*

Children learn more from parents' example than by their words. It is important that parents model the behavior they desire from their children. A parent that lives out his Christian faith on a daily basis and never says a word about his faith is more likely to have his children follow in that faith than the parent the preaches it daily, but does not live it.

Impressionable young minds need to see their parents walking closely with the Lord, surrendering their lives to Him and making the Bible the source of guidance and direction for their daily life. It is important that parents exhibit a strong prayer life and the same values privately and publicly. Parents need to model Christ to their children.

Children will learn more about Biblical roles in the home by watching their mother and father than listening to a hundred sermons on the subject. A couple that demonstrates respect, love, honor, admiration and acceptance to each other teaches their children those qualities. The importance of a healthy, fortified marriage in children's lives cannot be overstated. They learn from what they see and seeing a healthy marriage lived out before them provides invaluable lessons.

> *"Marriage is our society's most pro-child institution. If you want kids to do well, then you want marriage to do well."*
> *~ David Blankenhorn*

For Discussion as a Couple

1. How have children changed your marriage relationship? (If you have no children, how do you anticipate it will change your relationship?)

2. What is your responsibility as a parent?

3. Why is it important that the marriage come first? How do you demonstrate this in your family?

4. Do you and your spouse work as a team? How can you better be united before the children?

5. What kind of example do you provide for your children? Do they see your Christianity lived out? How?

Parenting Background Questionnaire

Think about how your parents raised you and your siblings. Answer the following questions honestly as an individual, and then discuss your answers with your spouse when you have time alone.

1. Did your parents work together as a team? How did you see this? ____________________

2. Were your parents overly strict? Lenient? How did this affect you? ____________________

3. Was there physical or sexual abuse in your home? Was it dealt with? How? ________________

4. Did your parents demonstrate love to each other? How? ____________________________

5. Did your parents fight in front of the children? How did they fight (argue, shout, physical)?

6. How did your parents demonstrate their faith in God? ____________________________

7. Were your parents the same in public as they were in the home? ______________________

8. How did your parents discipline the children? __________________________________

Parenting Background Questionnaire *(continued)*

9. Did you play games or do activities as a family? ______________________________

10. Were your parents involved in your school or extracurricular activities? How? ______________________________

11. Were you a priority in your parents' lives? How did you see this? ______________________________

12. Did you feel loved by your parents? Why or why not? ______________________________

13. How did your parents train their children? Was there formal training? Did they talk about life issues? When? How? ______________________________

14. How much did your parents control your life as a teenager? Did you have a lot of freedom? ______________________________

15. What responsibilities in the home did you have as a teenager? ______________________________

Additional notes about how your parents raised you: ______________________________

Parenting
Study 37
The Goal of Parenting

Only be careful, and watch yourselves closely so that you do not forget the things your eyes have seen or let them slip from your heart as long as you live. Teach them to your children and to their children after them.
~ Deuteronomy 4:9

The Importance of Being a Parent

Parenting is an incredibly important vocation. More than any other factor, parents determine whether a child will be a positive or negative influence on society once he reaches adulthood. Productive, sound adults are not produced by churches, schools, government, or society, but by parents. Parents are imperfect human beings and will fail in many ways, however, they consciously attempt to love and guide their children the best they can. The problem is that most parents have not learned how to properly raise a family, and, without knowledge, it is difficult to fulfill their parental roles.

Most couples just happen into parenthood. They are untrained, ill equipped and have little idea of the tremendous responsibility they face with this baby coming into their lives. Very few people take the opportunity to learn about parenting before the baby comes. Even if they are not prepared before, they have the nine months of pregnancy to begin preparation for parenthood.

It is never too late to begin learning Godly principles of parenting. Your parents may be divorced, you may come from a single parent home, your grandparents might have raised you, or your home growing up may have been very dysfunctional and hurtful. You may now be the type of parent you did not want to be; just like your parents. No matter how bad your childhood was or how bad a parent you may be now, God can change the legacy you will leave for your children. Your children can become Godly, healthy, balanced adults.

'Not by might nor by power, but by my Spirit,' says the LORD Almighty.* ~ *Zechariah 4:6

Parents are the source of life and the providers of love, growth, nurture, training and education for their children. Parenting is not an easy task. Children enter the world with a blank slate and a propensity for sin. It is the parents' responsibility to give their children the tools they need to function in life and make good choices that will help them mature and be productive. Parents need help, first through God's power and His Spirit and then with training, education and support. The school system can help with education and training and the church can help with spiritual training, but parents must also be willing to learn and grow and be able to provide for their children's needs.

Parental Responsibility

Views of parental responsibility and the goal of parenting may vary depending how one is raised. Some parents just get by and live one day at a time or seek to endure until their children are old enough to leave the home and take responsibility for their own lives. Or they may have no goals and decide to be their children's buddies and just get along.

Others detest the childhood they had and seek to do everything they can to make their children's childhood different. Their parents may have been overly strict, so they compensate by being overly lenient with their own children. Still others are overly strict thinking they can ensure that their children do not stray from the straight and narrow. It is important that parents find a balance and raise their children according to Biblical principles rather than their own ideas about parenting.

> *...Because he was seeking godly offspring.*
> *~ Malachi 2:15*

The Bible states that God brings a man and woman together because He seeks Godly offspring. These are children who love the Lord and desire to serve Him. They will live according to the Spirit rather than the flesh or the world. Raising children to be Godly adults is more difficult than it appears, and it takes a lot of work.

Dr. Henry Cloud and Dr. John Townsend state that mature character is the real goal of parenting.[1] It is the parent's responsibility to prepare their children for the life ahead of them and to guide their children in developing the attributes that will help them become responsible adults. Character in a person means that he has moral qualities, integrity and that he takes responsibility for his life. It can be defined as the sum of a person's abilities to deal with life as God designed him to.[2] Parents need to help their children become functioning, healthy adults.

Character Attributes

Research, study and life experience reveals three important characteristics to cultivate a mature character in children:

- Love for God
- Healthy boundaries
- Self-discipline

Parents need to instill a love for God into their children by word and example. They cannot force their children to love God, but they must lead their children into an understanding of God's love for them and their need for Him. Parents help their children mature to a point where they seek God and His guidance on their own.

A child's relationship with God will eventually become personal as the parents demonstrate God's love and their dependence on Him. Children who develop a strong walk with the Lord will develop their own conscience; the internal sense of right and wrong that will help build character into their life.

Healthy boundaries give a child the ability to make appropriate choices in life, develop healthy relationships, and take responsibility for their actions. Children with healthy boundaries are better able to cope with problems in life and can make choices that will help them avoid many trials and tribulations.

Developing self-discipline is important, but not always enjoyable—for parents or children. Children do not naturally know how to wait for what they want and often will not understand why they must delay gratification. Society and often, parents, teach children by their example that instant gratification can be expected. Yet, the Lord often asks His children to wait. Parents need to help their children learn to persevere and work toward goals in their lives. Healthy self-discipline helps children become competent in skills that will help them in a career, but also helps them fulfill responsibilities and remain in their walk with the Lord.

Cultivating these attributes in children will build character that will help young adults face a world that is hostile to everything good and right. It will help them become the Godly people God desires them to be. It will not guarantee that they will not fall to sin or even continue a walk with the Lord, but it certainly will help.

Boundaries with Kids

Boundaries are extremely important in a child's life, first, to protect him from harm and then to help him make good decisions. Children are not born with an ability to set healthy boundaries. They learn boundaries from their parents as their parents set boundaries for them and then help them learn to set their own boundaries. It begins at a very young age as children learn to accept "no" when there is danger or during inappropriate behavior. Developing healthy boundaries requires that children's boundaries be respected as appropriate for their age. Forcing children to show affection when they don't want to violates their boundaries and potentially sets them up for abuse at some point in their life.

Parents must model healthy boundaries themselves to be able to help their children develop healthy boundaries. The parent who cannot say, "no" to his child does not do the child any favors. Indulged children do not learn boundaries easily later in life. Parents who set healthy boundaries help children become responsible and make better choices, as they get older. They learn to live with both freedom and responsibility in their lives.

Parental Control

Children are born completely dependent on their parents. Parents provide food, love, care, safety, and direction, everything a child needs for life. They also make all of the decisions for the child, when they go to bed, wake up, are fed, what and whom they see. Essentially, at the beginning of a child's life, parents control a child's life completely. Parents pour themselves into the child in the first months of life, demonstrating love and helping him learn about the world he has just entered. It is a huge responsibility to have another human being so dependent on you, but it also can be a wonderful joy.

Parents are stewards of the children God has given them for a certain amount of time. Children do not belong to parents; they belong to God. He may have involved the parents in the creation of the child, but that life is a gift from God. The Lord created his inmost being and knit him together in his mother's womb (Psalms 139:13). Parents have a responsibility to care for their children, prepare them for life according to God's principles, teach them to live on their own and help them learn to serve their Creator.

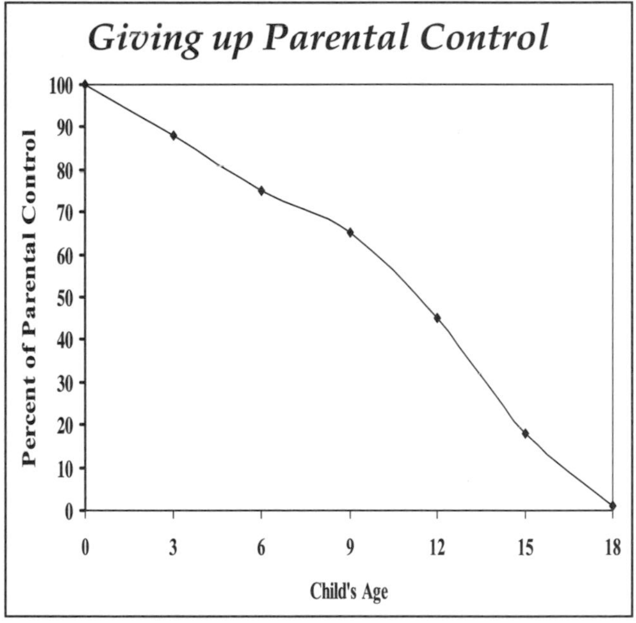

Parents should begin giving up control gradually in a child's life. They are pleased when their child begins feeding himself and can go to the restroom without Mom or Dad. Parents also must allow their child to begin making some of his own decisions and setting his own boundaries. The chart above is not scientific, but is meant to be a point of discussion for parents. Parents are to gradually give more control and responsibility to their children as the children age and demonstrate their responsibility. Different children in a family will not receive the same freedoms at the same age. They are all different. Birth order, personality and biological factors will affect how they adjust to responsibility.

Sheltering children from the problems of the world does not prepare them to eventually live in the world themselves. Relinquishing control to children may bring some physical or emotional injury. They need the freedom to fail, so they can learn from their mistakes and mature through them. Gradually giving up control helps minimize injury while still allowing children to learn.

God gives His children the freedom to make their own choices, and parents gradually must do the same, as children are able to make their own choices. Children grow up and eventually must bear the ultimate responsibility for their lives. No parent is perfect, and all children will suffer hurt as they grow up. Parents should use every possible opportunity to help their children learn to make good choices in life.

For Discussion as a Couple

1. What is your main goal of parenting? Why do you say this?

2. What is your responsibility as a parent?

3. How can you cultivate the three character attributes into your children?

4. Why are boundaries important in a child's life?

5. What are your thoughts about parental control? How do you know when to give your child more control?

Parenting
Study 38
Guiding Your Children

> *Train a child in the way he should go, and when he is old he will not turn from it. ~ Proverbs 22:6*

It Takes Two

Parenting requires both husband and wife working together. Many men believe their job is only to provide financially for their family and leave parenting to their wives. The husband may spend little or no time with his children, working long hours and claiming it is for his family. The husband's Biblical responsibility is for the physical, emotional and spiritual needs of his family, but he cannot provide for those needs if he is not present. The wife's Biblical responsibility is to help her husband and to love and nurture her family. She also cannot accomplish this if she is not present. Many women want it all, a career, motherhood and self-improvement. They have bought into society's dream of a perfect world and leaving their children for others to raise. Guiding children to mature character requires the active participation of both parents.

Today, many children do not have close contact with their parents on a daily basis. Is it any wonder that they are turning to drugs, alcohol, sex and gangs for fulfillment? It was bad enough when the father was not available and now in the name of equality, children have neither parent available to them. Parenting is a huge responsibility; it is more than one person can handle. It is difficult for children to achieve maturity in character without the involvement of both father and mother. Both parents need to work together as a team to provide a balanced, healthy environment required for children to grow into the Godly offspring God desires.

God uses a couple's differences to provide the balance needed to effectively raise their children God's way. Children can gain the advantage of healthy and balanced discipline, love, nurture, training and education in their lives through the differences of their parents. It is very difficult for one parent to provide that balance. Statistics reveal that in 80 percent of unwed pregnancies, the father is absent either emotionally and/or physically from the young lady's life.[1] People wonder about the rise in homosexuality and why men are not the Godly husbands they should be, yet generations of males have been raised without the involvement of a male role model in their lives. It is difficult for women to teach boys to be men and day care personnel will not care for children or provide the same positive influence as their parents.

It's amazing how little children can teach parents that the parents still have a lot to learn.

Recognizing a Child's True Potential

No parent wants to think that his child can be evil, but because of the sin of Adam, every child has the potential for any and all sin. They do not have an in-born potential for Godliness or righteousness. Humans are not born neutral; they are born sinners. Children do not go

bad because of something their parents did; children's sinfulness manifests itself because of what their parents do not do. Children do not have to be taught to be selfish and self-centered; it comes naturally for them. It is a parent's responsibility to guide his children toward God and the righteousness that only comes from knowing Jesus Christ.

> *"There is no one righteous, not even one; there is no one who understands, no one who seeks God."*
> *~ Romans 3:10-11*

Armed with the knowledge that every child has the potential to be a horrible mass murderer, parents can begin the work of molding their child into a person who will successfully become a productive part of society and, more importantly, someone who will serve God. Children are naïve and inexperienced, but they have their parents' genes and inclination toward sin.

Many apparently normal families and even some pastors' families produce children who seem to have no morals and demonstrates poor behavior. Tolerance and passivity tend to define society's method of parenting today. Parents, too often, are absent from their children's sphere of moral influence, or they do not correct wrong behavior. Discipline is viewed as punishment instead of an opportunity to teach children. Parents cannot back away and allow their children to determine their own direction in today's world. They must be involved in their children's lives, and this takes time.

Isolating children from the world will not keep them safe from sin. Nor will strict discipline and control of every aspect of a child's life keep him from straying. Relinquishing control as children mature does not mean that parents are not involved in their lives. Parents must be involved even as children reach the teenage years and are close to venturing out into the world on their own. Knowing what is going on in your child's life and using every opportunity to give training does not have to be control. Involved parenting is purposeful about leaving a legacy for your children. Parents are not to compromise what goes on in their home and they need to stand firm in the truths of the Bible. They are to consistently love, guide and direct their children according to God's principles.

Whatever parenting problems parents have had in the past, it is never too late to begin correcting errors. Parents need to draw a line in the sand and say from this day forward, "Me and my house will serve the Lord." Older children may reject or resist their parents' new commitment, but as the parents demonstrate God's love and a changed life, prayerfully, their children will see change and be drawn to Christ.

The Truth About Discipline

Discipline is not a popular term in today's society. People tend to reject discipline based only on the extremes they have seen or heard about. Yet, discipline is extolled throughout the Bible and self-control listed as a fruit of the Spirit (See Galatians 5:22-23). Discipline is key to preparing children for adulthood and helping them develop character. Helping children develop self-discipline is a primary responsibility of parents. Children will not learn self-discipline on their own.

> ***Discipline your son, for in that there is hope; do not be a willing party to his death.***
> ***~ Proverbs 19:18***

Discipline is defined as, "training by instruction and control. The biblical concept of discipline has both a positive side (instruction, knowledge, and training) and a negative aspect (correction, punishment, and reproof)."[2] It is not being harsh and rigid – it is being consistent, loving and firm. The Lord admonishes fathers to not exasperate or embitter their children (Ephesians 6:4 and Colossians 3:21). Discipline in anger hurts and discourages children. When disciplined in love, children are built up and encouraged even while inappropriate or unacceptable behavior is addressed.

Reasonable boundaries and expectations must be established before children are disciplined. It is impossible to define every situation that will arise, but it is possible to give children age-appropriate guidelines for what the parents expect of them. Written guidelines may be appropriate for older children. This preempts misunderstandings and misinterpretation. Patience and working with younger children will help them learn what is expected of them.

Discipline must be fair, loving and consistent. Children must be held accountable for the guidelines they have been given. Allowing repeated infractions because you don't want to take the time to discipline a child doesn't help him. Often, parents allow a child to push and push until they react out of impatience or anger and effective discipline does not occur. Appropriate consequences must be established and given when children misbehave. Children need to know that certain behaviors always bring consequences. Parents cannot evade this responsibility because they are busy or because it occurs at an inconvenient time. The security gained by knowing the boundaries in the home will help a child know he is loved and cared for.

Remember that children are children. They are not naturally responsible and self-disciplined. Children will forget to complete chores or absent-mindedly do dumb things. It is important to differentiate between childish irresponsibility and willful defiance. Defiance must be confronted, again, not with anger, but with a balance of love and firmness. Children must know that they are loved and accepted no matter what. Parents need to address behavior and refrain from tearing down their children's character or using absolute statements like "you always" or "you never."

> ***Encourage the young men to be self-controlled. In everything set them an example by doing what is good. In your teaching show integrity, seriousness and soundness of speech that cannot be condemned, so that those who oppose you may be ashamed because they have nothing bad to say about us. ~ Titus 2:6-8***

Training Children

There is no formula to develop mature character in children. It takes a lot of work and creativity. Each child will be different; they learn differently and react to discipline differently. A lot of factors enter into training children for life in the world. Paul tells Titus to encourage young men to be self-controlled. Healthy boundaries and self-discipline are two important aspects of mature character. It begins with parents setting a good example. Parents' lives are the primary teacher of their children. Children will become what you are more than what you teach.

Training children involves more than being a good role model. Parents must be purposeful about teaching their children. There may be times of formal instruction, but often, parents will use "teachable moments" to train their children. Life situations very often provide opportunities for parents to make a point or explain some Biblical principle to their children. Imparting wisdom and knowledge to children does not happen in one session, it takes time and it is important that the parents use the eighteen years they have with their children to build a foundation that will help the children enter adulthood with tools and resources to help them walk with God and meet the challenges of daily life.

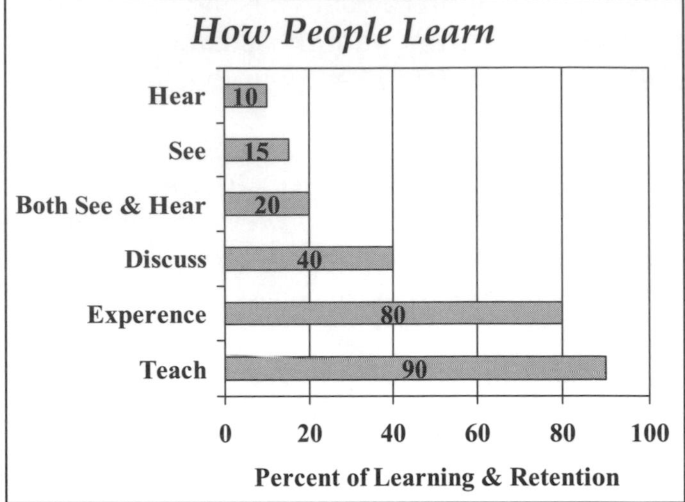

Learning requires much more than an occasional lecture on important life principles. People learn more when they are involved in the process. Children will be able to understand life principles when they gain experience with them. It is a process that begins shortly after birth and continues for as long as parents have the opportunity to give input to their children. Ideally, children begin learning about the different aspects of life at an early age. Children become more involved as they get older and even at some point may begin to teach some life principles to younger children.

Teaching children about relationships with other people is an important aspect of parenting. Parents teach their children how to get along and play nicely with other children, but do they teach how to develop friendships and the communication tools needed for resolving conflicts? Children need to learn how to effectively handle emotions and eventually, about relationships with the opposite sex. They also need to understand the physical and relational aspects of sex by the time they become teenagers and begin thinking about the opposite sex. Excellent, age appropriate materials are available to help parents in this area as noted in the endnotes for this study.

It is important that children begin learning Biblical principles about finances at a young age. Unfortunately, many parents do not teach their children about the financial aspects of life. Children enter the adult world thinking a credit card gives them extra funds or carrying debt is an acceptable way of life. They need to learn about all aspects of finances: income, budgeting, saving, debt and giving. Parents should model Biblical financial management and help their children experience the different aspects of finances.

Earning a small income or receiving an allowance will help children learn to manage their finances according to God's principles. Parents can guide their children in budgeting their income to accomplish the things they want to do or save for things they want to purchase. Children should be taught that there is a cost to borrowing money and that it is difficult to get out of debt. They also need to be taught the principles of giving both to God's work and to help others. Children can be given increased responsibilities with money as they age and parents may even want to let their children take care of the household finances (with close supervision of course!) for a period of time so that they can see what it takes to live in the real world.

Children are the only things you can take with you to Heaven. Faith and trust in Jesus Christ is the most important thing parents can teach their children. Not a superficial, religious faith, but a personal relationship with the living God. Children need Jesus Christ in their lives and need to see His love demonstrated by their parents.

Parents should be purposeful about transmitting their faith to their children. Reading Bible stories to children helps them learn about God. Sharing what God is doing in your life and demonstrating a close walk with Christ will bring the God of the stories to life. Praying for and with your children and worshipping God together will help them understand what it means to be a Christian. One of the most meaningful blessings in life is to lead your child in a prayer of accepting Jesus into his life and begin a life long relationship with Him.

Children left to themselves, will not go in the right direction. Parents today are not helpless in their effort to raise their children. The fast pace of life and ever-changing technologies are here to stay, but that doesn't mean that parents don't have something to offer their children. Children need their parents' love, guidance and direction to meet the challenges of the world today. Be an involved parent and help your children prepare for whatever life God has in store for them.

> ***These commandments that I give you today are to be upon your hearts. Impress them on your children. Talk about them when you sit at home and when you walk along the road, when you lie down and when you get up. Tie them as symbols on your hands and bind them on your foreheads. Write them on the doorframes of your houses and on your gates.***
> ***~ Deuteronomy 6:6-9***

For Discussion as a Couple

1. Why does it take two parents to effectively raise children? How are you and your spouse working together to guide your children?

____

____

____

____

2. How does knowledge that all children have a sinful nature give you purpose and direction for raising your children?

____

____

____

____

3. What misconceptions have you had about discipline? How can you use discipline to help guide your children?

____

____

____

____

4. What is the importance of discipline in a child's life? How do you (or would you) administer discipline?

____

____

____

____

5. How can you train your children so they will develop character and a trust in God?

____

____

____

____

____

Acceptance Inventory

Circle the number that best describes your interaction with your children in each area below.

	Almost Never	Rarely	Often	Almost Always
1. I tell my children that I am proud of them.	1	2	3	4
2. I hug my children.	1	2	3	4
3. I tell my children I love them.	1	2	3	4
4. I take an interest in what my children do.	1	2	3	4
5. I talk to each child individually.	1	2	3	4
6. I try to encourage my children.	1	2	3	4
7. I encourage my children to express their point of view.	1	2	3	4
8. I give my children my undivided attention when they speak.	1	2	3	4
9. I play with my children.	1	2	3	4
10. I show affection to my children.	1	2	3	4
11. I discipline my children when I am angry.	4	3	2	1
12. I tell my children to act their age.	4	3	2	1
13. I demonstrate impatience with my children.	4	3	2	1
14. I nag my children to get them to do their work.	4	3	2	1
15. I yell at my children.	4	3	2	1
16. I punish my children without explaining why.	4	3	2	1
17. I threaten my children.	4	3	2	1
18. I get emotional to get them to do what I want.	4	3	2	1
19. I show my disappointment to my children.	4	3	2	1
20. I do not allow my children to speak when disciplining them.	4	3	2	1

Total your score here: ________

A score of 65—80 indicates that you are very accepting of your children—continue to work to be involved with your children. If your score is 50—64, you are accepting, but may be able to use this inventory to increase your level of acceptance. Below 50: Please evaluate how you are dealing with your children. It is likely you are too harsh and do not demonstrate acceptance to your children. Parental acceptance is extremely important to the healthy development of children. If they don't have your acceptance, they will look for acceptance elsewhere.

Parenting

Study 39

Loving Your Children as They Are

Love is patient, love is kind. It does not envy, it does not boast, it is not proud. It is not rude, it is not self-seeking, it is not easily angered, it keeps no record of wrongs. Love does not delight in evil but rejoices with the truth. It always protects, always trusts, always hopes, always perseveres. ~ 1 Corinthians 13:4-7

The Importance of Love

Character development, discipline, training and guidance are all very important aspects of parenting, but if your children do not know they are loved, the work of parenting will not matter. Raising children in a Christian home does not guarantee Godly offspring. There are children who have rejected the faith of their parents and lived destructive lives that would break any parent's heart. Those children did not go astray for lack of material possessions or discipline, but because they did not know they were loved.

How important is love? Christians serve a God of love; He loved the world so much that He sent His only Son to die on a cross so people could be reconciled to Him. The Bible consistently speaks of the need to love God and love others, and it also puts a high premium on children. It is necessary that parents consistently demonstrate unconditional love for their children on a regular basis. Does this mean that parents don't discipline their children? Certainly not! God disciplines those He loves (Hebrews 12:6) and parents should also discipline their children in love. Unconditional love and acceptance is critically important to raising healthy children. Parents must separate who their children are from any misbehavior. Correct misbehavior, but do it in such a way that the child is absolutely sure of your love for him.

A child needs love the most when he least deserves it. ~ Anonymous

Parents often exasperate or embitter their children through expectations and demanding too much from them. Children usually are very different than their parents. Even if they have the same personality traits, they have the biological differences received from the other parent and they are a new and different generation. Not understanding that your children are created different and who they are as a person can cause both parents and children a lot of frustration. Understanding your children's personalities and their needs is an important part of the parenting process. You are better able to love them when you accept them for who they are, not whom you think they should be.

Fathers, do not embitter your children, or they will become discouraged. ~ Colossians 3:21

Parents are to guide their children to mature character. This guidance must be in the framework of who they are as a person. It is important for parents to help their children understand the strengths and weaknesses of their personality types. Children need to discover the unique plan God has for them and if parents are to effectively guide their children, it must be according to each child's unique personality.

Use the chart on the following page to help you determine the personality of each of your children.[1]

Golden Retriever or Peaceful Baby	*Beaver or Perfect Baby*	*Otter or Popular Baby*	*Lion or Powerful Baby*
Easy-going	Serious	Bright & wide-eyed	Adventuresome
Understanding	Quiet	Curious	Energetic
Happy	Likes a schedule	Gurgles & coos	Born leader
Adjustable	Looks sad	Wants company	Strong-willed
Slow	Cries easily	Shows off	Demanding
Shy	Clings	Responsive	Loud
Indifferent		Screams for attention	Throws things
		Knows they are cute	Doesn't sleep

Golden Retriever or Peaceful Child	*Beaver or Perfect Child*	*Otter or Popular Child*	*Lion or Powerful Child*
Watches others	Thinks deeply	Daring and eager	Daring and eager
Easily amused	Talented	Innocent	Productive worker
Little trouble	Musical	Inventive	Goal oriented
Dependable	True friend	Imaginative	Moves quickly
Lovable	Perfectionist	Cheerful	Self-sufficient
Agreeable	Intense	Enthusiastic	Competitive
Selfish	Dutiful	Chatters Constantly	Assertive
Avoids work	Responsible	Energized by people	Trustworthy
Fearful	Moody	No follow-through	Manipulative
Quietly stubborn	Whines	Disorganized	Temper tantrums
Lazy	Self-conscious	Easily distracted	Constantly going
Retreats to TV	Too sensitive	Short interest span	Testing
	Hears negatives	Emotional ups and downs	Stubborn

Golden Retriever or Peaceful Teen	*Beaver or Perfect Teen*	*Otter or Popular Teen*	*Lion or Powerful Teen*
Pleasing personality	Good student	Cheerleader	Aggressive
Witty	Creative—likes research	Charms others	Competent
Good listener	Organized	Daring	Organizes well
Mediates problems	Purposeful	Joins clubs	Assumes leadership
Hides emotions	High standards	Life of the party	Problem solver
Leads when pushed	Conscientious	Creative	Self-confident
Casual attitude	On time	Wants to please	Stimulates others
Quietly stubborn	Neat and orderly	Apologetic	Excels in emergencies
Indecisive	Sensitive to others	Deceptive	Great potential
Unenthusiastic	Thrifty	Creative excuses	Too bossy
Too compromising	Depressed	Easily led astray	Controls parents
Unmotivated	Withdrawn	Craves Attention	Looks down on others
Sarcastic	Inferiority complex	Needs peer approval	Unpopular
Uninvolved	Inflexible	Con artist	May become a loner
Procrastinates	Critical	Won't study	Judgmental
	Negative attitude	Immature	Unrepentant

What a Golden Retriever/ Peaceful Child Needs

A Golden Retriever child seems to have few or no needs. However, they do have needs for peace and calmness, and do not react well when pressured. Golden Retriever children seek to avoid conflict and may make poor choices (such as lying) rather than face conflict. They are not motivated by confrontation and parents need to be especially careful to discipline this child calmly and rationally.

Golden Retriever children have a high need for significance and self-worth. They need to know they are important and have a place in the family and world. Their slower pace and easy-going style can make them seem to be lazy and unmotivated. Parents need to give specific instructions regarding responsibilities and at the same time, not push them too hard.

What a Beaver/Perfect Child Needs

Beaver children need stability and order in their life. They will have a hard time handling chaos and constant activity. Routines and schedules work well for beaver children. They tend to dislike noisy parties and a house full of people. Quiet time is very important and when possible, parents need to give this child time away from the busyness of the day.

Parental support is very important to beaver children, and they need to know that their parents are on their team. Achieving excellence builds a beaver child's self-esteem, especially when they know that their parents are proud of them. These children like specific instructions and lots of details. Show that they are important to you, but don't gush all over them.

What an Otter/ Popular Child Needs

Otter children need lots of activity. They need to be kept busy or they will get distracted and may be led astray. They are not good with details and don't do well with routine tasks. Otter children will perform chores and responsibilities better if they can be creative and have fun while working. Changing responsibilities often will help keep the Otter child from getting bored.

Otter children thrive on attention. They will put on a show for anyone who will watch. They need their parents' approval and affection, and if they don't get it, they will look for it elsewhere. If they are constantly criticized and find that they cannot make their parents happy, they will give up and quit trying. Structure will tend to stifle otter children's creativity; they need discipline and guidance with a light touch. Whenever possible; make activities fun and adventuresome for these children.

What a Lion/ Powerful Child Needs

Strong willed children often have a lion personality, and they can certainly keep parents busy. All children will test parents, but the term "terrible twos" probably was meant for a Lion child. Many parents will be tempted to give in and let their Lion child have his way. Every aspect of life seems to be a battle with this type of child, but the parent who can direct his child's energies and keep him challenged can maintain control.

Lion children need appreciation, activity and something to control. Parents need to keep them busy and directed. Allow them the opportunity to exercise leadership and control in some area of their life. Their own pet may be an excellent opportunity to give the lion child control while teaching him responsibility. Demonstrate genuine appreciation for their achievements and keep them involved and active.

Each Child is a Unique Individual

No two children are alike and parenting must be adapted to each child based on his specific personality, strengths and weakness. Children do not fit nicely into one personality type, and parents must learn about each of their children. Children will each learn, interact with people and respond to discipline differently. It is important to guide them in the way they should go, not try to conform them into who parents think they should be.

Children are motivated differently. What works for one child may not motivate another child at all. Disciplining an Otter child by making him sit quietly in his room alone can really get his attention. But a Beaver or Golden Retriever child will enjoy sitting in his room alone— it will do little to make him realize that his behavior is unacceptable. Parents must find out what will motivate each child to achieve their greatest potential and what will encourage them to not misbehave.

Comparing one child to another will not accomplish anything good. Each child is unique and different. To say, "Why can't you be like your brother?" does not motivate a child to do better, but demonstrates that he is not accepted and loved as he is. Parents must handle each child individually, without comparing one to another.

There should be certain guidelines in the household for all children, but there will be some instances where each child will have guidelines specific for him. It will take less work to get a Beaver child to keep his room clean than an Otter child. Similarly, a Golden Retriever child will be less likely to misbehave in a restaurant than a Lion child. Parents must develop a system of rewards and punishments that recognizes the differences of each child. When parents guide their children in the direction they should go according to their personality, children will be more likely to feel loved and cared for by their parents.

"Wow, Tommy, I'm sure glad you're the one motivated by money. Dad's going to be really mad and I need my allowance to buy that bicycle I've been wanting."

Children's Love Languages

Love is the foundation to a secure child who will grow into a responsible adult. Children's different personalities affect how parents interact with them, and they also have different love languages. They receive love differently than their brothers and sisters and quite possibly than their parents. When a child feels loved, he is easier to discipline and train than when he does not feel loved.

A parent's unconditional love gives a child the feelings of security and safety he needs. Words and actions are both required to demonstrate love for children. Children need love spoken to them through all of the love languages, but, like adults, they will have a primary love language, one that speaks love more loudly than the others. It is important to discover your child's primary love language to effectively meet his need for love.

Speaking a child's love language does not guarantee that he will behave and be the perfect child. Problems will arise on his way to adulthood, but a child who has no doubt of his parent's love will be able to navigate through the minefields of life better than the child who does not have that assurance.

Discovering Your Child's Primary Love Language

It will take time and some work to determine your children's primary love language. They may or may not give clues; if not, keep searching until their love languages become clear. According to Dr. Gary Chapman, the love languages are:[2]

- Touch
- Words of Affirmation
- Quality Time
- Gifts
- Acts of Service

Begin by watching your child and see how he expresses love to you. Is he touchy or does he seem to receive joy by doing things for you? Does he say, "I love you" a lot or does he want to spend time with you? Does he like to give you little gifts? You can tell a lot by observing your child's interaction with you, your spouse and others. Watch him play with a friend from a distance and take note of how he expresses himself to his friend. What does your child request from you? Your time, attention, or things? Observe how he reacts to gifts, the things you do for him, time spent together, when touched, or words of affirmation.

You also can give your child a choice between two options. The choices will depend on your child's age and interests. Choices should compare two of the love languages such as, "would you like to put together a puzzle?" (Quality time) or,"would you like me to fix your bicycle?" (Acts of service). There are many ways to test your child's reception of love. Once you determine your child's love language and begin to speak it on a regular basis, he will feel loved.

Teenagers Need Love Too!

It is never too late to begin demonstrating love to your children. They will respond, although it may take a while, especially if they have experienced negativity, a lack of love or improper love. Asking for forgiveness may be required and demonstrates humility and a willingness to admit mistakes. The parent-child relationship can change drastically when a parent admits that he was wrong and has acted badly. Rather than weakness, this actually is a sign of strength and humility.

The teenage years are often the most difficult time for parents and their children. There is a certain amount of stress between parents and a child as the child attempts to break free and become independent. Today's rapidly changing culture focused on sex, violence, drugs and alcohol presents a difficult challenge for many teenagers and parents. The promiscuity, permissiveness and absence of moral absolutes in society today create an external environment that is tearing at the moral fabric of Christian belief. Guiding children toward adulthood is a very challenging task for parents today.

Teenagers need the love and guidance only parents can give. They need parents to be involved in their lives, to set boundaries, to care about them and to love them. Love is the foundation of the parent-child relationship. Parents who have nurtured and helped their children go in the right direction often become enemies fighting over every aspect of life during the teenage years.

Chances are, if a teenager's emotional need for love is met through the adolescent years, he will make it through this difficult time and emerge as a healthy young adult. Teenagers are searching for independence and identity. Parents need to have a balance between allowing independence and remaining involved in their teenagers' lives. Demonstrating love by knowing each child's personality, bents and speaking his love language will do much to help a child feel accepted, loved and significant.

Remember, a child left alone, will go in the wrong direction.

It is imperative that parents know their children and love them as they are, not as they should be or could be. You can have a positive parent-teen relationship. When teens are secure in the love of their parents, they will have confidence to face the negative influences in the culture that would keep them from becoming mature, productive adults. Teenagers are far more likely to succumb to the evil influences of drugs, perverted sex and violence without the Godly love of parents. They will feel loved when they are connected, accepted and nurtured by their parents. Parents must gradually let go of their children and give them freedom to learn on their own, even if they experience some pain along the way. Their parents' love and acceptance gives children a soft place to fall when they make a wrong choice or get hurt.

Children's personalities and how they receive love profoundly affects their lives. How they learn and how parents discipline and motivate them is determined, in part, by their personalities and primary love languages. A child to whom gifts speak love very loudly will be more motivated to get good grades by the promise of a present more than a child to whom words of affirmation speak love. It is important to understand each of your children, to know them and love them as they are.

Do you pray for your children daily?

Do you pray over them on a regular basis?

For Discussion as a Couple

1. Are you purposeful in showing love to your children? How do you show love to them? What can you do to make your children feel more loved?

____

____

____

____

2. Why is it important to understand the personalities of your children? How can you know what personality they are?

____

____

____

____

3. How does your personality type affect your parenting? Does your personality type conflict with your children's?

____

____

____

____

4. Do you agree that it is important to deal with children differently, according to their personality type? Why or why not?

____

____

____

____

5. What is each of your children's primary love language? How can you use their love language in your parenting?

____

____

____

____

Parenting
Study 40
Special-Needs Children

Jesus said, "Let the little children come to me, and do not hinder them, for the kingdom of heaven belongs to such as these." ~ Matthew 19:14-15

A Special Calling

Children are a joy and a blessing from God. The birth of a child can be very emotional for both parents, and watching their child grow, learn and develop is a constant joy. Parents feel a wonderful sense of pride as their child develops a personality and exhibits his traits. This is how it is supposed to be, but on occasion the birth of a new life does not work out this way. Many parents know the heartache of the birth of a child with disabilities. Their child may experience one of many syndromes, including down syndrome, suffer sensory challenges such as vision or hearing impairment, experience long-term illness with cancer or other diseases, or they may have serious physical challenges; cerebral palsy, heart problems, or physical deformity. Developmental challenges, Autism or ADD/ADHD are usually not discovered until a child begins developing. Some challenges can be corrected, some can be overcome, and some affect the child and family for life.

Parenting children without special needs is a challenge; special-needs children present even greater challenges to parents. "When parents learn that their child has a disability or a chronic illness, they begin a journey that takes them into a life that is often filled with strong emotion, difficult choices, interactions with many different professionals and specialists, and an ongoing need for information and services."[1] The initial shock and denial, and then coping with shattered dreams can be very draining and emotional. Yet, the emotions do not stop with the discovery of a child's disabilities. Anger, blame, guilt, disappointment and even depression can affect parents profoundly. Day to day living can be overwhelming for parents caring for a child with disabilities. It is not unusual for a parent to wish that his child would die. He must then deal with the guilt from having such a thought. Parents must forgive God, themselves and their child for the trouble they face with a disabled child.

"Shall we accept good from God, and not trouble?" ~ Job 2:10

Parents of special-needs children often are angry with God. "How could a God of mercy do this to my child? To our family?" "Why would an all-knowing, all powerful God create a child like this?" Perspective and focus are important, especially when asking, "why Lord?" Job lost his children, possessions, and health, yet he would not blame God. He kept the perspective that God was in control and remained focused on God more than his circumstances. The Lord may not change the situation and make your child whole, but He will empower you and your child to endure and achieve victory in spite of the situation. Parenting a special-needs child is a special calling many cannot handle. To successfully navigate through this life, parents must give their anger to God and allow Him to empower them to meet the challenges ahead of them.

Guarding Your Marriage

> *God is our refuge and strength, an ever-present help in trouble.*
> *~ Psalms 46:1*

Most couples are not prepared for the challenge of special-needs children. The stress of caring for a special-needs child will tend to drive a couple apart. They must work especially hard to remain close and remain a team working together to meet the challenges and the emotional strain they will go through. Unfortunately, the divorce rate for couples with special-needs children rises dramatically over the divorce rate of the general population. Couples with special-needs children must commit to guarding their marriage and educate themselves regarding their child's disability and how to cope with it as quickly as possible.

Every child presents unique challenges to parents. A special-needs child may have a relatively minor learning disability, or they may have severe disabilities that will require constant care for life. More severe disabilities will require greater involvement, but every disabled child needs two parents working as a team to help him deal with his challenges. Every parent of a special-needs child experiences a wide range of emotions. The emotions are normal and healthy as long as a couple works through the emotions together. Counseling may be required to survive and hold the marriage together while helping the child through his difficulties.

> *In the day of my trouble I will call to you, for you will answer me.*
> *~ Psalms 86:7*

Long-term or permanent disabilities demand that husband and wife push themselves beyond their natural tendencies to help each other with the challenges they face. Both parents need to help and support each other with all aspects of the child's care. One or both parents will burn out and find it difficult to continue without this support.

A strong husband – wife team who stand together to face the challenges that come their way will tend to gather more support for those challenges from professionals and educators. United, a couple is more confident and better able to present their requests and needs to the officials who can help their child. When a couple is divided and in conflict, they are not able to present unified requests to receive the help, information or resources they need.

Some parents find extraordinary strength to cope with the challenges of a special-needs child. Others react very differently and will want to run from those challenges. Love, encouragement and striving to meet each other's needs will help both parents cope with the problems they face daily. Parents must allocate time for each other. Support groups, family members and support agencies can provide aid so parents can take a break and spend some time together. There will be times when it seems like the whole world is against them and no one will help or give support. Standing together helps a couple get through those times and continue fighting for their child. They also can help each other remain focused on God and His promises. He enables parents to cope when it seems that they can no longer continue.

Special-needs children need healthy, loving parents. Couples must support each other, but they also need to take care of themselves individually. Respite programs aid parental physical, emotional and spiritual health by relieving couples of the burden of caring for a special-needs child. Utilize those services or seek out aid from your church or support groups so you can have time individually and as a couple to refresh and strengthen yourself.

Praise be to the God and Father of our Lord Jesus Christ, the Father of compassion and the God of all comfort, who comforts us in all our troubles, so that we can comfort those in any trouble with the comfort we ourselves have received from God. For just as the sufferings of Christ flow over into our lives, so also through Christ our comfort overflows. If we are distressed, it is for your comfort and salvation; if we are comforted, it is for your comfort, which produces in you patient endurance of the same sufferings we suffer. And our hope for you is firm, because we know that just as you share in our sufferings, so also you share in our comfort. ~ 2 Corinthians 1:3-7

Family Support

Special-needs children profoundly affect every person in the family. It is very easy for parents to focus so much on their special-needs child that they neglect the other children in the family. Some unwittingly place demands on their "normal" children or allow them to care for themselves. They forget that the other children have needs, feelings, and their own emotions regarding the disability of their brother or sister. Parents must help their children process their feelings and deal with the issues of having a special-needs sibling.

Parents will help their non-special-needs children greatly if they help them honestly express their feelings respectfully. When children are not allowed to express their feelings or their feelings are invalidated, they will internalize those feelings, and it can injure their emotional health and lead to depression. It is not easy being the sibling of a special-needs child. They will lose parental time and may face the negative reaction of their peers. Often, they lose much of their childhood, as they must help take care of their special-needs sibling. Love and acceptance are necessary even if children express negative feelings toward their sibling.

Educating your children will help them accept their special-needs sibling. It is important to give age-appropriate information regarding their sibling's disability as soon as the children are able to understand. Family meetings are an excellent way to provide information and allow children to express their concerns and fears. Open communication will help the parents aid their special-needs child as their well-children provide observations and information from their point of view.

It is important for parents to achieve a balance working with all of their children. The support of well-children can help parents with the challenge of a special-needs child, but the well-children each need support also. They need their parents' time, attention, love and involvement. Parents constantly face the challenge of having time for everyone. It is not easy, but it is possible as parents commit themselves to meeting the needs of each other and all of their children and then strive to meet those commitments.

The extended family can be a source of support or a source of tension. "A grandparent's grief is usually more involved than the parent's because there is sadness for the adult child and the grandchild."[2] They also must deal with lost dreams and unmet expectations. Parents of a special-needs child must educate their parents and extended family members to dispel any prejudices and misinformation they may have and to help them adjust to having a special-needs child participate in family functions.

Your Special-Needs Child

All children grow at their own pace, and special-needs children may grow at a much slower pace. Activities or events that happen in a well-child's life often take much longer for the special-needs child. Some activities and events may never take place for the special-needs child, depending on the severity of the disability. Patience and love are vital to a special-needs child's growth. It may be difficult to love a child who is unable to love back or expresses love in very limited and non-traditional ways. Any child responds to unconditional love, even if they are not able to show love. People have a limited capacity to love, but, in Christ, all things are possible, even loving the unlovable.

> *The more a child is loved, the more lovable that child is.*
> *~ Robert Naseef*

Understanding a special-needs child is vitally important to the relationship and to helping the child develop. Parents should learn as much as they can about their child's disability. An incredible amount of information is now easily accessible to help parents understand almost every aspect of a disability. The Internet, libraries and various agencies can provide the information needed. Parents can utilize this information to become as well informed as possible so they can help their child and effectively relate with him and the people who will help care for him.

One way or another, special-needs children touch everyone they come in contact with. Unfortunately, many prejudices exist regarding people with disabilities. Most people simply do not want to take the time to deal with disabilities. Some actually will taunt or make fun of a disabled person. Ignorance breeds most of these attitudes. When possible, parents need to inform and educate these people. Those who will stop and take the time to learn about a special-needs child are usually blessed by their interaction.

Parents must do what they can to protect their special-needs child and help him grow and learn to fulfill his potential. Unfortunately, many disabled people suffer mental, physical or sexual abuse from the very people who are responsible to care for them. Special-needs children often learn not to question caregivers or others in authority. Parents should help their children learn healthy boundaries as much as possible and learn to recognize potential abuse patterns. Potential care providers must be interviewed and prayerfully considered before children are left in their care.

Therapy for a special-needs child should always begin as soon as possible. There are many types of therapy available to enhance auditory processing, attention, thinking abilities, regulation of behavior, speech or physical movement. Beginning the right therapy quickly aids development and gets the child moving in the right direction. Research possible therapists, talk to them about your child, and get recommendations. Remain in close contact with the therapist to stay informed and aware of your child's therapy and progress.

Floor time is important to special-needs children. This is unstructured time when a parent follows the child's lead and interests. The child is allowed to direct the activities they do together. Parents will actually get on the floor with smaller children and play with them. Unstructured time with older children may involve playing games, sitting, walking or whatever activity the child chooses. Floor time builds relationship abilities for the child and builds the relationship between parent and child. It should be a regular, ongoing occurrence.

"When did we add a clown to our care team?"

Building a Team

Effective parenting of special-needs children is almost impossible without help. It is important that parents build a team to assist the care, education and growth of their child. This team should include medical doctors, educators, therapists, specialists, counselors, program administrators, and people in the parent's support system. The team may vary and change depending on the needs of the child, parent and family. Parents need to be the team leaders and remain in charge of their child's care. Parents, not administrators or educators should decide what is best for their child, self and family.

> *Blessed is he who has regard for the weak; the LORD delivers him in times of trouble.*
> *~ Psalms 41:1*

Parents should be their child's advocates with the care system. They spend the most time with the child and love the child as no one else will. They must know their child's disabilities well enough to discuss them with care team members. Dealing with professionals, educators or medical personnel can be intimidating. There are some professionals who may attempt to intimidate parents purposefully. Parents must be polite, respectful, firm and remain in control of their child's care. They may not have the university degrees, but they know their child better than anyone else.

The cost of care for a special-needs child can be overwhelming. Parents of special-needs children may qualify for financial aid, even if they have a good income. It is important that parents inform themselves about the programs and the possible financial aid available. Program administrators and support groups can often assist with information regarding aid available. Parents must be persistent about getting help. Keep searching until you get the assistance you need.

Parents need to set goals and make plans for their child and his development. It would be helpful to include the care team in the goal-setting process. Remember, goals and plans need to be flexible. When goals become the mission or plans become too rigid, people often experience frustration and anger. Look at the big picture of where your child is and what you would like him to attain. Don't get bogged down in the details of day-to-day care and forget about the direction you are headed in. Utilization of the strengths of both parents is essential in this effort. One may handle details well, while the other is able to see the vision. If both parents have similar strengths and weaknesses, find a team member to help you in the areas you lack.

A support group is an important part of the care team. They can be an excellent source of information and aid to meet the challenges parents will face with a special-needs child. Support groups need to be a safe place to discuss feelings and problems without fear of criticism. Once relationships and trust are built, the support group can be a good source of respite time as parents watch each other's children and provide time alone.

Parents should be involved with every decision made regarding their child. Involvement in education, therapy and medical attention will help parents remain informed. They need to be knowledgeable and cautious about medication to be given to their child.

Choosing a school is important and requires careful investigation. Parents should visit classes and observe teacher—child interaction. Are the teachers able to effectively interact with the children? Are the children able to work at their own speed? Does the school provide a variety of features to help children? Finding the right school for your child may take time and effort, but will aid your child's development.

God does have a plan, even though you may not see it for your special-needs child. Rejoice with your child in every victory and success. Look for the good in your child and your situation and continue to work on your relationship with the Lord and your spouse. Parenting a special-needs child can be very demanding, challenging and stressful. Do not allow this challenge to tear apart your marriage and family. Work together to meet this challenge and do not forget to work on your marriage! May the Lord bless you as you persevere with your special calling.

For Discussion as a Couple

> *For I know the plans I have for you," declares the LORD, "plans to prosper you and not to harm you, plans to give you hope and a future.*
> *~ Jeremiah 29:11*

1. Do you see parenting a special-needs child as a special calling? Why or why not?

 ____

 ____

 ____

 ____

2. What emotions did you experience as you went through the process of learning about and accepting your child's disability?

 ____

 ____

 ____

 ____

3. How can you guard your marriage and ensure the challenges of parenting a special-needs child does not tear you apart?

 ____

 ____

 ____

 ____

4. How can you ensure that all of your children get the time they need with you?

 ____

 ____

 ____

 ____

5. Do you have a care team? Why would this be important? What can you do to put a care team together?

 ____

 ____

 ____

 ____

Special Section: Educating Your Children

Parents are responsible for their children's education. They may utilize the public school system or a private school to help educate their children, or they may home school their children. Whichever option parents choose, they must remain involved in their children's education.

Children require a thorough education to effectively interact in the adult world. Their education should include academic, vocational, relational, social, cultural, family and spiritual training. Parents provide much of this education through life experiences, and formal and informal training. A natural part of parenting is to begin teaching children their "A,B,Cs," how to count and elementary writing skills. Teaching more than elementary, basic educational skills, advanced or specialized skills is more than many parents have the time or ability to accomplish. This is where parents can enlist the aid of schools to help them educate their children.

Choosing a School

Parents have alternatives today for their children's education. Some factors may limit those alternatives, but there are many resources available to help parents provide the education they desire for their children. Public school or expensive private schools are not the only options available today. Homeschooling, charter schools, lower cost private schools and alternative public schools present several options for parents to consider as opposed to only sending children to the local public school.

Many parents have become disillusioned with the public school system today. Moral and educational decay, violence and a loss of focus have driven many parents to search for an alternative for their children's education. Concerned parents can find alternatives, but are those alternatives best for their children? Parents must honestly analyze their situation and prayerfully seek God's guidance before making a decision regarding a school for their child.

"Mom, err, I mean, teacher. I don't think Rover understands this math lesson."

Public schools usually have the most opportunities and the greatest variety of programs available for students. Many children do very well in the public school system and emerge well educated and prepared to move on to university or specific career training. Public schools may provide vocational training allowing students to move directly from school into the career of their choice. The public school environment may not be the first choice for parents, but with parental guidance, children can navigate through the negative aspects of public schools. Parents must decide between cost, program availability and the educational environment for their children.

Private schools often provide the environment parents desire, but may not provide the broad education or specific programs their children need. Parents must carefully research possible private schools; a poor moral environment can exist even at "Christian" schools. Private schools frequently are more focused and dedicated to the education of students and often have a lower teacher to student ratio. They also allow parents to choose curriculum (such as Bible or spiritual training) for their children that would not be available in public schools. Cost often is the drawback to private schools. Parents desiring this alternative should check into possible sources of financial aid.

Homeschooling offers the greatest amount of parental control, but it also involves a great deal of time, energy and discipline by the parents. Homeschooling associations provide socialization for children and can offer a wider variety of programs than previously available. Parents teach the exact curriculum they want for their children and can tailor studies to meet each child's interests and needs. Parents must be able to teach a variety of subjects to children of different ages at one time. It is a difficult task, but not impossible with some training and support from others involved with homeschooling.

Making a decision about your children's education is not always easy. There are pros and cons to every option. Do not assume that every public school is bad or that every Christian school provides excellent education. Parents must research the alternatives and determine what is best for each child. Different children will react differently to educational alternatives. Both parents must be involved in the decision of how to educate their children. They must weigh all of the alternatives and costs involved with each. Talk to other parents, school administrators, and teachers about the options available to you. Make a choice based on God's direction, your child's needs and family resources.

Parental Involvement

Parents homeschooling their children are obviously involved with their children's education. These parents must remember that it takes both parents to effectively homeschool children. It is a huge commitment and while dad may be working to support the family, he must also help mom teach the children. She will burn out quickly if she must be teacher and mom all day, every day of the week. Parents must find creative ways to ensure that both parents are involved in the process.

It is easy to abdicate the children's education to the professionals in private or public schools. Parents must resist this temptation and remain involved in their children's education. Meet with teachers and administrators whenever possible. Find out what your children are being taught by questioning your children about educational practices and curriculum. Examine books and curriculum and research anything you find questionable. You don't have to be the crusading parent trying to change the educational system, but you can work within the system to obtain the best possible education for your children within the framework of your values and beliefs.

Parents can hold schools responsible for their part in a child's education. Work with administrators and teachers to ensure your children receive the best education possible. Find out the alternatives available for your children. If your child is struggling, find out why. Talk to the teachers and work with your child to help him make progress toward achieving his goals and objectives in education.

Educating your children is not an impossible task. It will take commitment and work, but your child can enter adulthood prepared to achieve all that the Lord wants for him.

Fortified Marriages
Chapter 9 Endnotes

Study 36: *When Children Arrive*

1. Harville Hendrix, Ph.D.; "Good Marriages Make Happy Children"

Recommended for further reading:
- Raising Responsible Kids by Jay Kesler
- The Complete Book of Baby and Child Care; Focus on the Family
- Growing a Spiritually Strong Family by Dennis & Barbara Rainey
- Becoming the Parent God Wants You to Be by Kevin Leman

For further information, see:
- Focus on the Family: ww.focusonyourchild.com
- Focus on the Family: www.family.org

Study 37: *The Goal of Parenting*

1. Dr. Henry Cloud & Dr. John Townsend; Raising Great Kids (Grand Rapids, MI; Zondervan Publishing House, 1999) p 29
2. Ibid

Recommended for further reading:
- Raising Great Kids by Dr. Henry Cloud & Dr. John Townsend
- Boundaries with Kids by Dr. Henry Cloud & Dr. John Townsend
- Setting Limits: How to Raise Responsible, Independent Children by Providing Clear Boundaries, by Robert MacKenzie

Study 38: *Guiding Your Children*

1. Nina Easton, The Invisible Dad, Los Angeles Times Magazine, June 14, 1992
2. Nelson's Illustrated Bible Dictionary; Copyright 1986, Thomas Nelsons Publishers

Recommended for further reading:
- Dare to Discipline by Dr. James Dobson
- Successful Christian Parenting by John MacArthur
- Learning About Sex; a seven book series, Concordia Publishing House
- God's Design for Sex Series, 4 volumes by Focus on the Family
- Financial Parenting by Larry Burkett and Rick Osborne
- Spiritaul Growth of Children, edited by John Trent, Rick Osborne and Kurt Bruner

For further information, see:
- Family Dynamics: www.familydynamics.net
- Family University: www.familyuniversity.com

Study 39: *Loving Your Children as They Are*

1. Donna Partow, A Woman's Guide to Personality Types (Bloomington, MN; Bethany House Publishers, 2002) pp 189—190
2. Gary Chapman; The Five Love Languages, How to Express Heartfelt Commitment to Your Mate (Chicago, IL; Northfield Publishing, 1992)

Recommended for further reading:
- How to Really Love Your Child by Ross Campell, M.D.
- A Woman's Guide to Personality Types by Donna Partow
- The Five Love Languages of Children/Teenagers by Gary Chapman
- Parents & Teenagers; Jay Kesler, General Editor

Study 40: *Special-Needs Children*

1. Joyce Brennfleck Shannon, editor; Mental Retardation Sourcebook (Detroit, MI; Omnigraphics, Inc, 1999) p 289
2, Becky Pruitt, quoted in Special Kids Need Special Parents (NY, NY; Berkley Publishing, 2001) p 32

Recommended for further reading:
- A Special Kind of Love; For Those Who Love Children with Special Needs, by Susan Osborn & Janet Mitchell
- A.D.D.: Wandering Minds and Wired Bodies, by Edward T. Welch
- My Child Has Special Needs: A Journey from Grief to Joy, by Sharon Hensely
- The Resilient Family: Living with Your Child's Illness or Disability, by Paul Power & Arthur Dell Orto
- Special Kids Need Special Parents: A Resource for Parents of Children with Special Needs, by Judith Loseff Lavin
- The Child with Special Needs: Encouraging Intellectual and Emotional Growth, Stanley Greenspan & Serena Wieder
- What To Do About Your Brain-Injured Child, by Glenn Doman
- You Will Dream New Dreams: Inspiring Personal Stories By Parents of Children with Disabilities, by Stanley Klein & Kim Schive
- Blinded by Grace: Entering the World of Disability, by Robert Molsberry
- Mental Retardation Sourcebook, Joyce Brennfleck Shannon, editor
- The Special-Needs Reading List: An Annotated Guide to the Best Publications for Parents and Professional, by Cory Moore

For further information, see:
- Information Center on Disabilities and Gifted Education; ericec.org
- Office of Special Education and Rehabilitative Services; www.ed.gov/about/offices/list/osers
- Mobility Internatiotional USA; www.miusa.org
- Special Needs Project; www.specialneeds.com
- Special Child; www.specialchild.com
- Family Voices; www.familyvoices.org
- Federation for Children with Special Needs; www.fcsn.org
- National Disability Rights Network; www.napas.org

- Association for Retarded Citizens; www.thearc.org
- Family Friendly Fun; www.family-friendly-fun.com
- Coping.org; www.coping.org
- Vision therapy & help; www.children-special-needs.org
- March of Dimes; www.marchofdimes.com
- National Center for Learning Disabilities; www.ncld.org
- Autism Society of America; www.autism-society.org
- Autism Today; www.autismtoday.com
- The National Down Syndrome Society; www.ndss.org
- National Federation of the Blind; www.nfb.org
- National Association of the Deaf; www.nad.org
- Muscular Dystrophy Association; www.mdausa.org
- United Cerebral Palsy; www.ucp.org
- The National Craniofacial Association; www.faces-cranio.org
- AboutFace USA; www.aboutfaceusa.org

Special Section: Educating Your Children

- Private School Review provides information about private schools throughout the United States: www.privateschoolreview.com
- Homeschool Information: www.home-school.com or www.homeschooling.com

Chapter 10
Parenting Adult Children

Study 41
Left, But Not Gone

Only be careful, and watch yourselves closely so that you do not forget the things your eyes have seen or let them slip from your heart as long as you live. Teach them to your children and to their children after them.
~ Deuteronomy 4:9

You Are Still a Parent

Children do not usually grow up, leave home and become totally independent people. God created people with a need for relationship and children still need their parents even after they move out on their own. The family should always be a source of support and aid and a safe place to turn in times of trouble. It is the parents' responsibility to raise children to be responsible adults, but does this mean that once they become adults, the parental responsibilities end? How much responsibility do parents have for their adult children? Do they support them financially? Give them instruction? Advice? Are parents only to be available for love and support? There are as many answers to these questions as there are sets of parents and adult children, and different children in the same family will often require different answers.

Society viewed parental involvement much differently in the past. Families were patriarchal in the Old Testament. Jacob's sons and their families followed him to Egypt and even as an elderly man; Jacob made the decisions for his family. His children, as adults followed his commands and his judgment, even though they were heads of their own households. Roman society, at the time of Jesus, also was patriarchal. The husband and father was the absolute authority in the home. He had to approve of a newborn child before it was allowed to live. His power continued as children reached adulthood, and he exerted control over many aspects of their lives.

The Bible does not teach absolute authority of the father, but does teach that parents have an ongoing responsibility to future generations.

Today, independence is the rule in society. Parental advice is viewed as an intrusion into the lives of their adult children. Children who remain close to their parents often are seen as different. Increasingly, parents are left totally out of the lives of their grown children. In fact, many writers (even Christians) state that parents do their best for 18 years and trust God for the rest. They say that parents have completed their job, but is the parents' job ever really finished? The Word of God says that parents are to teach His ways to not only their children, but to their children's children as well. Western society does not condone patriarchy as much as eastern cultures or societies of old, but the Bible teaches that the older are to teach the younger. It is important that Christian parents carefully balance truth and grace while respecting their adult children's independence.

Changing Roles

> ***Parental responsibilities for adult children are not easily definable.***

The parental role changes drastically as children enter adulthood, but it is not the end of parental involvement. Parents will always mean more to their children than simply friends, encouragers or counselors. They are Mom and Dad, and neither distance nor neglect can break the bonds that tie parents to their children. Obligations to children change dramatically as they enter adulthood, and the status of the relationship will depend a lot on the relationship parents have with their children during the teen years.

Parents are involved in their children's lives with decreasing levels of control as the children grow up and there is a point where this involvement should change dramatically. This may be at a specific point in time, such as when the child moves out of his parents' home or it may be very gradual as the child becomes increasingly independent. Many say that parental interjection should stop once a child becomes an adult, that the child must now determine where and when parental love, wisdom and skills are needed. Parents need to be sensitive to their adult children's independence, but there is a time when circumstances necessitate interjection whether their children want to hear it or not. Parents still have some responsibility in their children's lives.

> *At that time I will carry out against Eli everything I spoke against his family-from beginning to end. For I told him that I would judge his family forever because of the sin he knew about; his sons made themselves contemptible, and he failed to restrain them.* ~ 1 Samuel 3:12-13

Eli judged Israel as a priest of God for forty years. Priests in the Old Testament mediated between man and God, but Eli didn't hear much from God, largely because he did not restrain his sons from abusing their priestly positions to enrich themselves. He honored his sons more than God, and the Lord judged him and his family because of it.

The Lord expects parents to remain involved in their adult children's lives. Once a parent, always a parent as the saying goes. Life as father or mother of adult children can be as interesting and challenging as it was raising children through the first 18 years. Parents of adult children have the opportunity to build new and different relationships with their children now that they are adults. Their job as parents now is to find the balance between maintaining a relationship and providing valuable input while allowing their adult children the freedom to live their own lives. It is never too late to become a good parent. Parents can maintain or revive a relationship with an adult child that will enrich both of their lives.

Communication Changes

Many parents think that once their children move out, they can stop learning and developing their parenting skills. Nothing is further from the truth. The Lord expects parents to continue teaching His principles to their children and grandchildren. The key to effective parenting of adult children is learning how to interact with them as adults rather than as children. Parents can not determine the path of their children's lives any longer or make decisions for them. Yet, it is important to remain in relationship with adult children and to communicate effectively.

Parents cannot communicate with adult children as if they are still young children living at home. Often, parent-child relationships are strained or broken because of the way parents communicate with their adult children. They must treat their children with respect and as adults. Commanding or demanding certain behavior or actions of adult children usually will not change their children's behavior. When parents treat their adult children more as peers than children, they are better able to communicate effectively with them.

They are Different!

There often are many similarities in a family, but there are also many differences. More than ever, parents must deal with their adult children as individuals. What is good for one child will not necessarily be good for another. One child may remain close physically and emotionally, while another may move across the country and not call for months. Parents must adapt to the changes that occur as their children begin to live their own lives.

Children belong to a different generation and life is very different for them and their children than it was for their parents. They do not live in the same world that their parents lived in as children or young adults. They must be able to interact with the world their way and according to their relationship with the Lord. Children will resent their parent's attempts to be the Holy Spirit and change their behavior. They must make their own life choices.

Yes, parents need to speak up when children go astray or are headed in the wrong direction, but the principles of boundaries teach that parents can not change their children. There may be a time when parents have to stand back and allow their children to learn the hard way. It will be hard and can be very frustrating, but they are adults and they have a right to make their own choices, even if they are the wrong choices.

Remain Connected

Far too often parents allow distance to grow between them and their children. One can not change the physical distance, but he can keep emotional distance from creeping into the relationship. Young adulthood is a busy time of life: building careers, family, ministry and adjusting to life as an adult. It is the parents' responsibility to remain connected with and available to their adult children and to find a balance in the relationship. Parents need to always reach out to their children, even when it is inconvenient and their children don't reach out to them.

Remaining connected with adult children is possible. It takes some effort and some creativity, but meaningful relationships can be built with adult children. Creating traditions around events and holidays does a lot to keep a family together. Parents must remember that adult children have a right to not participate and do not need to explain their reason. Using guilt and manipulation to encourage participation will not build relationships. Mandatory participation causes bitterness and resentment and will often lead to a break in the parent-child relationship. Use the following list to begin thinking about ways to bring your family together and then find out what your whole family can agree to do.

- Special occasions: maybe pizza after grandchildren's soccer or little league games or desert after recitals or other special event.
- Holidays: birthdays—any or even all holidays. Get together as much as you can.
- Family work day: get together once a month or every other month and rotate having a work day at each family's home. The host family provides lunch and everyone helps clean, paint or does whatever is needed around the house.
- Pool your resources to provide Christmas for a family in need. This could be a Thanksgiving tradition or even another day. It is a great ministry to do something for someone else as a family.

Evaluate your family gatherings and make sure they are working for everyone in the family. If they aren't working, change them or do something else.

What Can Parents Do?

Parents of adult children are in a new era of their lives. There will be a lot of change and parents need to learn to adapt to the changes they see in their children. Seek God's will and His power and you can continue to be a positive influence in your children's lives. In summary, parents need to:

- Pray for your children.
- Adapt to your new parental roles.
- Communicate with your adult children as adults, not children.
- Understand and respect their differences.
- Seek to remain connected with your children.

For Discussion as a Couple

1. Do you agree or disagree with the statement, "Once a parent, always a parent?" Why or why not?

2. How do you see your parenting role changing as your children become adults?

3. Why must you be concerned about your child's differences? How does this affect your relationship with them?

4. Why is it important to communicate with your adult children differently than when they were young?

5. How can you remain connected with your adult children?

Parenting Adult Children

Study 42

Love & Support, Not Control

Fathers, do not embitter your children, or they will become discouraged. ~ Colossians 3:21

It is possible to give adult children advice and the benefit of your life experiences without intruding in their lives.

A Change in Relationship

Healthy families are a source of support and acceptance that benefits all family members. Parents must find the balance between controlling their adult children's lives and enabling them to live dysfunctional lives. There are limits both to their authority and their responsibility which legally ends when children officially become adults. Finding that balance can be very difficult as lives and needs change. Some situations may call for more parental involvement while others will warrant less. There is a point where parents are available for support, encouragement and advice, but at the same time allow their children to live independent lives.

Accepting the change in relationship with their children often is hard for parents. They want to help and guide their children with their greater experience and wisdom. They know the solutions for many of the problems that arise in their children's lives and they often can see the direction their children should go or the decisions they should make. Yes, parents usually know better than their children, but this does not give parents the right to interject their advice any time they feel the need. Parents need to learn to stop and think about what they are going to say to their adult children. Using words like *should, must,* and *ought* bring the relationship back to a parent-child relationship and will damage the relationship with their adult children.

Some parents consciously or subconsciously encourage their children to become dependent on them. They will take care of their children and attempt to shield them from the harshness of the world. A dependent child may give parents the warm feelings of being needed, but the relationship does little to help the child become an independent, mature adult. Parents will not live forever, and children who do not become independent, sooner or later will have to take responsibility for their own lives. Adults who remain emotionally or financially dependent on their parents are rarely equipped to live life on their own when they finally have to accept responsibility for their lives. It may be painful to allow children to suffer the consequences for bad decisions, but the growth they receive will help them handle life's situations when their parents are gone.

"The other night you were out until 10:00, at lunch, yesterday you didn't drink milk and this morning you didn't brush your teeth. Your father and I are afraid that you are going the wrong direction."

It is possible to give adult children advice and the benefit of life experiences without intruding in their lives or making them dependant. Parents need to remember that, as adults, their children are now peers in many ways. They may be younger and less experienced, but adult children must live their own lives, their way. Parents must consider their words and how they communicate with their children. Communicating with your adult children as if they are young children living at home will tend to alienate children rather than build the relationship.

Time to Speak Up

There are times when parents do need to speak up and confront their children. They can not be like Eli of the Old Testament and stand by as their children reject God and pursue sin or injurious activities. Christians have a duty to speak up when anyone strays from the faith, but parents must remember that they have to treat their children as adults, not children.

> ***Brothers, if someone is caught in a sin, you who are spiritual should restore him gently. But watch yourself, or you also may be tempted.***
> ***~ Galatians 6:1***

The Bible states that those found to be in sin should be restored gently, not harshly. Parents need to keep this in mind when they confront adult children. Is the issue sin or a problem that must be addressed? Attacking, demanding or criticizing children will not bring about repentance as much as reaching out in love and concern for their well being and success in life. Or is it a matter of simply having a difference of opinion? You may not like what your child is doing, but that doesn't make it a problem that must be addressed. Parents who talk to their children about everything they disagree with will usually find that they will see less and less of their children.

Parents need to speak to their adult children as they would a friend or a peer. They can offer advice or their insight into an issue, but then must allow their child to make his or her own decision. When considering whether or not to bring up an issue, you might ask yourself, "Is this issue important enough that I would bring it up to a friend?" Unless the issue directly affects you or your relationship with your adult child, you would probably not bring up something that you wouldn't bring up with a friend.

Letting Go

Letting go means that parents allow their children to make their own life decisions, and it should begin soon after birth as parents slowly relinquish control of their children's lives. Parents are responsible to prepare their children for adulthood, and that preparation involves increasing a child's level of responsibility and allowing them to make more of their own decisions. This process continues through childhood with parental guidance until the child becomes an adult and is in total control of his or her life. This is the point when a parent must really let go and surrender his child to the Lord.

This final letting go of an adult child can be difficult for parents. Understanding the following four steps will help parents as they seek a balanced relationship with their adult children.

- ➢ Understanding that some separation is inevitable and necessary.
- ➢ Allowing for a grieving period as you adjust to your new role in your child's life.
- ➢ Actively seek to redefine your parental role.
- ➢ Letting go of control of your child's life.

Accepting the separateness of grown children allows parents to express and expand their own individuality. They can now think more of themselves and do the things they want to do. Energy can now be directed toward the interests they desire to pursue now that they do not have daily parental responsibilities. They can focus on personal endeavors, while maintaining a balance in family relationships. Their work is never complete as a parent, but the day-to-day "hands-on" experience of parenting has ended.

Boundaries

Parenting adult children is an exercise in building and maintaining healthy boundaries. Parents must take responsibility and ownership for what they can control, while allowing their adult children to have responsibility and control for their own lives. Taking their children's responsibilities keeps the children from growing and maturing. Attempting to control their lives will cause animosity and possibly even a break in the relationship. Parenting adult children is a balancing act requiring prayer, thought and working together as a couple to have the right mix of providing aid and yet, allowing growth.

> ***It is difficult finding the balance between assisting adult children and enabling inappropriate behavior.***

Occasionally, parents will have good intentioned input received as attempted control. Sometimes, it may require parents to back off and allow their adult child to do his own thing, even if it means doing the wrong thing. Once the child realizes he is able to make his own decisions without parental commentary, criticism or judgment, he will often allow his parents back into the decision-making process. Parents must realize that if their adult children think they are breaking boundaries, they are breaking boundaries. Perception is the key and the child's perception may come from tight parental control during adolescent years. It may seem unfair, but adult children often will receive well intentioned input as criticism or control.

Married Children

When your adult child marries, much of the work you have done to establish healthy, working relationships will change. The son-in-law or daughter-in-law brings many new variables to your relationship. His or her parents, family, background, culture, values, and personality will have an affect on your relationship with your child. For better or worse, your child has decided to commit his life to this person. Your rejection usually will drive your child away from you, rather than prompting him to make a better choice. It is important for parents to make the effort to get to know their new "in-law" and make him or her feel accepted into the family.

Family life becomes much more complicated when children marry and have their own children. Another family is now involved, and they have their own traditions and ways of doing things. Parents must share their child with that other family. The young couple must build their own life together, which will pull the child away from parents at times. Parents must resist the urge to place expectations or demands on their married children. Help your children find the balance of time for their own families while still having time for each extended family.

How Much is Too Much?

How much involvement should parents have in their adult children's lives? The answer will vary greatly from family to family and even from child to child within the same family. One adult child may have daily contact with her parents, while another may not call at all, leaving it to the parent to initiate contact. Parents should not know everything going on in their adult children's lives, and they need to especially remain out of husband—wife difficulties, unless they are invited to mediate and work with both. There will be times in the lives of both parents and adult children when communication becomes difficult, yet even through those times, parents must ensure that contacts remain consistent. Again, it is a matter of finding a balance between being available and connected versus meddling or controlling your children's lives.

The Question of Money

Providing financial assistance for adult children can be an issue. Today's unstable society often places people in difficult circumstances financially. Many adults are irresponsible and cause their own difficulties, but unexpected problems and trials do arise, and parents should assist their children as much as they are able. It is also important that parents do not become enablers, holding their children back from learning from their mistakes. Experience often is the best teacher in this area, and if parents continually rescue their children from financial irresponsibility, they will not learn to manage their finances well. It is also very important that parents of adult children approach financial issues with their children as a team, and they must agree together whether they will help, how much and when they will help their adult children financially.

It is the parent's responsibility to learn Biblical relational principles and work with their children to develop balanced, healthy relationships. Again, it may not seem fair, but remember, you are the parent! Your children will continue to learn about life from you as long as you live. You have the opportunity to demonstrate maturity and how to develop healthy parent-child relationships. A life-long, growing relationship with your children is a wonderful legacy to leave to your children and grandchildren.

For Discussion as a Couple

1. How can you know when to speak up and when to say nothing to your adult children?

   ____
   ____
   ____
   ____

2. Have you let go of control of your adult children's lives? Why is it important to go through this process?

   ____
   ____
   ____
   ____

3. How have you overstepped your adult children's boundaries? What can you do to uphold their boundaries?

   ____
   ____
   ____
   ____

4. What areas do you need to be aware of when your children are married?

   ____
   ____
   ____
   ____

5. When would you help your adult children financially? When would you say "no?"

   ____
   ____
   ____
   ____

Parenting Adult Children

Study 43

Adult Children Living at Home

He who fears the LORD has a secure fortress, and for his children it will be a refuge. ~ Proverbs 14:26

So he got up and went to his father. "But while he was still a long way off, his father saw him and was filled with compassion for him; he ran to his son, threw his arms around him and kissed him. "The son said to him, 'Father, I have sinned against heaven and against you. I am no longer worthy to be called your son.' "But the father said to his servants, 'Quick! Bring the best robe and put it on him. Put a ring on his finger and sandals on his feet. Bring the fattened calf and kill it. Let's have a feast and celebrate. For this son of mine was dead and is alive again; he was lost and is found.' So they began to celebrate. Luke 15:20-24

Adult Children Returning Home

The idea of adult children moving back home is an interesting concept in today's society. Children did not leave home for much of history. Males remained in their parents' household and brought wives into the family, and wives moved into their husband's household. Generations of families remained together; older caring for young until the younger cared for the older in their declining years. The industrial revolution changed the family dramatically as families moved from rural areas to cities and worked in factories or service industries. Young adults moved out largely due to space limitations in their parent's homes. It has only been in the past couple of generations that there has been an expectation of children moving out and living independently of their parents.

The story of the Prodigal Son illustrates the differences that can occur in a family. One son demanded his inheritance and left home while the other remained at home with his parents. The culture of the time influenced this difference in part because the oldest son would inherit the family land and younger sons often inherited nothing or very little, so they would move out to make a future for themselves. The prodigal son did not build his future, but squandered his inheritance. Similar to some adult children today, he made a mess of his life and then moved back home in an attempt to get back on his feet. Many young adults today find it difficult to live on their own. They move back home or may remain home and not move out at all.

There are several reasons why adult children may return home: economics, break up of a marriage, limited availability in the job market, irresponsibility or a lack of maturity. It can be difficult today for young adults to obtain stable employment and succeed financially. Company shutdowns and "downsizing" with little or no notice are not unusual, and a person may find himself out of work and with few options available. Marital break-up can lead to the same results leaving an adult child with nowhere to live. There are also times when adult children just feel more comfortable at home. They make the attempt to live on their own, but they don't have the resources to succeed. The security of Mom and Dad's house can be very appealing.

Another interesting phenomenon in today's society is the fierce independence of young adults even when they live at home with their parents. Many adult children view any questions about their lifestyle as an intrusion, yet they have no problem living at home and not paying their own expenses. Some parents have middle aged children living in their home with no apparent interest in moving out. They want their freedom and no intrusions, but they are making no move toward independence.

Confusing Roles

Parent-child roles are most confusing when an adult child lives at home. The parents own the home and pay the bills, but their child is an adult and technically responsible for his own life. What expectations can the parents have of their child? What responsibilities should he have in the home? Do parents have a right to tell their child living at home anything? These can be tough questions as parents attempt to work out the answers in the midst of conflict in the home.

Biblically, parents have a responsibility to take care of their young children. There are some responsibilities for adult children, but parents are not financially responsible for their adult child who has the ability to earn his way in life. Couples must work together to decide the parameters of when they will allow an adult child to live at home. They also need to decide under what conditions he may continue to live at home. Those conditions can be negotiated, but, in the end, the parents will decide the expectations of their child while he is living at home.

Certainly, there are times when parents need to be available for their children. When they have been responsible and yet, something beyond their control happens to put them in a position where they need assistance. But what about the adult child who has been irresponsible and made poor choices? There is no set of rules to objectively decide what constitutes valid needs and what doesn't. Also, there is no checklist to tell parents when they qualify as a loving supporter of their adult child and when they are foolishly supporting an irresponsible, unmotivated adult who has no intention of supporting himself.

Healthy boundaries are absolutely necessary to making an adult child's stay in his parent's home a productive endeavor. Parents must seek God's guidance and wisdom, the input of trusted friends and maintain open communication with each other. They need to look at each situation as objectively and fairly as possible and make the best decision they can. Children differ and parents must make their decisions based on what they feel the Lord wants them to do for each child individually, even if the other children don't agree.

> *"We are the only animals that let our kids come back home."*
> *~ Bill Cosby*

Before They Move Home

Even if a child shows up at the door late one night saying; "Mom, Dad, I have nowhere to live," there are some things parents must do before they allow their adult children to move home. If they have had problems with irresponsibility, parents should have this discussion as a couple before the child is standing at the door late one night so that as husband and wife, they know what to say if their child shows up. Some things to consider before allowing an adult child to move home are:

1. Why is he coming home?
2. What is his purpose for coming home?
3. How long will he be at home?
4. What are the plans to fulfill his purpose for moving home?

Parents have a right to have all of their questions answered if their child is going to move into their home. They will want to talk to their child and ask for honest answers to their questions about his desire to live with them. Time at home should be for a specific duration with plans in place for how and when he will move out again. It is important that parents pray together about the situation before answering their child's request to move home.

Together, make a list of expectations that the adult child must meet while living at home. This must be written and should include:

- Behavior such as smoking, drinking, and friends of the opposite sex in the house.
- Financial; rent, food, utilities.
- Communication; information regarding schedule and when everyone can be expected home.
- Household work; what is expected of the adult child?
- Privacy; working out alone time for both parents and child.
- Sleep time, respecting each other's schedule.
- Discussion time; a scheduled time to work through issues.
- Time frame; how long will he stay?
- Accountability; how will parents hold their child accountable for the plan to fulfill his purpose at home?

The goal is to make life together smooth and a positive experience for everyone. Husband and wife must be in agreement with the conditions for their child coming home and the child must agree to abide by those conditions or not come home. The conditions must be in writing and although it seems harsh, having the adult child sign the conditions is a good idea. Those conditions may be reviewed and changed from time to time, but at least both parties understand the conditions prior to misunderstandings. Whether their child moves home because of bad choices or unfortunate circumstances, clear expectations before he moves in will save many problems later.

An agreement also will help keep the adult child from becoming a permanent fixture in his parent's home. A purpose, plan and accountability will help keep him on track and making progress toward accomplishing the purpose of his coming home.

While They are at Home

An adult child living at home can be a great experience. It allows parents and child the opportunity to grow together in a whole new way. Do things together, cultivate the relationship and have fun together. Play games or find a common interest that you can do together. It is an opportunity to reconnect with each other and also a chance for parents to influence their adult child in a new environment. Parents have less direct responsibility for their adult children and they can build a new relationship without the stress they had when the children were young.

> ***Make time for the two of you to have husband-wife time together—alone.***

Remember that as husband and wife, your first priority is to maintain a strong relationship between the two of you. Do not let the intrusion of an adult child living at home come between you. Time alone as a couple is important, especially if your child moves back home after a period of no children at home. Schedule occasional evenings or even weekends for just the two of you. The marriage relationship cannot be put on hold because an adult child lives with you.

It is important to quickly resolve issues that arise. Unresolved conflict with your adult child can ruin the experience and damage your relationship. If things aren't going right, sit down and talk about them. The adult child needs to live within the expectations agreed to. If it becomes a major point of contention that can not be resolved, he may need to make the choice to live elsewhere. Some flexibility is necessary, but it is your house and you do not have to compromise your values for your child. Make the most of the experience and a different, stronger relationship with your child can be built.

For Discussion as a Couple

1. What are your thoughts about the fact that for much of history, children did not move out of their parent's home? Is a multi-generational home feasible today?

2. Why do you think roles would tend to be confusing with an adult child living at home? What could you do to help define roles?

3. What would you do if you answered the door late one night to find your adult child standing there, asking to move in?

4. Why is it important to talk to your spouse and to be in one accord regarding your adult children living with you?

5. Do you agree that it is important to have written expectations of your adult child while they are living with you? Why or why not?

Acceptance Inventory - Your Adult Children

Circle the number that best describes your interaction with your adult children in each area below.

	Almost Never	Rarely	Often	Almost Always
1. I tell my children that I am proud of them.	1	2	3	4
2. I hug my children.	1	2	3	4
3. I tell my children I love them.	1	2	3	4
4. I take an interest in what my children do.	1	2	3	4
5. I show interest in what my children talk about.	1	2	3	4
6. I try to encourage my children.	1	2	3	4
7. I listen to my children's views without judging them.	1	2	3	4
8. I give my children my undivided attention when they speak.	1	2	3	4
9. I spend time with my children doing what they like to do.	1	2	3	4
10. I show affection to my children.	1	2	3	4
11. I let my children know that I disagree with their choices.	4	3	2	1
12. I remind my children that they should act like adults.	4	3	2	1
13. I demonstrate impatience with my children.	4	3	2	1
14. I push my children to do better in life.	4	3	2	1
15. I yell at my children.	4	3	2	1
16. I will purposefully not call my children to make a point.	4	3	2	1
17. I use money to get my children's attention.	4	3	2	1
18. I get emotional to get them to do what I want.	4	3	2	1
19. I show my disappointment to my children.	4	3	2	1
20. I am not open to discussion when we disagree.	4	3	2	1

Total your score here: _______

A score of 65—80 indicates that you are very accepting of your children—continue to work on your relationship with your children. If your score is 50—64; you are accepting, but may be able to use this inventory to help increase your level of acceptance. Below 50: Please evaluate how you are dealing with your children. It is likely you are harsh or uninvolved and do not demonstrate acceptance to your children. Parental acceptance is extremely important to healthy relationships with adult children. If they don't have your acceptance, they will look for acceptance elsewhere.

Parenting Adult Children

Study 44

Grandparenting

Children's children are a crown to the aged, and parents are the pride of their children.
~ Proverbs 17:6

A child needs a grandparent.

The Joy of Grandparenting

Perfect love sometimes does not come until the first grandchild. ~ Welsh Proverb

Grandparenting can be one of the great joys of life, but it can also be frustrating and discouraging. Grandparents have the opportunity to help their children and impart wisdom from a completely new point of view. They also have the opportunity to pour their love into grandchildren and positively influence a new generation. Frustration can also arise through miscommunication or expectations regarding the grandchildren and grandparent's role in their lives. It is important that there be open and honest communication regarding grandparent's roles in the grandchildren's lives. Achieving positive grandparenting roles and relationships will take some work.

Grandparents have a new and very different role than they did as parents. Usually, grandparents are in a position to devote more time to their grandchildren without having to worry about the daily problems of life. They can have fun with their grandchildren, while always remembering that it is their adult child who is the parent. The love shown to grandchildren must be grounded in support for their parents. Almost certainly, grandparents know more about parenting than their adult children, because they have already raised children. But knowledge is not the issue—responsibility, freedom, boundaries and control are the issues. Parents have raised their children, it is the children's turn to raise their children and grandparents must respect their parenting or expect to not see very much of the grandchildren. Grandparents are to give love to their grandchildren and love and support their adult children.

Being Involved

Participation in the grandchildren's activities is very important, even though it may not always be possible to attend all of their events. Setting aside time to attend concerts, games, dances and a host of other activities will mean a lot to both the grandchildren and adult children. Grandparents have the opportunity to be a part of their lives and it would be a loss to miss out. You may have missed out on many of your children's activities and feel bad about it. Apologizing and asking forgiveness of your adult children may be appropriate, but don't let mistakes of the past keep you from participating now.

Distance may present challenges to being involved with grandchildren. A little creativity allows grandparents to be involved even when they do not live near their children. Sending cards of encouragement before events and phone calls immediately following events will do much to keep grandparents close and involved in their grandchildren's lives. Video cameras can help grandparents feel involved. If your children don't own a video camera, consider purchasing one for them. Unless

travel is impossible, grandparents need to make the trip to see their children and grandchildren on occasion. Inconvenience is a poor excuse for not spending time with the family.

Grandparent, Not Parent

Yes, you know more about parenting than your adult child. Many grandparents *tell* their adult children what they need to do with the grandchildren, a confrontation ensues, and then the grandparents wonder why they don't see their grandchildren for a long time. The child's parents may have different ideas for raising children than their parents do. When the grandparents offer their suggestions about how to raise the children, the parents may get offended and resist the intrusion into their family. Grandparents must realize that different is not necessarily wrong and their children may raise the grandchildren very differently than they raised their children.

It is important for grandparents and parents to discuss the role of the grandparents in the lives of the grandchildren. Do not make assumptions about what your role will be and work with your children discussing any differences you may have. Grandparents must always defer to the parents' authority over the grandchildren and not usurp that authority by asking the grandchildren about doing fun things before asking their parents. Showing respect for the parents will build the relationship and benefit all three generations. Parents of the grandchildren need to know that they have their parents' support and love without control and intrusion into their lives. Some points to keep in mind when interacting with your children and their children:

- Support your child and spouse in their roles as parents.
- Follow the rules set by the parents.
- Love your grandchildren, don't compete for their love.
- Do not take a stand between your grandchildren and their parents.
- Do not criticize your adult children, especially in front of the grandchildren.

"We'll be home by midnight, Dad. Now, don't let Paul smoke, drink or do drugs. Don't let him get mixed up with the wrong type of girls and don't let him join a gang."

Helping Adult Children Parent

It is possible to give adult children pointers about parenting, even if they don't ask for advice. Parents must remember that they cannot control or force their adult children to do what they think is best. When your child brings up an issue, ask if you can give some advice. If they say "no," keep the information to yourself, but if they say "yes," give advice for that specific situation. Do not take the opportunity to give an hour long lecture about the finer points of parenting. Parents can also watch for those "teachable moments," when they can use a life experience to make a point about parenting.

The best thing parents can do for their adult children is to be available. Demonstrating availability will build the parent-child relationship and promote a closeness that will allow the parent the opportunity to interject advice in addition to support. Parents available to help with babysitting, errands, hosting parties and other activities will more likely be the people children will turn to when issues arise.

Helping adult children maintain perspective quite possibly is the most important aspect of a parent's availability. Parents who have raised children know well the tremendous task their adult children have raising children, building a career, working on a marriage and serving the Lord. Pointing the way to the Lord and providing continued support and encouragement can help adult children maintain perspective, even when there are problems in life.

Potential Issues

There are times where the grandparents' over-control is not the issue—the adult child's lack of control is the issue. Some people, even though they are adults, are not ready for parenting. The grandparent may become the major caregiver for the grandchildren. Boundaries can become a major issue when the adult child doesn't take responsibility of caring for their children. While it is important that parents do not undermine their child's responsibility and authority as parent, it is also important that they do not relieve them of their responsibility as parent and do the parenting for them as they live an irresponsible life. Grandparents generally make the best babysitters, but grandparents can also be taken advantage of if their children dump the grandchildren so that they can play and avoid their parental responsibilities.

Becoming grandparents when an unmarried daughter becomes pregnant can be a huge issue in the home. It is important that the parents not overreact to their daughter's sin. Yes, it is a serious issue, but throwing their daughter out of the house or writing her off is not the answer. This is a problem that comes with long-lasting consequences, but it does not have to destroy a family. Remember, every child is precious to God, even those conceived in sin, and it is not the grandchild's fault! Couples must work together and seek to love and guide their daughter through this time.

Physical, sexual or serious substance abuse issues may require intervention and at times, even the removal of the grandchildren from their parents' home. This has to be the hardest issue to face as a grandparent, and it must be faced with much prayer and a good system of support. The grandparent in this situation will often be vilified as a traitor and a terrible parent for betraying their child. Yet, God can use this situation to turn the lives of adult children around. Grandparents should be open and honest with their grandchildren about the issues without putting down the character of the parent or parents. They must honestly confront their child's issues in love.

It is imperative that husband and wife stick together through all of the problems they experience with their children and grandchildren. Strong communication is essential, and parents must refrain from blaming each other for the issues and at the same time, accept responsibility where they have responsibility. Problems with children can be the biggest issues in love and usually will either drive a husband and wife apart or bring them closer together. A couple who depends on the Lord, remains focused on Him and goes through the trials together can grow in their marriage relationship through any issues that may arise.

> A good man leaves an inheritance for his children's children, ~ Proverbs 13:22

The inheritance left for grandchildren may involve some money, but it is primarily the legacy that grandparents leave. How have the grandparents blessed and strengthened their grandchildren's lives? It is a blessing to give grandchildren gifts, but material gifts will never compare to the gifts of love, time, encouragement and being available. Passing along faith, love and history will build up grandchildren and help them prepare for adulthood. Contrary to the belief of some, it is not the grandparents' job to spoil the grandchildren. It is their job to love the grandchildren so much that they will always know that love and acceptance are waiting for them at their grandparent's home. This will be an inheritance that is much more valuable than any monetary inheritance.

Parents are busy with life as they raise their children. Grandparents have the chance to slow down and take time for their grandchildren. They are not in the battle on a daily basis and often can build a relationship with their grandchildren that parents could never have. Grandparents must make the effort to build this relationship. They must be more concerned about being involved in their grandchildren's lives than about their own convenience. Yes, the work never stops, but God's blessings never stop either, because grandchildren are a wonderful blessing from the Lord.

> *"Grandchildren are God's way of compensating us for growing old."*
> *~ Mary H. Waldrip*

Having Fun with the Grandchildren

Grandchildren present the opportunity for grandparents to enjoy more of the benefits of children without many of the responsibilities. Their parents are often busy building a home, career, family, ministry and grandparents can be the respite in the storm. The relationship they have with their grandparents can positively affect children for the rest of their lives.

Grandparents must learn about their grandchildren. It is important to understand their personalities and love languages to love them as they are. This may take more time when the grandchildren don't live with them, but a weekend or two should give grandparents a good idea of how to demonstrate love for each of the grandchildren.

Remaining in contact with grandchildren is not hard to do even if separated by great distances. Grandparents can send cards, letters or small gifts to stay in touch. They can send videos of themselves, making it fun by dramatizing how much they miss their grandchildren or even doing silly things that only grandchildren would appreciate. The electronic age makes it even easier to stay in touch with email and the ability to send pictures or videos instantly via computer. Purchasing a video or digital camera for your children could be a great investment to help remain connected to your grandchildren.

There are more things a grandparent can do to remain close to his grandchildren than there is time in the day. Have fun with your grandchildren! Use the list below as a starting point for ideas and then add your own so you can affect your grandchildren's lives with the love only a grandparent can give.

Things to do with Your Grandchildren[1]

- ☆ Spend time with them without their parents.
- ☆ Read stories to them, designate a bookshelf in your home just for the grandchildren.
- ☆ Take them to historical sites and museums.
- ☆ Take them on vacation with you.
- ☆ Play games; card games, board games, the more the better.
- ☆ Do different creative things, painting, drawing, pottery or woodworking.
- ☆ Go fishing together.
- ☆ Collect bugs in a jar.
- ☆ Tell them stories about their parents when they were little.
- ☆ Teach them about their ancestors.
- ☆ Build castles out of blocks or cards.
- ☆ Tell them all the important Bible stories.
- ☆ Play hide and seek with them.
- ☆ Take them to a park and play with them.

- ☆ Be interested in what they are interested in. Ask them questions about what they do and like and listen.
- ☆ Build a playhouse with them.
- ☆ Collect rocks.
- ☆ Take them on field trips to a fire station, airport or other places.
- ☆ Teach them to cook.
- ☆ Take them camping.
- ☆ Go to the zoo.
- ☆ Have them choose the activity to do on certain days.
- ☆ Put together a puzzle.
- ☆ Take a craft, music or some other class together.

There are many more activities than this, but you get the idea. Be a part of your grandchildren's lives and demonstrate God's wonderful love to them.

> ***What a bargain grandchildren are! I give them my loose change, and they give me a million dollars' worth of pleasure. ~ Gene Perret***

For Discussion as a Couple

1. Do you think grandparenting is more important today or less important than in the past? Why or why not?

   ____
   ____
   ____
   ____

2. What are some things you can do to be supportive of your adult children as they raise their children?

   ____
   ____
   ____
   ____

3. How would you handle your grandchild telling you that there is physical abuse going on in their home? Substance abuse?

   ____
   ____
   ____
   ____

4. What is the inheritance you can leave for your grandchildren?

   ____
   ____
   ____
   ____

5. What are some fun things you will commit to doing with your grandchildren?

   ____
   ____
   ____
   ____
   ____

Fortified Marriages
Chapter 10 Endnotes

Study 41: *Left, But Not Gone*

Recommended for further reading:
- Once a Parent Always a Parent; by Stephen Bly
- Parent's Work is Never Done; by James Haines & Margery Neely
- Parents Forever—You and Your Adult Children; by Sidney Callahan

For further information, see:
- Focus on the Family: www.family.org

Study 42: *Love & Support, Not Control*

Recommended for further reading:
- Parenting Your Adult Child: How You Can Help Them Achieve Their Full Potential; by Ross Campbell & Gary Chapman
- Becoming a Wise Parent For Your Grown Child; by Betty Frain & Eileen Clegg
- Give Them Wings; by Carol Kuykendall
- Getting Along Almost With Your Adult Kids; by Lois & Joel Davitz

Study 43: *Adult Children Living at Home*

Recommended for further reading:
- How to Talk to Your Adult Children About Really Important Things; by Theresa DiGeronimo
- Grown-up Children, Grown-up Parents; by Phyllis Lieber, Gloria Murphy & Annette Schwartz
- You and Your Grown-up Child; by Howard Halpern

Study 44: *Grandparenting*

1. Adapted from; 41 Things Grandparents Can Do With Grandchildren by Susan Alexander Yates

Recommended for further reading:
- Essential Grandparent: A Guide to Making a Difference; by Lillian Carson
- The ABCs of Christian Grandparenting; by Robert & Debra Bruce
- The Power of Grandparenting; by Robert Strand
- Creative Grandparenting Across the Miles; by Patricia Fry

For further information, see:
- Christian Seniors Association: www.christiansenior.org
- AARP: www.aarp.org/grandparents
- Grandparent World: www.grandparentworld.com
- Granparent Foundation: www.grandparenting.org

Chapter 11
Marital Challenges

Study 45
Resisting Attacks on Your Marriage

Every marriage will experience attacks, problems, setbacks or crises, and, unfortunately, many do not survive serious difficulties. Your marriage can survive and even grow through any problems you experience. Problems in marriage are nothing new; they have been around since the creation of man and the first marriage. Whether it is sin or the effects of a fallen world, couples must prepare for difficulties in life.

Marriage represents the relationship between God and His people, and Satan desires its destruction. He often attacks marriages through the temptation to sin and turn away from God. A couple's selfish, self-centered behavior also can destroy their marriage, if they allow it. The Lord provides the strength to stand up to any temptation or attack when a couple lives their lives according to Biblical principles and His power.

Be self-controlled and alert. Your enemy the devil prowls around like a roaring lion looking for someone to devour. Resist him, standing firm in the faith, because you know that your brothers throughout the world are undergoing the same kind of sufferings. And the God of all grace, who called you to his eternal glory in Christ, after you have suffered a little while, will himself restore you and make you strong, firm and steadfast. To him be the power for ever and ever. Amen.
~ 1 Peter 5:8-11

"To Love at all is to be vulnerable. Love anything, and your heart will certainly be wrung and possibly be broken. If you want to make sure of keeping it intact, you must give your heart to no one, not even to an animal. Wrap it carefully round with hobbies and little luxuries; avoid all entanglements; lock it up safe in the casket or coffin of your selfishness. But in that casket—safe, dark, motionless, airless—it will change. It will not be broken; it will become unbreakable, impenetrable, irredeemable... The only place outside Heaven where you can be perfectly safe from all the dangers and perturbations of love is Hell."[1]

There is Evil in the World

One does not have to look far to discover evil in the world. Horrible child abuse, genocide, slavery, murder, rape and the general lawlessness of mankind reveal the evil in the world. Anytime law and order are removed from an area, the depravity of human nature takes over. This is evidenced during floods, natural disasters or riots when police forces are overwhelmed until reinforcements can be brought and order restored.

Be very careful, then, how you live-not as unwise but as wise, making the most of every opportunity, because the days are evil.
~ Ephesians 5:15-16

Sin brought evil into the world and it affects every person in the world in one way or another. Sin of a spouse, children, or others can cause suffering and grief. No one is exempt; neither the faithful nor evil. Disease, illness, and natural disasters also affect many families and marriages everywhere. The world is full of trouble and couples must be care-

ful, living wisely with Jesus Christ at the center of their marriage. Only then will they be able to make the most of every opportunity as they obey and follow the Lord.

Trouble Will Come

Jesus told His disciples they would have trouble in this world. Persecution would come because of their faith, but also because of the problems of a fallen world. Christians are not exempt from the problems of the world. It doesn't seem fair or right that wonderful, giving people should suffer and die at the hands of evil men, but it happens... often. The fact that trials come should not surprise anyone. Married couples must be ready to face the trials and problems they that will experience in their lives.

In this world you will have trouble. ~ John 16:33

Physical pain may come through injury or illness. An accident, one moment of carelessness, can change lives forever. The brutality of sin is seen everywhere, from abuse suffered at home, to crime on the streets and war around the world. Cancer affects millions of people each year and it is difficult to watch a loved one go through the pain and suffering.

Emotional pain can be as difficult as physical pain. At times it can be even more difficult to endure. Emotional abuse can leave scars as deep as any physical scar. Human beings seem to have an incredible capacity for hurting others. The pain of depression can be a devastating experience that affects the whole family. Financial loss caused by loss of a job, theft, or bad investments can profoundly affect a couple. Any of these emotional hurts will affect a marriage.

Dear friends, do not be surprised at the painful trial you are suffering, as though something strange were happening to you. ~ 1 Peter 4:12

A growing problem is the need to care for elderly parents. Dr. Terry Hargrave states that this will become one of the biggest problems faced by couples in coming years as medicine keeps people alive longer, while not necessarily increasing their quality of life. Long term care giving can drain a couple and damage the marriage relationship.

The world is full of temptation and most people are much closer to falling to sin than they would like to believe. All marriages and families experience the affects of sin. Sexual or physical abuse in the home or by someone outside the home, adultery, addictions, rebellious children or teenage pregnancy will greatly affect any marriage.

The bad news is that, most likely, your marriage has endured or will experience at least some of these problems during your years together. Life in this fallen world means that every person is subject to the possibility of some sort of pain and loss during his lifetime. There will be natural disasters, disease, injury, hurt, and sin in life. The Lord did not promise His children wouldn't have problems, but He promised that He would be with them through it all.

Couples must also realize that love alone will not get them through the trials that they will face. Ninety percent of couples who lose a child divorce and couples facing other trials also face a much higher rate of divorce than the general population. It is unfortunate that many husbands or wives walk away from their hurting spouse rather than working to keep the marriage and family together during their crisis. It is important that a couple depend on the Lord when experiencing trials and problems in life. His strength will help them endure even when the love of their spouse is not enough.

"Love cannot protect a marriage from harm, and love by itself, is not enough to sustain even the most loving couples.
~ Drs. Les & Leslie Parrott

Persevering Through the Storms

Commitment is important to a marriage and will help a couple get through the storms of life, but commitment alone will not get them through. Couples must cling to the Lord and seek Him through every trial they face. God seals the commitment and strengthens a couple for the trials they will face. The marriage built on the foundation of the Rock—on Jesus Christ, can weather any storm.

God is our refuge and strength, an ever-present help in trouble.
~ Psalms 46:1

Satan does not cause every problem a couple will experience, but he certainly will attempt to use any problem to cause division in a marriage. He is that prowling lion looking for someone to devour. Couples must take a stand against him remembering that their struggle is not against the things they can see, but the spiritual forces that want to destroy their lives, marriage and family. Standing together and trusting totally in God gives a couple strength they can not have alone. The cord of three strands is not easily broken (Ecclesiastes 4:12) and a couple clinging to the rock of Jesus Christ will not be easily dragged away.

For our struggle is not against flesh and blood, but against the rulers, against the authorities, against the powers of this dark world and against the spiritual forces of evil in the heavenly realms. ~ Ephesians 6:12

Sometimes there are reasons for the problems a couple may experience, but sometimes there is no clear answer as to why there is a problem. Sin brings consequences even when there is repentance, forgiveness and restoration. Adultery of one spouse will definitely bring trouble into the home. Cancer, accidents or some senseless act of violence do not have easy answers and possibly no answer at all. Human tendency is to attempt to find answers for all suffering. Too much time and energy looking for answers will tend to draw a couple away from clinging to Christ and persevering through the trouble. Do bad things happen to good people? Yes. Is God all powerful and all knowing? Certainly. Does God love mankind with an everlasting love? Of course. Remember, this is a fallen world groaning under the weight of sin and depravity (Romans 8:22). All creation awaits the return of the King of kings and Lord of lords. God is in control even when the world seems out of control.

Peace I leave with you; my peace I give you. I do not give to you as the world gives. Do not let your hearts be troubled and do not be afraid. ~ John 14:27

A couple enduring the suffering of a trial must get support and help. One person cannot care for a hurting spouse alone day after day and when both husband and wife go through a trial they will be hard pressed to be able to encourage each other. Involve family, friends and the church to help with responsibilities and also to give emotional support. If the trial is sin, it is necessary to confront sin and deal with it. Couples cannot allow the sins of each other, children or others against their family to be forgotten without dealing with them. Abuse victims usually can deal with the abuse, but the lack of protection and care profoundly wounds a person already suffering from a sinful act. Get the help you need whether it is support, counseling or even protection through government agencies.

Couples must stand together and take on every trial as a "we" experience. A husband may

not feel the physical pain his wife feels dealing with cancer, but by walking with her through the trial, they will grow together and experience intimacy. When possible, they need to encourage and strengthen each other to persevere through their trial. When both do not have the strength to be available for each other, they need to get outside help.

...we rejoice in the hope of the glory of God. Not only so, but we also rejoice in our sufferings, because we know that suffering produces perseverance; perseverance, character; and character, hope. And hope does not disappoint us, because God has poured out his love into our hearts by the Holy Spirit, whom he has given us.
~ Romans 5:2-5

Hope is the aspect of the Christian faith that changes trials and suffering for Christians. Throughout the history of Christianity, Christians have suffered for their faith and suffered through earthquakes, floods, plagues, wars and everything else the world suffers through. If anything, God's people are singled out for destruction as Satan seeks to destroy their lives, marriages and families. Hope is the confident expectancy that God will do what He has promised to do. It sustains Christians through the worst of circumstances as they focus on the Lord and cling to Him.

Blaming God, spouse or others for trials does not help. Blame can tear couples apart as they focus on the object of blame rather than on the Lord. Yes, sin must be confronted and dealt with, but a person fixed on blaming someone else for his trouble and suffering is not showing grace or relying on the Lord. The victim mentality also puts focus in the wrong place as it focuses on self rather than the Lord. Being a victim does not help a person handle suffering and can even make the situation worse.

Who shall separate us from the love of Christ? Shall trouble or hardship or persecution or famine or nakedness or danger or sword? As it is written: "For your sake we face death all day long; we are considered as sheep to be slaughtered." No, in all these things we are more than conquerors through him who loved us. For I am convinced that neither death nor life, neither angels nor demons, neither the present nor the future, nor any powers, neither height nor depth, nor anything else in all creation, will be able to separate us from the love of God that is in Christ Jesus our Lord. ~ Romans 8:35-39

Perspective is important and can be the difference between growing through a trial and just surviving another day. Those who suffer with God's perspective do not look inward, but upward to the Lord for the strength to persevere through the trial. Peter walked on the water as long as he focused on Jesus. When he took his eyes off the One who sustained him and looked at his circumstances, he quickly began to sink (Matthew 14:28-32). Those going through trials must also remain focused on Jesus Christ.

Mankind does not understand God's ways and suffering may seem unfair and arbitrary at times. God did not answer Job's complaints and desire for fairness. He simply declared who He is. God did not rescue Jesus from the cross, but allowed Him to suffer so the His relationship with mankind could be restored. Because of sin, every person deserves death and eternal separation from God. His grace and mercy saves those who call upon His name and the suffering they may endure is only for a little while compared to the eternity promised in Heaven. The scars left by pain and suffering identify Christians with their Savior.

"Scars are evidence that you were hurt and evidence that the Lord healed you." ~ Dave Roever

Prepare Now

Storms, trials and tribulations will come in life. Couples must prepare before they come. Preparing means that they build the foundation for a strong, solid marriage. That foundation must be Jesus Christ. The marriage relationship that is not grounded in Jesus Christ will whither and dry up and then will blow away at the first major trial that comes at it. Do not allow your marriage to get to that point. Continue the work to build your relationship, first with the Lord and then with your spouse. Develop intimacy and closeness so that when the storms come, you will be able to stand together and remain focused on the God who loves you and will always be available for you.

> *You, dear children, are from God and have overcome them, because the one who is in you is greater than the one who is in the world. ~ 1 John 4:4*

For Discussion as a Couple

1. Do you believe that Satan wants to destroy your marriage? How would he attempt to do this?

____
____
____
____

2. Why is it important to rely on God rather than love and commitment when going through trials?

____
____
____
____

3. What does it mean for you and your spouse to stand together through trials?

____
____
____
____

4. Why must sin be confronted when it attacks your marriage or family? How do you confront it?

____
____
____
____

5. How can you prepare for the trials that will come to your marriage relationship?

____
____
____
____
____

Trials and Tribulations

Trials are adversity that will test an individual's faith. Tribulations are great adversity and anguish; intense oppression or persecution.[2] Answer the following questions honestly and openly. The purpose of the exercise is not to open old wounds, but help you work together as a couple in future trials. When discussing your answers, do not judge or attack your spouse. Accept the answers and thank him or her for being willing to share those answers with you.

---

1. What was your greatest trial or tribulation before you married? How did you get through it?

   ____
   ____
   ____

2. What was the most difficult trial you have experienced together? Did you stand together through it? What could you have done better? ______________________________

   ____
   ____
   ____

3. How do you tend to react to crisis and stress in your life? What could you do to respond better?

   ____
   ____
   ____

4. How does your spouse tend to react to crisis and stress in his or her life? How have you been hurt by that reaction? ______________________________

   ____
   ____
   ____

5. How has your sin affected your marriage? How have you and your spouse been able to move past it? ______________________________

   ____
   ____

6. How has your spouse's sin affected your marriage? How have you been able to get through it?

   ____
   ____
   ____

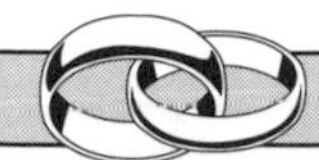

Challenges in Marriage

Study 46

When Children Go Astray

Jesus continued: "There was a man who had two sons. The younger one said to his father, 'Father, give me my share of the estate.' So he divided his property between them. "Not long after that, the younger son got together all he had, set off for a distant country and there squandered his wealth in wild living.
~ Luke 15:11-14

There is a way that seems right to a man, but in the end it leads to death.
~ Proverbs 14:12

Children going astray put an enormous amount of stress on a marriage. Parents tend to blame themselves or each other and often spend as much time fighting with each other as they do with their child. Children choosing a wrong path are difficult for all parents. Parents want their children to make good choices and hold to sound values, but the reality is that many will choose their own way. Parents may be able to see that their child is headed for problems, but they can not force him to make good decisions. They should continue to work with the child whenever possible, while remembering to keep their marriage relationship a priority.

No parent is perfect and no matter how well a couple raises their children, children can and do make bad decisions. Parents make mistakes and may do things wrong. Some may be abusive, too permissive or do very little to help their children grow and mature. Parents may need to repent of things they have done in the past and perhaps ask forgiveness from their children, but a child's poor choices are his decision. Parents should only take responsibility for the areas under their control, not their child's poor decisions.

Parents of children who go astray often are left hurt and confused over what happened and what might have caused their child's poor behavior. They can be like survivors of a tragedy, wondering why this happened to them. Who is to blame? Or what is the purpose of it all? Society's tendency is to blame-shift, but putting the blame on someone else does not help parents properly handle the situation. Rebellious children often will blame their parents for their problems, but accepting the blame for their child's consequences of poor behavior does not help the child.

When Your Teenager Makes Wrong Choices

When children become teenagers, parents often wonder what happened to their happy, contented, cooperative pre-teen. Somehow, their child was replaced by a sullen, angry, uncooperative teenager who doesn't want anything to do with his parents. They may not show it, but teenagers need their parents more than ever. Their hormones may be going crazy and they may be desperately attempting to find their place in the world, but a parent's love, support and encouragement is needed more than ever.

Too often, teenagers and parents become adversaries, fighting over virtually every aspect of home life. It is a natural part of God's order for teenagers to break free from parental bonds. It doesn't have to be a contentious, troubled time, but in many families, that is exactly what it becomes. Even with a teen in open rebellion, it is never too late to begin building a positive relationship and give unconditional love.

Parents need to work together to establish different levels of boundaries for their teens. Teens should be making many of their decisions. Parents need to decide where the boundary lines will be and then communicate those lines to their teenager. Levels of boundaries are necessary because the teen needs to know what is absolute, what is negotiable and what will be left to his discretion. Drugs, alcohol and sex in the home should not be negotiable. Parents have a right to decide what goes on in their home. Dating, driving, curfew times, etc. are areas that can be negotiated with the teen. Choice of music, clothes and hairstyle (all within some defined boundaries) can be left to the teen's discretion. Husband and wife should establish the boundaries together and then work with their teen to implement them.

> ***A child needs love the most when he least deserves it.***
> *~ Anonymous*

Parents must confront issues that come up with their teenagers as one. Divided parents will have difficulty affecting their teenager positively and bring about changed behavior. Working together and presenting a united front to a teenager is critical to helping their child get back on track and going in the right direction. When your teen is not willing to conform and is going in the wrong direction, it may be necessary to involve the church, friends, a counselor or even the authorities. This is not the time to give up or give in; you may be fighting for the very soul of your child. Shouting matches, name calling, or angry confrontations with your teenager are not productive and will not resolve problems. Speak to your teen in love, adhere to healthy boundaries and attempt to enlist his input in resolving the issues you face.

It is important that parents not overreact when problems arise. Poor grades on a report card do not necessarily mean a child will be a failure in life or consuming alcohol one time doesn't mean he will become a drug addict. Making such exaggerated statements will tend to drive children toward the extremes rather than drawing them back. Showing respect and being willing to negotiate on the negotiable items will serve to open teens up rather than drive them away.

"Remember Dad, the Bible says, 'in your anger do not sin.'"

When Children Choose a Different Path

Parents must weigh the seriousness of problems with their children. Children may choose not to pursue the dream they had growing up. They may find life working menial jobs fulfilling and choose not to go to college. Parents must resist the temptation to push their child to achieve what they think he should achieve. Are their choices "bad?" Or are they just different than what you want for them? Parents must examine their own motives before confronting decisions made by their older children.

Potentially harmful choices made by a teenaged child require confrontation by parents. A child may be developing the wrong kind of friends, poor spending habits or a sinful life style. Parents can express their fears, make positive recommendations and set healthy boundaries, but they can not force their children to make right choices. Constantly rescuing children from the consequences of their poor choices does nothing to help them learn. It is important that parents define the consequences for breaking the rules and then follow through.

Extreme problems have no easy solutions. There are many parents who wonder where their child will sleep at night or what kind of trouble he is in now. There may be child or spousal abuse, neglect, sexual abuse or severe drug or alcohol abuse. Getting involved is never easy and often very painful, but parents cannot stand by and watch one of their children throw his life away. They need to pray fervently, work together as a team and again, involve other mature Christians when going through serious problems with teenagers or adult children.

> ***Parents cannot control their adult children—no matter how bad the choices they make are.***

It is difficult to know when to get involved and when to stand aside and allow children to learn from the consequences of their poor choices. No parent wants to see his child suffer the consequences of his actions, but there are times when this is the only way a child will learn. Suffering consequences will usually teach a child more than any lecture a parent can give, in fact, parents may keep their child from learning by intervening and mitigating the consequences of poor decisions.

Letting Go of Adult Children

There is a time when parents must back off and give their adult child to the Lord and trust Him. Some people simply must learn the hard way. It is difficult for many parents to allow their children to make their own decisions, but, just as God does not violate mankind's right to choose, parents must also relinquish their control over their children. Parents who attempt to coerce or manipulate their children into making good decisions usurp God's authority. Often, parents' attempts to get their children to make right choices push the children further away and hardens their hearts. The father of the prodigal son did not chase after his son to help him make better decisions, he simply let him go.

Letting go means that parents give their children to the Lord and allow Him to work in their lives. They accept reality when they accept the fact that they cannot hold, train or protect their children any longer. Parents should pray diligently for their children, let go of control and attempting to guide their children. They let go of the dream they had for their child and allow the Lord to work in his life, but they do not let go of their faith, hope and love.

The Broken Hearted Parent

Letting go does not take away parents' pain when children have gone astray. A child's rejection can be the most painful experience a parent will endure. This is not the time to blame or attack each other for the failures of a child. There is enough pain without making it worse with accusations and hurt coming from a spouse. Husbands and wives will handle the pain differently, and they must be sensitive to each other as they go through this trial. Comfort must be found within the marriage relationship.

> ***Remember not the sins of my youth and my rebellious ways; according to your love remember me, for you are good, O LORD.***
> ***~ Psalms 25:7***

Parents have experienced heartache over the behavior of their children since the beginning of time. Adam and Eve grieved the loss of two sons, one murdered and the other exiled for the murder of his brother. King David's household experienced rebellion, murder and terrible abuse. King Hezekiah's son Manasseh led Judah into horrendous sin. Evangelists Billy Sunday and Billy Graham both experienced rebellious children. The heartbreak of children gone astray affects most families in one way or another.

It is important for parents to not allow their wayward child to negatively affect their marriage relationship. The pain and suffering parents experience cannot be minimized, but the question is, will a couple draw closer to the Lord or move away from Him as they experience trials? Will they cling to each other, or allow their tribulations to drive them apart? Parents must cling to the Lord and each other as they endure trials and tribulations with their children.

> *Love must be sincere. Hate what is evil; cling to what is good. Be devoted to one another in brotherly love. Honor one another above yourselves. Never be lacking in zeal, but keep your spiritual fervor, serving the Lord. Be joyful in hope, patient in affliction, faithful in prayer. ~ Romans 12:9-12*

Setting Boundaries

Parents with healthy boundaries will not allow their children to ruin their marriage and family or crush their spirits. Parents should not permit rebellious children to damage normal family life. They have to continue to give the other children the attention they need and protect their family as much as possible from the problems caused by a wayward child. Siblings should not be told all the details of the wayward child's problems. They already know there are problems to be worked through and need to know that their parents are committed to resolving those problems. The siblings also must be assured of their parents' love for them and each other.

> *We are hard pressed on every side, but not crushed; perplexed, but not in despair; persecuted, but not abandoned; struck down, but not destroyed. ~ 2 Corinthians 4:8-9*

Marriages under this kind of stress will either become stronger or weaker; they will not remain the same. Parents must work even harder to keep their marriage together. Ideally, issues of guilt and blame will not be a problem; if so, they must be worked through. It may be necessary for spouses to begin each day saying, "You are not my enemy" to each other. A system of support is important to help parents cope through such times.

Parents have to decide together what they will and will not allow in their home and how much they will support their children. Teenage children unwilling to obey even the most basic rules in the home are extremely difficult to handle. When do parents give in? When do they refuse to compromise their values? When do they get the authorities involved? These are difficult questions and parents must make these decisions together. Adult children can present equally difficult problems. What do you do when your grandchildren go hungry because their father spends everything on alcohol, drugs or gambling? What should parents do when their daughter brings home a boyfriend with no means of support and no apparent desire to earn any? There are no easy answers to these questions and the many more that could be asked, but together, with God's help and direction, parents can endure and see their family emerge from the trials stronger.

Acceptance

What if your child never becomes a God fearing, moral, self-supporting adult? Can you love him anyway? Some say that parents must love and accept their children exactly as they are, but in truth, they don't. Parents have the choice, but if they fail to love and accept their children, what will happen? Children will find it difficult to remain connected when they know their parents disapprove of them. Exhibiting God's love means that parents love and accept their children no matter what.

Does this mean parents must accept sinful behavior and poor life choices? No, parents cannot support or condone sinful or wrong behavior. They can, however, love their children in spite of that behavior. They can express God's truths and their views in love and then they can give their children to the Lord and allow Him to work in their lives. They can set and communicate healthy boundaries that will protect them, their home and other children and then work with their wayward child within those boundaries to build as much of a relationship as they can.

Parents need to be as inclusive as possible. They do not have to allow their child's sin into their home, but they can reach out to them and their chosen partner (no matter how ungodly or unholy) in God's love. It may be difficult, but a parent can find some commonality in which to build a relationship, even if it is a superficial relationship in the beginning. People are won to Jesus Christ more by God's love than by condemnation. Together a couple can find the balance and develop life-changing relationships with their children.

Prayerfully, there will be a day when that wayward child repents and returns home. Then parents can rejoice and celebrate the greatness of their God.

> ***So he got up and went to his father. "But while he was still a long way off, his father saw him and was filled with compassion for him; he ran to his son, threw his arms around him and kissed him. ~ Luke 15:20***

For Discussion as a Couple

1. How has a wayward child affected your home (or how do you think one could affect your home)?

   ____
   ____
   ____
   ____

2. What would you do if your teenager came home and announced they didn't have to obey your rules any longer?

   ____
   ____
   ____
   ____

3. What does it mean to let go of your wayward child? How can you do this?

   ____
   ____
   ____
   ____

4. Why is it important to have healthy boundaries when dealing with a wayward child?

   ____
   ____
   ____
   ____

5. How can you accept your child without accepting his sin or poor choices?

   ____
   ____
   ____
   ____
   ____

Where is God in your suffering and pain? Right there with you...

Psalms 23; a psalm of David.

The LORD is my shepherd; I shall not be in want.
He makes me lie down in green pastures,
He leads me beside quiet waters,
He restores my soul.
He guides me in paths of righteousness for his name's sake.

Even though I walk through the valley of the shadow of death,
I will fear no evil, for You are with me;
Your rod and Your staff, they comfort me.

You prepare a table before me in the presence of my enemies.
You anoint my head with oil; my cup overflows.
Surely goodness and love will follow me all the days of my life,
and I will dwell in the house of the LORD forever.

Challenges in Marriage

Study 47

Why Divorce is Not an Option

To the married I give this command (not I, but the Lord): A wife must not separate from her husband. But if she does, she must remain unmarried or else be reconciled to her husband. And a husband must not divorce his wife.
~ 1 Corinthians 7:10-11

"To get divorced because love has died, is like selling your car because it's run out of gas."
~ Diane Sollee

Too Many Couples View Divorce as an Option

Divorce shatters, rejects and invalidates one of the deepest spiritual experiences in a person's life.

Couples do not enter into a marriage relationship expecting to divorce, but unfortunately, many couples view divorce as an option from the very beginning of their marriage. They feel that if things don't work out, they always have an out. When the hard times come (and they always do), couples leave, rather than work through the problems they face.

Married couples also face an incredibly fast-paced society today that makes it difficult to concentrate and work on their marriage relationship. Whether it takes one or several years, sooner or later, the feelings of love fade away and couples drift apart. Too often, a couple divorce rather than rekindling the relationship or spending the time getting to know each other again.

Divorce today is easy, acceptable, and perceived as no big deal. Society, and often the Christian church, does not take strong stands against divorce. Yet, the Bible does take a strong stand against divorce. The Book of Malachi states that God hates divorce and in 1 Corinthians 7, God commands Christians not to divorce. Christians are also commanded to love others, including their spouse. Society may not view divorce as a problem, but God does.

Has not [the LORD] made them one? In flesh and spirit they are his. And why one? Because he was seeking godly offspring. So guard yourself in your spirit, and do not break faith with the wife of your youth. "I hate divorce ," says the LORD God of Israel, "and I hate a man's covering himself with violence as well as with his garment," says the LORD Almighty. So guard yourself in your spirit, and do not break faith.
~ Malachi 2:15-16

Couples will divorce because they do not feel love any longer. Their concept of love is that it is a feeling and if the feeling is gone, there is no other option but to leave and find a person they feel love for. Yet, Biblically, divorce is a violent tearing apart of a relationship and a family. God says that divorce is breaking faith with one's spouse. Malachi points out that the Lord views man's divorce of his wife as covering himself with violence just as he puts on his garment. This should be a good reason to remain together, yet Christian couples continue to leave their marriages.

Couples usually do not really look into the realities of divorce. They do not think about what it will do to their children, parents, extended family, the friends of their children, and even generations to come. They leave the marriage and often do not worry about the hurt that will result later. People going through divorce usually are just reacting and not thinking clearly.

There are many reasons given for the breakdown of marriages that result in divorce. Some say finances cause the biggest problems; others say communication or sex or a lack of togetherness. But James, chapter 4 really says it all. People are selfish! They have a sin nature and are, at their core, selfish and self-centered. Too often, people only want their needs met and are not willing to work to meet the needs of their spouse. They are too consumed with feeling good and taking care of self.

> ***What causes fights and quarrels among you? Don't they come from your desires that battle within you? You want something but don't get it. You kill and covet, but you cannot have what you want. You quarrel and fight. You do not have, because you do not ask God. When you ask, you do not receive, because you ask with wrong motives, that you may spend what you get on your pleasures. ~ James 4:1-3***

This selfishness and self-centeredness may eventually lead to divorce and the resulting consequences. Many people are not thinking rationally and leave a marriage for any and every reason without regard for the devastation and long-term affects divorce has on lives.

The Cost of Divorce

Linda Waite and Maggie Gallagher; in their book, *The Case for Marriage*, argue that married people are happier, healthier and better off financially. Marriage is an important institution, and if it is weakened or destroyed, society as a whole will suffer. The destruction of the family costs all of society through higher crime, welfare, education and health-care expenditures.[1]

Judith Wallerstein conducted an in-depth 25-year study of the children of divorce and found the cost to be extremely high. Her book, *The Unexpected Legacy of Divorce*, details the lives of several of the children in her study. She argues that the harm caused by divorce is deeper and longer lasting than anyone thought. For adults, divorce is a conclusion, but for children it is the beginning of uncertainty and fear. Children don't usually adjust well to the new situation, and they are often left behind as their parents attempt to put their lives back together. Most have trouble with relationships well into adulthood and, at times, throughout life.[2]

> ***The idea that a couple can separate amicably and even be better friends apart than when they were living together is a myth for most couples.***

Even the most amicable of divorces cause distress for the children. People think that if they don't fight and get along for the sake of the children, everyone will come through the divorce without too many problems. Through Dr. Wallerstein's and other research, this is found to simply not be true. In the best of circumstances, the children still are divided between parents, siblings, grandparents and friends. They have to make choices they should not have to make as children and lose out on many aspects of their childhood.

E. Mavis Hetherington, in another study about divorce; *For Better or For Worse: Divorce Reconsidered*, declares that 75% to 80% of children of divorce are functioning well, with little long-term damage. Her study found that 25% of children from divorced families have serious social, emotional or psychological problems, as opposed to 10% of kids from intact families.[3] Dr. Hetherington finds this number reasonable and acceptable. But think about this for a moment. There are approximately one million children entering into divorce each year. That is, by Dr. Hetherington's own admission, 150,000 additional children each year heading for serious social, emotional or psychological problems every year because of divorce. This is a huge cost!

A large number of men disconnect from family life after a divorce. Once divorced, men rarely remain involved with their children. Adolescent crime, drug and alcohol abuse and teenage pregnancy increase dramatically due to the absence of the father. A million additional children each year go to bed without their father in the house.[4]

Should a couple remain in a miserable marriage? Does a woman have to put up with abuse so that her children will not experience these problems? Is divorce ever OK? The quick answer is "no" to all three questions. Couples do not have to remain in a miserable marriage, they can turn it around and with God's power make their marriage good. No woman should put up with abuse, but that doesn't mean she has to divorce her husband. God hates divorce and Christians should do everything possible to save the marriage. They may need to seek counseling and set boundaries to protect themselves, but they should seek reconciliation and restoration of the marriage relationship. God can restore any marriage if given the opportunity.

What about adultery in the marriage? Yes, Matthew, Chapter 19 states that divorce is permitted in the case of marital unfaithfulness. Yet, many marriages rebound and become a wonderful testimony for God's work even through marital unfaithfulness. Where there is repentance and commitment, anything is possible with God!

You may have a "right" to divorce your spouse, but is it the "right" thing to do?

Some Pharisees came to Him to test Him. They asked, "Is it lawful for a man to divorce his wife for any and every reason?" "Haven't you read," He replied, "that at the beginning the Creator 'made them male and female,' and said, 'For this reason a man will leave his father and mother and be united to his wife, and the two will become one flesh'? So they are no longer two, but one. Therefore what God has joined together, let man not separate." "Why then," they asked, "did Moses command that a man give his wife a certificate of divorce and send her away?" Jesus replied, "Moses permitted you to divorce your wives because your hearts were hard. But it was not this way from the beginning. I tell you that anyone who divorces his wife, except for marital unfaithfulness, and marries another woman commits adultery." ~ Matthew 19:3-9

Saving a Marriage

God wants marriages to not only survive, but to grow and thrive. It is not an easy process and couples must overcome their ignorance, misconceptions, selfishness, and bad habits developed over the years. They must be willing to change and live their lives God's way and not their way.

Couples must understand who they are as people if they desire to have productive and strong marriages. Once a couple learns who they are individually and appreciate each other, they can better discern God's will for their lives and marriage. Then, they can begin to understand boundaries, communication and needs. The foundation must be laid before the home can be built.

Couples need to be willing to repent and ask for forgiveness when necessary and offer forgiveness when asked. They will have to work through the issues in their marriage and remain committed to completing the work to turn their marriage around. Mentoring or counseling may be necessary to get through some issues. It is not an easy task to work through years of hurt and pain. Yet, the incredible blessing of a restored marriage and family will positively affect the immediate family and the generations to come. It blesses God's heart to see a husband and wife turn from the selfishness of divorce and decide that, with His strength, and in obedience to their promises, they are going to rebuild their relationship and continue in the commitment to their marriage.

> *"Nearly all marriages, even happy ones, are mistakes: in the sense that almost certainly (in a more perfect world, or even with a little more care in this very imperfect one) both partners might be found more suitable mates. But the real soul-mate is the one you are actually married to. "*
> *~ J.R.R. Tolkien*

> *But from everlasting to everlasting the LORD's love is with those who fear him, and his righteousness with their children's children — with those who keep his covenant and remember to obey his precepts.*
> *~ Psalms 103:17-18*

For Discussion as a Couple

1. Is divorce an option for you in your marriage? Why or why not? What do you think that you can do to ensure that this is not an option for your marriage?

2. Do you agree that divorce is a big deal to God? What are your thoughts about this?

3. What do you think about the cost of divorce? What would divorce cost you and your family?

4. Two different views about how well children handle divorce have been presented. Do you agree that staying together for the kids is worthwhile? Why or why not?

5. Do you believe God can turn around any marriage, no matter how bad it is? How could this happen?

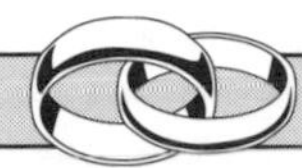

Challenges in Marriage

Study 48

The "Blended" Family

"Isn't this the carpenter's son? Isn't his mother's name Mary, and aren't his brothers James, Joseph, Simon and Judas? Aren't all his sisters with us?
~ Matthew 13:55-56

Learn to do right! Seek justice, encourage the oppressed. Defend the cause of the fatherless, plead the case of the widow.
~ Isaiah 1:17

Blended Families

"Well, I'm shuffled between two sets of parents and I have a brother, a half-brother, a step-brother, and a step-sister. I have a dog and a step-hamster, four grandmas and three grandpas. Christmas can be at any one of six houses; I never know until a couple of days before. But really, my life is OK. I think I have it all straight."

A "blended family" can be defined as a family created by the marriage of a couple where one or both of them have children from previous relationships. Blended families have been part of society for thousands of years. In a sense, some of the dynamics of them can be seen in Abraham, Jacob and David's families. Although divorce was not part of the equation, there were rivalries and contention between the children of their different wives to the point of murder. Jesus experienced the blended family also as his father was different than the father of His brothers and sisters. The Gospels bring out some of the stress there must have been in what is commonly called the "Holy Family". (See Luke 2:48-49, Matthew 12:46-50 and John 7:3-9)

The difference today is the numbers of families experiencing the stress of "blendedness". Some of the drama can be seen played out in airports or bus terminals as children are literally torn out of their parent's arms to be put on an airplane or a bus and sent back to their other parent. The cost of divorce is devastating and it is heart-wrenching to see the effects it has on many children, but the fact is that divorce happens frequently in society and sad to say, even in the Church.

Whatever reason a couple might have a "blended family," through divorce and remarriage, or through the death of a spouse and remarriage, it is a fact that parenting will be more complicated. The new parent must now learn about children who have already been shaped to some extent and may also have to deal with the influence of the other parents. That influence will be felt even if the parent died or has never interacted with his children. Biological factors and the feelings children have for their absent parent will affect the children and a couple's parenting.

Regardless of the reason for the remarriage, one must commit to conducting his marriage God's way. The cycle of divorce and remarriage must stop now. It will take a greater commitment and more work to make this marriage work, but by the grace and help of God, you can do it and do it right. Blended families face all the stresses that "traditional" families face—and more. If there are ex-spouses involved, it is important to be open to input from your present spouse regarding your interaction with the "ex". Very often, couples developed bad communication habits that continue after the divorce. Whether it is giving in to "get them off your back", screaming and yelling in your communication, or the "silent treatment", you now need to work on boundaries and practice good principles of communication. Your current spouse may be the person to help you develop in these areas. The key is to work together to improve your communication and to set healthy boundaries.

It is important to treat your ex-spouse with respect. You may never say a bad thing about the "ex" in front of your children, but they will know if you harbor enmity toward him. This applies to your spouse's ex-spouse as well. Tearing down the character and "bashing" the "other" parent never accomplishes anything positive. You don't have to tell your children how terrible their "other" parent is. If they are "terrible", the kids will figure it out. Using the children to get back at your "ex" or to manipulate them into doing what you want them to do (even if it is the right thing) is wrong. You can only control what you can control and an ex-spouse is definitely out of your area of control.

Work on Your Marriage

Building a strong relationship with your spouse is critical to having a healthy "blended family". You entered the marriage relationship with a ready-made family and time alone is extremely important since there was no time to develop the relationship with your spouse before children entered the family. Communicationskills, roles and responsibilities, boundaries and getting to know your spouse must be done under fire. Often, parents in blended families will feel guilty about not giving enough time to their children and will neglect working on their marriage relationship. The marriage relationship cannot survive if it is neglected and another divorce will be much more traumatic to the children than having lost some time with their parent.

"Mom, I know Joe is your husband, but do you really have to spend time with him? Couldn't you just see him every other weekend, like we see Dad?"

"Blending" a Family Takes Time

When a person chooses to marry another with children, the children are a part of the package. He is, in fact accepting parental responsibility for those children. Very often a man or woman will get involved with someone with children and not take the children into account at all. The children do not go away and they are not "yours" and "mine" — they are "ours." It is important that the stepparent accept responsibility to be the parent of his new children. At the same time, if the stepparent is not allowed to be a parent, relationships with the children will not develop.

Building a sense of identity and a history together takes time and it takes a blended family several years to fully integrate. Individual stepparent-stepchild relationships develop differently. Young children (ages 5 and under) very often become attached to a stepparent very quickly. Stepparent relationships with older children and teens can require years to develop. In fact, older teens may never really "bond" with a stepparent, maintaining only a "distant family member" connection. It is important for parents and stepparents to remember that the closeness of relationships with stepchildren is not indicative of their success as a stepfamily. Healthy blended families have varying degrees of connection and they need to accept things as they are without great disappointment. A child will let the stepparent into his life over time as trust develops. Stepparents need to learn to get along and allow the children to set the pace for development of the relationship.

The stepparent must remember that he is not a replacement for the absent biological parent, even if that parent is dead, but they are the parent in their home. Often fathers will abdicate their parental role and attempt to be buddies with their children who live in another household. Getting drawn into a competition of "who can be the child's best buddy" is a lose-lose proposition. When the stepparent loves his stepchildren as his own and displays that love, even as he disciplines and corrects the stepchildren, a healthy parent-child relationship will develop.

Stepparents should begin parenting based on borrowed authority from the biological parent (as does a baby-sitter) and gradually take on authority as the relationship with each child grows. Moving into the house and stating, "I'm the father (or mother) of this house now" or, "Things are going to change around here, right now!" will only serve to alienate the children and new spouse. Relationships need to be built before stepparents can effectively discipline their stepchildren.

The new parent in the household is at a disadvantage, because he doesn't know the dynamics of the relationships and interaction between the existing family members. Children coming with the stepparent also have to learn the ways of the new home and it can be a frightening experience for everyone involved. Children may feel like they are tossed together rather than blended. Learning the personalities, love languages and bents of each new child takes time and work.

Active Participation is Important

Involvement in the activities of your children is extremely important to both the biological children and stepchildren. It may not always be comfortable if your stepchild's "other" parent also attends the child's events, but it is important for you to attend, and to be respectful of the other parent. Attending your own child's events may not be convenient, but it is important that you attend your children's events whenever possible. Involvement in the children's lives and their interests is a bonding agent that will help make your relationship strong.

It is very likely that a stepparent has interests and talents that his stepchildren have not experienced. Sharing these with the children and allowing them to get involved as they desire will also build the relationship. Playing games, getting involved in service projects and serving the Lord as a family will integrate the family together.

Fun family activities reduce the anxiety children may feel about being involved with a "stepparent". The children need to have time to feel comfortable with the stepparent. Often children will feel that they betray their absent parent by entering into a relationship with their stepparent. Whenever possible, parents need to reassure their children that both parents will remain in their lives and the stepparent is another person to care for them, not a replacement.

Children coming to the home for visitation need to be included as part of the family, not an outsider intruding on the family occasionally. Do not make it a vacation for them either. They are part of the family and should participate with the chores and work that need to be done in the household. Helping the visiting child to find friends and get plugged into the neighborhood will help him to feel a part of the family also.

> ***Trust in the LORD with all your heart and lean not on your own understanding; in all your ways acknowledge him, and he will make your paths straight. ~ Proverbs 3:5-6***

Maintain the Course

Entering a marriage relationship is always a big transition, but blending a family together can be overwhelming. Couples in this situation need help and must rely on the Lord to guide them through the minefield they have entered. There are many snares in the blended relationships, but also many blessings. Couples should be quick to seek counseling when issues arise so they do not get out of control.

Working closely together as a couple is imperative in a blended family. There are so many stresses in a blended family that a couple can be driven apart very quickly. Children may experience different rules and values at their "other" house. The absent parent may even instigate trouble through his child. Couples should not get involved in competition with other parents and resist quarreling with them as much as possible. Healthy boundaries and mature reactions will draw your family together and be a witness to others.

It is important that parents apply Biblical principles and stick with them. The children may rebel or they may threaten to leave for the "other" parent's home, but it is possible to successfully raise children in a blended family. Cling to the Lord and communicate with your spouse. Hold meetings with your spouse and children to discuss family situations and improve family life overall.

Healthy boundaries and displaying consistent love for all of your children will bring unity and hold the family together. Husband and wife must maintain the course and persevere through the hard times, even though they may not see the fruit of their effort for many years.

For Discussion as a Couple

1. What are some of the problems "blended families" face that traditional families do not face? What is necessary to overcome those problems?

____

____

____

____

2. How can you balance a respectful attitude toward your ex-spouse and not allow them to cause problems in your present marriage and family?

____

____

____

____

3. Why is it so important to work on your marriage and have time for just the two of you? What can you do to ensure that this happens?

____

____

____

____

4. Do you agree that "blending" a family takes time? Why or why not? What do you need to do to bring that blending about?

____

____

____

____

5. What does it mean to "maintain the course?" What can you do to stay on course?

____

____

____

____

Fortified Marriages
Chapter 11 Endnotes

Study 45: *Resisting Attacks on Your Marriage*

1. C.S. Lewis; quoted by Steven Tracy; Mending the Soul (Zondervan, 2005) p 115
2. Nelson's Illustrated Bible Dictionary, Copyright © 1986, Thomas Nelson Publishers

Recommended for further reading:

- Take Back Your Marriage; Sticking Together in a World That Pulls Us Apart by William Dherty
- Where is God When Bad Things Happen? by Luis Palau
- God Will Make a Way by Dr. Henry Cloud & Dr. John Townsend
- Why? Trusting God When You Don't Understand by Anne Graham Lotz
- Experiencing Grief by H. Norman Wright
- Love Must Be Tough: New Hope for Marriages in Crisis by Dr. James Dobson
- Where is God When It Hurts? By Philip Yancey
- How to Talk to Your Senior Parents about Really Important Things by Theresa Foy DiGeronimo
- Eldercare 911: The Caregiver's Complete Handbook for Making Decisions, by Susan Beerman & Judth Rappaport-Musson

Study 46: When Children Go Astray

Recommended for further reading:

- When Our Grown Kids Disappoint Us by Jane Adams Ph.D.
- Parents with Broken Hearts by William L. Coleman
- Parenting the Prodigal by S. Rutherford McDill Jr.
- Parenting the Wild Child by Miles McPherson
- Surviving the Prodigal Years/How to Love Your Wayward Child Without Ruining Your Own Life by Marcia Mitchell

For further information, see:

- Focus on the Family: www.focusonthefamily.org

Study 47: *Why Divorce is not an Option*

1. Linda J. Waite & Maggie Gallagher; The Case for Marriage (NY, NY; Doubleday, 2000)
2. Walter Kirn, Should You Stay Together For The Kids?; Time Magazine, September 25, 2000.
3. Richard Corliss, Does Divorce Hurt Kids?, Time Magazine, January 28, 2002
4. Nina Easton, The Invisible Dad, Los Angeles Times Magazine, June 14, 1992

Recommended for further reading:

- The Case for Marriage; Linda J. Waite & Maggie Gallagher
- The Unexpected Legacy of Divorce; Judith Wallerstein, Julia Lewis & Sandra Blakeslee
- The Case Against Divorce by Diane Medved
- Before a Bad Goodbye; Dr. Tim Clinton
- The Divorce Remedy: The Proven 7-Step Plan for Saving Your Marriage by Michelle Weiner-Davis

For further information, see:
- Divorce Busting: www.divorcebusting.com

Study 48: *The "Blended" Family*

Recommended for further reading:
- The Stepfamily Survival Guide by Natalie Nichols Gillespie
- The Smart Stepfamily: Seven Steps to a Healthy Family by Ron Deal
- Willing to Try Again: Steps Toward Blending a Family by Dick Dunn

For further information, see:
- Successful Stepfamilies: www.successfulstepfamilies.com
- Stepfamily Association of America: /www.saafamilies.org/

Chapter 12
Married For Life

Study 49
Growing in Maturity

Brothers, I do not consider myself yet to have taken hold of it. But one thing I do: Forgetting what is behind and straining toward what is ahead, I press on toward the goal to win the prize for which God has called me heavenward in Christ Jesus. All of us who are mature should take such a view of things. And if on some point you think differently, that too God will make clear to you.
~ Philippians 3:13-15

Many people today enter marriage before they are prepared, before they are whole, healthy, and independent adults. They do not understand who they are and where they are going in life. Many are immature, selfish and self-centered. The problem is compounded when couples begin having children before they are ready to unselfishly give their lives to guiding little ones to mature character. Their marriage is not strong enough to withstand the stress and pressures of daily living, marriage and raising children. They seek to get their needs met and when they do not find it in the marriage relationship, they begin looking elsewhere. People desire a long lasting, fulfilling marriage, but they often leave the marriage when the feelings of love seem to have disappeared or it becomes too difficult.

Very often people go their own way, then invite God to join them, and then are dismayed when life doesn't work out according to their plans. Rather than seeking God's direction, they pursued their own vision for their life. Similar to the consumerist, throwaway society they live in, they are shortsighted and lack perseverance. Couples too often pursue their own goals and objectives without regard for the Lord or their spouse.

Maturity in the Believer's Life

Maturity is defined as "reaching full growth or development."[1] No one reaches complete maturity in this lifetime, but there should be a difference in the Christian's life as he gets older. Christians mature into who they are in Christ. It is a matter of bringing your daily life into alignment with who you are positionally because of what Christ did for you. Mature Christians look forward to what God has called them to do rather than focusing on past failures and problems in their lives.

His divine power has given us everything we need for life and godliness through our knowledge of him who called us by his own glory and goodness. Through these he has given us his very great and precious promises, so that through them you may participate in the divine nature and escape the corruption in the world caused by evil desires. ~ 2 Peter 1:3-4

God gives the believer everything he needs for life and godliness. The power is available, but it is up to the believer to appropriate that power to walk closely with the Lord. It is God's power at work in the believer who trusts in Him. This power enables the believer to grow in maturity and his walk with the Lord. Beginning with faith and then adding goodness, knowledge, self-control, perseverance, godliness, brotherly kindness and love, a Christian grows in maturity in His relationship with the Lord. One must trust in God, and, as he walks in faith and obedience, maturity will come.

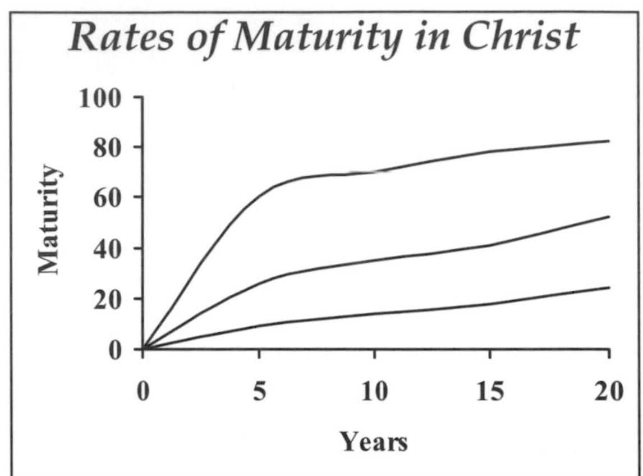

People mature at different rates. The graph above diagrams a generalization of the growth rates of believers in Christ. There tends to be three general rates of maturity. Some people become Christians, give their lives totally to God and begin growing very quickly. Others mature at a slow steady rate; taking many years to reach the higher levels of maturity. Finally, there are Christians who mature at a very slow rate. They may not be able to get past the emotional hurt of the past or they may find it difficult to give up the lure of the world. Their growth is slow and they often seem to have troubles in their lives. Everyone will experience setbacks in their walk with the Lord, but there should be evidence of continuing progress over time.

Characteristics of Maturity

Several characteristics are evident in the mature Christian's life. Every person is different, but as each one matures, there will be change in these areas.

- Submission
- Sacrificial Love
- Self-control
- Perseverance
- Walking in the Spirit

Submission

Mankind naturally has a rebellious spirit. People do not like to submit to authority and tend to rebel against parents, government, church and God. Point out a shortcoming to a spouse, friend or family member and most likely he will become defensive, or tell you to, 'mind your own business.' Rebelliousness doesn't have to be taught to children, it is evident in their lives from a very young age. Parents may not like their child's rebelliousness, but often will reinforce it by demonstrating their own rebellious spirit in day-to-day life.

But solid food is for the mature, who by constant use have trained themselves to distinguish good from evil. ~ Hebrews 5:14

Mature Christians submit to the Lord, obey Him and seek to conform their lives to His will. They do not seek to explain away their poor behavior or claim God's grace and then continue in their sin (see Romans, chapter 6). Submission can be explained as going in the same direction. When a Christian moves in God's direction and not his own, he can be confident in his submission to the Lord. It is a matter of giving every area of one's life to the Lord and following His guidance and direction. Submission to God's will is a characteristic of a mature Christian.

Sacrificial Love

Jesus Christ demonstrated sacrificial love for the entire world to see. He took on the sins of the world and died a horrible death so that mankind could be reconciled to God. No human will ever be asked to make such a sacrifice, yet the Bible tells Christians to love others as Jesus loves them.

Be imitators of God, therefore, as dearly loved children and live a life of love, just as Christ loved us and gave himself up for us as a fragrant offering and sacrifice to God. ~ Ephesians 5:1-2

The Apostle John's first letter points out that Christians are to be known by their love; not just words of love, but deeds demonstrating love (see 1 John 3:16-18 and 4:19-21). Mature Christians set aside their wants and desires, and even their needs to demonstrate love for others. Saying yes to every request made of a person is not setting healthy boundaries. There will be times when one must say, "No," but there is a difference between the Christian who lives a life of sacrificial love and the Christian who tends to live for himself.

Self-Control

Self-control is a fruit of the Spirit and means that the Christian is governed by God, not self or the flesh. He denies the desires that would draw him away from God's will for his life and submits his will to the Lord. A mature Christian finds the balance between trusting God, doing it himself and doing nothing. No one can make himself presentable before God by his own effort. Yet, he seeks to be transformed by the renewing of his mind (Romans 12:2). Renewing of the mind comes through a close, growing relationship with the Lord and involves prayer, worship, meditation on His Word, and fellowship with other believers.

> ***If anyone considers himself religious and yet does not keep a tight rein on his tongue, he deceives himself and his religion is worthless. ~ James 1:26***

Christians should control their tongues and not allow hurtful speech in their lives. Too often husbands and wives hurt each other, their children, family, or friends with their words. Mature Christians speak the truth in love, seeking to build others up according to their needs (Ephesians 4:29). They encourage others in their walk with the Lord and always seek to communicate the love of God to everyone.

Perseverance

> ***Perseverance must finish its work so that you may be mature and complete, not lacking anything. ~ James 1:4***

Perseverance is defined as a patient enduring or waiting. Society today tends to expect immediate fulfillment of every desire, but many aspects of life involve waiting. Financial problems often result because people are not willing to wait and save for the things they want. When people wait on the Lord and allow Him to work in situations, He will bless, and maturity will develop in the process. Mature Christians remain focused on the Lord and wait for Him to work in their lives, provide for their desires and bring them through trials and problems. They seek the Lord and His will for their lives and pursue it.

Few children have the patience to wait for a present or treat. They want it immediately and may throw a fit if they have to wait. How many adults are just like that impatient child? Many Christians run ahead of the Lord without waiting for His direction and then wonder why their plans go astray. Many times, God's answer to prayer is, "wait," but very often people are not willing to wait. They charge ahead and deal with the consequences later. Mature Christians will experience fewer problems because they are patient and willing to wait on the Lord.

Walking in the Spirit

> ***So I say, live by the Spirit, and you will not gratify the desires of the sinful nature. ~ Galatians 5:16***

The Christian's walk (the way he conducts his life[2]) reflects his relationship with God. A relationship with the Lord is not built by human effort. It is impossible to please God without faith in Christ (Hebrews 11:6) and a relationship with Him is built on faith and trust in Him. Yet, it is important that Christians mature in their relationship with the Lord. God loves His children as they are, but wants to see them grow up in their salvation (1 Peter 2:2).

Living the life God desires requires faith, trust and focus on Him. It is a matter of trusting and relying on Him for every aspect of life. The Apostle Peter walked on water as long as he remained focused on Jesus (Matthew 14:28-31). When he took his eyes off the Lord, he sank like a rock. Mature Christians focus on the Lord and surrender to Him daily, at times even moment by moment, as they trust God for direction and guidance. They practice the spiritual disciplines of prayer, worship, Bible study and fellowship on a daily basis, not only at Sunday worship services.

The Mature Marriage

> *"Marriage is our last, best chance to grow up." ~ Joseph Barth*

Couples will grow, mature and become more like Christ as they face both the joys of life and the trials and problems of life together. "A marriage needs to do more than endure, it needs to grow and mature. Time alone will not strengthen a marriage."[3] Working together as a team to meet the challenges of life brings a couple together and shapes their lives individually and as a couple. These challenges are used by God to build the couple up in maturity as they persevere and trust in Him.

Knowing each other's weaknesses and struggles, and yet, focusing on each other's strengths rather than on each other's weaknesses is evidence of a mature marriage. A mature couple uses their differences to build the relationship and serve God rather than as points of contention and reasons for attacking each other. They use their strengths individually and as a couple to grow in their relationship with God and each other, and they become better spouses and parents.

Connection to God and with each other is necessary for maturity to develop individually and as a couple. It is important that a couple prays, worships and studies the Bible together to build their relationship with the Lord and each other. Individuals may grow and mature in the Lord without their spouse, but the marriage relationship will lack spiritual intimacy if they are not growing together.

The health of the marriage relationship is directly tied to a couple's closeness with God. Couples struggling in their marriage relationship very often are also struggling in their spiritual life. They usually deny this in counseling sessions, but it is often true; one or both spouses will have a shallow, neglected relationship with the Lord. All three connections between husband, wife and God need to be strong to maintain a healthy marriage.

A productive, fortified marriage requires diligence and care. Husband and wife both need to be faithful in the little things on an ongoing basis. Connecting spiritually, praying together, sharing spiritual insights and maintaining fellowship with other Christians may not always be conve-

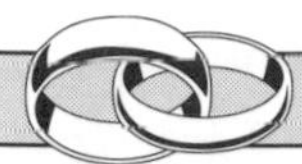

nient, but as a couple perseveres in these disciplines, they will see God's work in their lives and marriage.

The principles of the parable of the talents in Matthew, chapter 25 applies to the marriage relationship. God gives gifts and abilities to people individually and as a couple. The couple that is faithful to serve God with what they have been given will flourish and progress in their relationship with God and each other. Those who bury their talents and do not use them will tend to be unprepared for the tribulations that will come in life. They will also miss out on opportunities to be used by God to affect the lives of people around them.

God will use the mature marriage in the lives of family, friends and others. Build maturity in your life and marriage by pursuing God, walking in the Spirit, practicing the spiritual disciplines and exercising your faith and trust in the Lord.

> ***Therefore let us leave the elementary teachings about Christ and go on to maturity, not laying again the foundation of repentance from acts that lead to death, and of faith in God, ~ Hebrews 6:1***

For Discussion as a Couple

1. Would you consider yourself a mature Christian? How is that seen in your life?

____

____

____

____

2. Which of the characteristics of maturity do you need to grow in?

____

____

____

____

3. How can you walk in the Spirit as a couple?

____

____

____

____

4. How would you define a mature marriage? Is your marriage mature? Why or why not?

____

____

____

____

5. How has God used your marriage in the lives of others? If He hasn't, how could you prepare yourself so He could use you?

____

____

____

____

____

Married for Life

Study 50

The Holiness of Marriage

"For this reason a man will leave his father and mother and be united to his wife, and the two will become one flesh." This is a profound mystery-but I am talking about Christ and the church.
~ Ephesians 5:31-32

God's Relationship with Mankind

Both the Old and New Testaments refer to God's relationship with mankind as a marriage. God calls His people His bride and chastises her for adultery when she follows after other gods. Jesus refers to Himself, in the Gospels, as the Bridegroom coming for His bride. The relationship Jesus has with the church speaks of the close, intimate relationship couples should have with each other and with God. The world should see the sacrificial, giving love of God exhibited in Christian marriage relationships. Sadly, few Christian marriages truly display this kind of love.

Very often Christian marriages are no better than marriages in the world. Physical, sexual, verbal and emotional abuse should not happen in Christian marriage, yet they occur far too often. It must break God's heart when marriages deteriorate and become battlegrounds. God created mankind for His glory (Isaiah 43:7), yet people have rejected God and His plan for their lives. The institution that should reflect His relationship with mankind too often does not display the grace, mercy or love God has for His people.

God takes marriage seriously even though mankind often does not. Too often, people treat their spouses horribly; taking everything they can get and giving nothing in return. They give little or nothing of themselves to the marriage and wonder why they have a shallow, distant relationship with their spouse. They wantonly destroy lives and generations as they plunge headlong into the abyss of adultery and sexual depravity attempting to get their needs met. Then they wonder why they have meaningless, hopeless lives devoid of love and appreciation. Galatians 6:7 says, *"Do not be deceived: God cannot be mocked. A man reaps what he sows."*

I will betroth you to me forever; I will betroth you in righteousness and justice, in love and compassion. ~ Hosea 2:19

God, the creator of heaven, earth and all life takes His people as His bride. He sets the standard for the marriage relationship and it is an everlasting marriage. He holds His bride in righteousness, justice, love and compassion. This is a high standard to measure up to. No person can accomplish this in his own strength; it requires the work of the Lord in a couple's lives and marriage. God's covenant with His spouse is sealed with the blood of Jesus Christ who paid the price for the unfaithfulness of His own bride and made a permanent relationship possible for all people who accept Him as Savior and Lord.

"God designed marriage to make you holy more than to make you happy." ~ Gary Thomas

Called to Holiness

God desires that His people live holy lives, set apart from the world for His purposes. Christians are to love God, serve Him and be a testimony of His love to the world. People were not created just to exist, live for themselves or to be satisfied and happy. Christians are to be conformed into the image of Jesus Christ. The Lord empowers His people to live this holy life He has called them to. No person can live this life on his own, but with Christ, all things are possible.

> ***Therefore, prepare your minds for action; be self-controlled; set your hope fully on the grace to be given you when Jesus Christ is revealed. As obedient children, do not conform to the evil desires you had when you lived in ignorance. But just as he who called you is holy, so be holy in all you do; for it is written: "Be holy, because I am holy."***
> ***~ 1 Peter 1:13-16***

Jesus' sacrifice on the cross reconciled mankind to God and sanctifies (or makes holy) His people before God. Sanctification is the process of a person being transformed into who Jesus has made him to be. A mature Christian is really a sanctified Christian, living a life walking in God's Spirit. He lives a life closer to the Lord and further from sin. He may not be sinless, but he does sin less.

> ***For God did not call us to be impure, but to live a holy life.***
> ***~ 1 Thessalonians 4:7***

> ***Therefore, since we are receiving a kingdom that cannot be shaken, let us be thankful, and so worship God acceptably with reverence and awe, for our "God is a consuming fire." ~ Hebrews 12:28-29***

The Holiness of God

People today often do not have a healthy fear of God. They do not reverence and hold Him in awe as the Creator of the universe, the Creator and sustainer of life, and the great and awesome God. It seems that some people view God as their buddy in Heaven, rather than a Holy God, a Consuming Fire and the Mighty One of Israel. No man can stand before the holiness and majesty of such an awesome God (see Isaiah 6) and remain the same. Reverence and respect come when one sees the incredible glory of God.

Jesus Christ was the sacrifice that reconciled mankind to God. People don't have to fear God as they would a judge waiting to pass sentence, but it is right to give the Lord the respect He is due. He is worthy of worship because of who He is and what He has done for His people. Nothing else on earth or in Heaven deserves the adoration and praise God deserves. Reverence, awe and a respect for God's holiness is the beginning of understanding (Proverbs 9:10) and couples need to understand that God is a holy God.

> ***"Great and marvelous are your deeds, Lord God Almighty. Just and true are your ways, King of the ages. Who will not fear you, O Lord, and bring glory to your name? For you alone are holy. All nations will come and worship before you, for your righteous acts have been revealed."***
> ***~ Revelation 15:3-4***

Holiness and the Marriage Relationship

Marriage is a covenant between a man and a woman, but it is also much more than that. It is a place where people are challenged to grow, mature and become conformed into the image of Jesus Christ. God uses the marriage relationship to train people, increase their understanding of what it means to be a follower of Christ and to sanctify them.

A man and woman in a marriage relationship are as close as any two human beings can be. They know more about each other than anyone else will know. Their differences should work together to bring balance to the relation-

> ***As iron sharpens iron, so one man sharpens another.***
> ***~ Proverbs 27:17***

ship and to both of their lives. Sparks may fly at times as God uses husband and wife in each other's life. Sharpening and growing do not come without some pain. Experiencing both the joys and trials of life together will help them become more like Christ and mature in their walk with Him.

"Marriage isn't supposed to make you happy and satisfied. It's your job to make your marriage happy and satisfying."
~ Diane Sollee

People today tend to have this fixation that marriage is supposed to make them happy. When their spouse and the relationship lose their appeal, they look for another relationship to make them happy. They desire satisfaction and fulfillment, meaning that they should be satisfied and fulfilled, not that they would attempt to be used by God to help their spouse feel satisfied and fulfilled.

Couples must be open to God's work in their lives and marriages, and they need to be willing to listen to what their spouse has to say to them. Who better is able to make a difference in a person's life than his spouse? Rather than getting defensive and rejecting what one's spouse has to say, people need to listen, think about it, and seek God's confirmation of the truth about what has been said. This takes humility and a willingness to take responsibility for one's own actions.

Building Character

Character identifies a person. It is the pattern of behavior or sum of qualities or features marking a person.[1] He may have a strong, moral character or a character lacking morals. Men and women of good character do the right thing whether or not others are watching. They do it, not because they have to, but because they want to please God. It has become a way of life. The person of character has surrendered his life and allows Jesus Christ to live through him.

"Worry more about your character than your reputation. Character is what you are, reputation merely what others think you are."
~ John Wooden

Marriage provides an excellent opportunity to develop character as a husband and wife live life together. The Lord will use one's spouse to point out those areas in his life that need to change. Some have likened it to holding up a mirror and seeing all the ugliness one has in his life. He then has a choice about doing something about it and allowing God to transform him more into the image of Christ. Or, he can ignore it and continue to live life his own way.

Faith in God and obedience to His word builds character and holiness into the Christian's life. It is impossible to please God without faith (Hebrews 11:6). A holy life is built on faith. Obedience also is an important part of the Christian's life. He cannot live a holy life on his own, but as he obeys the Lord and relies on God to empower him, the Christian's character will grow. There must be a balance; works will not save a person, only faith, but, as James 2:18 says, works demonstrate the faith a person has.

Most people don't have as much of a problem discerning God's will for their lives as they do fulfilling His will. Often, people will say they can't do something, when in fact; they won't do it. The Bible says that all things are possible in Christ (Philippians 4:13). God will empower people to do the right thing if they have the desire to do it. Often, people will make promises or sacrifices to God, but He would rather have their obedience (1 Samuel 15:22).

> *It is God's will that you should be sanctified: that you should avoid sexual immorality; that each of you should learn to control his own body in a way that is holy and honorable, not in passionate lust like the heathen, who do not know God;*
> *~ 1 Thessalonians 4:3-5*

God clearly states His will at times and can be rather vague at other times, but the Bible provides the guidelines of how Christians are to live their lives. It does no good to pay homage to the Bible and acknowledge it as the Word of God without allowing it to change your life. Jesus said, "If you love Me, you will obey what I command" (John 14:15). It means setting boundaries and saying, "As for me and my house, we will serve the Lord." God will honor the person who desires to follow Him.

Glorifying God

The mystery of marriage is that it is representative of the relationship of Jesus Christ and the Church. The family is the primary ingredient of the church. Couples should build their relationship with the Lord daily, not just on Sundays while in church. The church of Jesus Christ is made up of people, not buildings or organizations. Jesus commissioned His church, His people to draw people to Him and to build them up in Him. The Christ-centered marriage should also draw people to Christ, beginning with the immediate family.

A person glorifies God by praising Him and honoring His commandments. Jesus glorified God through His perfect obedience and His sacrificial death for mankind (John chapter 17).[2] Again, it is not about legalistically obeying the rules, but Christian obedience comes from a love for God and what He has done for His people. Christians are to be conformed into the image of Jesus Christ and a Christian marriage should represent Christ. Jesus came to serve, not to be served. He did God's will even to the point of dying on the cross. Husbands and wives are also to seek to serve not be served. They are to seek to meet their spouse's needs and help others, not spend their life seeking met needs for themselves.

> *"I know that it is far more important to be the right kind of person than it is to marry the right person. In short, whether you married the right person or wrong person is primarily up to you." ~ Zig Ziglar*

The couple that works together to serve God and live lives according to His precepts will glorify Him in their marriage. They are intent on serving God rather than serving themselves. They should not be fighting for control in the marriage, but working together to meet the challenges of daily life. Husbands and wives who listen to each other and take each other's suggestions into account will have more unity in their marriages than those who don't. Those who are willing to learn, change and grow will glorify God in their lives and marriages.

A Marriage that is a Testimony

The marriage that glorifies God will be a testimony of God's love and faithfulness. It would be a great compliment to have another couple come up to you and your spouse and say, "We've been watching you and your marriage is an inspiration to us." The fact is that people do watch you and make a judgment about you, your marriage and the God you proclaim by the way you treat each other. The oneness of a strong, growing marriage will glorify God.

Do you want to change the world? Live a life for God, serve Him and love your spouse and children as God loves you. Your fortified marriage standing strong will affect generations as you persevere and grow through the trials and problems that will come against your marriage. The world today desperately needs couples that not only will persevere together, but also will be that example, that light that will draw people to God.

> *"You are the light of the world. A city on a hill cannot be hidden. Neither do people light a lamp and put it under a bowl. Instead they put it on its stand, and it gives light to everyone in the house. In the same way, let your light shine before men, that they may see your good deeds and praise your Father in heaven.*
> *~ Matthew 5:14-16*

Charles Spurgeon said, "What is the value of the grace we profess to receive which leaves us exactly the same kind of people as we were before we received it? An unholy life is evidence of an unchanged heart and an unchanged heart is evidence of an unsaved soul." Strong words to be certain, but words that need to be heard. Christians cannot be light when their marriages are no different than anyone else's. God will empower you to live holy lives and have a marriage that will make a difference when you surrender your lives to Him.

For Discussion as a Couple

1. Do you believe you are called to holiness? How should this affect your marriage?

   ____
   ____
   ____
   ____

2. How can God use your marriage to make you more holy?

   ____
   ____
   ____
   ____

3. Why is a strong moral character important to the marriage relationship?

   ____
   ____
   ____
   ____

4. How can you glorify God through your marriage?

   ____
   ____
   ____
   ____

5. Is your marriage a testimony to God's love and faithfulness? Why or why not?

   ____
   ____
   ____
   ____
   ____

The Deeper Truths of Marriage

Answer the following questions and share your answers with your spouse. Give the questions some thought and answer honestly. Your marriage will mature as you dig deeper into Biblical truths and stretch yourself.

---

1. Why are you married? ______________________________

2. What would please God in your marriage today? ______________________________

3. What is one thing you can do to bless your spouse daily? ______________________________

4. What does God want for your marriage? ______________________________

5. What does it take to have a maturing marriage? ______________________________

6. How is your marriage similar to the church's relationship with Jesus Christ? ______________________________

7. What plans to do you have to make your marriage last for life? ______________________________

Married for Life
Study 51
Protecting Your Marriage

> *... So guard yourself in your spirit, and do not break faith with the wife of your youth.*
> *~ Malachi 2:15*

Marriage Under Attack

There is a war going on in society today and marriage is under attack. The institution of marriage is the earthly representation of God's relationship with man and both the devil and ungodly people desire to see it destroyed. Also consider that when a marriage fails, a family and the following generations will suffer greatly. Society has bought into the lie that divorce and remarriage is no big deal. They believe that children are resilient and that they will get over it. Studies prove that this is not true. While parents are trying to put their own lives back together, children are often left without proper parental care and guidance. Some learn to cope; others begin a downward spiral that can continue throughout their lives.

> *Be on your guard; stand firm in the faith; be men of courage; be strong. ~ 1 Corinthians 16:13-14*

There is great danger to complacency. Couples tend to let their guard down when things are going well in their marriage. They don't see the point of working on their marriage because they are in love, and think they don't have to prepare for the storms that will come their way. They do not invest time or money into their marriage relationship. Too often, couples that would not spend money for a marriage seminar end up with serious marital problems or even divorced several years later. Couples must not allow themselves to become complacent. They must actively protect their marriage or it may not survive the challenges they will see in the life of their relationship.

Commitment Required

> *"I read somewhere that wolves mate for life. Which sort of surprised me, because I used to have this nagging feeling that it was the adventurous wolflike side of me that wanted to keep my options open, and the more passive, meeker side of me that craved the closeness and security of being with just one woman. Now I think it's just the opposite. Servicing the flock may be a pleasant occupation, but it doesn't call for any great distinction in character; any second-rate Billy goat can do it. It's commitment that calls for fierceness and vigilance and all the other qualities that make us think of the wolf as noble."[1]*

Marriage requires the strong commitment of both spouses. Commitment to love one's spouse as he is and to stand by him as he matures and grows into the person the Lord wants him to be. Society tends to be fascinated with the so called wolves, those who look after themselves and play the field, but the reality is that God created the wolf as one that is committed to one mate for life and to its pack. A wolf will fiercely defend the pack's territory, and a couple's commitment to their marriage today requires some of that fierceness and vigilance to protect it from the evils that want to see it destroyed. Couples must consider marriage a life-long commitment, not a commitment that can be broken for any and every reason.

A couple's commitment must be more than a casual acknowledgement of the concept. Commitment is an obligation or pledge to fulfill a promise or responsibility. There should be action in fulfilling a couple's commitment to each other and their marriage relationship. Demonstrating commitment involves including your spouse in your life and making him feel a part of every aspect of your life. Couples may have some separate interests and yet maintain a healthy marriage, but when connection is the exception rather than the rule, one wonders if they are committed to each other or their own activities.

Demands of Daily Life

> *"When a girl marries, she exchanges the attentions of many men for the inattention of one."*
> *~ Helen Rowland*

People today tend to get extremely involved in their daily lives and neglect maintaining their marriage relationship. The incredible pace of life in society can easily draw anyone into the trap of just trying to keep up. Demands of career, children, activities, church and ministry, and maintaining home and vehicles can consume people. They become overcommitted with a lot of activities and do not take care of the most important commitment of their life.

> *"It's not good enough that we do our best; sometimes we have to do what's required."*
> *~ Sir Winston Churchill*

The marriage relationship must be a priority. Commitment is demonstrated when one puts his spouse first before all other people and endeavors. It is challenging to live busy, full lives and maintain right priorities. The tyranny of the urgent does not have to rule their lives, but they must make the decision to do what is required and not just their best. They have to learn to say, "No" at times and do what is necessary to protect and build their marriage relationship.

Martha is not quite sure about Joe's new effort to protect their marriage.

Fortifying Your Marriage

The couple that seeks to strengthen and secure, reinforce, invigorate, and enrich their marriage will reap benefits and blessings. Their life together will be more productive and satisfying, and it will also have a positive affect on their children and the generations after them. Nothing on earth should take precedence over the marriage relationship: not career, friends, family, hobbies, or even service in the church. Too often, people neglect their spouse and family "serving God" when they are really serving self or others. One serves God by taking care of his family and then helping elsewhere as he is able.

The marriage relationship can be a battleground or a fortress of blessing and God's work. Couples make the choice whether they are going to fight against each other or fight together to protect their marriage and family. The couple who fights against each other is the house divided that will fall. Their house is built on sand that will wash away when the storms come against it. Couples must stand together and build a fortress that will be a light to the world and a refuge for those who need help.

> *Fight the good fight of the faith.*
> *~ 1 Timothy 6:12*

The Bible says that the battle is not against flesh and blood, but against spiritual forces of evil in the heavenly realms (Ephesians 6:12). The battle to protect your marriage is a spiritual battle, and victory only comes through Jesus Christ. The battle is not won by human effort, but by surrendering to the Lord and walking in the Spirit. It is important that a couple seeks the Lord together and stands together as they face daily problems and trials they will face.

Boundaries, hedges and moats protect an area or territory. They are the outer defenses to keep attackers from assaulting the main fortress. Similarly, couples need defenses set up for their marriage. Many Christians think of defenses as legalistic, radical or even silly and ridiculous, but the marriage relationship must be protected as fiercely as wolves protect their territory. It is better to be thought of as legalistic or ridiculous than to experience the consequences of sin and divorce.

> *Above all else, guard your heart, for it is the wellspring of life. ~ Proverbs 4:23*

Husbands and wives need to know and acknowledge their own and each other's weaknesses. They have to agree to be accountable to each other and work together to avoid falling to temptation. Wives need to help their husbands avoid the pitfalls of pornography and the visual temptations they face by speaking up when she detects something wrong. Husbands also need to help their wives avoid the emotional traps they can fall into with other men by being a safe emotional place for their wives. Whatever temptations each face, spouses must help protect each other from them. Set up safeguards for your marriage together. Use the following list to give you ideas.

- No compromise in what you see, say and hear.
- No secrets from your spouse.
- No separate friendships with the opposite sex.
- No activities that would draw you away from the Lord.
- Not too much idle time that could invite temptation.
- No dwelling on the negatives about your spouse.

- Reserve frequent times of connection.
- Maintain total honesty and openness.
- Build accountability with each other and other Christians into your lives.
- Regularly attend marriage enhancement, re treats, classes or seminars.
- Pray daily, individually and as a couple.
- Spend time with the Lord in His word daily.
- Reconcile and forgive each other readily.
- Serve God.
- Make time to relax, individually and as a couple; have fun together.
- Support, encourage and respect each other.
- Flee temptation.

Christians say faith and family are important, but often, their lives do not show it. Their faith is only seen on Sunday mornings and they do not seek God and His plan for their marriage and family. Only a small percentage of couples pray together, and often couples do not communicate more than a few minutes a day. Fortifying and protecting a marriage requires faith expressed in obedience to God's will.

> ***So then, brothers, stand firm and hold to the teachings we passed on to you, whether by word of mouth or by letter. ~ 2 Thessalonians 2:15***

Stand Firm

Standing firm is a recurring theme throughout the Bible. It also may be translated steadfast and means to be resolute in commitment. Couples need to stand firm, to be resolute in their commitment to their relationship. They need to be determined to make their marriage last for life. Sadly, many couples exist together for a lifetime, often because they don't know any other

way. A mature, growing marriage that can be used by God takes work and has to be guarded. It is imperative that couples stand firm together to build that kind of marriage.

When God tells His people to stand firm, He tells them to stand firm in Him. Faith and trust in the Lord and resolutely clinging to Him allows one to resist temptation and face the problems of life. There are times when people gain some victory over temptation and begin to think they can stand on their own. No one is immune to sin, and, in this fallen world, the right temptation at the right time might bring any Christian down. This doesn't mean that couples should dig moats or trenches and remain hidden behind high walls. Serving God and living life creates some exposure to society and temptation. Couples need to learn to protect themselves so they can be more effectively used for the Kingdom of God.

Value Your Spouse

> ***Couples must make a conscious decision to value each other and treat each other as the most valuable person in the world.***

The Bible tells both husbands and wives to respect the other (1 Peter 3:7 & Ephesians 5:33). The marriage relationship should be a place of safety where couples know they will be respected and valued. Value means, attributed worth, usefulness or importance.[2] Couples may complement, care for, and work with each other, yet often, they don't demonstrate that their spouse is valuable to them. Discontentment and complacency creep into their marriage and their spouse only hears the complaints and criticisms.

The story is told of a young man in the South Pacific who paid the incredible sum of eight cows for his wife when, according to the culture, his rather plain, unimpressive young wife would have brought perhaps two cows. His wife blossomed into a beautiful, self-confident young woman over time and the writer wondered how someone could be so different. "Do you ever think," the young man asked, "what it must mean to a woman to know that her husband has settled on the lowest price for which she can be bought? In her hometown, my wife believed she was worth nothing. Now she knows she is worth more than any other woman in the islands."[3] This young man placed a very high value on his wife; it changed her view of herself and her life.

There is power in the demonstration of love through giving value to a spouse. The husband or wife who knows that he or she has high value with his spouse doesn't have to look elsewhere for affirmation and worth. He knows that he is important to his spouse and that he has a part in his life. The marriage relationship is protected as they demonstrate respect and love to each other.

Demonstrating your spouse's value requires:

- Valuing his opinion.
- Valuing his efforts to fulfill his or her role.
- Valuing his gifts.
- Focusing on the good points.
- Respecting him or her.
- Valuing him or her even when you don't feel like it.
- Treating him as something very valuable.

These actions will build your relationship and draw the two of you closer together. Both will tend to want time together, not apart.

> ***"Let the wife make her husband glad to come home and let him make her sorry to see him leave." ~ Martin Luther***

> ***Therefore, my dear brothers, stand firm. Let nothing move you. Always give yourselves fully to the work of the Lord, because you know that your labor in the Lord is not in vain. ~ 1 Corinthians 15:58***

God Honors Vigilance

God will protect your marriage from the attacks of the world and Satan, but not from your own poor decisions. Couples who do not set up boundaries or take steps to guard their marriage usually will see failure and problems in their marriage. There are too many potential temptations in the world today. Those that are unprepared simply cannot navigate through the temptations they will encounter as they progress through life. God is always with you and will guide you when you look to Him for guidance.

God's Word is the light for the path through life. Couples who use that light more easily get through the tough periods of life they will face. The blessings of a strong, fortified and protected marriage are incredible. The confidence you will gain will enable you to better serve God and your spouse and allow Him to use your marriage to touch other lives.

For Discussion as a Couple

1. Is your marriage safe? Can you say it will never fail? Why or why not?

   ____
   ____
   ____
   ____

2. Why is commitment important for protecting your marriage?

   ____
   ____
   ____
   ____

3. How can the busyness of daily life leave your marriage unprotected?

   ____
   ____
   ____
   ____

4. What can you do to fortify and protect your marriage?

   ____
   ____
   ____
   ____

5. What can you do to demonstrate that you value your spouse?

   ____
   ____
   ____
   ____
   ____

Be Careful

God tells people to be careful throughout the Bible, meaning that people need to give attention to something or be cautious, mindful or wary. Couples need to guard their hearts, minds and marriage. They need to carefully watch over their marriage and protect it from the harm of sin, selfishness and the attacks of the world. Read the following Bible verses and consider how they apply to your marriage.

"Be careful to do everything I have said to you." ~ Exodus 23:13

You must obey my laws and be careful to follow my decrees. ~ Leviticus 18:4

Only be careful, and watch yourselves closely so that you do not forget the things your eyes have seen or let them slip from your heart as long as you live. ~ Deuteronomy 4:9

Be careful that you do not forget the LORD. ~ Deuteronomy 6:12

Be careful that no one entices you by riches; do not let a large bribe turn you aside. ~ Job 36:18

"Be careful not to do your 'acts of righteousness' before men, to be seen by them. ~ Matthew 6:1

"Be careful, or your hearts will be weighed down with dissipation, drunkenness and the anxieties of life, and that day will close on you unexpectedly like a trap." ~ Luke 21:34

Be careful to do what is right in the eyes of everybody. ~ Romans 12:17

Be careful, however, that the exercise of your freedom does not become a stumbling block to the weak. ~ 1 Corinthians 8:9

Be careful that you don't fall! ~ 1 Corinthians 10:12-13

Be very careful, then, how you live—not as unwise but as wise, making the most of every opportunity, because the days are evil. ~ Ephesians 5:15-16

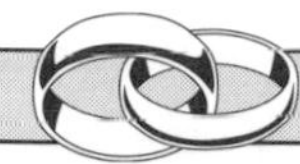

Married for Life

Study 52

Continuing the Work

I consider my life worth nothing to me, if only I may finish the race and complete the task the Lord Jesus has given me-the task of testifying to the gospel of God's grace. ~ *Acts 20:24*

Marriage is Important

Many people today say that marriage is a dead institution. They reject the commitment and values of marriage without realizing that marriage is the foundation of society and that without the institution of marriage, society is in trouble. Marriage holds the fabric of society together. Outside of marriage, males are more likely to be violent and anti-social, and less likely to be stable, positive influences on society. Children raised with their biological parents in a committed marriage relationship have a greater chance of becoming independent, productive adults than children raised in homes without both parents. The importance of marriage to children and society is not only a Christian view, but also the result of secular scholarly research.[1]

"Anyone who has been married more than five minutes realizes that it takes so much more than we were ever told. More than love. More than sincerity. More than compatibility, know-how, good communication skills, or hard effort. More than healthy self-esteem or good upbringing. More than a romantic nature, a willingness to listen, or mega-doses of "quality time." These alone will eventually prove inadequate to bind one imperfect person to another, forever.[2]

A marriage does not last simply because of a couple's love. It lasts because they have made a commitment and covenant to each other, and work to maintain a strong, growing marriage relationship. They nurture and take care of their marriage like they would a beautiful garden and fortify it against the attacks and difficulties they will face in life. Marriage relationships last because couples protect their marriage and work together as a team to meet the challenges of life together. The marriage built on the Rock, on Jesus Christ, will not crumble and fall when the storms rage against it. It is a beacon shinning the light of God's love to the world.

Life in God's creation is an incredible adventure. Sharing the adventure with a spouse makes the adventure more enjoyable and worthwhile. Maturing into the oneness only found in a committed marriage relationship is an adventure in itself. Each new season of life brings a newness and freshness to the marriage. Once a couple begins using their differences to strengthen their marriage and serve God, they will experience intimacy, closeness and blessing. The couple who remains together for a lifetime has the blessing of being able to look back at their marriage and see what God has done in their lives; carrying them through the difficult times and blessing them in the good times. Too often, people miss out on the adventure of a life-long, committed, growing relationship because they are only focused on their own happiness and self-fulfillment.

It Takes Work!

A wonderful marriage and a great life do not come without work, just as the sharpening of iron does not come without grinding and sparks. The pain and problems of life help mold and mature people. Enduring trials, persevering through problems, and remaining committed to God and spouse builds a character that will positively affect lives and generations as a couple leaves a godly legacy. God's grace, love and strength help a couple through the problems and to build a strong, mature marriage. They work at it, but it is not them, it is the grace of God working in and through them that brings about successful, productive lives and marriages.

> ***But by the grace of God I am what I am, and his grace to me was not without effect. No, I worked harder than all of them-yet not I, but the grace of God that was with me. ~ 1 Corinthians 15:10***

Remaining close to the Lord and daily nurturing a relationship with Him is necessary to have a mature marriage relationship. Praying together connects a couple with God and each other. Couples need to continue developing communication skills that will encourage open communication and keep the couple connected with each other. It is important to take the time to work on their relationship, with God and each other. Intimacy is not found and kept for life; it must be continually cultivated and nourished. They have to make their relationship with the Lord and each other a priority.

> ***"Never, never, never, never give up." ~ Sir Winston Churchill***

Couples cannot ever give up on the Lord or each other. There will be times when you do not think you have the strength to continue another day. It may seem like your spouse, child or the circumstances will never change. Do not give up! God never gives up on you, and, statistically, most couples in an unhappy marriage find that when they remain in the marriage, they are much happier five years later. The Lord will sustain you and help you get through the rough times and see wonderful blessings once you get past the problems.

Couples don't achieve life-long, fulfilling marriages based on the work of one spouse. It takes two to build a strong marriage. Fulfilling their Biblical roles will bring harmony and strength to their marriage and enable them to better meet the challenges of life. The couple that learns to work together as a team handles crises and problems better and can accomplish much more than the couple that works against each other.

Getting somewhere takes teamwork and sometimes a little extra work.

Plan to Have a Good Marriage

> ***"If you don't know where you are going in your marriage, you will end up going somewhere else." ~ Scott Morgan***

A healthy, productive marriage takes more than work; it takes planning. Couples need to have a purpose and a vision for their lives and marriage. They need to be going in the direction God wants them to go and toward a goal. Goals and objectives help a couple achieve the mission God has for their lives. It is very easy to end up where you don't want to be without a plan.

When a couple's lives and marriage are submitted to God, He can guide and direct them to where He wants them to go. Remember, submission is going in the same direction as the Lord. A couple with purpose and direction in their lives will work better together to accomplish what

God wants them to do, and their children will have more stability and security in their lives. Couples need to take the time to prayerfully examine their mission, goals, objectives and plan to ensure it is what God wants them to accomplish.

> ***By wisdom a house is built, and through understanding it is established; through knowledge its rooms are filled with rare and beautiful treasures.***
> ***~ Proverbs 24:3-4***

A couple's plans should include plans for their marriage. Plans to protect their marriage with boundaries and safe guards around it. They also need plans to learn and continue to grow, mature and remain connected. Seminars, retreats and on-going study need to be built into the plan for their marriage. No one ever knows it all about life, relationships, parenting or marriage. Life continually changes, and couples need to continue learning and growing in faith and knowledge of God and each other.

> ***The grass is greener on the other side of the fence only when you are looking through the glasses of discontentment.***

Jerry Jenkins, in his book, Hedges, states that he desires to make the grass of his marriage so green that the grass on the other side of the fence will always look brown in comparison. It takes planning and work to meet your spouse's needs, build an intimate relationship, and maintain contentment within your marriage. Looking elsewhere for happiness and contentment will only bring pain and despair. Couples must continually seek to keep their love strong; it is a choice they make every day.

The Power of Hope

Hope keeps people going and at times even keeps them alive. Prisoners in concentration camps with hope would survive while others, sometimes with better health or resources would not survive. The difference is what they had to look forward to. A Christian has the hope of salvation and eternal life in Heaven with God. He knows that his life is not without purpose, and he can look forward confidently to what he cannot yet see. When there is no hope, people tend to withdraw and lose all desire to move forward.

> ***Love does not delight in evil but rejoices with the truth. It always protects, always trusts, always hopes, always perseveres. ~ 1 Corinthians 13:6-7***

Hope is very important in the marriage relationship. The Bible says that love always hopes; that it is looking to the future and not stuck in the past. Love looks for the best in others and with forgiveness does not hold past failures against them. Couples can hope because of their faith in God. They see a future together even when they go through the toughest trials. Couples must believe in each other and that God will bring them through any problems they will face.

Many people abandon their marriage when their spouse fails. The challenge is to stick with the marriage and trust God for a future together even when there is failure by one spouse. Yes, sin can be very destructive and cause great pain. Adultery is a particularly difficult sin to forgive. One woman committed adultery, became pregnant and gave birth to a child that was of a different race and looked nothing like her, her husband or their other children. Yet, her husband forgave his wife and accepted the child, even to the point of giving him his name. Was it easy to get past this terrible sin? Certainly not, but by the grace and power of God, this couple has a tremendous testimony of God's love, faithfulness and power. When a couple works through their problems, puts their hope in Christ, and continues to work at their marriage God will empower and bless them.

Maintaining Balance

A relationship with Jesus Christ and with your spouse is about balance. Yes, it takes work and doing something on your part, but you cannot do it on your own strength. One spouse may do everything he can to make his spouse happy, only to have her walk away from the marriage. Making a spouse happy isn't the key to a good marriage. It is important to meet his or her needs, not necessarily his or her wants and desires. Healthy boundaries and the truth of God's word must be balanced with love and grace.

- Relationships of truth without grace dry up.
- Relationships of grace without truth blow up.
- Relationships of truth and grace grow up.[3]

> ***Enjoy life with your wife, whom you love,***
> ***~ Ecclesiastes 9:9***

Marriage should consist of more than raising children, career and meeting the challenges of life. Couples need to take time to relax, have fun, and enjoy each other. It is crucial that couples make time for themselves without having to worry about the responsibilities of life. There may be opportunities to get away on a vacation together, but they should not wait only for a dream vacation together, they need to spend time together on a regular basis. Going for a walk in the park or window-shopping downtown are two of many ideas for inexpensive, relaxing times for a couple.

It is also vitally important that people work on their relationship with the Lord. God's grace and love restored His relationship with mankind. People accept God's grace and by faith seek to walk in a relationship with God. It is not just a matter of accepting God's mercy and then living life your own way. The Lord expects obedience and growth, and there is a balance between God's grace and a person's works. The book of James says, "I will show you my faith by what I do." It is important to obey, but obedience cannot happen without God's strength and power.

Being Used By God

> ***Let us not become weary in doing good, for at the proper time we will reap a harvest if we do not give up.***
> ***~ Galatians 6:9-10***

The purpose of building a strong marriage is so a couple can be used by the Lord to help others and give them hope. Many couples raise their children build a comfortable life and then sit back to enjoy it. It certainly could be tempting to relax as a couple ages and has fewer responsibilities, but it would be better to discover ways a mature couple can be used by God.

Jesus said that to whom has been given much, much would be demanded (Luke 12:48). God expects that His people will use the gifts, abilities and resources He has given them to help others. A huge need exists for men and women mature in their walk with the Lord who are available to be used by Him. There are many areas a couple can serve, individually or as a couple. They may want to help children or adults, singles or married couples. A couple should seek the Lord's guidance and get involved in ministering to others.

The couple who has built a strong, fortified marriage will be a role model for others. They will be a testimony to their children, friends and those they come in contact with. Many marriages are suffering and in need of help, and a couple with a strong marriage has the opportunity to help other couples achieve stability and productivity in their marriages and lives. They can mentor a younger couple and help them by just being a part of their lives. Or, with some training, they can counsel and help couples experiencing problems by coming along side of them, sharing their lives and pointing the way to Jesus Christ.

Most people don't feel qualified for ministry. God does not seek qualified people as much as He seeks available people. God will guide and direct those who desire to serve Him. If a couple's ministry should be to other couples, the Lord will bring couples to them asking for help. Training and education for whatever ministry God calls you to will be helpful, but your availability and openness to God's calling is more important.

Finishing Well

> *Consider him who endured such opposition from sinful men, so that you will not grow weary and lose heart. ~ Hebrews 12:3*

Jesus Christ endured much to pay the price for the sin of mankind. He continued steadfastly to His appointed goal without wavering. Couples can take heart and remain strong in their commitment to continue in their walk with the Lord and each other because of what Christ has done for them. Jesus did not promise it would be easy and in fact, He told His disciples that the way would be hard. It is not enough to just survive until the end. There is a great testimony of God's love and power when a couple lives their lives victoriously for Him. It will be wonderful to stand before the Lord Jesus Christ and hear Him say "well done, good and faithful servant."

> *"I will make you a wall to this people, a fortified wall of bronze; they will fight against you but will not overcome you, for I am with you to rescue and save you," declares the LORD. ~ Jeremiah 15:20*

Couples who finish strong, who remain faithful to God and each other leave a legacy and a testimony that will live long after they are gone. They stand firm in their faith and do not give in to the temptations of the flesh or the world. They are not perfect, but they strive to grow and mature into whom God wants them to be. God empowers them to stand against the storms that come against them and their marriage. God rescues them and uses them to help others grow in their relationship with the Lord.

> *"People die in the way they have lived. Death becomes the expression of everything you are, and you can bring to it only what you have brought to your life."[4]*

Think of your life as an open book. What do people read about God's love and power from the life you live? Do they see commitment, love, forgiveness and hope? Do they see a marriage that glorifies God and spouses who work together for God's purposes? Run with perseverance, the race God has set before you and live a life worthy of the grace you have received. Love your spouse as God loves you and look forward to the day when the great God of the universe welcomes you into Heaven.

> *"I'm not the man I would be, or the man I should be, but thank God Almight, neither am I the man I once was!" ~ Dr. Martin Luther King*

Joe and Martha Today

Remember Joe and Martha from the *Introduction*? The couple that was on the verge of divorce? Their lives and marriage have changed dramatically. They now understand who they are, in Christ and as God has created them. This alone has given them more confidence in God and themselves, and they are able to work together rather than fight over their differences. They also have a purpose and a vision for their lives and marriage and strive to work toward them.

Applying boundaries and the principles of communication has helped them to communicate better and work through the problems in their marriage. They received counseling to help with some of the tough issues they faced and joined a couples Bible study group, which has helped them apply the principles they have learned.

Application of these principles has helped them grow, mature and handle the pressures of daily life better than they did before. Their lives and marriage today are much more meaningful, purposeful and fulfilling. They don't always do everything right, but they have a peace that, although they may require some help, they will be able to get through any problems they might face together. *Divorce* is no longer a part of their vocabulary. It has been replaced by the principles of *forgiveness, love, patience, teamwork, maturity, growth,* and more importantly God.

Joe and Martha now have a Fortified Marriage.

> ***May our Lord Jesus Christ himself and God our Father, who loved us and by his grace gave us eternal encouragement and good hope, encourage your hearts and strengthen you in every good deed and word.***
> ***~ 2 Thessalonians 2:16-17***

For Discussion as a Couple

1. How is your life and marriage an adventure? If it isn't, what can you do to make it an adventure?

____
____
____
____

2. How can you plan to have a strong, lasting marriage? What will you include in those plans?

____
____
____
____

3. How can you maintain hope and remain focused on the Lord in spite of your circumstances?

____
____
____
____

4. Why is it important to maintain a balance in your life and marriage? How can you maintain a balance?

____
____
____
____

5. Are you being used by God? If not, how can you get involved in a ministry and be used by God?

____
____
____
____

Fortified Marriages
Chapter 12 Endnotes

Study 49: *Growing in Maturity*

1. Collier's Dictionary; William D. Halsey, Editorial Director (NY, NY; Macmillan Educational Company, 1986)
2. Nelson's Illustrated Bible Dictionary, Copyright © 1986, Thomas Nelson Publishers

Recommended for further reading:
- Becoming a Couple of Promise by Dr. Kevin Leman
- The Marriage Book by Nicky and Sila Lee
- See Dick and Jane Grow Up: Seven Growth Steps to Marital Maturity by Dr. David Hawkins

Study 50: *The Holiness of Marriage*

1. Collier's Dictionary; William D. Halsey, Editorial Director (NY, NY; Macmillan Educational Company, 1986)
2. Nelson's Illustrated Bible Dictionary, Copyright (c)1986, Thomas Nelson Publishers

Recommended for further reading:
- Sacred Marriage; What if God Designed Marriage to Make us Holy More Than to Make us Happy? By Gary Thomas
- Louder Than Words: The Power of Uncompromised Living by Any Stanley
- Cultivating Christian Character by Michael Zigarelli

For further information, see:
- The Center for Evangelical Spirituality: www.garythomas.com

Study 51: *Protecting Your Marriage*

1. Laurence Shames, Esquire, quoted by Art Carey, In Defense of Marriage (USA, Walker Publishing Company, 1984) p 103
2. Collier's Dictionary; William D. Halsey, Editorial Director (NY, NY; Macmillan Educational Company, 1986)
3. Patricia McGerr, Johnny Lingo's Eight-Cow Wife, Reader's Digest: February 1988

Recommended for further reading:
- Hedges: Loving Your Marriage Enough to Protect It by Jerry B. Jenkins
- Guard Your Heart by Dr. Gary Rosberg
- Divorce Proof Your Marriage by Gary & Barbara Rosberg
- Safe Haven Marriage: Building a Relationship You Want to come Home To by Dr. Archibald Hart & Dr. Sharon Hart Morris

For further information, see:
- Dr. Gary & Barbara Rosberg: www.americasfamilycoaches.com

Study 52: *It is Never Finished*

1. Linda J. Waite & Maggie Gallagher; The Case for Marriage (NY, NY; Doubleday, 2000)
2. Dr. Ronn Elmore, An Outrageous Commitment (NY, NY, Harper Collins Publishers, 2003) pg XIII
3. Jimmy Evans, & Secrets of Successful Families (Amarillo, TX, Marriage and Family Today, 2001, pg 18
4. Michael Roener, quoted by Philip Yancey, Where is God When it Hurts (Grand Rapids, MI, Zondervan, 1997)

Recommended for further reading:

- The Marriage Masterpiece: a bold new vision for your marriage by Al Janssen
- Why Marriage Matters by Glenn Stanton.

Marriage Resources

The following pages list some of the many books that can help you grow in your marriage.

100 Fun and Fabulous Ways to Flirt with Your Spouse by Doug Fields
10 Great Dates to Energize Your Marriage by David & Claudia Arp
101 Nights of Grrreat Romance by Laura Corn
400 Creative Ways to Say I Love You by Alice Chapin
52 Fantastic Dates for You and Your Mate by David & Claudia Arp
5 Essentials for Lifelong Intimacy by Dr. James Dobson
7 Secrets of Effective Fathers by Ken Canfield
A Woman's Guide to the Personality Types by Donna Partow
The ABCs of Christian Grandparenting by Robert & Debra Bruce
A.D.D.: Wandering Minds and Wired Bodies by Edward T. Welch
Becoming a Wise Parent For Your Grown Child by Betty Frain and Eileen Clegg
Becoming the Parent God Wants You to Be by Kevin Leman
Becoming One Financially by J. Andre Weisbrod
Becoming One/Emotionally, Spiritually, Sexually by Joe Beam
Before a Bad Goodbye by Dr. Tim Clinton
Biblical Foundations for Manhood and Womanhood, Wayne Grudem, Editor
Blinded by Grace: Entering the World of Disability by Robert Molsberry
Boundaries by Dr. Henry Cloud and Dr. John Townsend
Boundaries in Marriage by Dr. Henry Cloud and Dr. John Townsend
Boundaries with Kids by Dr. Henry Cloud and Dr. John Townsend
Building Your Mate's Self-Esteem by Dennis & Barbara Rainey
Captivating by John & Stasi Eldredge
The Case Against Divorce by Diane Medved
The Case for Christ by Lee Strobel
The Case for Marriage by Linda J. Waite and Maggie Gallagher
The Child with Special Needs: Encouraging Intellectual and Emotional Growth by Stanley Greenspan and Serena Wieder
The Christ Centered Marriage by Dr. Neil T. Anderson and Charles Mylander
Communication; Key to Your Marriage by H. Norman Wright
The Complete Book of Baby and Child Care; Focus on the Family
The Complete Idiots Guide to Managing Your Money by Robert K. and Christy Heady
The Complete Marriage Book, edited by by Dr. David & Jan Stoop
Creating a Successful Marriage by Cleveland McDonald and Philip McDonald
Creative Counterpart by Linda Dillow
Creative Grandparenting Across the Miles by Patricia Fry
Cultivating Christian Character by Michael Zigarelli
Dare to Discipline by Dr. James Dobson
Different by Design by John MacArthur
Discovering Your Spiritual Gifts by J. E. O'Day
Discover Your God-Given Gifts by Don & Katie Fortune

Divorce Proof Your Marriage by Gary & Barbara Rosberg
The Divorce Remedy: The Proven 7-Step Plan for Saving Your Marriage by Michelle Weiner-Davis
Eldercare 911: The Caregiver's Complete Handbook for Making Decisions by Susan Beerman and Judth Rappaport-Musson
Essential Grandparent: A Guide to Making a Difference by Lillian Carson
Evidence that Demands a Verdict by Josh McDowell
Experiencing Grief by H. Norman Wright
Financial Parenting by Larry Burkett and Rick Osborne
Finding Freedom in Forgiveness by Charlie "T" Jones and Daniel R. Ledwith
Finding Your Spiritual Gifts Questionnaire by C. Peter Wagner
First Things First by Stephen Covey
The Five Love Languages by Gary Chapman
Five Steps to Forgiveness: the Art and Science of Forgiving by Everett Worthington
For Women Only by Shaunti Feldhahn
The Gift of Sex by Clifford & Joyce Penner
Give Them Wings by Carol Kuykendall
God's Design for Sex Series; 4 volumes by Focus on the Family
God's Plans for Your Finances by Dwight Nichols
God Will Make a Way by Dr. Henry Cloud and Dr. John Townsend
Good Marriages Take Time, Bad Marriages Take More Time by David & Carole Hocking
Growing a Spiritually Strong Family by Dennis & Barbara Rainey
Grown-up Children, Grown-up Parents by Phyllis Lieber, Gloria Murphy and Annette Schwartz
Guard Your Heart by Dr. Gary Rosberg
Guiding Your Family by Tony Evans
Hedges: Loving Your Marriage Enough to Protect It by Jerry B. Jenkins
The Heritage by J. Otis Ledbetter and Kurt Bruner
His Needs Her Needs by Willard F. Harley, Jr.
Holding onto Romance by H. Norman Wright
How to Manage Your Money by Larry Burkett
How to Really Love Your Child by Ross Campell, M.D.
How to Succeed at Being Yourself by Joyce Meyer
How to Talk to Your Adult Children About Really Important Things by Theresa DiGeronimo
How to Talk to Your Senior Parents about Really Important Things by Theresa DiGeronimo
If Only He Knew by Gary Smalley
Intended for Pleasure by Ed Wheat
Intimate Encounters by David & Teresa Ferguson and Chris & Holly Thurman
Learning About Sex; a seven book series,Concordia Publishing House
Learning to Live With the Love of Your Life by Neil Clark Warren
Liberated Through Submission by P.B. Wilson
Love Life for Every Married Couple by Ed Wheat
Love Life for Parents by David & Claudia Arp
The Love List/Eight Little Things That Make a Big Difference in Your Marriage by Drs. Les & Leslie Parrott
Love Must Be Tough: New Hope for Marriages in Crisis by Dr. James Dobson
Louder Than Words: The Power of Uncompromised Living by Andy Stanley

Made to be Loved by Steve & Valerie Bell
Making Your Love Last Forever, A Book for Couples by H. Norman Wright
Making Sense of the Men in Your Life by Dr. Kevin Leman
Man and Woman in Christ by Stephen B. Clark
The Marriage Book by Nicky & Sila Lee
The Marriage Builder by Larry Crabb
Marriage Clues for the Clueless; Developed and produced by the Livingstone Corporation
The Marriage Masterpiece: a bold new vision for your marriage by Al Janssen
Men and Women: Equal Yet Different by Alexander Strauch
Men are from Mars, Women are From Venus by John Gray, Ph.D.
Men Who Won't Lead and Women Who Won't Follow by James Walker
Mental Retardation Sourcebook, Joyce Brennfleck Shannon, editor
More Than a Carpenter by Josh McDowell
More than Married; the Keys to Intimacy for Lasting Marriage by David & Teresa Ferguson
Money Talks and So Can We by Ron & Judy Blue
Muriel's Blessing by Robertson McQuilken, Christianity Today, February 5, 1996
My Child Has Special Needs: A Journey from Grief to Joy by Sharon Hensely
Ordering Your Private World by Gordon MacDonald
Once a Parent Always a Paren by Stephen Bly
An Outrageous Commitment; The 48 Vows of an Indestructible Marriage by Dr. Ronn Elmore
Parenting the Prodigal by S. Rutherford McDill Jr.
Parenting the Wild Child by Miles McPherson
Parenting Your Adult Child: How You Can Help Them Achieve Their Full Potential by Ross Campbell and Gary Chapman
Parents Forever—You and Your Adult Children by Sidney Callahan
Parents with Broken Hearts by William L. Coleman
Parent's Work is Never Done by James Haines and Margery Neely
Parents & Teenagers, Jay Kesler, General Editor
Personality Plus by Florence Littauer
Personality Plus for Couples by Florence Littauer
The Power of Forgiveness: Keep Your Heart Free by Joyce Meyer
The Power of Grandparenting by Robert Strand
Powerful Personalities by Tim Kimmel
The Practice of Godliness by Jerry Bridges
The Purpose Driven Life by Rick Warren
Raising Great Kids by Dr. Henry Cloud and Dr. John Townsend
Raising Responsible Kids by Jay Kesler
Relationship Rescue by Dr. Phil McGraw
The Resilient Family: Living with Your Child's Illness or Disability by Paul Power and Arthur Dell
Rocking the Roles: Building a Win-Win Marriage by Robert Lewis and William Hendricks
Sacred Marriage; What if God Designed Marriage to Make us Holy More Than to Make us Happy? by Gary Thomas
Safe Haven Marriage: Building a Relationship You Want to come Home To by Dr. Archibald Hart and Dr. Sharon Hart Morris
The Second Half by David & Claudia Arp

See Dick and Jane Grow Up: Seven Growth Steps to Marital Maturity by Dr. David Hawkins
Setting Limits: How to Raise Responsible, Independent Children by Providing Clear Boundaries by Robert MacKenzie
The Seven Principles for Making Marriage Work by John M. Gottman and Nan Silver
Sex, Romance and the Glory of God by C.J. Mahaney
The Smart Stepfamily: Seven Steps to a Healthy Family by Ron Deal
Simply Romantic Nights by Dennis & Barbara Rainey
Special Kids Need Special Parents: A Resource for Parents of Children with Special Needs by Judith Loseff Lavin
A Special Kind of Love; For Those Who Love Children with Special Needs by Susan Osborn and Janet Mitchell
The Special-Needs Reading List: An Annotated Guide to the Best Publications for Parents and Professionals by Cory Moore
Spiritual Growth of Children, edited by John Trent, Rick Osborne and Kurt Bruner
Staying Close by Dennis Rainey
The Stepfamily Survival Guide by Natalie Nichols Gillespie
The Strong Family by Chuck Swindoll
Successful Christian Parenting by John MacArthur
Surviving the Prodigal Years/How to Love Your Wayward Child Without Ruining Your Own Life by Marcia Mitchell
Take Back Your Marriage; Sticking Together in a World That Pulls Us Apart by William Doherty
Total Forgiveness by R.T. Kendall
The Two Sides of Love Gary Smalley and John Trent
The Unexpected Legacy of Divorce by Judith Wallerstein, Julia Lewis and Sandra Blakeslee
Using Your Money Wisely by Larry Burkett
Victory Over the Darkness by Neil T. Anderson
Victorious Christian Faith by Alan Redpath
What Does She Want From Me, Anyway? by Holly Faith Phillips
What To Do About Your Brain-Injured Child by Glenn Doman
When Bad Things Happen to Good Marriages by Drs. Les and Leslie Parrott
When Two Become One; Enhancing Sexual Intimacy in Marriage by Christopher & Rachel McCluskey
When Our Grown Kids Disappoint Us by Jane Adams Ph.D.
Where is God When Bad Things Happen? by Luis Palau
Where is God When It Hurts? by Philip Yancey
Whole Marriages in a Broken World by Gary Inrig
Why Marriage Matters by Glenn Stanton
Why? Trusting God When You Don't Understand by Anne Graham Lotz
Willing to Try Again: Steps Toward Blending a Family by Dick Dunn
A Woman After God's Own Heart by Elizabeth George
The Wonderful Spirit Filled Life by Charles Stanley
The World's Easiest Guide to Finances by Larry Burkett with Randy Southern
You and Your Grown-up Child by Howard Halpern
You Will Dream New Dreams: Inspiring Personal Stories By Parents of Children with Disabilities by Stanley Klein and Kim Schive

Marriage and Family Resource Organizations

CLASS; Christian Leaders, Authors & Speaker Services: Speakers bureau, training seminars and resources, CLASS helps people train and develop their speaking and writing skills. 800-433-6633, 505-899-4283, www.classervices.com

Answers in Genesis: An apologetics (i.e., Christianity-defending) ministry, dedicated to enabling Christians to defend their faith, and to proclaim the gospel of Jesus Christ effectively. Providing Biblical education and resources. 800-350-3232, 859-727-2222, www.answersingenesis.org

AMFM; Association of Marriage and Family Ministries: To serve, encourage, equip and partner with those who are called to the vital area of Marriage and Family ministry. 480-585-0109, www.amfmonline.com

Smart Marriages; Coalition for Marriage, Family and Couples Education, LLC: The Coalition for Marriage, Family and Couples Education serves as an information exchange and clearinghouse to help couples locate marriage and relationship courses; to help mental health professionals, clergy, mentor couples and lay educators locate training programs and resources; to connect those with an interest in the continuing development of the field; to support community initiatives, legislation and research; and to promote the effectiveness of the courses and increase their availability in the community. 202-362-3332, www.smartmarriages.com

The Family Research Council (FRC): Champions marriage and family as the foundation of civilization, the seedbed of virtue, and the wellspring of society. FRC shapes public debate and formulates public policy that values human life and upholds the institutions of marriage and the family. Believing that God is the author of life, liberty, and the family, FRC promotes the Judeo-Christian worldview as the basis for a just, free, and stable society. 202-393-2100, www.frc.org

Marriage Movement.org: Pledged to turn the tide on marriage and reduce divorce and unmarried childbearing, so that each year more children will grow up protected by their own two happily married parents, and so that each year more adults' marriage dreams will come true. Provides resources for the Marriage Movement. 212-246-3942, www.marriagemovement.org

Covenant Marriage Movement: Seeks to restore churches and society to an understanding and practice of marriage as covenant by applying timeless the principles of God's Word. 800-311-1662, 434-525-1080, www.covenantmarriage.com

Focus on the Family: "Turning hearts toward home" by reasonable, biblical and empirical insights so people will be able to discover the founder of homes and the creator of families: Jesus Christ. Education and resources for marriage and the family. 800 A-FAMILY (232-6459), 719-531-3400, www.family.org

FamilyLife: Bringing timeless principles home. Marriage conferences, education and resources. 800-FL-TODAY (800-358-6329), www.familylife-ccc.org

National Association of Marriage Enhancement (NAME): Provides effective, proven tools for reaching out to the community. Trains lay marriage counselors and provides the resources for NAME counseling centers within the local church. Promotes Biblical marriage principles. 888-262-NAME (6263), 602-404-2600, www.nameonline.net

Marriage Savers: A ministry that equips local communities, principally through local congregations, to help men and women to: Prepare for lifelong marriages, Strengthen existing marriages, and Restore troubled marriages. 301-469-5873, www.marriagesavers.org

The Council on Biblical Manhood and Womanhood (CBMW): Studies and sets forth the Biblical view of the relationship between men and women, especially in the home and the church. Promotes the publication of scholarly and popular materials representing this view. Encourages the considered and sensitive application of this Biblical view in the appropriate spheres of life. 888-560-8210, 502) 897-4065, www.cbmw.org

Freedom in Christ Ministries: Equipping the Body of Christ to be alive, free, and complete in Him. Supplying resources to Christian leaders world-wide to help them establish their people free in Christ. 866-462-4747, 865-342-4000, www.freedominchrist.com

Cloud-Townsend Resources: Helping people find solutions to life's challenges. Equipping people to make better decisions, find personal fulfillment, and grow spiritually. Provide and distribute the many resources developed by Dr. Henry Cloud and Dr. John Townsend. 800-676-HOPE (4673), www.cloudtownsend.com

American Association of Christian Counselors (AACC): Committed to assisting Christian counselors and the entire 'community of care,' licensed professionals, pastors, and caring church members with little or no formal training. It is our intention to equip clinical, pastoral, and lay care-givers with Biblical truth and psycho-social insights that ministers to hurting persons and helps them move to personal wholeness, interpersonal competence, mental stability, and spiritual maturity. 800-526-8673, 434-525-9470, www.aacc.net

Crown Financial Ministries: Equipping people worldwide to learn, apply, and teach God's financial principles so they may know Christ more intimately, be free to serve Him, and help fund the great commission. 800-722-1976, www.crown.org

Focus on Your Child: Provides resources and information for parenting. 800 A-FAMILY (232-6459), 719-531-3400, www.focusonyourchild.com

Crisis Resources

Immediate help is available for those who need it. Family, close Christian friends, your pastor or a Christian counselor often can help during a crisis or at least point you in the right direction. When you have no one to call, the following list can be of help in your crisis. It is general and only has numbers that are available nationwide in the United States. Many websites below do have international resources, check the applicable sites if needed. There are also many local ministries or agencies that also can help, but are too numerous to print here.

If you are in a life-threatening, dangerous situation, call the emergency number in your area (911 in the United States).

Many states now have 211 services to provide information and resources for people in need. Visit www.211.org or more information or consult your local telephone book for *Community Information and Referrals*. There is information for basic human needs, physical and mental health resources, employment supports, older or disability supports and support for children and families.

Alcohol Abuse

National Institute on Alcohol Abuse and Alcoholism (NIAAA)
www.niaaa.nih.gov
National Drug and Alcohol Treatment Referral Routing Service provides a toll-free telephone number, 1-800-662-HELP (4357), offering various resource information.

Alcoholics Anonymous: www.alcoholics-anonymous.org
Phone: 212-870-3400 or 800-252-8336

Al-Anon/ Alateen: www.al-anon.alateen.org / Phone: 757-563-1600

National Council on Alcoholism and Drug Dependence: www.ncadd.org
Phone: 800-622-2255

Child Abuse

Childhelp USA: www.childhelpusa.org
Phone: 800-4-A-CHILD (800-422-4453)
For child abuse victims, parents, concerned individuals.

Youth Crisis Hotline: www.1800hithome.com
Phone: 800-HIT-HOME (800-448-4663)
For individuals reporting child abuse, youth ages 12 to 18.

Child Sexual Abuse - Stop It Now! www.stopitnow.com
Phone: 888-PREVENT (888-773-8368)
For child sexual abuse victims, parents, offenders, concerned individuals.

Children with Disabilities

National Dissemination Center for Children with Disabilities (NICHCY):
www.nichcy.org / Phone: 800-695-0285

Counseling	*American Association of Christian Counselors:* www.aacc.net 800-526-8673
	Focus on the Family Counseling Department: Phone: 800-A-FAMILY (232-6459) or 719-531-3400, ext. 7700, Monday-Friday 9 a.m. - 4:30 p.m. Mountain time.
Crime Victims	*National Center for Victims of Crime:* Phone: 800-FYI-CALL (800-394-2255) For families, communities, and individuals harmed by crime
Crisis Pregnancy	*Pregnancy Centers:* www.pregnancycenters.org Phone: 800-395-HELP (800-395-4357)
	Heartlink, Focus on the Family's Pregnancy Resource Center: www.heartlink.org /Phone: 800-A-FAMILY (232-6459) or 719-531-3400
Drug Abuse	*National Institute on Drug Abuse:* www.nida.nih.gov 301-443-1124 National Drug and Alcohol Treatment Referral Routing Service provides a toll- free telephone number, 1-800-662-HELP (4357), offering various resource information.
	U.S. Department of Health and Human Services: Alcohol and Drug Information: www.health.org /Phone: 800-729-6686
Emergency Assistance	*America's Second Harvest Network:* www.secondharvest.org Phone: 800-771-2303 Referral to local food banks and relief organizations.
	Canadian Association of Food Banks: www.cafb-acba.ca Phone: 877-535-0958
	MercyCorps: www.mercycorps.org / Phone: 800-292-3355 Helping distressed families
	Salvation Army: www.salvationarmyusa.org Help for people in distress; consult telephone directories for local community centers.
Family Violence	*National Domestic Violence Hotline:* www.ndvh.org Phone: 800-799-SAFE (800-799-7233)
	For children, parents, friends, offenders *National Coalition Against Domestic Violence:* www.ncadv.org Phone: 303-839-1852
Grief	*Compassionate Friends, Inc.* www.compassionatefriends.org / 877-969-0010 *Grief Recovery:* www.grief.net /Phone: 818-907-9600
Legal Aid	*Christian Legal Society:* www.clsnet.org / Phone: 703-642-1070
	Christian Law Association: www.christianlaw.org /Phone: 727- 399-8300

Mental Health — *National Institute of Mental Health:* www.nimh.nih.gov
Phone: 866-615-6464

Missing/ Abducted Children — *Child Find of America:* Phone: 800-I-AM-LOST (800-426-5678)
For parents reporting lost or abducted children.

Child Quest International Sighting Line
Phone: 888-818-HOPE (888-818-4673)
For individuals with missing child emergencies and/or sighting information; victims of abduction.

National Center for Missing and Exploited Children
Phone: 800-THE-LOST (800-843-5678)
For families and professionals (social services, law enforcement).

Operation Lookout National Center for Missing Youth
Phone: 800-LOOKOUT (800-566-5688)
For individuals with missing child emergencies and/or sighting information (for children ages 18 and under).

Natural Disasters — *Federal Emergency Management Agency (FEMA):*
ww.fema.gov / 800-621-FEMA (3362)
Red Cross: www.redcross.org / 202-303-4498

Rape/Incest — *Rape and Incest National Network:* www.rainn.org
Phone: 800-656-HOPE; Ext. 1 (800-656-4673; Ext. 1)
For rape and incest victims, media, policy makers, concerned individuals.

Relief for Caregivers — *National Respite Locator Service:* www.respitelocator.org
Phone: 800-677-1116
For parents, caregivers, and professionals caring for children and adults with disabilities, terminal illnesses, or those at risk of abuse or neglect

National Family Caregiver Support Program (NFCSP)
www.aoa.gov/prof/aoaprog/caregiver/overview/overview_caregiver.asp
Phone: 202-619-0724

Youth in Trouble/ Runaways — *Girls and Boys Town:* www.girlsandboystown.org/home.asp
Phone: 800-448-3000
For abused, abandoned, and neglected girls and boys; parents; family members

Covenant House Hotline: www.nineline.org /Phone: 800-999-9999
For problem teens and homeless runaways (ages 21 and under), family members, youth substance abusers.

National Referral Network for Kids in Crisis:
Phone: 800-KID-SAVE (800-543-7283)
For professionals, parents, adolescents

Youth in Trouble/ Runaways (cont.)

National Runaway Switchboard: 800-621-4000
For runaway and homeless youth, families

National Youth Crisis Hotline (Youth Development International)
www.1800hithome.com / Phone: 800-HIT-HOME (800-448-4663)
For individuals wishing to obtain help for runaways; youth (ages 12 to 18) experiencing drug abuse, teen pregnancy, homelessness, prostitution, or physical, emotional, or sexual abuse

Suicide Prevention

Suicide Hotlines: www.suicidehotlines.com
1-800-SUICIDE/ 1-800-784-2433 or 1-800-273-TALK /1-800-273-8255

American Foundation for Suicide Prevention: www.afsp.org
888-333-AFSP (888-333-2377)

Befrienders Worldwide: www.befrienders.org/index.php
In the United Kingdom - multi-lingual, excellent information with referrals worldwide.

Chris & Carmen Garner
Fortified Marriages Ministries
www.fortifiedmarriages.com
info@fortifiedmarriages.com
866-263-5638

Dear Reader,

Our prayer is that the Lord has blessed you abundantly through this book. This is the fruit of many years of work and it is our hearts' desire to see individuals, couples, families and even churches and communities strengthened and built up in the Lord. We know the Lord can use this information to transform lives, marriages and families.

Helping couples is our passion; we have experienced and know the heartache of a dysfunctional, unproductive marriage and now experience the joy of a strong marriage used by God in the lives of others. You can also have a meaningful marriage relationship as you apply the Biblical principles in this book to your life and marriage.

If God touched and changed your life and marriage as a result of working through this marriage manual, we would love to hear from you.

Also, please contact us for:

Additional *Fortified Marriages* Manuals.
Marriage workshops.
Training to lead *Fortified Marriages* classes or studies.

We are here to serve the Lord.

May the Lord, God of Heaven bless you and your marriage.

Love in Christ,

Chris N. G.
Carmen Garner